Keynote

4

Teacher's Edition

Colleen Sheils

NATIONAL GEOGRAPHIC LEARNING | CENGAGE Learning

Australia • Brazil • Mexico • Singapore • United Kingdom • United States

Keynote Teacher's Edition 4
Colleen Sheils

Publisher: Andrew Robinson

Executive Editor: Sean Bermingham

Senior Development Editor: Derek Mackrell

Associate Development Editor: Yvonne Tan

Director of Global Marketing: Ian Martin

Senior Product Marketing Manager:
    Caitlin Thomas

IP Analyst: Kyle Cooper

IP Project Manager: Carissa Poweleit

Media Researcher: Leila Hishmeh

Senior Director of Production: Michael Burggren

Senior Production Controller: Tan Jin Hock

Manufacturing Planner: Mary Beth Hennebury

Compositor: MPS North America LLC

Cover/Text Design: Brenda Carmichael

Cover Photo: A robot drone hovers above a
    hand: © Yash Mulgaonkar

For product information and technology assistance, contact us at
Cengage Learning Customer & Sales Support, 1-800-354-9706

For permission to use material from this text or product,
submit all requests online at **cengage.com/permissions**
Further permissions questions can be emailed to
permissionrequest@cengage.com

ISBN-13: 978-1-337-10425-8

National Geographic Learning
20 Channel Center Street
Boston, MA 02210
USA

Cengage Learning is a leading provider of customized learning solutions with office locations around the globe, including Singapore, the United Kingdom, Australia, Mexico, Brazil, and Japan. Locate your local office at **international.cengage.com/region**

Cengage Learning products are represented in Canada by Nelson Education, Ltd.

Visit National Geographic Learning online at **NGL.cengage.com**
Visit our corporate website at **www.cengage.com**

Printed in the United States of America
Print Number: 01   Print Year: 2017

Contents

Scope and Sequence

	LESSON C	LESSON D		LESSON E	
	READING	TED TALK	PRESENTATION SKILLS	COMMUNICATE	WRITING
	The stressed-out generation	**HOW TO MAKE STRESS YOUR FRIEND** *Kelly McGonigal*	Involving the audience	Dealing with stress	Writing a letter giving advice
	Are superheroes good role models?	**HOW MOVIES TEACH MANHOOD** *Colin Stokes*	Knowing your audience	Assessing movies	Writing a movie review
	The economics of happiness	**GLOBAL POPULATION GROWTH, BOX BY BOX** *Hans Rosling*	Using props	The distribution of wealth	Writing about how wealth is distributed in your country
	Lies we need to tell	**HOW TO SPOT A LIAR** *Pamela Meyer*	Beginning with a strong statement	The lying game	Expressing an opinion on lying
	Magic man	**HOW I HELD MY BREATH FOR 17 MINUTES** *David Blaine*	Explaining technical words	Talking about big achievements	Comparing people's achievements
	Giving something back	**WHY GIVING AWAY OUR WEALTH HAS BEEN THE MOST SATISFYING THING WE'VE DONE** *Bill and Melinda Gates*	Being authentic	Convincing people to give to your project or charity	Writing about a charitable project

Scope and Sequence

LESSON C	LESSON D		LESSON E	
READING	TED TALK	PRESENTATION SKILLS	COMMUNICATE	WRITING
Just press "print"	**THE SORE PROBLEM OF PROSTHETIC LIMBS** *David Sengeh*	Body movement and gestures	Pitching an invention	Writing a letter to a potential investor
The defining decade	**WHY 30 IS NOT THE NEW 20** *Meg Jay*	Using a case study	Giving advice	Writing an advice column
Drones are here to stay	**ROBOTS THAT FLY ... AND COOPERATE** *Vijay Kumar*	Referring to visuals	Debating	Writing about the applications of drone technology
The lost art of listening?	**FIVE WAYS TO LISTEN BETTER** *Julian Treasure*	Using acronyms to summarize	How good are your listening skills?	Summarizing the results of a survey
Your brain on nature	**CLOUDY WITH A CHANCE OF JOY** *Gavin Pretor-Pinney*	Being enthusiastic	Slow movement organizations	Writing an advertisement for an organization
Whistleblowers	**DARE TO DISAGREE** *Margaret Heffernan*	Using pauses	A company meeting	Writing an email to a company CEO

Keynote Pacing Guide

Keynote can be adapted to courses of any length. The following examples show course options to cover one level of Keynote.

TOTAL COURSE LENGTH: 45 HOURS	TOTAL COURSE LENGTH: 60 HOURS
1 x 90 minute class x 30 weeks	Option 1: 4 x 50–60 min classes x 15 weeks Option 2: 2 x 50–60 min classes x 30 weeks
One unit is covered in two weeks, i.e. the core Student Book content is covered in 24 full teaching weeks (36 hours). Remaining time allowance (9 hours) can be used for: *Presentations, exams/review,* and/or *school vacations.*	One unit is covered in either one week (option 1), or two weeks (option 2), i.e. total class time approximately 4 hours. The Student Book content is covered in either 12 or 24 full teaching weeks (48 hours). Remaining time allowance (12 hours) can be used for: *Presentations, exams/review,* and/or *school vacations.*
Class 1: Opener Lesson A: Vocabulary, Listening, Speaking Lesson B: Language Focus, Speaking **Class 2:** Lesson D: TED Talks Lesson E: Communicate	**Class 1:** Opener Lesson A: Vocabulary, Listening, Speaking **Class 2:** Lesson B: Language Focus, Speaking **Class 3:** Lesson D: TED Talks **Class 4:** Lesson E: Communicate Writing task The four classes can be taught over one or two weeks.
This option assumes the reading lessons (Lesson C) are set for students to complete on their own at home. The writing task of Lesson E can also be set as homework.	This option assumes the reading lessons (Lesson C) are set for students to complete on their own at home. Responses to the reading can be elicited at the start of Class 3. The Lesson E Writing task is started in class, and completed for homework.

TOTAL COURSE LENGTH: **90 HOURS**	TOTAL COURSE LENGTH: **120 HOURS**
2 x 90 minute classes x 30 weeks	4 x 50–60 min classes x 30 weeks
One unit is covered in four classes taught over two weeks. The Student Book content is covered in 24 full teaching weeks (72 hours). Remaining time allowance (18 hours) can be used for: *Presentations, exams/review, use of additional materials/ancillaries,* and/or *school vacations.*	One unit is covered in two weeks, i.e. total class time approximately 8 hours. The Student Book content is covered in 24 full teaching weeks (96 hours). Remaining time allowance (24 hours) can be used for: *Presentations, exams/review, use of additional materials/ancillaries,* and/or *school vacations.*
First week: Lessons A–C **Class 1:** Opener Lesson A: Vocabulary, Listening, Speaking Lesson B: Language Focus **Class 2:** Lesson B: Speaking Lesson C: Reading *Second week: Lessons D–E* **Class 3:** Lesson D: TED Talks **Class 4:** Lesson E: Communicate Writing task	*First week: Lessons A–C* **Class 1:** Opener, Lesson A: Vocabulary, Listening **Class 2:** Lesson A: Speaking, Lesson B: Language Focus **Class 3:** Lesson B: Speaking, Lesson C: Reading **Class 4:** Lesson C: Reading (continued, including Vocabulary) *Second week: Lessons D–E* **Class 5:** Lesson D: TED Talks: Previewing, Viewing, **Class 6:** Lesson D: TED Talks: Vocabulary in Context, Presentation Skills, Lesson E: Communicate (preparation) **Class 7:** Lesson E: Communicate **Class 8:** Lesson E: Writing task

Course Overview

What is TED?

TED is a non-profit, global organization with a simple goal: to spread great ideas. Every year, hundreds of presenters share ideas at TED events around the world. Millions of people watch TED Talks online, inspiring many to change their attitudes and their lives.

Why use TED Talks in English Language Teaching?

TED speakers use authentic language, model best practices in presentation delivery, and bring real and fascinating ideas to the classroom. These ideas inspire learners to form opinions that they want to share. National Geographic Learning materials can help them do that in English.

How does Keynote use TED Talks to teach English?

Learners develop English language skills, presentation literacy, and explore great ideas through authentic TED Talks. Each unit helps learners build an understanding around a TED speaker's main idea.

How is using Keynote different than using a TED Talk found online?

National Geographic Learning is the only publisher able to curate TED Talks for English language learners. The TED Talks selected for NGL materials are fascinating, language-level appropriate, and supported by a one-of-a-kind curriculum. In Keynote, TED Talks are broken into manageable segments that are used as springboards for language learning.

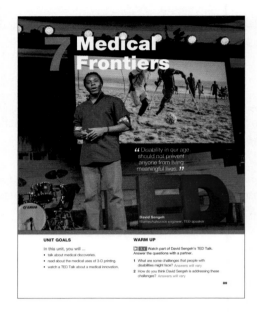

Each unit develops appropriate language-learning goals supported by a carefully segmented TED Talk. The **unit opener** uses a compelling excerpt to introduce the main idea, engage learners, and encourage discussion.

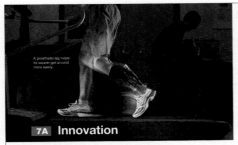

Vocabulary sections teach key words and phrases needed to talk about the main idea presented in the unit.

Listening sections feature audio and video interviews with real people from around the world, including psychologists, aid workers, and marathon runners.

In the **Language Focus** section, an engaging infographic provides real-life context for key grammar points. Students then listen to the grammar presented in context.

The **Language Focus Chart** provides explicit language instruction, while the **Grammar Summary** section at the end of the student book provides additional support for the lesson's target language.

In the **Speaking** section, learners practice grammar communicatively through a controlled task.

NATIONAL GEOGRAPHIC LEARNING | CENGAGE Learning

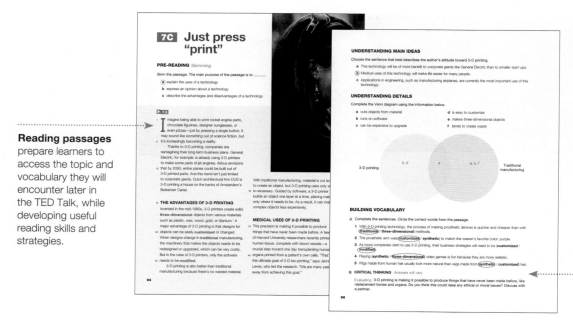

Reading passages prepare learners to access the topic and vocabulary they will encounter later in the TED Talk, while developing useful reading skills and strategies.

Critical Thinking activities develop skills like applying, evaluating, and interpreting information to help learners achieve a deeper understanding of the main idea.

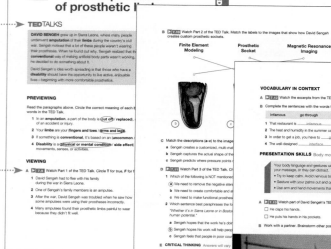

Lesson D uses an authentic **TED Talk**, which is divided into shorter parts to enable learners to better understand and respond to a TED speaker's idea worth spreading.

Activities related to each part of the TED Talk reinforce vocabulary, assess comprehension, and develop listening and viewing skills.

Vocabulary in Context sections guide learners to review excerpts from the TED Talk to identify the meaning of useful spoken expressions and idioms.

Using TED Speakers as models, **Presentation Skills** sections guide learners to watch and note best practices speakers use to deliver their ideas.

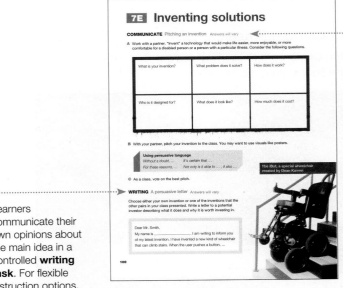

A **communicative task** guides learners to collaborate in pairs and groups to discuss and think creatively about the theme and topic of the unit.

Learners communicate their own opinions about the main idea in a controlled **writing task**. For flexible instruction options, this task is further supported in the print workbook.

Located after every three units, **Presentation** units review the presentation skills presented in the previous units and guide learners to apply those skills as they create and deliver their own presentations.

A **model presentation** gives students a model to consolidate language and presentation skills from preceding units.

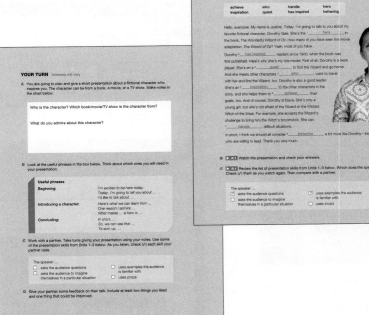

Using prompts and relevant language, learners create their own short presentations.

When delivering their own presentations, learners integrate the presentation skills presented in the previous units and give constructive feedback on their peers' presentations.

Keynote Technology Components

My Keynote Online

My Keynote Online provides:

- reinforcement activities tied to each lesson in the Student Book

- a smart learning path that automatically provides additional support in grammar and vocabulary as needed and point-of-use access to all of the videos and the Student eBook

Classroom Presentation Tool

The **Classroom Presentation Tool** for each level brings the classroom to life through:

- complete, interactive versions of the Student Book pages featuring point-of-use access to all of the videos

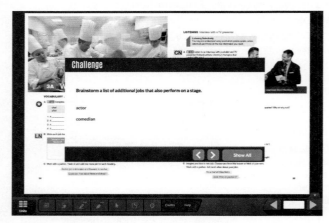

- additional communicative classroom activities

- instructional support

- animated videos that support the listening activities

1 Embrace Stress!

TED

" I have changed my mind about stress, and today, I want to change yours. **"**

Kelly McGonigal
Health psychologist, TED speaker

UNIT GOALS

In this unit, you will ...

- talk about dealing with stress.
- read about how stress affects young adults.
- watch a TED Talk about dealing with stress.

WARM UP

▶ **1.1** Watch part of Kelly McGonigal's TED Talk. Answer the questions with a partner.

1 Do you think stress is harmful for your health?
   Answers will vary.
2 What do you think Kelly McGonigal will say to change your mind about stress? Answers will vary.

13

---

1 Embrace Stress!

WARM UP

Have students look over the picture, caption, and quote on the page. Read the quote aloud. Note that students will hear the quote in the video clip. If necessary, explain that a *psychologist* studies the human mind with a focus on mental health, meaning how our attitudes and characteristics affect our actions. Write the expression *change someone's mind* on the board.

▶ **1.1** Play the preview clip of the TED Talk.

For question 1, ask students to brainstorm a list of negative impacts of stress that they've heard or read about. Then have pairs share some examples with the class. Write a mind map or list of the ideas on the board. Note that stress is often named as a cause of health problems, sleeping issues, emotional issues, and so forth.

For question 2, elicit or explain the meaning of *change someone's mind*. When you change someone's mind, you convince them to think differently about something. Tell partners to look at the ideas they brainstormed for question 1 as they think about how their perspective about stress could be changed. Point out that students gave negative viewpoints about stress for question 1. Ask them to consider if there are any positive viewpoints.

⊙ EXTENSION ACTIVITY Have students work in pairs. Ask them to make a list of things that they do when they feel stressed. Tell them to decide together if these habits are positive or negative ways of coping with stress. Ask them to organize their coping strategies into positive and negative categories to use for a later activity.

UNIT GOALS

In this unit, students will read, watch, and talk about the impact of stress on our lives. Students are asked to think about and discuss how they deal with stress. Students will read about the effect of stress on younger generations and watch a talk about shifting our mindsets regarding stress.

TED Speaker

Kelly McGonigal is a health psychologist at Stanford University, an author, and a speaker.

TED Talk Summary

Kelly McGonigal used to teach her patients about the negative impact of stress on their health and lives, but one day she read a study that changed her way of thinking about stress, and now she wants to change how others view it as well. She shares that the study revealed that it is our mindset about stress that determines whether it affects us negatively or positively, so if we simply change how we *feel* about stress, we'll change its effect on us.

Idea Worth Spreading

If we see stress as something natural and helpful, it has a positive impact on us.

Iranian women practice parkour for stress relief in Tavalod Park, Tehran.

1A Dealing with stress

1A

Dealing with stress

1A Dealing with stress

LESSON OVERVIEW

Aims: Learn language for talking about stress; listen to a psychologist talk about stress; practice talking about dealing with stress

Target Vocabulary: cope with, experience, feel, handle, reduce, relieve

VOCABULARY

A Have students work individually to read the words and decide which category they fit in. Check answers as a class, going over meaning when necessary.

B Have students work in pairs. Read the two questions aloud. Ask students to brainstorm both reasons and coping strategies. Point out that there are both positive and negative ways to cope with stress, and positive and negative situations that cause stress. If they did the **Extension Activity** in **Warm Up**, they can use their lists here. After pairs discuss, elicit a class discussion. See **Content Note** for possible answers.

VOCABULARY Stress collocations

A Read the paragraph below. Then add the **bold** words to the column that describes their meaning.

Many college students **experience** stress. Being away from home for the first time is one major cause; the pressure of exams is also a factor. Since **feeling** stress is common to college life, counselors often recommend that students find ways to **cope with** it. There are many techniques for **reducing** stress. Physical exercise is one. Listening to music is another. In addition, talking to people—especially friends and family back home—can be an excellent way to **relieve** stress. Even though it is a fact of college life, having ways to **handle** stress can help give students a sense of control over their lives.

have stress	manage stress	lower stress
experience, feeling	cope with, handle	reducing, relieve

B Work with a partner. Discuss your answers to these questions. Answers will vary.

1 What are some other reasons students feel stress?

2 What are some other ways students can cope with stress?

14

Content Note

Possible reasons students may feel stress: lifestyle changes, new roommates, new relationships, and exams.

Some positive ways of coping with stress: visiting friends, getting enough sleep, going for a walk, stretching, eating well, and taking deep breaths.

Some negative ways of coping with stress: avoiding the situation, eating junk food, acting cranky with others, and withdrawing from friends and family.

● EXTENSION ACTIVITY Ask

students to write a story about a recent stressful experience and how they dealt with it. Explain that it can be a positive or negative story. Tell students to use the language from **Vocabulary** in their stories.

> **Showing contrast**
> Contrast words are used to transition from one topic or point to another.
> Here are some words that signal contrast.
>
> *However, …   Nevertheless, …   Despite (this), …*

A ▶ **1.2** Watch psychologist Dr. Trudi Edginton talk about stress. Why is it important to effectively manage stress?
For our physical and emotional well-being

B ▶ **1.3** According to Dr. Edginton, what activities might help us relieve stress? Watch and check (✓) your answers.

- ☑ painting
- ☑ meditation
- ☐ healthy eating
- ☑ sleeping
- ☑ walking a dog
- ☐ volunteer work

C **CRITICAL THINKING** Answers will vary.

Reflecting Which of the activities suggested by Dr. Edginton do you think would work best for you? Why? Discuss with a partner.

Dr. Trudi Edginton teaches cognitive neuroscience at the University of Westminster, U.K.

SPEAKING Talking about stress

A ▶ **1.4** Why does Speaker B feel stressed? Because of an important test tomorrow

A: Hey, what's wrong? You look really stressed!

B: I have an important test tomorrow. I've been studying for it all week, but I feel like I don't remember anything. I just can't seem to focus.

A: Maybe you need to take a break. Whenever I feel stressed, I go for a run or do some yoga. Exercise is a good way to unwind and take your mind off things.

B: I'm too tired to exercise. Besides, I still have a few more chapters to read.

A: Have you been getting enough sleep?

B: Not really. I've only had about four hours of sleep each night this week.

A: No wonder you're so stressed out! I usually get at least seven hours of sleep every night. Why don't you take a quick nap? Then you'll be able to focus better when you start studying again later.

B: Yeah. You're probably right. Thanks.

B Practice the conversation with a partner.

C Work with a partner. What types of activities help you deal with stress? Use the expressions in blue above to help you. Answers will vary.

> How do you deal with stress?

> Whenever I feel stressed, I play video games. What about you?

15

SPEAKING

A Ask students to read along as they watch.

▶ **1.4** Play the audio/video.

Check answers as a class. Elicit the ideas for coping with stress that the friend talks about (*go for a run, do yoga, sleep more*).

Point out the phrase *You look really stressed*. Explain that saying "You look …" is a common expression for commenting on someone's state at the time. It is a useful conversation opener for talking to someone that you know well. Note that this expression is only used with people we know well as it could be interpreted as too direct by people we don't know well.

B Model the conversation aloud with a student. Then have students work in pairs to practice. Make sure they alternate between A and B roles.

➕ **SUPPORT** Play the audio/video again, pausing after each sentence so students can repeat.

C Model the example with a volunteer. Encourage students to use content from the lesson about their ways of coping with stress. Encourage partners to ask each other questions to get additional information. Ask for pairs to repeat their conversations for the class. Have students raise their hands if they cope with stress similarly.

➡ **EXTENSION ACTIVITY** Have the class play a game of charades to act out both positive and negative ways of coping with stress over an exam. Ask pairs to think of one coping strategy and act it out silently for the class while students call out their guesses.

LISTENING

A Read **Showing contrast** aloud as students read along. Explain that each of these phrases introduces a clause that presents a contrast. For example, *Stress can be difficult. However, new studies show that it has some benefits, too.*

Elicit any other words or expressions that students know to show contrast. Read the question aloud and tell students to listen for the answer.

▶ **1.2** Play the video. Check answers as a class.

B Have students preview the task.

▶ **1.3** Play the video. Check answers as a class.

C **CRITICAL THINKING** Read the question aloud. Give students time to consider their answers and discuss in pairs. Encourage them to share personal stories of coping with stress. If students did the **Extension Activity** in **Vocabulary**, point out that they may be able to use these stories as an example.

LESSON OVERVIEW

Aims: Read an infographic about jobs and stress levels; talk about jobs and stress

Infographic Summary: A list is introduced of the six most stressful jobs and the six least stressful jobs. According to the infographic, military personnel have the most stress at work, while university professors have the least.

LANGUAGE FOCUS

A Read the question aloud.

▶ **1.5** Play the audio/video as students read along. Then give them additional time to look over the infographic.

Have students discuss their answers in pairs. Note that the most stressful jobs involve a high level of risk to other people. For example, if a pilot, firefighter, or someone in the military makes a mistake, others could die as a result.

B Read the question aloud and tell students to listen for the answers.

▶ **1.6** Play the audio/video. Check answers as a class. Elicit more details about the conversation. Ask: *What does William work as?* (a professor)

How does William feel about his job? (He loves it.)

C Have students read over the language chart for **Talking about jobs and stress**.

▶ **1.7** Play the audio/video. Ask students to pay close attention to the verb usage. Go over the formation and use of gerunds and infinitives. Direct students to page 183 for more information.

1B High- and low-stress jobs

LANGUAGE FOCUS Stress and work

A ▶ **1.5** Read about high- and low-stress jobs. What do the most stressful jobs have in common?
High degree of personal risk; responsibility for public safety

HIGH- AND LOW-STRESS JOBS

All jobs can be stressful, but some jobs are much more stressful than others. Below are some high- and low-stress jobs, along with their annual median salaries.

6 MOST STRESSFUL JOBS

1. **Military Personnel** $41,998
2. **Firefighter** $45,250
3. **Commercial Airline Pilot** $92,060
4. **Newspaper Reporter** $36,000
5. **Taxi Driver** $22,440
6. **Police Officer** $55,010

6 LEAST STRESSFUL JOBS

1. **University Professor** $62,050
2. **Seamstress / Tailor** $25,850
3. **Jeweler** $35,170
4. **Dietician** $53,250
5. **Hair Stylist** $22,500
6. **Librarian** $54,500

B ▶ **1.6** Listen to the conversation. Why does Sophie find being a pilot stressful?
The long hours; being in charge of the safety of all the passengers

C ▶ **1.7** Watch and study the language in the chart.

Talking about jobs and stress

If you can't imagine having a stressful job, you shouldn't join the military.		
If you like working in a relaxing environment, you should consider becoming a librarian.		
Do you enjoy working outdoors?		

Daniel plans to be a dietician.		
Lara expects to work long hours at her new job.		
Anna hopes to have a career in medicine.		

He	likes / loves	being a teacher.
She	prefers / wants	to work with children.

For more information on **gerunds and infinitives**, see Grammar Summary 1 on page 183.

16

Grammar Note

Note that the language in the chart introduces some verbs for talking about jobs and stress. While the focus of the sentences in the chart is jobs, note that these verbs can be used to talk about other situations as well.

When two verbs are paired together, the second one can appear in the *-ing* form (gerund) or the infinitive form depending on the verb that comes first. In the chart, the verbs *imagine, enjoy, like*, and *love* are followed by the *-ing* form. And *plan, expect, hope, prefer,* and *want* are followed by the infinitive.

However, please note that some verbs can actually be followed by either the *-ing* form or the infinitive, including these verbs from the chart: *like, love, prefer.*

D ▶ **1.6** Listen to the conversation in **B** again. Complete the sentences from the conversation.

1 "I thought you always ____wanted to be____ a pilot."

2 "I didn't ____expect to work____ such long hours."

3 "I can't ____imagine writing____ papers and ____having____ people evaluate them."

4 "Good thing I didn't encourage you ____to become____ a professor then!"

E Complete the sentences. Circle the correct words.

1 Jae wants ((to avoid)/ avoiding) working in an office, so he plans ((to be)/ being) a dietician.

2 Elise considered (to become /(becoming))an emergency room doctor, but she doesn't enjoy (to be /(being))under pressure.

3 The university encourages students ((to take)/ taking) internships, especially if they plan ((to work)/ working) in business.

4 If you are considering (to have /(having))a career in medicine, expect ((to go)/ going) to school for several years.

5 Wei can't imagine (to run /(running)) into a burning building, so he doesn't want ((to be)/ being) a firefighter.

F ▶ **1.8** Complete the information using the correct form of the verb in parentheses. Then listen and check your answers.

Many college students ¹ ____take____ (**take**) a semester off from school if they want ² ____to get____ (**get**) some work experience. They often prefer ³ ____to find____ (**find**) internships in the types of companies or organizations that they hope ⁴ ____to work____ (**work**) for after they finish college. This way, they can learn more about the industry and find out if they'll enjoy ⁵ ____working____ (**work**) in that field in the future. Most students shouldn't expect ⁶ ____to get____ (**get**) paid if they find an internship. However, even if an internship is unpaid, students should still consider ⁷ ____doing____ (**do**) it. The work experience gained will increase their chances of getting a permanent job in the future, and make the job search process less stressful.

Career counselors help students apply for internships and jobs.

SPEAKING Ways to relax   Answers will vary.

You are going to ask your classmates how they deal with stress. Turn to page 165.

17

SPEAKING

Have students preview the task and read the chart. Explain that they are going to walk around the classroom to find individuals who use each of the activities in the chart to cope with stress. Model the example with a volunteer. Point out that students will ask follow-up questions to find out more information from those who answered yes.

➕ **SUPPORT** Give students time to look over the situations to ask questions about in more detail, and to take notes on possible follow-up questions.

★ **CHALLENGE** Have each student introduce another to the class by sharing their ways of coping with stress. Or play a guessing game where students give information about someone and the rest of the class has to guess who it is.

D Have students preview the task.

▶ **1.6** Play the audio/video. Have students work individually to complete the activity. Have students check answers in pairs.

E Have students work individually. Tell them to use the information in the language chart to help them. Check answers as a class, going over the use of gerunds and infinitives.

F Have students work individually to complete the paragraph.

▶ **1.8** Play the audio/video to check answers.

The stressed-out generation

1C The stressed-out generation

LESSON OVERVIEW

Aims: Read and comprehend an article about stress in the younger generation; understand main ideas and details

Target Vocabulary: anxiety, generation, recession, responsibility

Reading Summary: People across all generations today report higher levels of stress than in the past, but it is Millennials that seem to be the most stressed-out of all. Growing up in a world where access to modern technology is the norm, Millennials are suffering stress from being overwhelmed by information. Additionally, they have come of age during an economic downturn, which has made it hard for them to find their career paths. Public awareness about mental health issues means that Millennials are more open about discussing stress, which is one reason why they may seem to have more of it than past generations. It also means that Millennials are more likely to seek help for their stress though, and ultimately develop useful coping strategies.

PRE-READING

Read the question aloud. Tell students to guess the answer based on their own background knowledge and ideas. Ask them to check their answer as they read.

▶ **1.9** Play the audio/video as students read along. Explain any key terms that students might not be familiar with.

PRE-READING Predicting

Look at the title. Which generation do you think is the most stressed-out?

(a) Millennials (born roughly between 1981 and 2004)

b Generation X (born roughly between 1965 and 1980)

c Baby Boomers (born roughly between 1946 and 1964)

▶ **1.9**

1 Each **generation**—from Baby Boomers to Generation X to Millennials—has its own set of values and characteristics. But one thing common to all generations is that they are suffering
5 from stress. In a recent poll by the American Psychological Association (APA), all age groups now report higher levels of stress than in the past. Baby Boomers (those born roughly between 1946 and 1964, and who are now moving into their retirement
10 years) said that they are stressed about money and health issues. Gen Xers (born roughly between 1965 and 1980) are concerned about work, money, and job stability. However, Millennials (born roughly between 1981 and 2004) are turning out to be
15 the most stressed-out[1] of all the generations. Poll results indicate that stress levels for these younger respondents are significantly above average. So what's worrying the Millennials?

STRESS AND MILLENNIALS

20 Millennials are the first generation to grow up with computers in the home and the classroom. Due to the rise of modern technology and social media, they are constantly bombarded with information. Over time, this information overload can become too much to handle
25 and can result in chronic stress, which in turn can cause serious physical, psychological, and emotional problems. Another contributing factor, according to author Michael D. Hais, is that many Millennials have lived sheltered lives due to overprotective parents.
30 These young adults lack problem-solving skills and may struggle with fear of failure once they leave home. Making matters worse, the 2008 **recession** occurred when many Millennials were graduating from high school or college. The resulting economic
35 slowdown reduced the number of available jobs for graduates. Sure enough, in the APA poll, Millennials said that work, money, relationships, family **responsibilities**, and the economy are the main stressors in their lives.
40 However, the poll results may be a bit misleading as they don't take into account public attitudes toward stress and mental illness. Ronald Kessler of Harvard Medical School, who has studied the prevalence of mental disorders in the
45 U.S., points out that changes in social attitudes have helped reduce the stigma attached to mental

18

Content Note

Giving nicknames to generations became a popular trend in the United States in the 1900s. The nicknames are often first given by academics or writers, and then catch on and become popularized in the media. The trend is said to have started when a writer, Gertrude Stein, referred to the generation of people born between 1880 and 1900 as the Lost Generation. The generations that followed are known as the Greatest Generation, the Silent Generation, Baby Boomers, Generation X, and Millennials.

People of the same generation are influenced by the historical period that they are born in and share similar characteristics with each other as a result.

The term *chronic stress* (line 25) refers to a condition where our bodies contain too many hormones to counter long-term stress. Note that *chronic* is a vocabulary word in Lesson D.

A *stigma* (line 68) refers to a negative public image. Something that has a stigma attached to it is typically not accepted by society.

The term *hypnotherapy* (line 74) refers to a hypnosis technique used to help people deal with emotional issues by putting the person in a trance or an altered mental state.

High school students take part in their end-of-term exam in Fengqiu County, China.

illness over the years. For example, the creation of health-related television programming and specialty magazines such as *Psychology Today* have
50 contributed to greater public awareness of mental health issues. It's possible that younger people now are more willing to admit to being stressed than in the past. "There is not a lot of evidence of true prevalence having gone up," Kessler says. "It
55 looks like younger people are in worse shape, but unfortunately, we just don't know."

AGE AND OPTIMISM
Despite the high levels of stress reported by Millennials in the APA poll, there is reason for
60 optimism. Many happiness and well-being surveys show that happiness generally increases as people grow older. This seems to imply that the ability to manage stress effectively comes with

age. As Millennials gain more life experience and
65 develop better problem-solving skills over time, they should become better at handling stress. Moreover, with the greater awareness surrounding mental health issues today, the stigma associated with seeing a psychiatrist or psychologist has
70 lessened. This means that people are more likely to seek professional help to reduce their stress and **anxiety** levels. There is now a wide range of stress management techniques available including exercise, meditation, and hypnotherapy. Millennials
75 must develop effective coping strategies to deal with stress in order to be productive members of their community. Once they do, they will be able to look back with satisfaction on the world they helped create.

¹ **stressed-out:** *adj.* experiencing stress

19

➡ **EXTENSION ACTIVITY** Ask students to think about whether or not the generation names explained in **Content Note** are appropriate for the generations in their home countries. Have them work individually to come up with a name for the most recent generation in their home country. Tell them to share the nickname with a partner and explain the reasoning.

Language Note

A person's *values* (line 3) are the ideas and behaviors that that person finds important.

To be *bombarded* (line 23) with something means to be overwhelmed to the point of feeling attacked.

The expression *information overload* (line 24) refers to the condition of having too much information or data. With the Internet, our access to information means that we can also easily become too informed with unhelpful information, causing us stress.

UNDERSTANDING MAIN IDEAS

Have students look over the diagrams in detail. Tell them to refer back to the passage if necessary. Have them check answers in pairs. Elicit a summary of the main idea as shown in the correct diagram.

UNDERSTANDING DETAILS

Encourage students to use the technique of scanning to find the information from the passage to answer each question. Point out that the subheadings are helpful for finding where specific information may be. Note that the questions are written in a style similar to those found on exams such as TOEFL®, TOEIC®, and so forth. Check answers as a class, eliciting the line in the passage where each piece of information was found.

⊙ **EXTENSION ACTIVITY** Divide the class into pairs or small groups based on home countries. Ask students to discuss whether the information in the reading passage is similar to or different from the Millennial generation in their home countries. Ask groups to list some common characteristics of the generation and the factors that cause stress in that generation's life. Is it the same? If time permits, have each group give a short presentation to the class.

BUILDING VOCABULARY

A Have students work individually to complete the activity. Check answers as a class. Elicit example sentences using each word. Write them on the board. See **Content Note** for more on various generations.

B **CRITICAL THINKING** Read the questions aloud as students read along. Have students work in pairs to first review the main ideas that they heard Dr. Trudi Edginton talk about in the video. Then ask them to write down some advice that they think she would agree with. Have pairs share one piece of advice with the class. Ask the class to comment on whether they think Dr. Edginton would agree with the advice or not. Model the example. Note that students can use this phrase to introduce their ideas.

UNDERSTANDING MAIN IDEAS

Which of the diagrams below best illustrates the results of the APA poll?

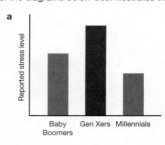
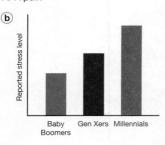

UNDERSTANDING DETAILS

Choose the correct options.

1 Which of the following is true about the results of the APA poll?

  a Stress levels are down for all age groups, but they're down the most for Millennials.

  b Millennials are experiencing more stress than before, but other age groups aren't.

  (c) All age groups are experiencing more stress than before.

2 Which of these is a cause of worry across all generations?

  a health

  b the weak economy

  (c) money

3 According to the passage, what is true about young people today compared to the past?

  a They are more likely to become psychiatrists or psychologists.

  (b) They are more willing to seek professional help to deal with stress.

  c They are more independent and have good problem-solving skills.

4 According to the passage, why might Millennials be right in feeling optimistic about the future?

  a The economy is improving.

  b Technology is helping to reduce stress.

  (c) Happiness tends to increase with age.

BUILDING VOCABULARY

A Match the words in blue from the passage to their definitions.

1 generation — a group of people about the same age

2 recession — a period when economic activity is not strong

3 responsibilities — things that a person must do as part of a job, role, or legal obligation

4 anxiety — a feeling of worry or nervousness

B **CRITICAL THINKING** Answers will vary.

Synthesizing What might Dr. Trudi Edginton (page 15) say about the poll results? What advice might she have for Millennials? Discuss with a partner.

> I think Dr. Edginton would say that …

20

⊙ **EXTENSION ACTIVITY** Have students work in pairs. Tell them to go online to find the article by Dr. Trudi Edginton titled "How to deal with stress and relax, according to a psychologist." Ask them to read the article and compare the strategies she gives versus the ones that they mentioned in their discussion in **Critical Thinking**. Note that Dr. Trudi Edginton was the speaker in the **Listening** section on page 15.

1D How to make stress your friend

TEDTALKS

KELLY McGONIGAL is a psychologist at Stanford University. She is interested in helping people understand and apply the latest scientific findings in psychology, neuroscience, and medicine.

Kelly McGonigal's idea worth spreading is that if we can view stress as our body's natural reaction to a difficult situation, it's better for our relationships, health, and happiness.

PREVIEWING

Read the sentences below and guess if they are correct. Circle **T** for true or **F** for false. Then match each **bold** word to its meaning. You will hear these words in the TED Talk.

1 **Chronic** stress can cause serious health problems.   Ⓣ   **F**

2 The way you view stress can **transform** the way your body reacts to it.   Ⓣ   **F**

3 Stressful **experiences** can increase your chances of dying by 30 percent.   Ⓣ   **F**

4 People who are closer to their loved ones live **relatively** stress-free lives.   Ⓣ   **F**

_____relatively_____	**a**	in comparison with
_____transform_____	**b**	to change significantly
_____chronic_____	**c**	long-lasting
_____experiences_____	**d**	events or occurrences

VIEWING

A ▶ **1.10** Watch Part 1 of the TED Talk. Choose the correct options.

1 What helped McGonigal change her mind about stress?

   a a personal experience

   ⓑ the results of a study

2 Who has the lowest risk of death?

   a people who don't experience a lot of stress but who believe that stress is dangerous

   ⓑ people who experience a lot of stress but who think that stress isn't harmful

21

1D

How to make stress your friend

PREVIEWING

Have students read the sentences and guess their answers. Tell them to pay attention to how each word is used in context in order to understand its meaning. Have students work individually before checking answers in pairs.

Remind students of the **Warm Up** preview clip. Tell them to use all the language and information they have learned about stress to support their viewing of Kelly McGonigal's TED Talk. If necessary, elicit additional example sentences with each vocabulary word.

VIEWING

A Have students preview the task. Tell them to listen selectively for the information that they need.

▶ **1.10** Play Part 1 of the TED Talk. Check answers as a class. Elicit or explain the meaning of any unfamiliar language. Suggestions for Part 1 include *cardiovascular disease, my whole approach, public records,* and *tracked.*

★ **CHALLENGE** Before students hear the rest of McGonigal's talk, ask them to share their general impressions and feelings about stress now. How does stress affect them specifically? Do they experience physical effects? How do they think long-term stress can affect people in general?

LESSON OVERVIEW	

Aims: Watch and understand a talk about rethinking stress; observe and practice involving the audience

Target Vocabulary: chronic, experience, relatively, transform

TED Talk Summary: Kelly McGonigal tells the TED audience that she spent ten years giving people the wrong advice about stress, and that her talk is one way for her to clearly explain the misconceptions that many have about how stress impacts us. Recent research, she explains, shows us that stress does not affect us negatively. Instead, it's our attitude toward stress that has a negative impact on us. Studies reveal that people who don't see stress as something negative are as a result not affected negatively by it. Conversely, those who see stress as negative may even die from it, as this attitude affects our body's physical reaction to stress.

B Have students preview the task.

▶ **1.11** Play Part 2 of the TED Talk. Check answers as a class or play the check-your-answers part of the video. Ask students to work in pairs to summarize the process of the social stress test. Ask them to explain what happened during the test in their own words.

McGonigal explains that the test involves first giving a speech about your weaknesses, while you're being filmed, for an audience that is not responding positively to what they hear. Note that students only hear part of the explanation of the social stress test. After this stressful speech experience, participants are then asked to do a math problem while someone keeps interrupting them and telling them to do better.

C Tell students to complete the task based on the information they heard in Part 2. Check answers as a class. Then elicit an explanation about why the picture on the right is better. Make sure students understand that the picture on the left shows the blood vessel getting narrower, which prevents the blood from flowing to the heart and can therefore lead to heart problems.

Write the following quote from McGonigal on the board and elicit the meaning of "make you better at stress": *So my goal as a health psychologist has changed. I no longer want to get rid of your stress. I want to make you better at stress.*

Note that she is saying that she wants to help us change the way we view stress so we can experience positive benefits of it instead of negative. Elicit or explain the meaning of any unfamiliar language. Suggestions for Part 2 include *nonverbal feedback, meet this challenge*, and *heart rate*.

D Have students read the statements. Note that students can infer the answers based on what they've heard and read so far in the unit.

▶ **1.12** Play Part 3 of the TED Talk. Check answers as a class. Ask students to specify what kind of social connections McGonigal says are helpful (those in which you help people you know or in your community).

B ▶ **1.11** Watch Part 2 of the TED Talk. Which option best summarizes the Harvard social stress test and its outcome?

(a) Participants were told that the symptoms of stress that they experienced during the test were positive. This led to them having relaxed blood vessels.

b Participants were asked to consciously lower their breathing and heart rate before taking part in the test. This led to them having relaxed blood vessels.

c Participants were categorized based on how they viewed stress. Those who viewed stress as positive had relaxed blood vessels.

C Label the diagrams below and complete the descriptions using the words from the box.

anxiety	healthy	joy	unhealthy	helpful	disease

¹ _____unhealthy_____ blood vessel

⁴ _____healthy_____ blood vessel

This is a typical stress response when you feel ² _____anxiety_____ . Over the long term, it can lead to cardiovascular ³ _____disease_____ .

This is what happens when people view their stress response as ⁵ _____helpful_____ . It looks a lot like what happens in moments of ⁶ _____joy_____ .

D ▶ **1.12** Watch Part 3 of the TED Talk. Check (✓) the statements that Kelly McGonigal would agree with.

☐ The harmful effects of stress on your health are inevitable.

☑ It's more important to view stress differently than to avoid stress.

☑ Forming greater social connections is a good way of dealing with stress.

☑ Individuals have the ability to control how stress affects them.

E **CRITICAL THINKING**

Evaluating/Reflecting Discuss these questions with a partner. Answers will vary.

1 Check your answers to the Previewing quiz on page 21. Did any of McGonigal's findings surprise you?

2 Have your views about stress changed? How do you think your body will respond to stress in future?

22

Elicit or explain the meaning of any additional unfamiliar language. Suggestions for Part 3 include *financial difficulties* and *resilience*.

E **CRITICAL THINKING** Read the questions aloud. Ask students to go back to their quizzes individually to check their answers. Give them a few minutes to also think about how their views of stress have changed before discussing their answers in pairs. Elicit a class discussion after pairs have talked. Ask for some specific examples of how students plan to change their approach to stress.

➡ **EXTENSION ACTIVITY** Have students work in small groups. Tell group members to brainstorm some ideas about how they can help others in their community. Give them time to go online to find some relevant organizations if necessary. Then have groups share one or two of their ideas with the class.

VOCABULARY IN CONTEXT

▶ **1.13** Watch the excerpts from the TED Talk. Choose the correct meaning of the words. 1.a; 2.b; 3.a; 4.c

PRESENTATION SKILLS Involving the audience

> Help your audience pay attention by involving them in your presentation. Here are some ways you can do this.
> - Ask them questions about themselves.
> - Ask them to make a prediction or guess facts.
> - Describe a situation and ask them to imagine participating in it.
> - Engage them physically by asking them to stand, raise hands, clap, etc.
> - Use a conversational tone rather than a formal "academic" tone.

A ▶ **1.14** Watch part of Kelly McGonigal's TED Talk. Which of the techniques above does she use?
She describes a situation and asks the audience to imagine participating in it, and uses a conversational tone.

B Work with a partner. What advantages are there to involving the audience in your presentation? Answers will vary.

C Work with a group. Brainstorm other ways to involve the audience in a presentation. Answers will vary.

23

VOCABULARY IN CONTEXT

▶ **1.13** Play the video. If necessary, play it again.

PRESENTATION SKILLS

A Read the Presentation Skills paragraph **Involving the audience** aloud. Note that this skill summarizes many different techniques that can be used to engage an audience by making them active participants in the presentation. Students will see many examples of how TED speakers do this throughout the textbook. In McGonigal's case, she involves the audience by having them imagine that they are participating in a social stress test.

▶ **1.14** Play the video. Check answers as a class. Ask students to comment on whether they found McGonigal's presentation easy to pay attention to or not.

B Read the question aloud. In pairs or as part of a class discussion, have students talk about the benefits of involving the audience.

C Divide the class into small groups. Tell groups to brainstorm ideas about other ways to involve the audience. Note that students will observe a range of techniques in the TED Talks throughout the textbook. Some other possibilities include: give a demonstration, ask the audience to calculate something, and have them play a game.

⊙ EXTENSION ACTIVITY Have students work in pairs. Tell them to go to the TED website and find a short talk to watch. Ask them to pay attention to the way that the speaker involves the audience. Have pairs report back to the class to share any new techniques that were demonstrated.

Language Note

Part 1

Cardiovascular disease is a medical term that refers to illnesses that affect the function of the heart.

When McGonigal says *my whole approach*, she is referring to the way in which she has dealt with stress-related issues with her patients so far.

Public records refer to information, usually documents, made public so anyone can access them. It is common in the United States for records of birth, marriage, and death to be publicly available.

To *track* people in a study means to follow them over a time period to stay aware of any updates or changes that are relevant for the study.

Part 2

Nonverbal feedback refers to a reaction expressed through body language. Note that McGonigal gives an example of nonverbal feedback in her speech.

To *meet a challenge* means to handle it successfully. A challenge usually means something that is difficult.

Your *heart rate* is how many times your heart beats in one minute.

Part 3

The term *financial difficulties* refers to money problems, such as not being able to pay monthly bills. Someone who has *resilience* is tough—able to recover from a hard situation.

Managing stress

Aims: Present a plan to help people cope with stress; write a letter of advice

COMMUNICATE

A Divide the class into groups. Give each group time to read over the profiles. Explain that they will be discussing how people can handle their stress better. Tell students to read individually and take notes before discussing as a group. Ask groups to go over each individual's situation. Tell group members to suggest at least one idea that might help each person.

Explain that they can give both general advice and more specific advice. For example, they can suggest that Silvie get exercise in the park nearby, or that she go for a one-hour walk every day in the park. Encourage students to discuss general ideas at first, and then get more specific. Tell them to use all the knowledge they've gathered about coping with stress in the unit when making suggestions. Explain that groups should be writing down their ideas because they are going to present them to another group next.

B Have each group join another group. Ask them to present their advice to each other. Tell the groups to also give reasons for their suggestions.

WRITING

Remind students that they have watched psychologists in the unit. Ask them to now pretend that it is their profession, too. Tell them to give advice based on the information they learned about how to handle stress in the unit.

COMMUNICATE Dealing with **stress** Answers will vary.

A Work in small groups. Read the profiles of four people who are experiencing stress. Suggest possible ways for them to deal with or manage their stress. Use the ideas you have learnt in this unit or your own ideas.

Silvie, 22
- a college student
- is stressed about applying for graduate school
- doesn't cook and eats a lot of junk food
- doesn't have much money saved
- lives near a park

Daisy, 23
- just started her first job
- is stressed because she often doesn't understand what she's supposed to do at work
- lives alone and far away from her family
- enjoys tech gadgets and has a lot of them

Rob, 17
- a high school student
- is stressed about his grades
- lives with his parents but isn't getting along with them right now
- has a few good friends
- loves playing guitar

Theo, 30
- an airline pilot
- is stressed because he works very long hours
- doesn't have a lot of free time to spend with his wife and kids
- likes exercising and being outdoors

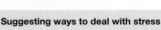

Suggesting ways to deal with stress
She could relieve stress by ...   *It may be good for him to ...*

B Compare your ideas with another group.

WRITING A letter giving advice Answers will vary.

Imagine you're a psychologist. Choose one of the people above and write them a letter giving your advice.

> Daisy,
> You're experiencing stress because you've just started a new job and it's challenging for you. In addition, you're far away from home. Since you're good with tech gadgets, I would recommend ...

24

Read the model letter aloud. Point out that in the example, the psychologist explains some reasons why the person is experiencing stress. Explain that they will also include ideas and suggestions about how to cope with the stress. Remind students to use the language and grammar in the unit.

⊙ EXTENSION ACTIVITY Have students work with a partner to role-play giving advice. Have them tell their partners to whom they wrote the letter. Then have them role-play a conversation between that person and a psychologist using the letters that they wrote as a guide for what they are going to say. Tell partners to switch roles so each has a turn to give advice. If time permits, ask for volunteers to act out their role plays for the class.

2 Media Influences

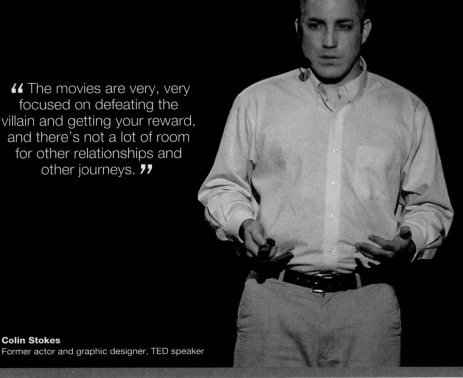

44 The movies are very, very focused on defeating the villain and getting your reward, and there's not a lot of room for other relationships and other journeys. **77**

Colin Stokes
Former actor and graphic designer, TED speaker

UNIT GOALS

In this unit, you will ...

- talk about movies and their effect on the audience.
- read about superheroes as role models.
- watch a TED Talk about how movies can provide positive messages for children.

WARM UP

▶ **2.1** Watch part of Colin Stokes's TED Talk. Answer the questions with a partner.

1 What were some of your favorite movies when you were a child? Why did you like them? Answers will vary.
2 Do you think movies affect people's attitudes and behavior? Answers will vary.

25

---

2 Media Influences

UNIT GOALS

In this unit, students will read, watch, and discuss how media and movies in particular influence our thinking. Students will talk about favorite movies they watched as children, and consider how these might affect them now.

TED Speaker
Colin Stokes is the director of communications at Citizen Schools, a nonprofit that aims to provide education opportunities for the underprivileged.

TED Talk Summary
Stokes shares insights that he's learned from watching movies with his daughter and son. He's realized that male characters are predominantly engaged in violence and that there is a real lack of empowered and complex female characters in movies.

Idea Worth Spreading
Male characters in movies should respect and act as a team with women.

WARM UP

Have students look over the picture, caption, and quote on the page. Read the quote aloud. Note that students will hear the quote in the video clip. Elicit or explain the meaning of *defeating the villain.*

▶ **2.1** Play the preview clip of the TED Talk.

For question 1, note that students' answers will be based on their own interests and experiences as children. Ask them to introduce their favorite movies, or movies that made an impact on them when they were growing up.

For question 2, ask them to consider how children and adults are affected by movies. Ask them to talk about whether movies influenced them more when they were children or now. Ask volunteers to share some points that they discussed with the class.

➲ **EXTENSION ACTIVITY** Have students work in pairs. Ask them to describe the plot of their favorite movie from childhood. Have students retell the stories in their own words. As partners listen, ask them to quickly draw pictures about what they hear. Tell them not to show their pictures to their partners yet. After students finish, have partners reveal their pictures. Was the story depicted accurately?

Content Note

Although Stokes's former acting career probably influenced his opinion about the movie industry, he explains in his talk that it was in his role as a father when watching movies with his young children that he really became aware of the stereotypes in movies.

2A

At the movies

LESSON OVERVIEW

Aims: Learn language for talking about influences from media; listen to a NASA engineer talk about a movie; practice talking about movie genres

Target Vocabulary: character, ideals, influence, inspiration, role model, hero

VOCABULARY

A Have students work individually to complete the sentences. Check answers as a class, going over meanings when necessary.

B Have students work individually. Have them check answers in pairs. Explain that the language in the lesson will help them talk about the impact and influence that movies or other stories have had on them.

C Read the questions aloud. Point out that the conversation continues the discussion they had in pairs in the **Warm Up** about their favorite movies and how movies influence us. Ask them to give more specifics about how the movies and TV shows influenced them.

⭐ **CHALLENGE** Ask students to also talk about movies that left a lasting negative impression on them, and why.

An actor dressed as Spider-Man entertains children at a museum in New York City.

2A At the movies

VOCABULARY Influences

A Complete the sentences using the correct form of the words from the box.

find	have	make

1 Many parents feel that some pop stars don't _____ make _____ good **role models** for their children.

2 Some parents want their children to _____ find _____ **inspiration** in real people, not fictional characters in movies.

3 _____ Having _____ a strong **character** means standing up for your beliefs and taking responsibility for your actions.

4 Studies show that even though movies aren't real, they can _____ make _____ us feel strong emotions and **influence** our behavior.

5 Christopher Reeve, the actor who played Superman, once said, "What _____ makes _____ Superman a **hero** is not that he has power, but that he has the wisdom and the maturity to use the power wisely."

6 People with high **ideals** _____ have _____ very strong beliefs about what is good and right.

B Cross out the word that is NOT a synonym for each **bold** word.

1	**role model**	hero	~~actor~~	idol
2	**inspiration**	encouragement	~~information~~	motivation
3	**character**	personality	~~body~~	moral strength
4	**influence**	determine	affect	~~help~~
5	**ideals**	ethics	morals	~~suggestions~~

C Work with a partner. What movies and TV shows had an influence on you as a child? How did they influence you? Answers will vary.

26

Language Note

If necessary, introduce or review language for movie genres: *action movie, animation, drama, fantasy, horror movie, mystery, musical, romance, romantic comedy, science fiction, thriller,* and *western.*

When talking about movie types in general, we usually make the noun plural: *I like thrillers/dramas/westerns/fantasies/romantic comedies.*

Exceptions to this include *animation* and *science fiction.*

When speaking about a specific movie, it is typical to use a singular noun: *My favorite movie is a western/musical/thriller.*

Some genres commonly appear as a collocation with *movie*, most notably *action movie* and *horror movie.*

LISTENING Movies and career choices

> **Focused listening**
> When you know what the speaker will talk about, you can form ideas. The aim of focused listening isn't to predict what you'll hear, but to help you identify the main points and ideas.

A ▶ **2.2** Watch aerospace engineer Mamta Nagaraja talk about how a movie changed her life. Which movie does she mention?
Space Camp

B ▶ **2.2** Watch again. Check (✓) the statements that Nagaraja would agree with.

- ☑ Movies can open your imagination to new ideas.
- ☑ Movies can provide role models.
- ☑ Movies can influence your career choice.
- ☐ Movies about space tend to appeal to boys, not girls.

C CRITICAL THINKING Answers will vary.

Reflecting Have any movies influenced your career aspirations? Discuss with a partner.

Mamta Nagaraja at NASA's Mission Control Center

SPEAKING Talking about movie genres

A ▶ **2.3** Why does Speaker A find action movies predictable?
Because the female characters in those movies usually need to be saved by a man.

A: What's your favorite movie genre?

B: I love action movies like *Transformers*. The special effects are great, and they keep me on the edge of my seat. I never get bored watching them.

A: Don't you find them a bit predictable?

B: Not at all. Do you?

A: Yes! The female characters in those movies are usually helpless "damsels in distress" who need to be saved by a man. Most action movies don't have positive role models for girls.

B: Well, what about *The Avengers*? Scarlett Johansson's in it.

A: But there are so many guys in that movie and only one girl. My favorite kind of movies are ones that have strong female lead characters, like *The Help*. That movie had a big influence on me. It's so inspiring.

B Practice the conversation with a partner.

C Work with a partner. Talk about different movie genres and why you like or don't like them. Use the expressions in blue above to help you. Answers will vary.

> What kind of movies do you like?

> I love science fiction movies because ...

27

LISTENING

A Read **Focused listening** aloud as students read along. Explain that being focused as a listener means that you are concentrating on what is being said. This helps to pick up the main ideas, but also in a conversation, it lets you show someone that you are an engaged and active listener. Read the question aloud and tell students to listen for the answer.

▶ **2.2** Play the video. Check answers as a class. Ask students to raise their hands if they've seen this movie.

B Have students preview the task. Point out that they will be inferring the answers based on what they can imply about the speaker's feelings about movies.

▶ **2.2** Play the video. Have students check answers in pairs. Ask them to point out what they heard that helped them infer what the speaker agrees with.

C CRITICAL THINKING Read the question aloud. Give students some time to consider their answers. Note that students can also talk about TV shows, books, or fiction stories. Tell

students to use the language in the lesson in their discussion. Tell them that if they don't have an example of a career choice being affected, they can talk about another way that a movie inspired a life change.

SPEAKING

A Ask students to read along as they watch.

▶ **2.3** Play the audio/video. Check answers as a class. Ask students to raise their hands if they agree with the speaker's views. Elicit some other movies with helpless female characters.

Point out the phrase *Well, what about ...?* Explain that this expression is useful when offering an example to oppose someone's view. In the conversation, the speaker uses the expression to introduce a movie that has a strong female character.

B Model the conversation aloud with a student. Then have students work in pairs to practice. Make sure they alternate between A and B roles.

➕ **SUPPORT** Play the audio/video again, pausing after each sentence so students can repeat.

C Read the task aloud. Elicit the names of movie genres to write in a word web on the board to support the discussion. See **Language Note**. Model the example with a volunteer. Point out that students will continue the conversation by giving reasons about why they like or don't like a genre.

➡ **EXTENSION ACTIVITY** Have students work in pairs or small groups. Ask them to think of a movie that they like and to describe the female characters in that movie. What kind of roles do the women in that movie have? Do they think the characters are positive or negative role models?

2B Media and the mind

LANGUAGE FOCUS How the media affects us

LESSON OVERVIEW

Aims: Read an infographic about how media affects us; talk about qualities that are important in a movie

Infographic Summary: Data is presented about how TV shows and movies influence our behavior, in both positive and negative ways. On the negative side, we can actually become more aggressive. On the positive side, we can become more altruistic.

LANGUAGE FOCUS

A Read the question aloud.

▶ **2.4** Play the audio/video as students read along. Then give them additional time to look over the infographic. Point out for Positive Content the study talks about the effect of laughing on our blood vessels, which is also something the Unit 1 TED speaker talked about regarding stress. Elicit a summary of what the speaker said about how our blood vessels are affected by stress. Have students discuss their answers in pairs. Note that they should talk about movies or TV shows that created either aggressive behavior, or positive social interactions and self-control. Ask them to also talk about how they feel when they laugh while watching a movie.

B Read the questions aloud and tell students to listen for the answer.

▶ **2.5** Play the audio/video. Check answers as a class. Elicit more details about the conversation. Ask: *Who did Steve take to see a movie?* (his little brother)

What movie does Jennifer recommend? (*Finding Dory*)

Ask students to share with the class any background information that they have about the movie *The Avengers*. Then ask the class if they think it's too violent for kids.

A ▶ **2.4** Read about how movies and TV can affect us. Can you think of a movie or TV show that affected you in a similar way? Answers will vary.

MEDIA AND THE MIND

People often watch movies to relax. However, movies can affect your mind and your body in ways you may not be able to detect.

NEGATIVE CONTENT:

A U.S. study showed that watching violent movies can lead to an increase in blood pressure and cause hostile behavior in both men and women.

Two psychologists found that elementary school children who watched many hours of violence on TV showed higher levels of aggressive behavior when they became teenagers.

POSITIVE CONTENT:

A study conducted at the University of Pennsylvania showed that watching pro-social TV shows and video clips can lead to positive social interaction and more self-control.

Researchers at the University of Maryland found that laughing while watching a funny film causes your blood vessels to dilate by 22 percent, which helps lower your blood pressure.

B ▶ **2.5** Listen to the conversation. Does Jennifer think it's OK for kids to watch violent movies? Why or why not? No. She's concerned that kids who watch violent movies may show higher levels of aggressive behavior once they grow up.

C ▶ **2.6** Watch and study the language in the chart.

Talking about media and inspirations
A role model is someone who provides an example of how to behave. The movies (that) children watch should be age-appropriate.
Superheroes, who are often based on comic book characters, are not always good role models for children. The survey, which included people from all over the world, showed that movies can influence behavior.
People participating in the study were all volunteers. The movie voted most inspirational that year was *The Theory of Everything*.

For more information on **relative clauses**, see Grammar Summary 2 on page 183.

C Have students read over the language chart for **Talking about media and inspirations.**

▶ **2.6** Play the audio/video. Ask students to pay attention in particular to the relative pronouns in the clauses. Go over the formation and use of relative clauses. Direct students to page 183 for more information.

Grammar Note

The language chart introduces relative clauses for adding information. In each sentence in the chart, the clauses are connected by a relative pronoun. The relative pronouns *who, that*, and *which*

are introduced for sharing more details in a sentence.

In the first two sentences, which have no commas, the information following the relative pronoun is essential to the sentence. However, in the next two sentences, the relative clauses are offset by commas, which indicates that the information is non-essential, meaning it is extra information. In the second two sentences, if the clause is removed, what remains would still be a complete sentence.

D ▶ **2.5** Listen to the conversation in **B** again. Complete the sentences from the conversation.

1 "I read an article recently about the impact _____that_____ violent movies can have on young children."

2 "It said that kids _____who_____ are exposed to violence in movies and on TV tend to show higher levels of aggressive behavior once they grow up."

3 "But I'd prefer it if my younger brother watches movies like *Finding Dory*, _____which_____ is funny and inspiring."

E Find and correct the mistake in each sentence.

1 Research suggests that watching horror movies releases ~~hormones, which~~ ^{hormones that} can increase your heart rate.

2 Children ^{who} ~~that~~ play a lot of violent video games may be more likely to engage in aggressive behavior.

3 One study revealed that movies that make you laugh can lower your blood pressure, ^{which} ~~that~~ in turn decreases the risk of cardiovascular disease.

4 Parents should be aware of the potential dangers ^{that} ~~who~~ violent TV shows can have on children.

F ▶ **2.7** Complete the information. Circle the correct words. Then listen and check your answers.

We all know the power ¹(**that** / **which**) a movie can have on its audience. Movies can inspire, enlighten, or enrage. In 2011, the Academy Award for Best Picture went to *The King's Speech*, a movie about one man's struggle with stuttering—a speech disorder. The movie, ²(**that** / **which**) helped raise awareness for the disorder, tells the story of King George VI, ³(**that** / **who**) overcame his stutter to become a great leader of the United Kingdom. Movie characters, ⁴(**which** / **who**) are often an inspiration for audiences, can help to change people's perceptions of society and the world we live in.

Colin Firth won an Academy Award for Best Actor for his performance in *The King's Speech*.

SPEAKING Ranking movies   Answers will vary.

A Work in small groups. Below is a list of qualities that are important in a movie. Add three more qualities. Then rank them in order from 1–8 (1 being the most important quality).

___ **a** The main character is inspirational.	___ **b** The movie evokes strong emotions.
___ **c** The movie has a strong social message.	___ **d** The movie's plot makes sense.
___ **e** The movie has actors who I like.	___ **f** _____
___ **g** _____	___ **h** _____

B Pick two of your favorite movies. How do they rate against your criteria above? Tell your group.

29

Explain that they should use relative clauses to give more information about the movies and the inspiration.

SPEAKING

A Give students time to preview the task and read the chart. Have them rank the qualities on their own before sharing their ideas with their group members. Explain that each aspect should be given a ranking from 1–8 and that no two aspects can have the same ranking.

Divide the class into small groups and have students discuss each aspect of a movie together and share their rankings. Encourage groups to debate before coming to a consensus on what ranking each aspect should have.

B Give students time to work individually. Tell them to think about two of their favorite movies and to use the charts that they made with their groups to evaluate the movies. Ask students to explain if any of their opinions about their movies changed after evaluating them using the chart.

⟳ **EXTENSION ACTIVITY** Have students work in small groups to repeat the **Speaking** activity using their favorite childhood movie, TV show, or video game instead. Ask them to rate it against their criteria in the chart and then discuss how it may have influenced them as children, or while growing up. Tell students to also refer to the information in the infographic during their discussions. Which category from the infographic does their favorite childhood movie/TV show/ video game fit into? What kind of impact do they think it had on them?

D Have students preview the task.

▶ **2.5** Play the audio/video. Have students work individually to complete the activity.

Check answers as a class. Point out the expression *I read an article recently about . . .* Explain that this is a useful expression for sharing information that supports your argument.

E Have students work individually. Tell them to use the information in the language chart to help them correct the errors. Check answers as a class, going over the use of relative pronouns together.

F Have students work individually to complete the paragraph.

▶ **2.7** Play the audio/video to check answers. Note that for item 1, in British English, *which* is an acceptable answer too, but in American English, only *that* is correct.

⟳ **EXTENSION ACTIVITY** Have students work individually to write a movie summary similar to the one in **F**. Ask them to explain the storyline of a movie that they consider inspiring. Tell them to include ideas about how the movie could change people's attitudes.

LESSON OVERVIEW

Aims: Read and comprehend an article about how superheroes influence us; understand main ideas and details

Target Vocabulary: dedicated to, exposure to, transfer, underlying, virtual

Reading Summary: Superhero stories are popular among children, yet how do these stories affect behavior? Opinions vary. Research shows that people who play a superhero in video games are more likely to help others. In regard to children, pretending to be superheroes is a way for them to be empowered; however, parents must be careful that this doesn't turn into aggressive behavior. Some experts say that modern superheroes are not good role models, unlike older superheroes such as Superman. However, others disagree with this assessment. Although opinions vary, what is clear is that the superheroes we are exposed to can influence our behavior.

PRE-READING

Read the question aloud. Tell students to read quickly to find the names of the superheroes mentioned. Check answers as a class, eliciting hints about how students found the names quickly. Point out that each name is a proper noun, which means it is capitalized. Scanning the text for capital letters is one strategy for finding the names quickly.

▶ **2.8** Play the audio/video as students read along. Explain any key terms that students might not be familiar with.

2C Are superheroes good role models?

PRE-READING Skimming

Skim the passage. Check (✓) the superheroes who are named as good role models.

- ☑ Superman
- ☐ Iron Man
- ☑ Spider-Man
- ☑ Daredevil

▶ **2.8**

1 Superheroes are everywhere: in comic books, movies, video games, and in posters on buses and trains. But what effect, if any, do superheroes have on our behavior?

5 A research team at Stanford University decided to explore this question by setting up a **virtual** reality experiment. In the study, people were given a mission—to find and rescue a sick child. One group of participants was made to feel as though

10 they could fly like Superman, while another group attempted the same task in a virtual helicopter. After the mission, each participant was interviewed.

During the interviews, the researcher pretended to accidentally knock over a cup filled with pens.

15 People who had just flown like Superman were not only quicker to help, but picked up an average of 15 percent more pens. Every "superhero" picked up at least a few pens, whereas some of the helicopter participants failed to offer any help at

20 all. This suggests that heroic behavior in a virtual environment might **transfer** to helpful behavior in the real world.

Superheroes may have a particularly important influence on children. Children have very limited

25 control over many areas of their lives. Therefore, pretending to be a superhero allows a child to act out and process any anxiety that they have, and thereby resolve or reduce **underlying** fears, claims Dr. Amy Bailey, a clinical psychologist at kidsFIRST

30 Medical Center, Dubai. "Children age three to four years find it difficult to differentiate between reality and fiction and, as such, the trait of superhuman strength is completely believable to them," she says. It "allows them to access some sense of power."

35 Bailey adds, "The risk to superhero play is that sometimes children's behavior can become out of control and escalate into chaotic play as a child becomes submerged[1] in these roles." She advises parents to limit **exposure to** more aggressive

40 shows and to have children focus on "other positive characteristics of their favorite hero, such as their clever thinking and care of others." Concern over the potential effect of aggressive behavior has led to some schools banning superhero play from the

45 classroom altogether.

Other psychologists share this concern. Some point to the evolution of the superhero over time, and are critical of modern renditions.[2] "There is a big difference in the movie superhero of today

50 and the comic book superhero of yesterday," says

30

Skill Note

Skimming involves reading quickly for main ideas. The first step of skimming includes quickly reading the title, subheadings, and captions, as well as looking at the pictures. The students should then read the entire first paragraph quickly, then the first and last sentence of each paragraph, and finally the entire last paragraph. Explain that students should be reading very quickly, and picking up on key words and phrases that can give them a general idea of what the passage is about. Note that scanning involves reading quickly for specific information, whereas skimming is done to get a main idea. While scanning, students should stop when they come to information that they think is relevant for what they are searching, and then read more carefully.

Batman impersonator Leonard Robinson visits a sick child at a hospital in West Virginia, U.S.A.

31

Language Note

To *knock something over* (line 14) means to make it fall down. It can be used in both intentional and unintentional situations.

A number that is *an average of* (line 16) is the median or most common value.

To *resolve* (line 28) means to handle or fix a problem.

The verb *claims* (line 28) is used to indicate that what a person is saying is not completely proven to be true, but is believed to be true by that person. It is a useful reporting verb when there is a degree of uncertainty.

When something *escalates* (line 37), it increases in intensity. The verb is often used to describe negative situations.

The word *banning* (line 44) refers to something being officially (or legally in some cases) not allowed.

To *exploit* (line 60) something or someone means to use them to your own advantage, especially without consideration for what is moral or right.

To *promote* (line 71) something means to encourage people to engage with it. The verb is often used to refer to advertising in businesses.

psychologist Sharon Lamb of the University of Massachusetts. "Today's superhero," Lamb says, is "aggressive, sarcastic, and rarely speaks to the virtue of doing good for humanity."

55 Lamb compares the selfish, playboy millionaire Tony Stark (Iron Man) to a superhero of the past, such as Superman. Superman, she points out, had a real job as a newspaper reporter and was **dedicated to** fighting injustice. More recent
60 characters such as Stark "exploit women, flaunt bling,[3] and convey their manhood with high-powered guns."

Jeff Greenberg, a social psychology professor at the University of Arizona, is less critical of modern
65 superheroes. According to him, superheroes give children confidence and can deliver a positive moral message. Many superheroes—such as Spider-Man or Superman—use their powers to protect the weak. And more modern superheroes such

70 as Daredevil, who is blind, and Charles Xavier (Professor X), who is paralyzed,[4] promote diversity and present positive images of disability.

It is becoming clear that superheroes offer us more than just entertainment. "If you design games
75 that are violent, people's aggressive behavior increases," claims Jeremy Bailenson, who led the Stanford University study. But he also believes that video games and other forms of superhero entertainment could be designed to train people to
80 be more empathetic[5] and helpful in the real world— perhaps giving us all the power to be a little more like Superman.

[1] **submerged:** *adj.* deeply involved
[2] **renditions:** *n.* versions or interpretations
[3] **flaunt bling:** *v.* to show off expensive jewelry, clothing, etc.
[4] **paralyzed:** *adj.* unable to move all or part of the body
[5] **empathetic:** *adj.* having the ability to understand someone else's feelings

Content Note

Historically, U.S. comics have been produced by two major publishing houses: Marvel Comics and DC Comics.

Of the characters mentioned in the reading, Iron Man, Spider-Man, Daredevil, and Professor X are creations of Marvel Comics, while Superman was created by DC Comics.

Fans of superheroes will notice the difference in characters coming from each publishing house. For example, DC characters tend to live in imaginary cities, while Marvel characters live in real cities. Most DC characters are born with their superpowers, while Marvel characters get theirs as a result of an accident. Most DC superheroes were created in the 1930s and 1940s, while Marvel Comics characters mostly came about in the 1960s and 1970s.

UNDERSTANDING MAIN IDEAS

Have students work individually. Check answers as a class. Direct students to paragraph 1 and ask them to find the sentence that introduces the main idea of the passage: *But what effect, if any, do superheroes have on our behavior?*

UNDERSTANDING DETAILS

A Elicit a review of the meaning of *pros* and *cons* (advantages and disadvantages). Have students work individually. Check answers as a class.

B Have students complete the activity without referring to the passage. Then have them check their answers by referring to the passage.

➡ **EXTENSION ACTIVITY** Have students work in pairs or small groups. Assign each pair or group one of the superheroes mentioned in the passage (Superman, Iron Man, Daredevil, Professor X) and ask them to go online to find out more about the character. Then have them report back to the class, giving a short presentation with pictures or other visual support.

BUILDING VOCABULARY

A Have students work individually to complete the activity. Check answers as a class. Elicit example sentences using each word. Write them on the board.

B **CRITICAL THINKING** Read the questions aloud as students read along. Have them work in pairs to first discuss what they know about the superheroes mentioned in the passage before evaluating the characterizations.

Then ask pairs to talk about other superheroes. Model the example with a volunteer.

Write useful phrases for discussion opinions on the board: *In my opinion …, I think …, I agree, but …, I disagree.*

UNDERSTANDING MAIN IDEAS

Choose the main idea of the passage.

a Parents should limit children's exposure to violent superhero movies.

ⓑ Superheroes can have a powerful impact on children's behavior.

c The concept of the superhero has evolved over time.

UNDERSTANDING DETAILS

A Complete the chart showing pros and cons of superheroes.

Pros	Cons
The heroic behavior of superheroes can encourage children to be more [1] __helpful__ in real life.	Imitating superheroes can sometimes lead to violent or [2] __aggressive__ behavior in children.
Superheroes give children [5] __confidence__ and send a positive message about protecting [6] __the weak__.	Some superhero characters exploit [3] __women__ and convey a narrow version of [4] __manhood__.

B Match the superheroes to the characterizations mentioned in the passage.

1 Superman ○ ——— ○ He is self-centered and is not a good role model for children.

2 Iron Man ○ ——— ○ He empowers children and stands for justice, fairness, and decency.

3 Professor X ○ ——— ○ He shows children that it's OK to be different.

BUILDING VOCABULARY

A Match the words in blue from the passage to their definitions.

1 virtual ○ ——— ○ having contact with something and being affected by it

2 transfer ○ ——— ○ existing only on computers or on the Internet

3 underlying ○ ——— ○ concealed but detectable

4 exposure to ○ ——— ○ committed to a task or purpose

5 dedicated to ○ ——— ○ to carry over from one situation to another

B **CRITICAL THINKING** Answers will vary.

Reflecting Discuss these questions with a partner.

1 Do you agree with the characterizations of the superheroes mentioned in the passage? Why or why not?

> In my opinion, Iron Man is a … because …

> I disagree. I think that …

2 Can you think of any other examples of superheroes who make good or bad role models?

32

Note that superhero characters are sometimes portrayed differently in movies than in the original comic books. If any students have background knowledge about the original characters from the comic books, have them share what they know with the class. Have pairs tell the class the name of one superhero they think is a good role model and explain why. Then ask the class to show if they agree or disagree by raising their hands.

➡ **EXTENSION ACTIVITY** Have students work in pairs or small groups to create a new superhero who will have a positive impact on kids. Tell them to decide their superhero's name and his or her superpower. Then ask students to make a poster with a picture and description of the hero. Have each group introduce their superhero to the class.

2D How movies teach manhood

TEDTALKS

COLIN STOKES is a former actor and graphic designer who currently divides his time between parenting and working for Citizen Schools, a nonprofit organization that helps to improve middle schools in low-income communities.

Colin Stokes's idea worth spreading is that movies should feature men who respect women and work with them, rather than men who use violence to rescue female characters.

PREVIEWING

Read the paragraph below. Match each **bold** word to its meaning. You will hear these words in the TED Talk.

As a parent of a girl and a boy, Stokes is interested in how movie characters and **themes** influence his children. In his TED Talk, he **assesses** recent and classic children's films. Several of these movies involve a **quest** where the characters go on a journey to accomplish a goal. However, Stokes is concerned that in most of these movies, both the **heroic** and the **villainous** characters are male. He would like to see more female characters. Stokes believes this is important not only for the girls in the audience, but also for the boys. He suggests that parents **seek out** movies with more female characters, so that both their sons and their daughters can have positive female role models.

1	a search for something, especially over a long time period	quest
2	to look for	seek out
3	having the qualities of a bad person	villainous
4	evaluates; analyzes	assesses
5	the central ideas of an artistic work, such as a movie or a novel	themes
6	having the qualities of a person admired for bravery or great deeds	heroic

VIEWING

A ▶ **2.9** Watch Part 1 of the TED Talk. Choose the option that best completes each sentence.

1 When Stokes refers to the "children's-fantasy-spectacular-industrial complex," he's describing an environment inspired by _____ .

   a movies made for children like *The Wizard of Oz*, with simple themes

   ⓑ entertainment designed for children that also markets products such as games and toys

   c entertainment that uses sophisticated technology, but is designed for adults

33

LESSON OVERVIEW

Aims: Watch and understand a talk about male role models in movies; observe and practice knowing your audience

Target Vocabulary: assess, heroic, quest, seek out, theme, villainous

TED Talk Summary: Colin Stokes shares insights he picked up about the movie industry while watching popular movies with his children. He sings the praises of *The Wizard of Oz*, which he says is full of strong female role models, is adventurous without being violent, and offers an encouraging message about being a leader and being

a friend. When it comes to movies like *Star Wars*, he is more critical. There is too much focus on the good guy beating the bad guy as well as on aggressive, go-it-alone male characters. Stokes says that *Star Wars* has informed the ways that movies have been made since the 1970s, but he thinks that *The Wizard of Oz* is a much better model to follow. He wants to see more movies that will teach his young son that women are strong leaders too, and that teamwork is valuable.

2D

How movies teach manhood

PREVIEWING

Have students read the paragraph. Tell them to pay attention to how each word is used in context in order to understand its meaning. Have students work individually before checking answers in pairs. Remind students of the **Warm Up** preview clip. Tell them to use all the language and information they have learned about movies and stories to support their viewing of the TED Talk.

VIEWING

A Have students preview the questions. Note that the question format is similar to comprehension questions on exams such as TOEFL® and TOEIC®. Note that the answer choices paraphrase what students will hear in the video, which requires an understanding of the overall meaning.

▶ **2.9** Play Part 1 of the TED Talk. Check answers as a class.

Elicit the movie that Stokes is referring to when he describes the plot as a metal guy and a furry guy rescuing a girl by dressing up as the enemy's guards (*Star Wars*). Ask students if they have seen *The Wizard of Oz*. Elicit a quick summary of the major plot points of both movies. Elicit or explain the meaning of any unfamiliar language. Suggestions for Part 1 include *complex* and *computer-generated*.

Content Note

The movie *The Wizard of Oz* came out in 1939, and it is one of the most well-known musical movies of all time. It is the fantasy story of a girl who finds herself lost in a magical land, and how she manages to get back home.

The movie is based on a book published in 1900, written by L. Frank Baum.

The action-adventure space fantasy movie *Star Wars* was released in 1977, and it was written by the movie's director, George Lucas. The story follows three space adventurers who try to win a war to defeat an evil empire.

B Have students preview the task. Explain that students will infer what the speaker thinks about some of the movies based on what they hear him say.

▶ **2.10** Play Part 2 of the TED Talk. Check answers as a class or play the check-your-answers part of the video.

Ask students to explain the answers for *Beauty and the Beast* and *The Hunger Games*. What thought process did they use to arrive at these inferences? Note that Stokes says he has positive feelings about Disney movies, and he uses the name of the lead character of *The Hunger Games* (Katniss) to comment on it being a war movie. Elicit or explain the meaning of any unfamiliar language. Suggestions for Part 2 include *supervision, imprinted, dopey,* and *patriarchy*.

C Have students complete the activity without watching Part 2 again. Play the check-your-answers part of the video. Note that the end of Part 2 is where they will get the information to infer the answer.

D Have students preview the task. Point out that question 2 is below the box.

▶ **2.11** Play Part 3 of the TED Talk. Check answers as a class.

Go over the three questions of the Bechdel Test and elicit students' thoughts and reactions. Explain that by introducing this test, Stokes is trying to show how ridiculous most movies are because they can't pass it. Elicit a quick discussion to check answers for question 2. Stokes says that he wants more movies with characters and messages that will make his son see women as courageous heroes and teach him to value a more team-oriented leadership style.

Elicit or explain the meaning of any additional unfamiliar language. Suggestions for Part 3 include *caught fire, lines, nudge,* and *identify with*.

E **CRITICAL THINKING** Read the direction line and questions aloud. Ask students to choose favorite movies or movies that they've recently seen so they remember the details of the story well enough. Read the example aloud with a volunteer. Explain that pairs will share their evaluations of the movies.

2 Stokes says that the wizard in a modern version of *The Wizard of Oz* might say, "Use your magic slippers to defeat the computer-generated armies of the Wicked Witch," because _____.

  a movies like *Star Wars* often feature the same magical weapons and enemies as in *The Wizard of Oz*

  b in *The Wizard of Oz*, Dorothy fought computer-generated armies using a pair of magic shoes

  ⓒ movies like *Star Wars* often feature a hero who has a magic weapon and fights computer-generated characters

B ▶ **2.10** Watch Part 2 of the TED Talk. Match the movies to what Colin Stokes might say about them.

  1 *Star Wars* — It's unlikely that boys will watch it.

  2 *The Wizard of Oz* — It has strong female characters but is still a war movie.

  3 *Beauty and the Beast* — It can be a great model for both boys and girls.

  4 *The Hunger Games* — It has a lot of violence and only a few female characters.

C Choose the ending Colin Stokes might most agree with.

We need more movies that _____.

  a focus on relationships and personal journeys

  b present positive messages and role models for girls

  ⓒ teach boys how to respect girls and women

D ▶ **2.11** Watch Part 3 of the TED Talk. Discuss these questions with a partner.

  1 What questions does the Bechdel Test ask? Complete the box below.

The Bechdel Test

  1 Are there at least two _____ women _____?

  2 Do they talk to _____ each other _____?

  3 About something other than a _____ man _____?

---

  2 What kind of movies does Stokes want for his son? Why?
  Movies that pass the Bechdel Test, so that his son can have positive female role models and learn to work with women

E **CRITICAL THINKING** Answers will vary.

  Applying **Work with a partner. Choose three movies and apply the Bechdel Test to each of them. Then discuss the following questions.**

  1 Do the movies pass the Bechdel Test?

  2 Why do you think these movies pass or fail the test? Could it be connected to who wrote or directed them? Or when they were made?

> All the movies we chose failed the Bechdel Test.

> It could be because of the movie genre. We only chose romantic comedies, and these kinds of movies are usually ...

34

Tell them to give details about the movie to explain why it passed the test or not.

Language Note

Part 1
The noun *complex* refers to a complicated system or network of things that are linked together.
The term *computer-generated* means digital, and Stokes uses it to refer to the computer graphics used as special effects in many movies these days.

Part 2
The noun *supervision* refers to the act of keeping watch over someone or something in order to keep it safe.

When something is *imprinted* on a person, it makes a strong, lasting impression.
The adjective *dopey* is a gentle euphemism for *stupid*.
The *patriarchy* refers to a male-dominated society, where positions of power are held by men.

Part 3
Something that *catches fire* becomes very popular in a short time.
In regard to movies, the term *lines* refers to what a character says.
To *nudge* means to push.
To *identify with* means to feel a connection with.

VOCABULARY IN CONTEXT

▶ **2.12** Watch the excerpts from the TED Talk. Choose the correct meaning of the words. 1.b; 2.c; 3.b; 4.a

PRESENTATION SKILLS Knowing your audience

> Speakers keep their audience in mind when they plan their presentations. When they want to illustrate an idea, they choose examples that they know their audience is familiar with.
>
> When preparing a presentation, think about the following:
> • Where does the audience come from?
> • Are they native speakers of the language you're presenting in?
> • What is their age group?

A ▶ **2.13** Watch part of Colin Stokes's TED Talk. Then read the information below and discuss the questions with a partner.

The first *Star Wars* movie appeared in 1977. People in Stokes's audience are probably familiar with it because they saw either the original movie or one of the many sequels that have appeared since then.

1 Why does Stokes refer to *The Wizard of Oz* and *Star Wars*? What does he assume about the cultural background of his audience? Because they are popular movies that his audience knows. He assumes that his audience is English-speaking and familiar with Western pop culture.
2 Are you familiar with *The Wizard of Oz* and *Star Wars*? If so, do you think you had a better understanding of the talk? If not, how did this affect your understanding? Answers will vary.

B If you were giving a presentation that compared an old movie with a newer one from your country or culture, which movies would you choose? Why? Would these movies work for Stokes's audience? Why or why not? Answers will vary.

C Look at the movie poster below. What do you know about this movie? What kind of audience would be familiar with it? Answers will vary.

IN THE LAST GREAT WAR ONE MAN DEFIED AN EMPIRE...

"THE BEST KUNG FU MOVIE IN A GENERATION" NEO

"MARTIAL ARTS CINEMA AT ITS FINEST" IMPACT

IP MAN

MENTOR OF ICONIC LEGEND BRUCE LEE

VOCABULARY IN CONTEXT

▶ **2.12** Play the video. If necessary, play it again.

PRESENTATION SKILLS

A Read the Presentation Skills paragraph **Knowing your audience** aloud. Explain that speakers should understand who they are speaking to and shape their content to resonate with that particular audience. An easy example of this is that a presentation given to an audience of children should be different from a presentation on the same topic given to adults. Remind students that the ultimate goal is to engage the audience to make the message memorable.

Have students preview the task. Note that they can probably answer the questions without watching the video, but it will provide an easy reference for the discussion to follow.

▶ **2.13** Play the video. Check answers as a class, eliciting a class discussion to hear students' ideas. Note that Stokes has chosen two widely popular movies that are known at least vaguely by both Western and non-Western audiences. However, he is making the assumption that his audience members are movie watchers, as well as fans of popular culture. Encourage students to also talk about a gap of understanding that might result from a generational difference. Would their grandparents know the movies? Would their younger relatives? And would someone who doesn't know these movies still be able to understand Stokes's talk?

B Read the questions aloud. Have students work in pairs. Tell students to describe the plot and message of both movies. Then tell them to talk about whether Stokes's audience would know the movies. If they wouldn't know them, could they still understand the message of the talk?

C Give students time to look over the poster. Then have them discuss in pairs. Ask them to decide if they think the movie would pass the Bechdel Test or not.

Content Note

Ip Man is a 2008 Hong Kong movie based loosely on the life of Bruce Lee's real-life martial arts teacher Yip Man. It is set in the Chinese city of Foshan during the Sino-Japanese war, and tells the story of how Yip Man became a kung fu grandmaster. The movie's great popularity led to the release of *Ip Man 2* and *Ip Man 3*.

⊙ **EXTENSION ACTIVITY** Have students work in small groups to create a movie that passes the Bechdel Test. Tell them to decide on the basic details of the movie as well as the storyline. Have groups describe their movie to the class. Then ask the class to comment on how well the movie seems to pass the Bechdel Test or what can be improved in the storyline.

2E

Analyzing movies

COMMUNICATE

A Have students work in pairs. Explain that they are going to create a test with three questions that can help assess whether a movie has a positive impact on its viewers. If necessary, review the questions in the Bechdel Test on page 34. Tell pairs to decide on a test name. Note that in the written example below, the partners use their names as the test name. Point out that the questions they ask should be related to the values that they list at the top of the chart. Give pairs enough time to write their questions.

B Have pairs get together with another two pairs to form a group of six. Ask each pair to decide on one movie to introduce to the group. Explain that each pair will present their tests to the group, and when they evaluate the movies, they should use that test. After groups have done all three tests, ask them to discuss the results and tests in more detail. Which questions do they think are useful? Which ones are thought-provoking?

C Have groups vote. Then ask them to think about how they can combine each other's tests or improve the test to make it better. Ask each group to present their favorite test to the class.

WRITING

Explain that students can use their own test or one of the tests they learned about in their groups. Point out that they need to give credit to the creators by using the test name in their review.

COMMUNICATE Assessing movies   Answers will vary.

A Work in pairs. Create a test—similar to the Bechdel Test—to decide whether a particular movie promotes positive values. First, give your test a name. Then, list some values you think are positive, and think of questions that can help you evaluate a movie in terms of those values.

Test name: _____

Positive values: _____

Test questions

1 _____

2 _____

3 _____

B Get into groups with two other pairs. As a group, choose three movies. Apply each test in your group to the movies chosen. Then compare the results of the tests.

Comparing test results

... did better on that test.   The ... test is more accurate.

C In your group, vote on the most useful test.

WRITING A movie review   Answers will vary.

Choose one of the tests above and apply it to a movie or a TV show. Write a review of the movie or TV show based on whether it promotes positive values. Include a brief summary of the movie (or TV show) plot, and describe how the test works.

Captain America: The First Avenger tells the story of Steve Rogers, a sickly man from New York who is transformed into super-soldier Captain America. The movie has many interesting themes and—according to the Martinez and Yan Test—it promotes positive values. The first question in the test is "Does the main character achieve an important goal?" In the movie, Captain America's goal is to ...

36

Chris Evans starred as Captain America in *Captain America: The First Avenger* and its sequels.

Ask students to choose a different movie or show from one that they talked about in their groups.

Explain that they should summarize the movie briefly, and then use the test to evaluate and review it. Read the model aloud. Note that the writing introduces the movie, then begins to assess it using the questions in the test. Remind students to use the language and grammar that they've learned in the unit to talk about media influence. If time permits, ask for volunteers to read their review aloud to the class.

⟶ EXTENSION ACTIVITY Have students trade reviews. Tell them to find a review of a movie that they've seen. Then ask them to review that movie as well and use their own test. Then have students get together to compare their reviews and discuss what they found positive or negative about the movie.

3 Development

" And the tragedy is that the two billion … struggling for food and shoes, they are still almost as poor as they were 50 years ago. "

Hans Rosling
Global health expert, TED speaker

UNIT GOALS

In this unit, you will …

- talk about what people want out of life.
- read about the relationship between wealth and happiness.
- watch a TED Talk about the connection between child survival and population growth.

WARM UP

▶ **3.1** Watch part of Hans Rosling's TED Talk. Answer the questions with a partner.

1 What is the world population now? What do you think it will be by 2050?   Answers will vary.

2 What are some problems that dramatic population growth can cause?   Answers will vary.

37

UNIT GOALS

The unit focuses on the situation of the increasing world population. Students will read, watch, and talk about how the economic map of the world has changed over the last 50 years, especially in regard to emerging economies. They will study research related to household expenditures in industrialized nations, and learn various theories about the relationship between wealth and happiness. By the end of the unit, they will have considered how the world's distribution of wealth must change in order for the population crisis to be controlled.

TED Speaker

Hans Rosling is a global health expert from Sweden. He has given several TED Talks.

TED Talk Summary

Hans Rosling explains the global population crisis by looking at how socioeconomic categories have changed over the last 50 years. The gap between the poorest two billion and the rest of the world has to be closed in order to stop the population growth, and it begins with education, alleviating poverty, and better healthcare so that the child survival rate can improve in poor countries.

---

3 Development

Idea Worth Spreading

Raising the income of the poorest people in the world can curb the global population crisis.

WARM UP

Have students look over the picture, caption, and quote on the page. Note that the quote on the page won't be heard in the video clip.

▶ **3.1** Play the preview clip of the TED Talk.

For question 1, have students discuss it in pairs to share any data they know about the world population. Note that Rosling's talk was given in 2010. As of December 2016, there are 7.4 billion people in the world. Later in the talk, Rosling explains that world population growth can stop by 2050 if the poorest people get out of poverty.

For question 2, elicit a class discussion after students discuss answers in pairs. Problems resulting from population growth include environmental problems, water and food scarcity, loss of farmland, climate change, rising energy prices, pollution, war, and more poverty.

◯ EXTENSION ACTIVITY Have students work in pairs to go online to learn more about Hans Rosling. Note that he has given several TED Talks on various topics related to global health, and he tends to rely on data and statistics to drive his talk. Tell pairs to find out what other topics he's spoken about to TED audiences.

Aspirations

Aims: Learn language for talking about goals and ambitions; listen to someone talk about a job; practice talking about volunteer work

Target Vocabulary: altruistic, aspiration, enduring, priority, trend

VOCABULARY

A Have students work individually to read the paragraph. Tell them to look at the context of how the word is used to guess its meaning. Remind students that they read about Millennials in **Unit 1**. Ask students if they agree with what the paragraph mentioned about Millennials having more altruistic aspirations than previous generations. Ask students to share what it's like in their own countries. Check answers as a class.

B Give students time to read the questions and think about their answers before discussing. Explain that for question 1, students should think about priorities in regard to goals and aspirations, and share personal stories to support their discussion points. For question 2, ask students to describe the altruistic actions the person has taken.

➡ **EXTENSION ACTIVITY** Have students continue their discussion. Tell them to share some of their goals for the next five years. Then ask them to talk about how they could change their priorities and goals somewhat to become more altruistic. Or if students are already altruistically minded, ask them to explain their altruistic goals for the next five years. How do they want to make a difference?

A volunteer doctor treats a survivor of the 2015 earthquake in Nepal.

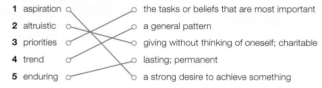

VOCABULARY Goals and ambitions

A Read the paragraph below. Then match each **bold** word to its definition.

What is the average Millennial's greatest **aspiration**? Research suggests that more and more Millennials are interested in pursuing **altruistic** goals, such as helping others. A study conducted by Harris Interactive found that young adults ages 21 to 31 are less focused on financial success than they are on making a difference. Their highest **priorities** seem to be giving back, and working to improve society. This seems to be a worldwide **trend** among young people. As a generation that came of age amidst a global recession, a global war on terrorism, and the Internet revolution, it's not surprising that Millennials tend to see themselves as part of the bigger picture. Many of today's young adults are therefore hoping to go into careers that make an **enduring** impact on others.

1 aspiration		the tasks or beliefs that are most important
2 altruistic		a general pattern
3 priorities		giving without thinking of oneself; charitable
4 trend		lasting; permanent
5 enduring		a strong desire to achieve something

B Work with a partner. Discuss your answers to these questions.   Answers will vary.

   1 What are your priorities right now?

   2 Do you know any famous person who is altruistic?

38

Language Note

Some useful expressions for talking about altruistic goals:

influence others, change thinking, effect change, give back, offer help, do volunteer work, make a difference, make an impact, pursue a higher purpose, work to improve society, live an altruistic life

LISTENING International development

> **Adding points**
> Here are some commonly used words or phrases for adding points.
> *Besides that, …*   *In addition, …*   *Also, …*

A ▶ **3.2** Watch Linda Steinbock talk about her work at Save the Children. What is the aim of the organization?
To support children affected by war and natural disasters.

B ▶ **3.3** Watch and check (✓) the things Steinbock says influenced her decision to work in international development.

☐ a natural disaster   ☑ volunteer work

☑ a trip to a developing country   ☑ an internship

Linda Steinbock is passionate about helping children fulfil their potential.

C **CRITICAL THINKING**   Answers will vary.

Reflecting Do you think you could get a job in international development? Why or why not? Discuss with a partner.

SPEAKING Talking about volunteer work

A ▶ **3.4** Why did Speaker B go to Nepal?
To teach English to children as part of an international volunteer program.
A: Hey, I heard you just got back from Nepal. What were you doing there?

B: I was teaching English to children. I joined an international volunteer program.

A: Really? I've been thinking about volunteering abroad too. How was it?

B: Great! I learned a lot about Nepal and its culture.

A: I've heard that Nepal's one of the poorest countries in the world, and its population has been steadily rising over the past few decades.

B: You're right. I met families who struggle to feed themselves every day. And many Nepalese people can't read or write, especially in the rural areas.

A: Well, hopefully the kids you taught will get good jobs one day. And who knows? They might even become leaders in their community.

B: I hope you're right. It's very rewarding to think that I might have made a difference in their lives. In fact, this experience has made me consider getting a job in international development.

A: That's a great idea! I'm glad you got so much out of the experience.

B Practice the conversation with a partner.

C Work with a partner. Talk about the types of volunteer work you've done or would like to do. Use the expressions in blue above to help you.   Answers will vary.

> Have you ever done any volunteer work?

> I'm a volunteer at the local dog shelter. I've learned a lot about …

39

LISTENING

Read **Adding points** aloud. Elicit other expressions that might indicate that more information is coming. Note that these phrases mostly come at the beginning of a sentence to indicate that another point to support an argument is following.

A Give students time to preview the task. Read the question aloud and tell students to listen for the answer.

▶ **3.2** Play the video. Check answers as a class.

B Give students time to preview the task.

▶ **3.3** Play the video. Check answers as a class. Elicit an overall definition of the *field of international development* according to what students heard in the video.

C **CRITICAL THINKING** If necessary, play the video again before students discuss. Ask pairs to think of any organizations they know in the field of international development and what kind of skills and experience they think that these organizations look for when hiring employees. Encourage students to also discuss whether they find international development an interesting field to work in and why or why not.

SPEAKING

A Have students preview the question. Tell them to read along as they listen.

▶ **3.4** Play the audio/video. Check answers as a class.

Ask some comprehension questions:

What benefits did the volunteer get from going to Nepal? (learned about Nepal and its culture)

How did the experience change the volunteer? (wants to work in international development)

B Have students work in pairs and alternate between A and B roles.

✚ **SUPPORT** Play the audio/video again, pausing after each sentence so students can repeat.

C Give students time to think about the question and write notes to refer to during their discussions. Model the examples. Elicit or explain the meaning of *dog shelter*. Explain that it is a place where abandoned dogs are taken care of.

Ask for volunteers to share the types of volunteer work they have done or are interested in doing.

The next economic giant

LANGUAGE FOCUS Economic trends

A ▶ **3.5** Read about changes in the world's largest economies. Which country has shown the biggest increase in wealth in recent years?   China

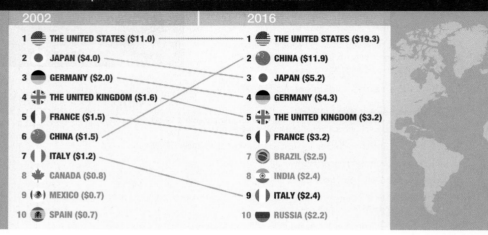

THE NEXT ECONOMIC GIANT

There have been some significant changes to the world's largest economies over the last few years. Below is a comparison in terms of GDP in trillions of U.S. dollars.

2002	2016
1 THE UNITED STATES ($11.0)	1 THE UNITED STATES ($19.3)
2 JAPAN ($4.0)	2 CHINA ($11.9)
3 GERMANY ($2.0)	3 JAPAN ($5.2)
4 THE UNITED KINGDOM ($1.6)	4 GERMANY ($4.3)
5 FRANCE ($1.5)	5 THE UNITED KINGDOM ($3.2)
6 CHINA ($1.5)	6 FRANCE ($3.2)
7 ITALY ($1.2)	7 BRAZIL ($2.5)
8 CANADA ($0.8)	8 INDIA ($2.4)
9 MEXICO ($0.7)	9 ITALY ($2.4)
10 SPAIN ($0.7)	10 RUSSIA ($2.2)

B ▶ **3.6** Listen to the conversation. What are the MINT countries?   Mexico, Indonesia, Nigeria, and Turkey

C ▶ **3.7** Watch and study the language in the chart.

Talking about change

The world's top ten biggest economies have changed since 2002.
Income inequality in the U.S. has increased significantly since the 1970s.
The world population has jumped to 7 billion.

The economy of China has been growing for a number of years.
Some traditionally strong economies have been shrinking recently.
According to statistics, global poverty rates have been falling steadily for over two and a half decades.

For more information on the **present perfect** and **present perfect progressive**, see Grammar Summary 3 on page 184.

LESSON OVERVIEW

Aims: Understand an infographic about the global economy; talk about change; discuss household expenses

Infographic Summary: Two lists, 2002 and 2016, of the world's top-ten global economic powers are compared. The most notable changes to the list come from developing nations. In 2002, China was ranked sixth, but by 2016 it was second in the world. And countries like Brazil and India, which weren't even on the list in 2002, are now on the list.

LANGUAGE FOCUS

A Read the question aloud.

▶ **3.5** Play the audio/video as students read along. Then give them additional time to look over the infographic. Check answers as a class. Ask students to share what may have surprised them about the change in rankings in the infographic. Point out that it's quite a significant change for a 14-year span.

B Read the question aloud.

▶ **3.6** Play the audio/video. Check answers as a class. Note that students should not only name the MINT countries, but explain their significance. They are considered to be the top emerging economies that will become the next economic giants.

C Have students read over the language chart and pay attention to the verbs in blue.

▶ **3.7** Play the audio/video. Go over the meaning and use of the present perfect and present perfect progressive to talk about change.

Grammar Note

Note that the language in the chart introduces the present perfect and present perfect progressive tenses to talk about change. The present perfect is used for changes that have already happened: *China's economy has grown*.

Note that *have/has* is usually contracted with a pronoun subject (*I've changed a lot this year*), except in cases when the verb is negative, and then *have/has* is contracted with *not* (*I haven't changed at all this year*).

The present perfect progressive uses *have/has been* + present participle (*-ing* form) to talk about ongoing change that is likely to continue: *China's economy has been growing*.

Note that the present participles of the following verbs are not typically used in the present perfect progressive: *know, like, be, have*.

D ▶ **3.6** Listen to the conversation in **B** again. Complete the sentences from the conversation.

1 "Also, all four MINT countries have a growing young population, which means that the labor force in these countries ____has been increasing____ ."

2 "Unfortunately, poverty and inequality ____have worsened____ in many emerging countries."

3 "The Indonesian government ____has been making____ significant efforts to reduce poverty levels in recent years."

E ▶ **3.8** Complete the information. Circle the correct words. Then listen and check your answers.

Krochet Kids International is a nonprofit organization that teaches crocheting to women living in Uganda, and then helps them sell their crochet products in the U.S. It aims to empower Ugandan women to break out of the poverty cycle. Since 2008, Krochet Kids [1](**has employed** / has been employing) 150 women in Uganda. It [2](**has increased** / has been increasing) the average worker's personal income by as much as 10 times. Krochet Kids also provides training in money management and business skills. More and more women [3](**used** / **have been using**) this training to set up their own businesses. Due to its success, the organization [4](**has opened** / has been opening) another branch in Peru. The women in Krochet Kids Peru [5](have made / **have been making**) hats and other items since 2011.

Every woman who works for Krochet Kids is taught how to crochet.

SPEAKING Talking about expenses Answers will vary.

Work in pairs. Look at the table below showing trends in U.S. household expenditure. Then discuss the questions below.

	Ten years ago	Today
Clothing	8%	8%
Education	5%	4%
Entertainment	8%	8%
Fast food	1%	3%
Groceries	15%	12%
Health and health products	3%	4%
Housing and utilities	22%	26%
Transportation	14%	18%

1 How have household expenses changed in the past ten years? With your partner, take turns describing the trend in each category.

> There hasn't been any change in the expenditure on clothing. It has remained at ...

> The expenditure on education has decreased from ...

2 Why do you think people are spending more money on fast food and transportation?

41

The economics of happiness

LESSON OVERVIEW

Aims: Read and comprehend an article about money and happiness; understand an argument

Target Vocabulary: correlation, decline, paradox, surge, threshold

Reading Summary: While we all need money to afford the basic necessities to lay the foundation for a good life, does having the basic requirements of well-being mean we are happier? There is a debate around this question. In 1974, the Easterlin paradox showed through research that more individual wealth only translates to a momentary, rather than long-term, rise in one's level of happiness. Yet a study from 2013 showed that happiness did improve as income rose. Psychologists say that our happiness level is also connected to those around us, so if wealth is not evenly distributed, we won't be as happy even if we are rich. This points to the importance of income equality in order for a society to be happy.

PRE-READING

Read the question aloud. Give students time to think about their answer before discussing in pairs. Ask them to explain how they think money and happiness may affect each other, and to offer any anecdotes or personal stories to support their views. Elicit some of the points that students talked about.

Point out the glossary at the end of the reading. Remind students to refer to it before or while reading.

▶ 3.9 Play the audio/video as students read along. Explain any key terms that students might not be familiar with.

3C The economics of happiness

PRE-READING Predicting

Do you think there is a relationship between money and happiness? Discuss with a partner.   Answers will vary.

▶ 3.9

There's little doubt that having enough money is important to your well-being. The ability to afford food, clothing, and shelter is essential to your quality of life. However, well-being is not the
5 same thing as happiness. Well-being is the state of being comfortable or healthy, while happiness is an emotion. So can money also buy happiness? And taking a broader perspective, do countries get happier when they get richer?

10 **THE EASTERLIN PARADOX**
The idea that richer countries are happier may seem intuitively obvious. However, in 1974, research by economist Richard Easterlin found otherwise. Easterlin discovered that while individuals with higher
15 incomes were more likely to be happy, this did not hold at a national level. In the United States, for example, average income per person rose steadily between 1946 and 1970, but reported happiness levels showed no positive long-term trend; in fact,
20 they **declined** between 1960 and 1970. These differences between nation-level and individual results gave rise to the term "Easterlin **paradox**": the idea that a higher rate of economic growth does not result in higher average long-term happiness.

25 Having access to additional income seems to only provide a temporary **surge** in happiness. Since a certain minimum income is needed for basic necessities, it's possible that the happiness boost from extra cash isn't that great once you rise
30 above the poverty line. This would explain Easterlin's findings in the United States and other developed countries. He argued that life satisfaction does rise with average incomes—but only in the short-term.

RISING INCOME, RISING HAPPINESS?
35 Recent research has challenged the Easterlin paradox, however. In 2013, sociologists Ruut Veenhoven and Floris Vergunst conducted a study using statistics from the World Database of Happiness. Their analysis revealed a positive
40 **correlation** between economic growth and happiness. Another study by the University of Michigan found that there is no maximum wealth **threshold** at which more money ceases to contribute to your happiness: "If there is a satiation[1]
45 point, we are yet to reach it." The study's findings suggested that every extra dollar you earn makes you happier. With so much debate about the relationship between money and happiness, it's

42

➡ **EXTENSION ACTIVITY** Have students work in pairs. Ask them to go online to find out about the Happy Planet Index (HPI). Tell them to read about this measurement of a country's happiness level. Then have them discuss their opinions. Do they think this is a useful measurement tool? Where do their countries fall in the ranking? See **Content Note** for more on the HPI.

Nyhavn, Copenhagen. Denmark was crowned the world's happiest country in 2016.

Language Note

Our *quality of life* (line 4) is a term that is used to refer to the general well-being of people in a society or community (or to individuals when used specifically), and takes into consideration aspects of everyday life such as wealth, education, job, housing, family, living environment, among others.

To know something *intuitively* (line 12) means that you know it based on feeling and logic, even if you don't have proof.

The *poverty line* (line 30) is the least amount of income that someone needs to have a comfortable life with basic necessities such as food and shelter.

After a *satiation point* (lines 44–45) is reached, benefit is no longer received.

When a government *implements* (line 62) a new policy, it means that it is enforced legally. In general, *implement* means to put something, such as a plan, into action.

clear that happiness itself is a complex concept and
50 depends on many factors.

IT'S ALL RELATIVE

According to psychologists Selin Kesebir and Shigehiro Oishi, happiness also depends on how your income compares to the people around you.
55 They argue that a country's economic growth only makes its citizens happier if wealth is evenly distributed. In emerging countries with high income inequality—where the rich get richer and the poor get poorer—average happiness tends
60 to drop because only relatively few people benefit from the economic prosperity. This suggests that governments should consider implementing policies to ensure a more equal distribution of wealth. The happier people are, the more

65 productive they are likely to become, thus leading to improved economic outcomes at the individual and national levels.

THE KEY TO HAPPINESS

There is continuing debate about the link between
70 wealth and happiness, with arguments both for and against the notion that richer countries are happier. However, it is clear that wealth alone isn't enough to make us happy. The effect of income inequality on happiness shows that happiness is a
75 societal responsibility. We need to remember the positive effects of generosity, altruism, and building social connections. Perhaps our focus should be less on how much money we have, and more on how we use it.

¹**satiation:** *n.* a state of being satisfied and not wanting more

43

Content Note

Statistician, TED speaker, and creator of the New Economics Foundation, Nic Marks, has created something called the Happy Planet Index, which he designed as a way to measure which countries' people are the happiest overall. It is calculated using the ecological footprint of a country, as well as the life expectancy and well-being of its people.

Marks believes this is a better measure of progress than more traditional indexes that look only at economic markers such as a country's GNP. At the time of his TED Talk, the country with the highest HPI in the world was Costa Rica.

UNDERSTANDING MAIN IDEAS

Have students work individually. Check answers as a class. Ask students to reword the main idea in their own words.

UNDERSTANDING AN ARGUMENT

Have students preview the task. Tell them to refer back to the passage if necessary. Check answers as a class, eliciting the line numbers where students found each argument in the passage. Ask students to expand on each argument by explaining the research results for each study in their own words.

BUILDING VOCABULARY

A Ask students to go back to the reading passage to see each word used in context. Have students work individually before checking answers as a class. Ask pairs to choose one word to write a sentence for. Elicit example sentences from each pair.

B Have students work individually to complete the sentences before checking answers in pairs.

C **CRITICAL THINKING** Read the questions aloud. Give students a few minutes to think about their answers. Tell them to consider all the material they've read and heard so far in the unit in regard to the link between happiness and wealth. Model the example with a volunteer. Elicit a class discussion to hear students' opinions. Tell them to give reasons for their viewpoints. Ask students if they think people in their own home countries are happy or not, and why.

➡ EXTENSION ACTIVITY Ask students to think about what they would do if they suddenly won a lot of money. Have them work in groups and share three things they would do with the money. Then after students hear everyone else's ideas, ask them if they want to make any changes to their three ways of how to spend their money.

UNDERSTANDING MAIN IDEAS

Which sentence best summarizes the main idea of the passage?

- **(a)** The relationship between happiness and wealth is complex—it involves many societal and economic factors.
- **b** Happiness means different things to different people, and there is no clear link between wealth and happiness.
- **c** People living in rich countries are happier and more productive than those in poor countries.

UNDERSTANDING AN ARGUMENT

Complete the sentences. Circle the correct words.

1 According to the Easterlin paradox, there is (**a** /**no**) positive correlation between a country's economic growth and average long-term happiness.

2 According to Veenhoven and Vergunst, people living in poor countries are (**not**/ **equally**) as happy as those in rich countries.

3 According to Kesebir and Oishi, people tend to be happier when there is (**high** /**low**) income inequality.

BUILDING VOCABULARY

A Match the words in blue from the passage to their definitions.

1 declined — a sudden increase
2 paradox — became smaller, fewer, or less; decreased
3 surge — the point at which something begins or changes
4 correlation — a puzzling statement that contains two opposing truths
5 threshold — a meaningful connection between two or more things

B Complete the sentences using the words in **A**.

1 Income grew in the U.S. during the 1990s, but it _____declined_____ in the 2000s.

2 Economists predict that the "Internet of Things" will lead to a _____surge_____ in productivity.

3 Researchers have found a direct _____correlation_____ between happiness and good health.

4 Easterlin's ideas are called a _____paradox_____ because he found that individual happiness does not correspond with the overall happiness level of a country.

5 Psychologist Daniel Kahneman found that the income _____threshold_____ for Americans is $75,000 a year. Beyond that, he believes, more money does not make them happier.

C **CRITICAL THINKING** Answers will vary.

Reflecting Do you think a person can have too much money? Why or why not? Discuss with a partner.

I don't think it's possible to have too much money because ...

I disagree. I think that ...

44

3D Global population growth, box by box

TEDTALKS

HANS ROSLING is a professor of International Health at the Karolinska Institute in Sweden. He also co-founded *Doctors Without Borders Sweden*. Rosling is known for the creative ways he presents information about global health and economic issues.

Hans Rosling's idea worth spreading is that if we want to manage population growth, we must raise the income of the world's poorest billion people.

PREVIEWING

Complete the sentences with the words from the box. You will hear these words in the TED Talk.

developing world	emerging economies	industrialized world

1 Developed countries that are part of the _____industrialized world_____ include Canada, Japan, and Germany. These countries have advanced technology and highly developed economies.

2 Countries such as Brazil and India have _____emerging economies_____; they once were part of the developing world but are now increasing in wealth.

3 The _____developing world_____ is a term that describes the type of economy in countries such as Haiti and Laos. These countries have low levels of technological or economic resources.

VIEWING

A ▶ **3.10** Watch Part 1 of the TED Talk. Complete the diagram below. Think of the props Rosling used to help you.

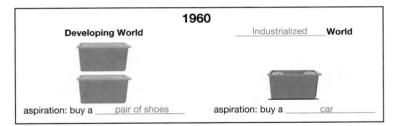

1960

Developing World   _Industrialized_ **World**

aspiration: buy a _____pair of shoes_____   aspiration: buy a _____car_____

45

LESSON OVERVIEW

Aims: Watch and understand a talk about the world's population crisis; observe speakers using props

Target Vocabulary: developing world, emerging economies, industrialized world

TED Talk Summary: Hans Rosling breaks down the global population crisis by looking at how socioeconomic categories have changed over the last 50 years. He first explains what the gap between rich and poor globally looked like when he was young—the wealthy aspired for cars, and the poor aspired for shoes. He explains that now the global map has changed considerably because of emerging countries with growing economic strength. However, there is still an expanding divide between the poorest and the richest. It is that gap between the poorest two billion and the rest of the world that has to be closed in order to stop population growth, and it begins with education, alleviating poverty, and better healthcare so that the child survival rate improves in poor countries. Once this improves, fewer people will be born and the world population will stabilize.

3D

Global population growth, box by box

PREVIEWING

Remind students that they saw the preview video in the **Warm Up**. Have them work individually to complete the sentences. Note that they have been exposed to the term *emerging country* and can likely infer that *emerging economy* means the same thing. Check answers as a class, eliciting sample summaries in students' own words of the meaning of each term. Elicit examples of each type of country.

VIEWING

A Have students preview the task.

▶ **3.10** Play Part 1 of the TED Talk. Then play the check-your-answers part of the video. Ask students if the personal story that Rosling opened with helped them engage with the talk. Note that Rosling's talk is somewhat technical, but as a skilled speaker he knows how to simplify a topic and make it relatable to the audience. Point out that he uses humor when bringing out the IKEA boxes (he is from Sweden), another technique to keep audience members engaged. Ask students to comment on why a demonstration and humor might help a technical subject like this.

Elicit or explain the meaning of any unfamiliar language. Suggestions for Part 1 include *analog*, *the West*, and *taxonomy*.

B Have students preview the task. Note that students can infer by the last line of Part 1 that Rosling is next going to talk about modern times.

▶ **3.11** Play Part 2 of the TED Talk. Check answers as a class or play the check-your-answers part of the video. Elicit an example of a remote destination.

Elicit or explain the meaning of any unfamiliar language. Suggestions for Part 2 include *staggering* and *remote destination*.

C Have students preview the task. Note that this is the same graph that students will see Rosling show his audience during his talk. Elicit the meaning of *child survival*. Note that Rosling defines the term as meaning that a child lives up to the age of starting school. Some students might also be familiar with the term *child mortality rate*.

▶ **3.12** Play Part 3 of the TED Talk. Check answers as a class.

⭐ **CHALLENGE** Have students work in pairs. Ask them to take turns explaining points they learned from the graph in their own words. After students discuss, elicit summaries of each point. Note that this will support their completion of the next activity in **D**.

D Have students work alone to complete the paragraph. Check answers as a class.

B ▶ **3.11** Watch Part 2 of the TED Talk. Complete the diagram below. Think of the props Rosling used to help you.

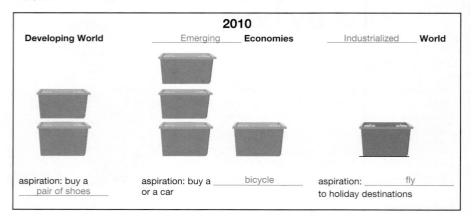

2010

Developing World	Emerging **Economies**	Industrialized **World**
aspiration: buy a ___pair of shoes___	aspiration: buy a ___bicycle___ or a car	aspiration: ___fly___ to holiday destinations

C ▶ **3.12** Watch Part 3 of the TED Talk. Look at the graph below showing the relationship between family size and child survival. Then complete the sentences.

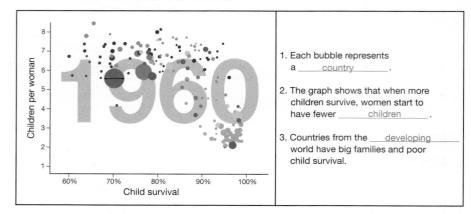

1. Each bubble represents a ___country___.

2. The graph shows that when more children survive, women start to have fewer ___children___.

3. Countries from the ___developing___ world have big families and poor child survival.

D Complete the summary below. Circle the correct words.

As the years pass by, more emerging economies are joining the Western world. This means that the child survival rate in these countries is [1](**improving** / worsening) and family size is [2](increasing / **decreasing**). However, there is still a wide gap between the richest and the poorest parts of the world. If the Gates Foundation, UNICEF, and other aid organizations invest in poor countries, we can raise child survival rates in those places, [3](encourage / **stop**) global population growth, and ensure sustainable development for all.

46

Language Note

Part 1
Something that is described as *analog* involves no technology or computers.

The term *the West* refers generally to the industrialized world. Rosling points out that this term is now very outdated since industrialized countries are not just in the Western world (Europe) anymore.

Taxonomy refers to the science of classification.

Part 2
Something that is described as *staggering* can be interpreted as shocking.

A *remote destination* is a place that is hard to get to. When Rosling refers to remote destinations as aspirations for wealthy people, he is referring to vacations on islands and other faraway places around the world.

Part 3
When a group of people is referred to as *(the/a) rainbow of*, it means that many ethnicities are being represented.

The term *hygiene* refers to cleaning habits that keep us healthy.

A *vaccination* is an injection that a person, often a child, gets to prevent disease.

To alleviate something means to fix a problem or make it somewhat better. When Rosling refers to alleviating poverty, he means putting an end to it.

E CRITICAL THINKING Answers will vary.

Inferring Discuss these questions with a partner.

1 Hans Rosling says, "Child survival is the new green." What does he mean by this?

2 Rosling describes himself as a "possibilist." What do you think a "possibilist" is? Give examples to support your answer.

VOCABULARY IN CONTEXT

▶ **3.13** Watch the excerpts from the TED Talk. Choose the correct meaning of the words. 1.b; 2.c; 3.a

PRESENTATION SKILLS Using props

Props are physical objects that you can use to illustrate your ideas in a presentation. They can also make your presentation more interesting. When you choose a prop, think about the following:

- Is the prop easy for everyone in the audience to see and recognize?
- Is the prop interesting enough to hold the audience's attention?
- Will the prop help your audience remember your main idea, or distract from it?

A ▶ **3.14** Watch part of Hans Rosling's TED Talk. Which of the criteria above do his props meet?
The boxes are easy to see and recognize, and the car is cute and grabs the audience's attention. All the props reinforce his main idea.

B Work with a partner. Discuss trends in one of the areas in the box by answering the questions below.
Answers will vary.

communication	food	transportation	money

- What props could you use to show the trends?
- Why would these props work?
- What criteria in the Tip box would the props meet?

A
Have students preview the task. Note that students will watch while keeping in mind what they learned about effective props above.

▶ **3.14** Play the video. Check answers as a class. Ask students to comment on whether they felt Rosling's props were effective or not, and why.

B
Read the direction line aloud. Explain that a *trend* describes the general direction that something is moving in, such as increasing or decreasing. Explain that students are going to discuss what kind of props might work for talking about each topic. Tell partners to think of a trend about each topic and then brainstorm some props that may work to visualize the trend.

Have each pair share one trend and the props they would use to talk about it with the class. Ask the class to evaluate whether the prop ideas are effective or not.

⊙ EXTENSION ACTIVITY
Have pairs prepare a presentation about one of the trends that they spoke about in **B**. Tell them to use one of the props that they discussed.

E CRITICAL THINKING
Read the questions aloud. Have students discuss in pairs before eliciting a class discussion. For question 2, Rosling is feeling positive because he knows a better future is possible, but he knows that we have to work hard to make the world he describes a reality.

VOCABULARY IN CONTEXT

▶ **3.13** Play the video. If necessary, play it again.

PRESENTATION SKILLS

Read the Presentation Skills paragraph **Using props** aloud. Explain that props both help an audience visualize and keep them engaged in the same way a demonstration does. Elicit what props Rosling used in his talk.

Rich and poor

LESSON OVERVIEW

Aims: Discuss and make predictions about economic issues in the United States; write a paragraph about wealth distribution

COMMUNICATE

A Give students enough time to look over the graph in detail. Then have them get in pairs to discuss. Tell them to summarize in their own words the details that are available on the graph. Then ask them to discuss their guesses about what the actual distribution of wealth is.

B Have color pencils or markers available for students to use. Give them time to color in their predictions that they discussed in **A**.

★ CHALLENGE Have pairs get together with another pair and share their predictions. Tell them to give reasons for their ideas.

C Have students check their predictions. Then ask pairs to discuss what they find surprising.

★ CHALLENGE Have a class discussion about the wealth distribution in the United States. Tell students to use what they learned in the unit to comment on the unfair distribution of wealth and offer ideas about how to change it.

WRITING

Have students read the direction line. Note that students are being asked to explain what they think the distribution of wealth is like in their home countries. Point out that they are not expected to research the actual statistics to support it. Tell students that they can write about the communities that they live in if they are all from the same country.

COMMUNICATE The distribution of wealth Answers will vary.

A Work in pairs. The graph below shows how Americans *think wealth is* distributed in America and how they *think it should be* distributed. How do you think wealth is *actually* distributed in America? Discuss with your partner.

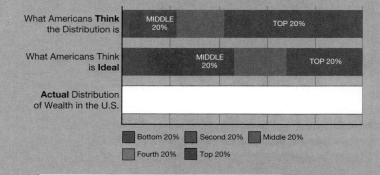

What Americans **Think** the Distribution is	MIDDLE 20% ... TOP 20%
What Americans Think is **Ideal**	MIDDLE 20% ... TOP 20%
Actual Distribution of Wealth in the U.S.	

■ Bottom 20% ■ Second 20% ■ Middle 20%
■ Fourth 20% ■ Top 20%

Making predictions about wealth distribution
I think the actual distribution is more equal than ...
I don't think the bottom 20% will own more than ...

B Draw your prediction in **A** on the graph above. Using the space provided, color in how you think the wealth is *actually* distributed among the five income brackets.

C Turn to page 165 to check your answers. Do you find this information surprising? Discuss with your partner.

WRITING Comparing wealth distribution Answers will vary.

Write a paragraph on how you think wealth is distributed in your country or community. Compare it to the actual distribution of wealth in America discussed above. Give examples to support your ideas.

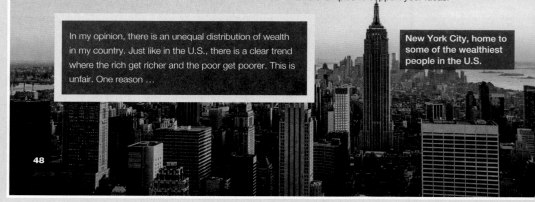

In my opinion, there is an unequal distribution of wealth in my country. Just like in the U.S., there is a clear trend where the rich get richer and the poor get poorer. This is unfair. One reason …

New York City, home to some of the wealthiest people in the U.S.

48

Read the model aloud as students read along. Explain that students should use the statistics that they learned about the United States as a comparison. Have students share their paragraphs with a new partner.

★ CHALLENGE Have students from the same country or community share ideas and discuss in groups what they think about the distribution of wealth in their own country or community.

Presentation 1

MODEL PRESENTATION

A Complete the transcript of the presentation using the words in the box.

achieve	who	handle	hero
inspiration	quest	has inspired	behaving

Hello, everyone. My name is Justine. Today, I'm going to talk to you about my favorite fictional character, Dorothy Gale. She's the ¹_____hero_____ in the book, *The Wonderful Wizard of Oz*. How many of you have seen the movie adaptation, *The Wizard of Oz*? Yeah, most of you have.

Dorothy ²__has inspired__ readers since 1900, when the book was first published. Here's why she's my role model. First of all, Dorothy is a team player. She's on a ³_____quest_____ to find the Wizard and go home. And she meets other characters ⁴_____who_____ want to travel with her and find the Wizard, too. Dorothy is also a good leader. She's an ⁵____inspiration____ to the other characters in the story, and she helps them to ⁶_____achieve_____ their goals, too. And of course, Dorothy is brave. She's only a young girl, but she's not afraid of the Wizard or the Wicked Witch of the West. For example, she accepts the Wizard's challenge to bring him the Witch's broomstick. She can ⁷_____handle_____ difficult situations.

In short, I think we should all consider ⁸_____behaving_____ a bit more like Dorothy—be brave team players who are willing to lead. Thank you very much.

B ▶ **P.1** Watch the presentation and check your answers.

C ▶ **P.1** Review the list of presentation skills from Units 1–3 below. Which does the speaker use? Check (✓) them as you watch again. Then compare with a partner.

The speaker …
- ☑ asks the audience questions
- ☐ asks the audience to imagine themselves in a particular situation
- ☑ uses examples the audience is familiar with
- ☐ uses props

B ▶ **P.1** Play the video to check answers.

C Have students preview the task.

▶ **P.1** Play the video again. Check answers as a class.

Elicit the presentation skills from Units 1–3:

1. Involving the audience
2. Knowing your audience
3. Using props

Elicit what question the speaker asked to involve the audience (*How many of you have seen the movie adaptation?*). Note that the speaker also uses a conversational tone in her talk, which is another way to involve the audience.

Review the presentation skills from Units 1–3 in more detail. Elicit the additional details and/or language options that students can use in **Your Turn**.

Involving the audience: Use a conversational tone to ask them questions about themselves, ask them to make predictions, describe a situation and ask them to imagine participating in it, and ask them to stand, raise their hands, clap, and so forth.

Knowing your audience: Think about where they are from, what their native language is, and how old they are.

Using props: Use props that are easy to see, are interesting, and help the audience understand the main idea.

Presentation 1

LESSON OVERVIEW

Aim: Students give a short presentation to a partner to introduce a fictional character who inspires them, using each of the presentation skills they've learned in Units 1–3.

MODEL PRESENTATION

A Have students work individually to complete the sentences. Elicit some basic points about the presentation:

1. Who is speaking? (Justine)
2. What is she talking about? (the character Dorothy Gale from *The Wonderful Wizard of Oz*)
3. What three things does the speaker find inspiring about the character? (She is brave, a team player, and a good leader.)

YOUR TURN

A Have students preview the presentation task. Point out that they can write about a character from a book, movie, or TV show. Give them time to write their speech notes. Point out that they can write linear notes or a mind map, whichever they prefer.

Tell them to think about their audience and if it is likely that their classmates will know the character or not. Tell them to provide more background information if it is likely that their audience will not be familiar with the story that the character is from.

B Read the useful phrases aloud as students repeat. Tell students to think about which ones would work best for their presentation content. Explain that they can also use other phrases that they learned in the units. Point out that students should have props in their presentations if possible. Remind them that the props should help the audience understand the main points, and not distract.

For support, go over the organization of Justine's speech in more detail. Ask:

How does she open? (She introduces herself.)

What language does she use to introduce her character? (Today, I'm going to talk to you about my favorite fictional character …)

How does she conclude? (In short, …)

C Tell students that they have two important roles in the activity: speaker and listener. Explain that they need to give their partner their full attention in order to evaluate in **C** and give effective feedback in **D**.

D Explain that when offering feedback after hearing a presentation, it's good to start with a short phrase of praise. Introduce some simple phrases for students to praise each other: *Well done; Good job; You did great; That was really good*.

Explain that after giving praise, students should offer some positive feedback (*You asked a good question to involve the audience*), and then offer any points that need to be improved (*Your props were a little distracting*).

A You are going to plan and give a short presentation about a fictional character who inspires you. The character can be from a book, a movie, or a TV show. Make notes in the chart below.

> Who is the character? Which book/movie/TV show is the character from?
>
> What do you admire about this character?

B Look at the useful phrases in the box below. Think about which ones you will need in your presentation.

> **Useful phrases**
>
> **Beginning:**
> *I'm excited to be here today.*
> *Today, I'm going to tell you about …*
> *I'd like to talk about …*
>
> **Introducing a character:**
> *Here's what we can learn from …*
> *One reason I admire …*
> *What makes … a hero is …*
>
> **Concluding:**
> *In short, …*
> *So, we can see that …*
> *To sum up, …*

C Work with a partner. Take turns giving your presentation using your notes. Use some of the presentation skills from Units 1–3 below. As you listen, check (✓) each skill your partner uses.

> The speaker …
> ☐ asks the audience questions
> ☐ asks the audience to imagine themselves in a particular situation
> ☐ uses examples the audience is familiar with
> ☐ uses props

D Give your partner some feedback on their talk. Include at least two things you liked and one thing that could be improved.

⭐ **CHALLENGE** Have students give their presentations to the entire class.

4 Secrets and Lies

" Trained liespotters get to the truth 90 percent of the time. The rest of us, we're only 54 percent accurate. "

Pamela Meyer
Professional liespotter, TED speaker

UNIT GOALS

In this unit, you will …

- talk about types of lies.
- read about situations where lying may be good.
- watch a TED Talk about how to spot a liar.

WARM UP

▶ **4.1** Watch part of Pamela Meyer's TED Talk. Answer the questions with a partner.

1 Would you describe yourself as a liar?
   Answers will vary.
2 Do you think it's important to be completely honest in a relationship? Answers will vary.

51

UNIT GOALS

In this unit, students will read, watch, and talk about deception in communication. They will read about situations where lying is considered acceptable, as well as learn some tips from a trained liespotter about how to catch a liar. Students are repeatedly asked to think about and discuss the lies that they tell on a daily basis, especially in regard to stretching the truth and telling white lies.

TED Speaker
Pamela Meyer is the CEO of Calibrate, a training center for detecting lies.

TED Talk Summary
As an experienced liespotter, Pamela Meyer knows how to recognize cues from language and body language that indicate someone is lying. She shares some of these cues with her TED audience, explaining they are probably not what most people think.

Idea Worth Spreading
If we all become better at spotting lies, we can build a more honest society.

4

Secrets and Lies

WARM UP

Have students look over the picture, caption, and quote on the page. Read the quote aloud. Note that students will not hear the quote in the video clip, but it introduces an interesting statistic about lying. Draw students' attention to the speaker's job, *liespotter*. Elicit guesses about what the job involves. A liespotter is a professional trained to detect when a person is lying by observing such details as body language, facial expressions, tone of voice, and so forth. Liespotters are called in to assist criminal and fraud cases, as well as to train police, lawyers, human resource professionals, and insurance claim workers, among others.

▶ **4.1** Play the preview clip of the TED Talk.

For question 1, note that students will hear in the video clip that we are all liars to some degree, which may influence how they answer the question. Note that the image of a liar is in general a negative one, so some students may be reluctant to describe themselves as one at first. If necessary, explain the concept of a *white lie*, and ask them to share some examples of times they think lying can be positive.

For question 2, ask students to also consider the statistic given in the quote on the page, which says that we're only getting the truth 54% of the time. Ask students to consider different relationships as they discuss.

➲ **EXTENSION ACTIVITY** Have students work individually to make a list of lies they've told in the last three days. Tell them to include small white lies said to make someone feel better as well as exaggerations. Explain that they can keep their list private for now, but they may refer back to it during the unit.

4A

Truth and lies

VOCABULARY

A Have students work individually to read the sentences and decide which category they fit into. Check answers as a class, going over the meaning and examples of each type of lie. Note that a *white lie* is usually told in order to prevent someone from feeling bad, while *stretching the truth* refers to making an exaggeration.

B Have students work individually before checking answers in pairs.

C Read the discussion questions aloud. If students did the **Extension Activity** in **Warm Up**, encourage them to refer to their lists to get examples of lies that they have told. Point out that the TED speaker says that we all lie quite often, which means that students will have examples of both white lies and stretching the truth.

Language Note

Give students an example situation about canceling a dinner plan with a friend. Here are examples of lies in each category for this situation:

Absolute truth: *I'd rather watch my favorite TV show at home.*
Element of truth: *Something else came up tonight, so I'd like to postpone.*
White lie: *I think I'm getting a cold, so I want to stay home to rest.*
Stretched the truth: *I'm a little low on money, so can we go next week?*
Total lie: *My mother asked me to help her repair her broken blender, so I can't go.*

A polygraph—or a lie detector—measures a person's physiological reactions when they respond to questions.

4A Truth and lies

VOCABULARY Collocations with *truth* and *lie*

A Read the sentences below. Check (✓) the correct description.

	Completely untrue	Somewhat true	Completely true
1 Her story had **an element of truth**.		✓	
2 She told **the absolute truth**.			✓
3 He told **a white lie**.	✓		
4 He told **a total lie**.	✓		
5 He **stretched the truth**.		✓	

B Match each example below to the correct descriptions (**1–5**) in **A**.

a __4__ He said he was at the office, but he was actually at home.

b __3__ He said, "I like your new hairstyle," because he didn't want her to feel bad.

c __5__ He said, "I have two Porsches," but one is his and one is his father's.

d __1__ It's true that she lives in New York, but every other part of her story is untrue.

e __2__ The CEO began her speech by saying, "I'm the CEO of a company."

C Work with a partner. Discuss your answers to these questions. Answers will vary.

1 Have you ever told a white lie to protect a friend's feelings? What happened?

2 Have you ever stretched the truth before? Why?

52

⊙ EXTENSION ACTIVITY Have students work in pairs. Tell them to come up with a situation in which someone tells a lie. Then ask them to write different lies for that situation according to each of the categories in **A**. Have them present their lies to the class and ask them to identify which category each lie belongs to. See **Language Note** for an example.

LISTENING Lying in a job interview

> **Giving examples**
> Here are some commonly used phrases that indicate examples.
> *For example, …*   *… such as …*   *… is a case in point.*

A ▶ **4.2** Watch recruiter Erin Wong talk about her experience with job applicants. According to her, why do people tend to lie in job interviews? *To increase their chances of getting a job.*

B ▶ **4.3** Watch and check (✓) the things Wong says people have lied to her about in job interviews.

- ☐ age
- ☑ reason for leaving a job
- ☑ computer skills
- ☐ previous salary
- ☑ having a certification
- ☑ work experience

C **CRITICAL THINKING**   *Answers will vary.*

Reflecting Do you think it's important to be completely honest in a job interview? Discuss with a partner.

Erin Wong is a recruiter for an international IT organization.

SPEAKING Talking about stretching the truth

A ▶ **4.4** Do the speakers think it's sometimes OK to lie in a job interview? *Yes*

A: Do you think you have to tell the absolute truth in a job interview?

B: Not always. I think sometimes it's OK to stretch the truth.

A: Can you give me an example of what you mean?

B: OK, imagine you want to quit your current job because you have a personality conflict with your boss. And an interviewer asks why you want to leave your current job. What would you say?

A: Hmm. I'm not sure. I wouldn't want to offend my current boss or make anyone feel uncomfortable. What would *you* say?

B: I'd probably say something like, "I'm looking for new challenges."

A: Oh, I think I see what you mean. It's probably OK to bend the truth a bit in that case.

B: Here's another question for you. What would you say if someone asked how long you worked for a certain company?

A: If it's a cold, hard fact, I think you should just tell the truth. Lying about how long you held a job isn't stretching the truth—it's lying.

B Practice the conversation with a partner.

C Work with a partner. Make a list of job interview questions. Which questions could you stretch the truth on? Which ones should you answer with absolute truth? Use the expressions in blue above to help you.   *Answers will vary.*

> Would you stretch the truth if an interviewer asked you …?

> I think it's important to tell the absolute truth here because …

LISTENING

A Read **Giving examples** aloud as students read along. Remind students that examples are one type of supporting evidence that can be offered in a conversation or in writing to make an argument or point more convincing. Read the direction line aloud. Elicit or explain the job of a recruiter. People who work in the human resources (HR) department of a company are in charge of managing all employee issues, including health care, salary, and hiring and firing staff.

▶ **4.2** Play the video.

B Have students preview the task.

▶ **4.3** Play the video. Check answers to **A** and **B** together as a class. Ask students if they know anyone who has stretched the truth in a job interview. Did that person get the job?

C **CRITICAL THINKING** Read the question aloud. Give students a little time to consider their answers. Then have them discuss in pairs. Encourage them to share any personal stories of job interviews as well. If time permits, elicit a class discussion to hear each pair's thoughts on the topic. Note that in most job interviews, the biggest issue is that candidates stretch the truth to make themselves sound more qualified. As the speaker explains, total lies are not very common.

SPEAKING

A Ask students to read along as they watch.

▶ **4.4** Play the audio/video. Check answers as a class. Elicit what things specifically the two speakers think are OK and not OK to lie about (*OK to lie about reason for leaving a job; not OK to lie about how long you worked somewhere*).

Note that the conversation builds on what students discussed in **Critical Thinking**. Ask them to comment on what they talked about versus what the two speakers said. It might be interesting to point out that the speaker doesn't directly say that lying about how long you've worked somewhere is bad, but instead that you should avoid doing so because it's an easy lie to trace. However, it can be inferred by the last line that the speaker thinks negatively of lying, but not so much of stretching the truth.

B Model the conversation aloud with a student. Then have students work in pairs to practice. Make sure they alternate between A and B roles.

➕ **SUPPORT** Play the audio/video again, pausing after each sentence so students can repeat.

C Read the direction line aloud. Tell pairs to write the questions first, and then go back and discuss possible ways to stretch the truth or tell another type of lie. Remind them to use the language from the lesson in their conversations. Model the example with a volunteer. Encourage partners to speak honestly about areas where they might be somewhat dishonest in an interview.

Truth, lies, and pictures

LANGUAGE FOCUS Making deductions

A ▶ **4.5** Read the information. Have you ever lied on social media, or do you think your friends have?

Answers will vary.

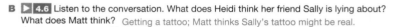

LIES PEOPLE TELL ON **SOCIAL MEDIA**

People tell all kinds of lies on social media. Here are some of the most common ones.

 6% posted pictures of expensive things that they didn't own — but said they did.

 10% lied in order to make themselves appear fashionable or attractive.

 8% used some kind of photo app to make their picture look better.

 16% of young adults actually believe their own lies after posting them. These are known as "false memories."

68% posted pictures to make their lives look more exciting than they actually are.

B ▶ **4.6** Listen to the conversation. What does Heidi think her friend Sally is lying about? What does Matt think? *Getting a tattoo; Matt thinks Sally's tattoo might be real.*

C ▶ **4.7** Watch and study the language in the chart.

Speculating about the truth
She might be telling the truth about meeting Will Smith.
He tells so many lies, he may or may not know what the truth is anymore.
The photo of her bungee jumping can't be real—I don't think she's really that adventurous.
He must have used a picture of someone else's car, because he doesn't own a Porsche.
She could have lied to us about her exam results.
He couldn't have been that close to a lion—the picture must be fake.

For more information on **modals of deduction and speculation**, see Grammar Summary 4 on page 184.

LESSON OVERVIEW

Aims: Read an infographic about lying on social media; talk about how people bend the truth on social media sites

Infographic Summary: Lies are commonly told by people on social media. Most notably, 68% of people post pictures that stretch the truth about their lives, making them appear to have more exciting lives than they actually do.

LANGUAGE FOCUS

A Read the question aloud.

▶ **4.5** Play the audio/video as students read along. Then give them additional time to look over the infographic. Ask students to share with the class an example of how they've lied on social media. Point out that the lies in the infographic are mostly about slightly misrepresenting yourself to make your life seem better than it is.

B Read the questions aloud and tell students to listen for the answers.

▶ **4.6** Play the audio/video. Check answers as a class. Elicit more details about the conversation.

C Have students read over the language chart for **Speculating about the truth**.

▶ **4.7** Play the audio/video. Ask students to pay close attention to the modal verbs. Explain that the modal verbs we use communicate the level of certainty we have about the truth of a topic. Go over the degree of certainty or possibility for each sentence. Direct students to page 184 for more information.

Grammar Note

Note that the language in the chart introduces modal verbs that can be used for making deductions about truth, in which you communicate what degree of certainty you have about something that you doubt is totally true.

Modal verbs don't have infinitive forms (~~to can~~) or participles (~~canning~~).

Regarding the degree of possibility or certainty, *might* is slightly less certain than *may,* and *could* is slightly less certain than *can.*

D ▶ **4.6** Listen to the conversation in **B** again. Complete the sentences from the conversation.

1 "There's no way Sally got one. It _____ must _____ be a picture of someone else's tattoo."

2 "But the tattoo is of a dog's paw print, and I know she loves her dog a lot. It _____ might _____ be real."

3 "She _____ could _____ have posted it just to see how people would react."

E ▶ **4.8** Complete the information. Circle the correct words. Then listen and check your answers.

Hubert Provand's 1936 photograph of the Brown Lady of Raynham Hall is one of the world's most famous "ghost" photographs, but you [1] (**couldn't** / **may or may not**) believe the image is real. Some experts have claimed that Provand used trick photography to create the image of the lady. It [2] (**couldn't** / **could**) have been faked with a computer, since it was taken before computers even existed. However, Provand [3] (**couldn't** / **could**) have combined two images to create the ghostly photograph. To this day, the photograph [4] (**might not** / **can't**) be satisfactorily explained. Even though the image [5] (**must** / **might**) not be real, many visitors to England's Raynham Hall still look for the ghost of the Brown Lady.

The Brown Lady of Raynham Hall

F Complete the sentences with the words from the box.

must have	may never	couldn't have	might actually

1 We _____ may never _____ know how Provand created the image.

2 Provand's photograph _____ couldn't have _____ been digitally altered.

3 The image of the ghost _____ might actually _____ be painted on the picture.

4 Some critics say Provand _____ must have _____ faked the image by putting grease on the camera lens.

SPEAKING Speculating about real and fake photographs

A Turn to page 166. Look at the two photographs. One of these photographs is real; the other is fake. Speculate about the two photographs, and decide which one you think is real and why.
Photo A is fake; Photo B is real.

B Work with a partner. Discuss your answers. Answers will vary.

> Photograph A must be real because …

> I'm not too sure about that. The image could have been …

55

SPEAKING

A Have students turn to page 166. Give them time to preview the photos and decide which one they think is real and which one they think is fake. Tell them to take notes. Explain that they will next talk about their speculations to a partner.

B Model the example with a volunteer without going into detail about the photos that students are using. Point out that students should come to an agreement about which photograph is fake and why. After students discuss, ask for volunteers to share their speculations with the class.

➡ **EXTENSION ACTIVITY** Ask students to discuss in pairs how they feel about the statistics in the infographic. Does it change their impression of social media? Ask them to go online and look at their friends' recently posted pictures. Tell students to pick one picture that stretches the truth about a friend's life. Note that students will learn in the reading passage in **Lesson C** that these misleading photos are actually anti-social because they create negative feelings of jealousy in those who view them, even though they are actually exaggerated versions of someone's life; therefore, they actually harm our relationships with one another.

D Have students preview the task.

▶ **4.6** Play the audio/video. Have students work individually to complete the activity. Have students check answers in pairs.

E Have students work individually. Tell them to use the information in the language chart to help them complete the paragraph.

▶ **4.8** Play the audio/video to check answers.

F Explain that the sentences relate back to the content that students read in **E**.

Have students work individually before checking answers as a class. Elicit reasons why students chose each answer, referencing back to the paragraph in **E**.

➡ **EXTENSION ACTIVITY** Have students work individually to write a paragraph similar to the one about the ghost picture in **E**. Ask them to write about a famous myth or legend that they know about and what may or may not be true about it. Ask them to use the language in the lesson to talk about why some people believe the legend and other people don't.

4C Lies we need to tell

PRE-READING Skimming

Skim the passage. Give an example of a pro-social lie that you have told. Share your answer with a partner.

Answers will vary.

▶ 4.9

¹ We often hear "**Honesty** is the best policy," and no one likes to be called a liar. But is **dishonesty** always wrong? Not necessarily, according to some psychologists.

² According to Oxford University psychologist Robin Dunbar, there are two types of lies: lies that help your relationships and the people around you, and lies that hurt them. Bad lies are lies that harm people; Dunbar calls these antisocial lies. Good lies are lies that make people feel better; Dunbar calls these pro-social lies.

³ How often have you clicked "Like" on Facebook, not because you actually like the picture of your friend's lunch or the cat video your cousin posted, but because you want to show your support? Psychology professor Larry Rosen says that we do this to show our friends that we have good intentions. This white lie is an example of a pro-social lie. According to Rosen, it's similar to saying "Yes" when someone asks, "Do you like my new shoes?" You're lying not to hide a secret or to protect yourself, but to avoid hurting someone's feelings.

⁴ But when people tell lies on social **networks** to make their own lives seem more exciting, or to make others **jealous**, this is antisocial lying. It doesn't bring friends closer, but instead creates negative feelings.

⁵ Workplace lies range from small, harmless lies to complete and destructive fabrications.[1] An example of a pro-social workplace lie is complimenting[2] someone on their presentation— even though it was only average—because you know they were nervous beforehand. In this case, your intention is simply to protect your colleague's

DAILY DISHONESTY: TOP LIES WE HEAR AND TELL

You look great!

My phone died.

I'm sick today.

I'm fine.

I've been really busy lately.

That was delicious!

We should have lunch soon!

Sorry, I didn't get your message.

56

Lesson page (left column)

LESSON OVERVIEW

Aims: Read and comprehend an article about dishonesty; understand main ideas and details

Target Vocabulary: deception, dishonesty, honesty, jealous, network

Reading Summary: Are there some situations where it's OK to be dishonest? Most psychologists say yes, if the lie is a pro-social one. Pro-social lies don't hurt others, while antisocial lies do. Sometimes we tell pro-social lies to show our support for others, such as liking a post on Facebook even if we aren't really interested in the content. Psychologists agree that sometimes white lies and stretching the truth are necessary in order to avoid hurting others. Lying may even be part of our biological wiring, since even young babies and apes have been caught in lies! While antisocial lies harm our relationships with others, pro-social ones tend to improve our social connections.

PRE-READING

Read the question aloud. Point out that students will need to skim the passage first to find out what a pro-social lie is and to read some examples. Give them one minute to do this. Then ask students to make a list of some pro-social lies that they have told recently. Have them share these with a partner.

▶ 4.9 Play the audio/video as students read along. Explain any key terms that students might not be familiar with.

➡ **EXTENSION ACTIVITY** Have students work in groups of four. Ask them to think of one pro-social lie that someone told them, which they discovered was not the truth. Tell them to explain the lie, describe the situation, and give the reason why they think it was told to them. Then ask the group to discuss whether they agree if it is a pro-social lie or not. Encourage students to also comment on how they felt after finding out they were lied to.

Koko the gorilla shares a drink with Wilbur Garrett from National Geographic.

Language Note

An *intention* (line 16) is the reasoning behind doing something. If someone has good intentions, it means that they were acting under the belief that they were doing something positive.

Something that is *destructive* (line 27) causes harm, usually to others. A *destructive fabrication* is a lie said with the purpose of hurting someone.

Something that is described as *average* (line 30) is considered normal, and does not stand out as being special.

If you are *on someone's good side* (line 35), they like you and think fondly of you.

To *resort to* (line 53) something means to do it in order to solve a challenge or problem.

When you do something *reflexively* (line 54), you do it without thinking.

To *master* (line 61) something means to be very skilled at it.

feelings. However, people sometimes tell bigger lies at work for the purpose of avoiding blame or to stay on the boss's good side. If your boss asks how a particular project is going and you say it's going well when it isn't, that's an antisocial lie. It's antisocial because your boss is likely to discover the truth, and as a result, will probably stop trusting you.

6 Author and TED speaker Pamela Meyer agrees that not all **deceptions** are harmful. If your partner asks, "Do I look fat in this?" the best answer is probably "No," even if it means stretching the truth. And many experts agree that for married people, keeping some secrets is completely healthy—as long as the secrets don't hurt anyone.

7 Of course, there are some things you should always tell a partner about: the loss of a job or a major health issue, for example. These could affect the future of both people, and living a lie is a bad idea in these cases.

8 Deception is also a significant part of the natural world, so it's little wonder we resort to it almost reflexively. Koko the gorilla learned to understand 2,000 words in English and to communicate using sign language. Occasionally, she's used this amazing language ability to lie. Human babies sometimes pretend to cry, check to see if anyone is listening, and then start crying again. By the age of five, children learn to say things that are completely untrue, and most nine-year-olds have mastered keeping secrets to protect themselves. As adults, we live in a world where we hear 10 to 200 lies from the people around us every day.

9 Lying can be incredibly harmful to our relationships and to the people around us. But that's only true for antisocial lies. Pro-social lies have the opposite effect—they can actually help us. Through pro-social lying, we can show our online connections that we support them, keep our professional relationships positive, and make our partners and loved ones feel happy and confident.

¹ **fabrications:** *n.* untruthful statements
² **complimenting:** *v.* praising or expressing admiration for someone

57

Content Note

In her TED Talk, speaker Pamela Meyer shares the famous instance of the gorilla Koko being caught in a lie.

Koko is a gorilla that lives in a research institute in California. She has learned to use sign language—over one thousand different signs—to communicate with her trainers. She loves kittens and has had a series of pet kittens over the years.

One day, Koko was alone in her habitat and acted destructively toward a sink. She removed it from the wall. When her trainer returned and saw the sink, Koko was asked what happened. In response, Koko signed "The cat did it."

UNDERSTANDING MAIN IDEAS

A Have students preview the task. Encourage them to complete the activity based on their first reading, and to not refer back to the passage. Have them check answers in pairs.

B Tell students to refer back to the passage to reread the paragraphs if necessary. Note that they can likely get the answer by reading only the topic sentence. Check answers as a class.

⭐ **CHALLENGE** Have students work in pairs to write new headings for each section. Then have them share their ideas with the class.

UNDERSTANDING DETAILS

Have students work individually. Check answers as a class, eliciting how to make each false statement true. Elicit the line in the passage where students found the correct information.

⭐ **CHALLENGE** Have students work in pairs to go back to each sentence in **Understanding Details**. Have them explain it using one of the modals in **Lesson B** for making deductions regarding the truth.

BUILDING VOCABULARY

A Have students work individually to complete the activity. Check answers as a class. Elicit additional example sentences using each word. Write them on the board.

B **CRITICAL THINKING** Read the question aloud as students read along. Have students work in pairs. Give them time to look more closely at the infographic on page 56. Ask them to decide which lies are pro-social and which aren't. Note that it may depend on the situation whether a lie is pro-social or not. Then ask students to describe times that they've used some of the lies listed. What was the situation? Did they hurt anyone with the lie? Did the lie have a benefit in the end?

UNDERSTANDING MAIN IDEAS

A Check (✓) the sentences that are supported by the passage.

☐ Lying always hurts someone in the end: either the liar, or the person being lied to.

☑ Sometimes, making people feel good is more important than telling the absolute truth.

☐ Lying on social media is pro-social, but face-to-face lying isn't.

☑ Some lies can make a marriage stronger.

☐ Babies and children don't lie.

B Match each section below to a suitable heading.

Paragraph 2   Why We Lie
Paragraphs 3–7   Good Lies and Bad Lies
Paragraphs 8–9   Lying Is in Our Nature

UNDERSTANDING DETAILS

Circle **T** for true or **F** for false.

1 We usually tell pro-social lies to protect people's feelings.   **(T)**   F

2 If you make your boss feel better by lying about your progress on a project, it's a pro-social lie.   T   **(F)**

3 Married couples should always tell the truth about big issues, but small lies are probably not harmful.   **(T)**   F

4 Animals are unable to lie.   T   **(F)**

5 Pro-social lying can strengthen our online and offline relationships.   **(T)**   F

BUILDING VOCABULARY

A Complete the sentences using the words from the box.

deceptions	dishonesty	honesty	network	jealousy

1 We typically post pictures online of our best or most exciting moments, which can sometimes lead to feelings of _____jealousy_____ in some people.

2 His many _____deceptions_____ did not become known until years after he had died.

3 The government official's _____dishonesty_____ over the financial scandal has led to his dismissal.

4 Through pro-social lying, we can strengthen our _____network_____ of family and friends.

5 Total _____honesty_____ is probably not important for most relationships. Some lies are helpful.

B **CRITICAL THINKING** Answers will vary.

Reflecting Look at the infographic on page 56. Which of these lies have you told and in what situations? Discuss with a partner.

➡ **EXTENSION ACTIVITY** Have students go online to a social media site. Tell them to write down four possible lies (two pro-social and two antisocial) that they see while browsing the feed page of their friends and family members. Then have a class discussion about communicating on social media. Ask students to share some of the examples that they found. Encourage them to also comment on why they think the lie was told (for example, to make themselves seem interesting, to make a friend feel loved, or to make others praise them).

4D How to spot a liar

TEDTALKS

PAMELA MEYER is the CEO of social networking company Simpatico Networks. She has researched lies for many years and has written a bestselling book called *Liespotting*.

Pamela Meyer's idea worth spreading is that by learning to recognize lies through speech and body language, we can help to build a more truthful world.

PREVIEWING

Read the paragraph below. Match each **bold** word to its meaning. You will hear these words in the TED Talk.

If we're all against dishonesty, Pamela Meyer asks, why is it so **prevalent**? It seems that everyone lies: men and women, **introverts** and **extroverts**, married couples, friends, and strangers. Meyer believes that understanding **body language** is one key to spotting lies. If we know what to look for, we can tell when someone is being **sincere** and when they are **faking** their emotions.

1	honest	sincere
2	common; widespread	prevalent
3	socially confident people	extroverts
4	people who feel most comfortable alone	introverts
5	pretending to feel or have	faking
6	the way we communicate using our face, hands, etc.	body language

VIEWING

A Guess the answers to the summary below. Circle the correct words.

Meyer says that ¹ (**everyone lies** / **most people lie**). We lie because we want to ² (**protect ourselves** / **be better people**). We usually lie three times within the first ten minutes of meeting ³ (**a stranger** / **an old friend**).

B ▶ **4.10** Predict. Complete the sentences below using the words in the parentheses. Then watch Part 1 of the TED Talk, and check your answers to **A** and **B**.

1 We lie more to ___strangers___ than we lie to ___co-workers___ . (**co-workers** / **strangers**)

2 ___Extroverts___ lie more than ___introverts___ . (**extroverts** / **introverts**)

3 ___Men___ usually lie about themselves, while ___women___ lie to protect others.
(**men** / **women**)

4 ___Unmarried___ couples lie to their partners more than ___married___ couples.
(**married** / **unmarried**)

59

4D

How to spot a liar

meaning. Have students work individually before checking answers in pairs. Remind students of the **Warm Up** preview clip. Tell them to use all the language and information they have learned about lying throughout the unit to support their comprehension of Pamela Meyer's TED Talk. If necessary, elicit additional example sentences with each vocabulary word.

VIEWING

A Explain that students will guess answers before watching. Tell them to rely on the background information on lying that they've gathered throughout the unit. Have them work individually. If necessary, elicit or explain the meaning of *stranger*.

B Tell students to also predict the answer for **B** using their background information. Give students enough time to guess which word goes in each blank. Ask students to check their answers as they watch.

▶ **4.10** Play Part 1 of the TED Talk. Ask students if any answers in **A** or **B** surprised them. Elicit or explain the meaning of any unfamiliar language. Suggestions for Part 1 include *alarm, recoil,* and *the plot thickens.*

Write the following quote from Part 1 on the board: *Now when we first hear this data, we recoil.*

Ask students to talk about how they felt when they heard the data. Did they recoil? Or did the information that they've learned so far in the unit prepare them?

Ask students if their real-life experiences support what Meyer is saying. Do they lie more to strangers than to co-workers?

LESSON OVERVIEW

Aims: Watch and understand a talk about liespotting; observe and practice beginning with a strong statement

Target Vocabulary: body language, extrovert, fake (v), introvert, prevalent, sincere

TED Talk Summary: Everyone lies. In fact, we can lie up to 200 times a day. As an experienced liespotter, Pamela Meyer knows how to recognize verbal and nonverbal cues that give away a liar. She shares some of these with her TED

audience, explaining that what reveals a lie is probably not what most people think. She explains that attitude is the most important indicator. When people lie, they give too much detail, they won't be able to retell their story the same way twice, they blink at an increased rate, and they lower their voices. By learning to spot a liar, we can all encourage a more honest world by not letting others get away with lies.

PREVIEWING

Have students read the paragraph. Tell them to pay attention to how each word is used in context in order to understand its

C Have students preview the task. Point out that they are predicting again. Give them enough time to make their guesses before watching the video.

▶ **4.11** Play Part 2 of the TED Talk. Check answers as a class, eliciting how to make each false statement true. (If liars don't fidget, what do they do?) For question 4, ask students what part of the face reveals a real smile? (the eyes)

Ask students to share how many predictions they got right. Note that Meyer says that many of us have misunderstandings about cues that liars give. Did students have misunderstandings, too? Ask students to share how their thoughts about lying have changed over the course of the unit. Elicit or explain the meaning of any unfamiliar language. Suggestions for Part 2 include *throw your assumptions out the door, fidget, spot something a mile away,* and *hot spot.*

D Have students preview the task. If necessary, for support, play the video twice before checking answers.

▶ **4.12** Play Part 3 of the TED Talk. Check answers as a class. Ask students what kind of situation Meyer is mostly describing in Part 3. They should pick up that she is talking about the interrogation of an accused criminal. Elicit or explain the meaning of any additional unfamiliar language. Suggestions for Part 3 include *cooperative, infuriated, herky-jerky, pepper, interrogator,* and *blink rate.*

E CRITICAL THINKING Read the questions aloud. Do not explain the meaning of *red flag* until after students have discussed and offered some possible meanings. Give them a few minutes to think about how their view of lying has changed during the unit. Elicit a class discussion after pairs have talked. Ask for some specific examples of how students plan to change their approach to communicating with others.

C ▶ **4.11** Can you predict a liar's body language? Circle **T** for true or **F** for false. Use a dictionary if necessary. Then watch Part 2 of the TED Talk and check your answers.

1 Liars tend to fidget a lot. T **(F)**
2 Liars will often freeze their upper body. **(T)** F
3 Liars usually avoid eye contact. T **(F)**
4 Picture B below shows a genuine smile. **(T)** F
5 Liars' actions tend to match their words. T **(F)**

A

B

D ▶ **4.12** Watch Part 3 of the TED Talk. Use the words in the box to complete the chart.

recommends strict punishment	withdrawn	speaks in a low voice
willing to brainstorm	gives lots of details	enthusiastic
tells their story chronologically	pauses	cooperative

Honest person	Liar
cooperative	withdrawn
enthusiastic	speaks in a low voice
willing to brainstorm	pauses
recommends strict punishment	gives lots of details
	tells their story chronologically

E CRITICAL THINKING Answers will vary.

Inferring/Evaluating Discuss these questions with a partner.

1 Pamela Meyer says that the behaviors and attitudes in **D** above are "not proof of deception"; they're "red flags." What does she mean by this?

2 Which facts about lying did you find most surprising? Do you think being aware of these facts can make you better at liespotting?

60

VOCABULARY IN CONTEXT

A ▶ **4.13** Watch the excerpts from the TED Talk. Choose the correct meaning of the words. 1.a; 2.b; 3.c; 4.c

B Work with a partner. Complete the sentences with your own ideas. Answers will vary.

  1 Someone went the extra mile for me when _____.

  2 A politician or other public figure was deceptive when _____.

PRESENTATION SKILLS Beginning with a strong statement

> The start of a talk is your opportunity to get the audience's attention and hold it. You can do this in a variety of ways.
> - Be surprising: Do or say something your audience won't expect.
> - Be controversial: Say something that some people might not agree with.
> - Be challenging: Say something to make your listeners question themselves or those around them.

A ▶ **4.14** Watch part of Pamela Meyer's TED Talk. Complete the opening sentence of the talk. Which of the techniques from the box above does she use? Be challenging.

"OK, now I don't want to alarm anybody in this room, but it's just come to my attention that
_____ the person to your right is a liar _____."

B ▶ **4.15** Watch the next part of Meyer's TED Talk. Circle any other sentences that use this technique.

"Also, the person to your left is a liar. Also, the person sitting in your very seats is a liar. We're all liars. What I'm going to do today is I'm going to show you what the research says about why we're all liars …"

61

VOCABULARY IN CONTEXT

A ▶ **4.13** Play the video. If necessary, play it again.

B Read the sentences aloud. Have students work in pairs to share answers. Check answers as a class.

PRESENTATION SKILLS

A Read the Presentation Skills paragraph **Beginning with a strong statement** aloud.

▶ **4.14** Play the video. Check answers as a class. Meyer uses a challenging statement to engage her audience immediately.

B Have students preview the task.

▶ **4.15** Play the video. Check answers as a class.

⊙ **EXTENSION ACTIVITY** Have students work in pairs to rewrite an opening to Meyer's talk that is a different kind of strong statement. Have pairs share their openings with the class.

Language Note

Part 1

To *alarm* someone means to make them aware of something disturbing or frightening. The expression *I don't want to alarm anyone, but …* is used to introduce news that is shocking and may affect the listeners in a negative way.

To *recoil* from something means to feel fear or disgust about it, to the point that you physically flinch.

The expression *the plot thickens* is used to explain that a story is more complicated than we might have first thought.

Part 2

The expression *throw your assumptions out the door* is a request to clear your mind of any preconceptions that you already have about whatever topic you are going to hear about.

When someone *fidgets*, they move their body nervously. It usually involves small movements of the hands and feet.

To *spot something a mile away* means you can predict or know that something is going to happen.

When Meyer uses the term *hot spot*, she is using a liespotting term that refers to verbal or nonverbal cues given that indicate someone is lying.

Part 3

To be *cooperative* means to be agreeable and to assist someone in getting something done.

To be *infuriated* means to be very angry.

Someone who moves or behaves in a *herky-jerky* way stops and starts a lot.

The verb *pepper* in regard to conversation refers to adding information in a scattered way.

An *interrogator* is someone who asks questions to a suspect in order to try to find out the truth.

A person's *blink rate* refers to the number of times he or she blinks during a set period.

A *red flag* is a warning of a possible negative outcome.

Liespotting

LESSON OVERVIEW

Aims: Consider the importance of body language in liespotting; write a paragraph about lying

COMMUNICATE

A Have students work individually to fill in the chart before getting into groups. Give them enough time, and tell them to mix up the truth and lies in the box. Point out the example ideas given in the direction line. Students can write about anything, but suggestions given include birthplace, hobbies, skills, and experiences. Have students get into small groups of three or four.

B Give students time to think individually about how they will present to their group the information that they wrote down. Remind them of the various liespotting techniques that they learned in the unit. Note that students should try to hide their lies, but that they also may try to project that they are lying when they are actually telling the truth.

C Have group members take turns sharing their information. Have each student share all six pieces of information at once so that their group members can compare cues between each piece of information. Tell group members to write down which two pieces of information they think the person was lying about, and why. After all group members have had their turn, then have the group share the result of their liespotting.

⭐ **CHALLENGE** Elicit a class discussion about the experience. Ask students to share how they felt while telling a lie as well as while liespotting. Was it easy to catch the lie? Why or why not? Which techniques from the TED Talk did they use?

WRITING

Read the question aloud. Note that students are being asked to give their opinions in their writing. Ask them to support their ideas with examples.

Read the model aloud. Point out that the writer states an opinion at the beginning. Then the writer gives a reason and begins to offer support. Remind students that support can come in the form of examples, anecdotes, quotes, or statistics.

Have students share their writing in pairs.

4E Liespotting

COMMUNICATE The lying game   Answers will vary.

A Work in groups of three or four. You are going to tell your group six facts about yourself. Two of them must be lies. Think about where you were born, experiences you've had, hobbies, skills and abilities, etc.

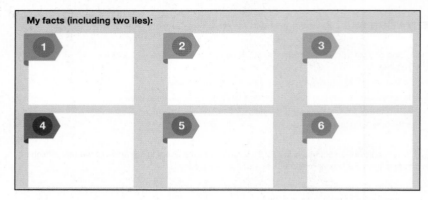

My facts (including two lies):

1   2   3

4   5   6

B Think about how you will try to hide your lies. Consider the following: your eyes, body language, and voice.

C In your group, take turns sharing your six facts. Your group members should try to spot which two statements are lies.

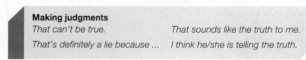

Making judgments
That can't be true.   *That sounds like the truth to me.*
That's definitely a lie because …   *I think he/she is telling the truth.*

WRITING Expressing an opinion   Answers will vary.

Do you think there is ever a good reason for lying? Explain your view and give an example to support your opinion.

> Although we often think of lying as a bad thing, there are many times when there may be a good reason for telling a lie. I think that sometimes, it may be better for people to not know the whole truth. For example, …

Some people give false information about themselves online.

62

⭐ **CHALLENGE** Have a class debate about whether or not there is ever a good reason to lie. Tell students to use the reasons and support from their writing as arguments and/or counterarguments in the debate.

5 To the Edge

66 Magic … is pretty simple. It's training and experimenting, while pushing through the pain to be the best that I can be. **99**

David Blaine
Magician, illusionist, TED speaker

UNIT GOALS

In this unit, you will …

- talk about significant challenges and achievements.
- read about David Blaine's endurance challenges.
- watch a TED Talk about achieving the impossible.

WARM UP

▶ **5.1** Watch part of David Blaine's TED Talk. Answer the questions with a partner.

1 What goal did Blaine have as a young man?
   To imitate Houdini's underwater challenges
2 What goals have you set for yourself—as a child or now? Answers will vary.

63

5

To the Edge

WARM UP

Have students look over the picture, caption, and quote on the page. Read the quote aloud. Note that students will not hear the quote in the video clip, but it gives the speaker's conclusion about his work. Draw students' attention to the speaker's job titles: *magician* and *illusionist*. Elicit the meanings of both and explain the difference.

▶ **5.1** Play the preview clip of the TED Talk.

For question 1, note that students will hear in the video that David Blaine was obsessed with Houdini and his underwater challenges, so he trained himself to hold his breath underwater. Students may not know who Houdini is, although his pictures are shown in the video clip. Houdini was a famous American magician and illusionist who lived during the early 1900s. He is considered one of the most famous magicians of all time and popularized magic as a performance, much like Blaine has done one century later.

For question 2, give students time to think about their goals. Then have them share with a partner.

➡ **EXTENSION ACTIVITY** Draw students' attention to the first unit goal and question 2, both of which discuss personal achievements. Ask students to make a list of their long-term goals. Then they should choose one goal from the list and make a plan for achieving it over the next five years. Note that they can refer back to this during the unit when asked to discuss personal goals and achievements.

Language Note

Illusionist or *magician* describes a person who does tricks to entertain an audience. An illusionist performs on large stages or to live audiences. David Blaine is known for his many televised public performances.

UNIT GOALS

The unit focuses on reaching personal goals and making major achievements. Students will be encouraged to share their personal goals as they read about and watch the extraordinary accomplishments of others. They will use collocations and the past perfect tense to discuss challenging achievements.

TED Speaker

David Blaine is a famous magician from the United States.

TED Talk Summary

David Blaine shares how, with serious training and practice, he broke the world record for holding his breath underwater. While people may think that magicians create illusions that aren't real, Blaine explains that he is focused on proving he can do what medical knowledge says humans cannot do. He claims he has learned to accomplish these tasks through dedicated study and preparation.

Idea Worth Spreading

Impossible goals can be achieved with dedication and commitment.

Unit 5 **63**

Challenge and success

VOCABULARY

A Note that each vocabulary term is a phrase or collocation for talking about challenges or achievements. Point out that most terms contain an action verb + object. Have students work individually to complete the sentences before checking their answers in pairs.

B Have students work in pairs to group together all the phrases that describe an achievement. Check answers by making a Venn diagram on the board of achievements and challenges. Elicit which category each phrase belongs in. Ask for an example sentence that makes the meaning of each phrase clear. Note that *overcome (a challenge)* describes facing a challenge successfully, so it can fit in both categories. Students may be able to argue even more overlap between challenges and achievements since the achievement often comes after a challenge.

C Read the questions aloud. For question 1, point out that students can talk about someone they know personally or someone famous. Note that not all records have to be sports-related. Tell students that they can talk about any kind of record that interests them.

For question 2, ask students to share a personal story about overcoming a challenge. Explain that it doesn't have to

High-wire artist Nik Wallenda set a world record as the first person to cross Niagara Falls on a tightrope.

5A Challenge and success

VOCABULARY Describing challenges and successes

A Complete the sentences with the words from the box.

against	break	milestone	overcome	pain	yourself

1 As soon as you **set a record**, someone else will try to ____break____ it.

2 To **face a challenge**, you have to ____overcome____ your fears and doubts.

3 In many cases, it's necessary to **push** ____yourself____ to win.

4 Athletes often **endure** ____pain____ **and suffering** on the way to success.

5 When you **reach a goal** or an important ____milestone____ in your life, it's a time for celebration.

6 Sometimes you **compete head-to-head with other people**, and sometimes you **compete** ____against____ **yourself**.

B Work with a partner. Which of the phrases in **bold** above describe an achievement?
set a record; reach a goal

C Work with a partner. Discuss your answers to these questions. Answers will vary.

1 Do you know of anyone who has set or broken a record?

2 Can you think of a time in your life when you had to overcome a challenge?

64

be a serious challenge but could relate to an accomplishment in school, work, or an activity where they set a goal. Ask students to also talk about whether they *competed against themselves* or against another person or group.

⭐ **CHALLENGE** Have students practice making comparisons between different challenges in their lives in order to review comparatives and superlatives: *For me, finishing the marathon meant enduring a lot of pain, but learning to drive was even more stressful and required me to push myself outside of my comfort zone.*

Language Note

When you *face a challenge*, you engage with it and try to deal with it. If this is done successfully, it is described as *overcoming that challenge*.

The term *compete head-to-head* means to have a direct confrontation. While it sounds like it applies to a meeting of two individual competitors, it can also be used to talk about teams or groups that compete against each other. *Competing against yourself* usually involves setting personal records in sports or overcoming personal challenges in other matters.

> **Listening for time expressions**
> Time expressions are used to sequence events and to make stories and anecdotes more interesting.
>
> *Back then, ...   After that, ...   I now ...*

A ▶ **5.2** Watch Nadia Ruiz talk about being a marathon runner. What is her biggest achievement?

(a) She has run more than 100 marathons.

b She broke a national record for the marathon.

B ▶ **5.3** Watch and check (✓) the challenges Ruiz mentions.

☐ breaking a speed record

☑ competing against yourself

☐ following a strict diet

☑ pushing through the pain

☑ being mentally strong

C **CRITICAL THINKING** Answers will vary.

Analyzing Work with a partner. Brainstorm five personality traits that a marathon runner must have.

Nadia Ruiz has participated in marathons around the world.

SPEAKING Talking about an achievement

A ▶ **5.4** Why does Speaker A congratulate Speaker B? Because Speaker B won a medal for powerlifting.

A: I heard you won a medal for powerlifting. Congratulations!

B: Thanks! It was really tough, but I'm glad that all my hard work and training paid off.

A: How did you train for it?

B: I practiced weight training every day of the week with my coach. It took time away from my friends and family, and I had to push myself to keep working out. But I'm proud of myself for sticking with it.

A: It must feel great now that you've reached your goal.

B: It does. This was definitely one of my biggest achievements. But now I need to focus my energy on next year's competition.

A: Good luck for next year! I'm sure you'll do well.

B Practice the conversation with a partner.

C Work with a partner. Talk about your biggest achievement in life so far. Use the expressions in blue above to help you. Answers will vary.

> One of my biggest achievements is winning a ...

> How did you prepare for it?

65

---

in **B** as a guide for discussion. Ask them what kind of person would succeed under such type of circumstances. Encourage students to also talk about whether it's a challenge they feel they could have overcome.

⊙ EXTENSION ACTIVITY Ask students to share the story of someone they know personally who has achieved a challenging sports-related goal. Ask them to tell the story of the challenge and achievement. Then ask them to talk about how the person's personality traits helped them overcome the challenge.

SPEAKING

A Read the question aloud. Ask students to read along as they watch.

▶ **5.4** Play the audio/video. Check answers as a class. Ask students to identify what Speaker B got for the achievement (a medal). Elicit or explain the sport of powerlifting. It is a competitive form of weightlifting where participants have to do three different kinds of lifts at the heaviest barbell weight possible. Point out that the conversation introduces additional language for talking about goals. Write on the board: *pay off, train for it, practice + -ing verb, stick with it, reach your goal,* and *focus my energy on.*

Note that many of the phrases introduced in the conversation can also be used to talk about general challenges and goals, not just sports-related ones.

B Model the conversation aloud with a student. Then have students work in pairs to practice the conversation. Make sure they alternate between A and B roles.

C Read the direction line aloud. Point out that students can talk about any kind of achievement and that it does not have to be sports-related. Ask them to share what they learned about themselves during the experience. Model the example with a volunteer. Point out that the student who is listening asks relevant questions to help guide the conversation. Encourage students to make it more of a conversation instead of one student telling a story and the other just listening.

LISTENING

A Read **Listening for time expressions** aloud as students read along. Point out that the first phrase is used to talk about past events, so a clause in one of the past tenses will follow. The last phrase deals with the present and will be followed by a clause in a present or possibly future tense.

▶ **5.2** Play the video. Elicit the expressions that students heard in the video that indicate a past experience. (*After that, I started training seriously and running more marathons every*

year. *In 2013, I became the youngest Latin-American woman in the world to run 100 marathons.*) Note that one more phrase is introduced: *In 2013, ...* Elicit the length of a marathon (26 miles or 42 km).

B ▶ **5.3** Play the video. Check answers to **A** and **B** as a class. Ask students to add some other challenges that a marathon runner might face. Encourage students who have run a marathon to share their experience with the class.

C **CRITICAL THINKING** Explain that students can use the list of challenges

LESSON OVERVIEW

Aims: Understand an infographic about record breakers; use the past tense

Infographic Summary: The incredible achievements of six people are introduced, from a woman in India with amazing calculation skills to a man in Japan who sliced a moving tennis ball in half with a sword. In all corners of the world, there are people with astonishing abilities.

LANGUAGE FOCUS

A Read the question aloud. Elicit or explain the meaning of *superhuman*. Remind students that they read about superheroes in **Unit 2**. In contrast to a superhero, a superhuman is a real person who has a unique and extraordinary skill.

▶ **5.5** Play the audio/video as students read along. Then give them additional time to look over the infographic.

B Have students preview the task. Explain that the audio is broken up into numbered pieces of information about each person.

▶ **5.6** Play the audio/video. Check answers as a class, eliciting some of the details that students heard about each person.

C Have students read over the language chart before playing the audio/video. Ask them to pay attention to the verbs in blue.

▶ **5.7** Play the audio/video and have students read aloud. Direct students to page 185 for more information on the past perfect and past perfect progressive.

5B Superhumans

LANGUAGE FOCUS Doing the impossible

A ▶ **5.5** Read the information. Which "superhuman" do you think is the most incredible? Answers will vary.

DOING THE IMPOSSIBLE

These six ordinary people have superhuman abilities.

28 SECONDS
The time it took **Shakuntala Devi** from India, to correctly calculate 7,686,369,774,870 × 2,465,099,745,779 — in her head!

-29°C
The temperature when Dutchman **Wim Hof** ran a marathon — without a shirt!

299 KILOGRAMS
The weight of a barrel **Sakinat Khanapiyeva** of Russia moved as a ten-year-old girl — equivalent to the weight of four grown men!

50
The number of marathons American **Dean Karnazes** ran in 50 days, in 50 states of the U.S.!

4,700
The number of words **Anne Jones** from England can read in one minute! Most people read 220–300 words per minute.

820 KILOMETERS PER HOUR
The speed of a tennis ball cut in half in mid-air by Japanese sword expert **Isao Machii**!

B ▶ **5.6** Listen. Match each piece of information you hear (**1–6**) to the correct person in the infographic.

Shakuntala Devi	3	Wim Hof	2
Dean Karnazes	6	Anne Jones	1
Isao Machii	4	Sakinat Khanapiyeva	5

C ▶ **5.7** Watch and study the language in the chart.

Describing accomplishments

She had turned 45 before she won her first speed-reading world championship.
He had completed his first marathon before he graduated from high school.
By the age of five, she had already started earning money for her family.
She hadn't known about her superpower before moving the heavy barrel.

When he set his world record, he had been practicing and training for many years.
He had been meditating for several years before he decided to climb Mount Everest wearing nothing but shorts and hiking boots.

For more information on the **past perfect** and **past perfect progressive**, see Grammar Summary 5 on page 185.

66

Grammar Note

The language chart introduces the past perfect tense (*had* + past participle) and past perfect progressive tense (*had been* + present participle (*-ing*)) to talk about events in the past.

The past perfect tense can be used to talk about completed actions that happened before another past event. (*By the age of 50, he had graduated from five different universities.*) It refers to a past event that happened before another past event.

The past perfect progressive tense is used to talk about ongoing situations that have since been completed. (*I had been training for months before the competition.*)

Note that for the past perfect tenses, when speaking, it is common to contract *had* and the subject. (*He'd been running for months beforehand.*) The sounds are commonly linked or reduced in speech. In cases when the verb is negative, *had* is contracted with *not*. (*He hadn't trained at all before competing.*)

Note that the present participles of the following verbs are typically not used in the past perfect progressive: *know* (~~had been knowing~~), *like* (~~had been liking~~), *be* (~~had been being~~), *have* (~~had been having~~).

D ▶ **5.6** Listen to the information in **B** again. Complete the sentences with the words you hear.

1 "She _____had turned_____ 40 when she learned to speed read."

2 "He _____had been studying_____ Eastern philosophy for several years when, in the winter of 1979, he decided to jump into some icy water."

3 "He _____had been running_____ regularly since kindergarten, and completed his first marathon before he graduated from high school."

E Complete the sentences. Circle the correct words.

1 Shakuntala Devi (**was** /(**had been**)) performing around the world for more than 50 years before she was studied by psychologist Arthur Jensen.

2 Sakinat Khanapiyeva (**lifted** /(**had been lifting**)) heavy weights for more than 60 years before she finally ((**received**)/ **had received**) the "World's Strongest Granny" award.

3 When Dean Karnazes ((**started**)/ **had started**) the New York Marathon, he (**ran** /(**had already run**)) more than 2,050 km in the previous 49 days.

4 Anne Jones (**hasn't** /(**hadn't**)) shown special reading ability before she ((**taught**)/ **had taught**) herself speed reading.

5 Isao Machii ((**began**)/ **had begun**) his training when he was five years old.

F ▶ **5.8** Complete the information using the correct form of the verb in parentheses. Then listen and check your answers.

In the 1970s, Diana Nyad [1] _____set_____ (**set**) many world swimming records—the final one in 1979, when she swam 164 km in the sea from the Bahamas to Florida. She [2] _____completed_____ (**complete**) the swim in 27.5 hours. Shortly after that, she retired from competitive swimming. However, in 2010, at the age of 60, Nyad decided to try a new challenge—swimming from Cuba to Florida—a task she [3] _____had failed_____ (**fail**) to complete 30 years prior. Before her first swim attempt in 2011, Nyad [4] _____had_____ already _____been training_____ (**train**) for several months. Swimmers in the Straits of Florida often swim inside a cage to protect themselves from shark attacks, but Nyad [5] _____chose_____ (**choose**) not to use one. The challenge wasn't easy; she failed several times. But on her fifth attempt on September 2, 2013, Nyad saw the lights of Key West, Florida on the horizon. At this point, she [6] _____had been swimming_____ (**swim**) for 38 hours. She pushed herself through the last 15 hours of her journey and finally achieved success, becoming the first person to swim from Cuba to Florida without the aid of a shark cage.

Diana Nyad is an American long-distance swimmer.

SPEAKING Talking about yesterday's activities Answers will vary.

You are going to talk about things you did yesterday. Turn to page 167.

EXTENSION ACTIVITY Have students write an imaginary story about Diana Nyad's training program based on what they read in **F**. Tell them to use the past perfect tense and the past perfect progressive tense to explain in detail what Nyad did to train for her historic swim from Cuba to Florida.

SPEAKING

A Have students preview the task and chart on page 167. Give them time to recall and write down some events from the previous day. Note that students should write about events that were completed or still in progress at each time in the chart. If necessary, write your own schedule yesterday on the board. Use it to also demonstrate how to talk about your activities from yesterday in **B** below.

B Model the example with a volunteer. Explain that group members should compare what they did with other members at certain times during the day. Encourage them to offer interesting reactions to each other's activities (for example, *You'd already gone to bed by 8 p.m.? Isn't that a little early?*).

C Have groups next discuss who had the most interesting day and who had the busiest day. Tell them to give reasons by mentioning events they heard each other talk about in their schedules.

EXTENSION ACTIVITY Have students work in pairs to go online and find out about another superhuman. Tell them to find a fascinating world record that someone holds, and to explain what they did to get it. (Students can check the Guinness World Records website for some unique records.) Have each pair make a poster about their record breaker. Tell them to include on the poster whatever key information they can find as well as any visuals that are available. Then have pairs present their posters to the class.

D Have students preview the task. Tell them to listen carefully for the verb that the speaker uses.

▶ **5.6** Play the audio/video. Check answers as a class, asking students to identify the verb tense and explain why it was used.

E Have students work individually. Note that this activity is a good chance for them to understand when to use past perfect versus simple past tense. Check answers as a class, eliciting an explanation of why the verb tense was used in each case.

F Have students work individually to complete the paragraph.

▶ **5.8** Play the audio/video to check answers. Then elicit a summary of the information in the paragraph. Who is Diana Nyad? What did she accomplish?

Magic man

5C Magic man

LESSON OVERVIEW

Aims: Read and comprehend an article about David Blaine; understand main ideas and details

Target Vocabulary: astonishment, endurance, reaction, stunt, transformed

Reading Summary: From a young age, David Blaine was fascinated both by magical performances and by tests of endurance. He was particularly focused on underwater challenges, and trained himself to stay underwater for as long as his idol, magician Harry Houdini, could. Blaine started his career as a street magician, but his entertaining performances soon landed him on TV and allowed him to elevate his shows into grander and riskier performances. He has since done a series of high-risk stunts live on television, most of which involved exciting endurance challenges. In the process, David Blaine has made magic a popular form of entertainment, as well as an exciting career choice.

PRE-READING

Have students preview the task. Tell them to read the passage quickly to find the information. Note that they will have to find two pieces of information in order to calculate the correct age. Point out that students should also read the sidebar on page 68.

Point out the footnotes at the end of the reading. Remind students to refer to it before or while reading.

▶ **5.9** Play the audio/video as students read along. Go over any unfamiliar language. See **Language Note**.

5C Magic man

PRE-READING Scanning

Scan the passage. At what age did David Blaine become a professional magician? 24

▶ **5.9**

He's been enclosed in a massive block of ice for three days and three nights, been buried alive for a week, lived in a glass box for 44 days with nothing but water, and spent one week inside a water-filled sphere—all in the name of entertainment. In less than three decades, David Blaine has **transformed** the world of magic. His unique and fascinating career as a magician, illusionist, and **endurance** artist has led critics to compare him with the greatest magician of them all, and Blaine's personal hero—Harry Houdini.

EARLY LIFE

At the age of four, Blaine saw a street magician performing in the New York subway and instantly became fascinated. He started practicing magic with a deck of cards given to him by his grandmother. From an early age, he was also interested in endurance challenges, like holding his breath. In 1987, when Blaine was 14, he heard a news story that really grabbed his attention. It was about a teenager who had fallen through ice and become trapped under a river for 45 minutes. Amazingly, he survived without brain damage.

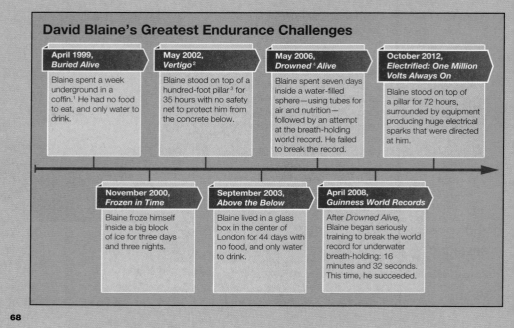

David Blaine's Greatest Endurance Challenges

April 1999, Buried Alive
Blaine spent a week underground in a coffin.[1] He had no food to eat, and only water to drink.

May 2002, Vertigo[2]
Blaine stood on top of a hundred-foot pillar[3] for 35 hours with no safety net to protect him from the concrete below.

May 2006, Drowned[1] Alive
Blaine spent seven days inside a water-filled sphere—using tubes for air and nutrition—followed by an attempt at the breath-holding world record. He failed to break the record.

October 2012, Electrified: One Million Volts Always On
Blaine stood on top of a pillar for 72 hours, surrounded by equipment producing huge electrical sparks that were directed at him.

November 2000, Frozen in Time
Blaine froze himself inside a big block of ice for three days and three nights.

September 2003, Above the Below
Blaine lived in a glass box in the center of London for 44 days with no food, and only water to drink.

April 2008, Guinness World Records
After Drowned Alive, Blaine began seriously training to break the world record for underwater breath-holding: 16 minutes and 32 seconds. This time, he succeeded.

68

➡ **EXTENSION ACTIVITY** Have students work in pairs. Ask them to read and summarize the information in the sidebar together. Tell them to also talk about which stunt they find most exciting. Would they have watched it? Would it be something they'd be interested in trying? After pairs discuss, ask students to share with the class which stunt of Blaine's they find the most exciting and why.

Skill Note

Scanning involves reading quickly for specific information. The first step of scanning includes quickly reading the title, subheadings, and captions, as well as looking at the pictures. The students should then read the passage quickly, stopping when they come to information that they think is relevant for what they are searching, and then read more carefully.

David Blaine as seen during *Electrified: One Million Volts Always On* in New York City, U.S.A.

When something is *enclosed* (line 1), it has something like a wall all around it. The verb is not often used with a person as the subject, but in the case of talking about magic tricks, magicians often perform tricks that involve enclosing themselves in small spaces.

When something is done *in the name of* (lines 5–6) something or someone, it means that the act has a significant meaning in how others will view that person or thing.

A *street magician* (line 13) is someone who performs magic shows for free in public places, such as on a street corner, or in a park, or in a subway station entrance.

The term *special* (line 36) refers to a television program that is a one-time program outside of regular programming. To have a *primetime special* (line 50) is very impressive because primetime television hours are the most expensive ones, so they are only given to popular shows.

A *sequel* (line 37) refers to a follow-up show after the first one.

When talking about Blaine's popularity, the author mentions quotes from the *New York Times* and *The New Yorker*. Both publications (the first is a newspaper, the second a magazine) are highly respected sources of news and commentary in the United States, so getting positive reviews would reflect very well on Blaine in the eyes of an American or international audience.

At the time, Blaine thought to himself that if the boy
25 could survive without breathing for that long, it must be possible for other people to do it. And he was determined to find out how.

THE START OF A CAREER

Twenty years after seeing the street magician in the
30 subway, Blaine became a professional magician himself. He started out as a street performer and gained instant popularity due to his exciting tricks and unique magic style. His success prompted him to make a tape of his performance, which he sent
35 to a TV network. Soon after, the television network aired his self-produced special, *David Blaine: Street Magic*, and its sequel, *David Blaine: Magic Man*. In these programs, Blaine was shown traveling across the country and entertaining unsuspecting
40 pedestrians. Unlike other magic shows where the focus was mainly on the magician, Blaine's shows focused on the audience's **reactions**. This forever changed the way magic was portrayed on television. Blaine had created a new style of magic,
45 and audiences loved it. The *New York Times* said that Blaine had "taken a craft that's been around for hundreds of years and done something unique and fresh with it." *The New Yorker* claimed that he had

"saved magic." Since then, Blaine has produced
50 eight additional primetime specials, including *Real or Magic*, in which he shocks celebrities in their own homes.

In 1999, Blaine was ready to face new challenges. It was time for him to explore his lifelong interest in
55 endurance. In April, he performed the first of a series of **stunts** that would finally lead to him challenging a world record. Blaine says, "As a magician, I try to create images that make people stop and think. I also try to challenge myself to do things that doctors say
60 are not possible."

WHAT'S NEXT?

Although he teases future plans, Blaine hasn't revealed his next big project. However, one thing is certain—Blaine will continue to set high goals
65 for himself and to push himself to do incredible, impossible things for the **astonishment** of audiences around the world.

¹ **coffin:** *n.* a long box in which a dead body is buried
² **vertigo:** *n.* the feeling you get when you look down from a great height
³ **pillar:** *n.* a tall stone, wood, or metal object that supports a building or holds a statue
⁴ **drown:** *v.* to die from being underwater and unable to breathe

69

Content Note

Illusionist and *magician* are often used interchangeably to refer to those who do tricks to entertain an audience, like Blaine. However, the difference is that an illusionist performs on large stages or to live audiences, and is viewed by a large group at once. Illusionists often have large props and perform very over-the-top stunts, like Blaine.

UNDERSTANDING MAIN IDEAS

Have students work individually before checking answers in pairs. Note that more than one idea will be checked. Check answers as a class, eliciting the line numbers in the passage where students found the information.

UNDERSTANDING DETAILS

Have students work individually. Tell them to refer back to the passage to find the details. Note that some of the details come from the information in the sidebar. Check answers as a class, eliciting the line from the reading where students found each detail.

Ask students to raise their hands if they have ever watched a David Blaine performance on TV or video. Ask those who have to share their impressions and explain what he did in the performance.

BUILDING VOCABULARY

A Have students work individually to complete the activity. Check answers as a class. Elicit additional example sentences using each word. Write them on the board. Note that *endurance* in this case refers to having the strength to physically and mentally go through a challenging situation successfully. Draw students' attention to item 2. Ask students to use the other vocabulary words to answer this question: *How did Blaine transform magic?*

B **CRITICAL THINKING** Read the questions aloud. For question 1, remind students to refer to the information in the sidebar during their discussion. For question 2, encourage students to talk about a famous magician from their home country. How is the magic performed in their own countries different from or similar to Blaine's style of magic?

UNDERSTANDING MAIN IDEAS

Check (✓) the sentences that are supported by the passage.

- [✓] Blaine's favorite magician is Harry Houdini.
- [ ] Blaine first became interested in magic when he was a teenager.
- [✓] Blaine has risked his life for his magic.
- [ ] Blaine usually competes against other magicians in his endurance challenges.

UNDERSTANDING DETAILS

Choose the correct options.

1 Blaine _____ survived underwater for 45 minutes.

   a once   **b** had a friend who   **(c)** heard about a boy who

2 Blaine's first TV show was called _____.

   (a) *Street Magic*   **b** *Magic Man*   **c** *Real or Magic*

3 Blaine's new style of performing magic for the camera showed _____.

   a only his hands   **b** Blaine with children   **(c)** the faces of the audience

4 In his TV special *Vertigo*, Blaine spent 35 hours _____ a pillar.

   a tied to   **(b)** standing on top of   **c** holding up

BUILDING VOCABULARY

A Complete the sentences using the words from the box.

astonishment	endurance	reaction	transformed	stunt

1 People who run long distances need a lot of ____endurance____.

2 David Blaine's TV specials have completely ____transformed____ people's understanding of what magic can do.

3 The crowd gasped in ____astonishment____ at the magician's skill.

4 Jumping a motorcycle over a moving bus is a very difficult ____stunt____.

5 After the performance, the illusionist received a positive ____reaction____ from the audience.

B **CRITICAL THINKING** Answers will vary.

Analyzing **Discuss these questions with a partner.**

1 David Blaine says, "As a magician, I try to create images that make people stop and think. I also try to challenge myself to do things that doctors say are not possible." What details in the passage support this statement?

2 What other famous magicians do you know of? In what ways are they similar to or different from Blaine?

➡️ **EXTENSION ACTIVITY** Draw students' attention to the quote in item 1 of **Critical Thinking**. Blaine says that he wanted to prove the doctors wrong. Ask students if there was ever a time where they challenged what an authority figure told them. Have students either write about the experience and what happened or discuss it with a partner.

5D How I held my breath for 17 minutes

TEDTALKS

DAVID BLAINE is a world-famous **magician** and endurance artist who became famous for doing street magic in the late 1990s. He then went on to perform amazing stunts. Blaine has been **obsessed** with both magic and endurance since he was a child—especially the **underwater** challenges of the great magician Harry Houdini.

David Blaine's idea worth spreading is that through training and dedication, we can achieve goals that others might consider **impossible**.

PREVIEWING

Read the paragraphs above. Match each **bold** word to its meaning. You will hear these words in the TED Talk.

1	below the water surface	underwater
2	a performer who does tricks	magician
3	unable to be done	impossible
4	continually thought about	obsessed

VIEWING

A ▶ **5.10** Watch Part 1 of the TED Talk. Circle **T** for true or **F** for false.

1 As a teenager, Blaine matched Houdini's personal record for underwater breath-holding. (**T**)   **F**

2 Static apnea refers to how deep underwater people can go while holding their breath.   **T**   (**F**)

3 Blaine learned how to remain still and slow his heart rate down underwater. (**T**)   **F**

4 Purging releases CO_2 from the body. (**T**)   **F**

B ▶ **5.11** Watch Part 2 of the TED Talk. Complete the Venn diagram using the information below.

a has the ideal body type for holding his breath underwater

b is over six feet tall

c had to change his eating habits

d trained for a breath-holding challenge on a TV show

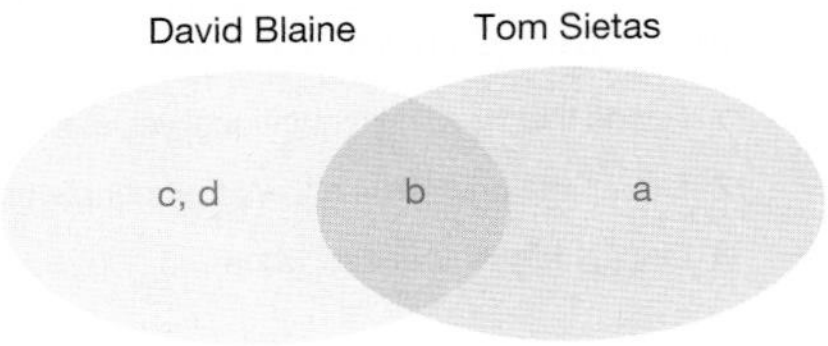

David Blaine   Tom Sietas

c, d   b   a

71

LESSON OVERVIEW

Aims: Watch and understand a talk about achieving a major goal; observe and practice explaining technical words

Target Vocabulary: impossible, magician, obsessed, underwater

TED Talk Summary: David Blaine tells the story of challenging the record for the longest time that a human has held their breath underwater. He goes into detail about how he trained for the stunt, and then explains the intense performance that led to him holding the world record. While people may think that magicians create illusions that aren't real, Blaine is focused on proving that he can do what medical knowledge says humans can't do. And he has learned to accomplish such tasks through dedicated training and physical and mental preparation.

5D How I held my breath for 17 minutes

PREVIEWING

Have students work individually before checking answers in pairs. Elicit additional example sentences for each vocabulary word.

⭐ **CHALLENGE** Have students go online and learn a little more about Harry Houdini, an important inspiration to David Blaine. Tell them to try to find out more about Houdini's underwater stunts in particular.

VIEWING

A Have students preview the task.

▶ **5.10** Play Part 1 of the TED Talk. Have students watch the check-your-answers part of the video. Elicit how to make false statements true. Elicit or explain the meaning of any unfamiliar language. Suggestions for Part 1 include *personal record*, *pearl divers*, *free-diving*, and *hyperventilating*.

Write the following quote by Blaine on the board: *Just hold and relax through all the pain*. Ask students if this is the kind of physical challenge that appeals to them. Elicit reasons.

B Have students preview the Venn diagram and the questions in **C** (on the next page) before watching the video. After students preview, ask them to guess who Tom Sietas is (the former world-record holder for holding one's breath underwater).

▶ **5.11** Play Part 2 of the TED Talk. Explain that students only need to write the letters in the diagram, not the words. Check answers as a class.

C Have students work individually. Point out these are all details they heard during Part 2. Check answers as a class or play the check-your-answers part of the video. Elicit or explain the meaning of any unfamiliar language. Suggestions for Part 2 include *lung capacity, resting heart rate,* and *under duress.*

Write on the board: *Individual results may vary.* Explain that Blaine is making a joke that not everyone may lose as much weight as he did if they follow the same diet. This expression is typically heard in commercials and advertisements by companies that provide lifestyle products promising to help you get into shape, lose weight, and so forth.

D Have students preview the timeline and list of events. Ask students to guess what event the timeline refers to (*his attempt to break the world record*).

▶ **5.12** Play Part 3 of the TED Talk. Check answers as a class. Elicit or explain the meaning of any unfamiliar language. Suggestions for Part 3 include *vital organs.*

Ask students to share what they thought and felt while watching Blaine's world-record performance. Why do they think he started to get emotional at the very end of his talk?

E **CRITICAL THINKING** Read the questions aloud. Note that David Blaine has come close to dying during some of his performances. Ask students to talk about the possible motivations he has for doing such dangerous stunts, and why we like to watch them. Students' opinions on whether his performances go too far or not will vary. Encourage them to give reasons for their opinions. If time permits, elicit a class discussion to hear students' thoughts.

C Choose the correct options.

1 Why did Blaine change his eating habits?
  (a) to lose weight   **b** to gain muscle mass   **c** to train his mind

2 Why did Blaine swim with sharks?
  a to be on TV   **b** to get used to the ocean   **(c)** to learn to relax even in scary situations

3 In what position was Blaine comfortable underwater?
  a floating faceup   **(b)** floating facedown   **c** floating upright

4 What was Blaine extremely nervous about?
  a being on live TV   **b** wearing a tight suit   **(c)** keeping his feet strapped in

D ▶ **5.12** Watch Part 3 of the TED Talk. Complete the timeline with the descriptions (**a–f**) of Blaine's challenge.

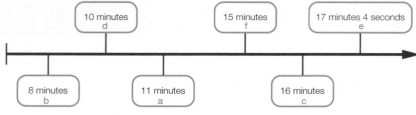

- 10 minutes — d
- 15 minutes — f
- 17 minutes 4 seconds — e
- 8 minutes — b
- 11 minutes — a
- 16 minutes — c

  a His legs and lips felt very strange.
  b He felt certain he wouldn't be able to complete the challenge.
  c He pulled his feet out of the straps.
  d He started to get strange feelings in his fingers and toes.
  e He set a new world record.
  f He experienced an irregular heartbeat.

E **CRITICAL THINKING** Answers will vary.

Reflecting Look back at David Blaine's endurance challenges on page 68. Given how dangerous they are, should we really be watching them? Do you think there is a point where entertainment like this becomes irresponsible? Discuss with a partner.

VOCABULARY IN CONTEXT

A ▶ **5.13** Watch the excerpts from the TED Talk. Choose the correct meaning of the words.
                                                          1.b; 2.c; 3.a; 4.b

B Work in pairs. Complete the sentences with your own ideas. Answers will vary.

1 Foods that have high nutritional value, such as _____, are good for our health.
2 One of the primetime shows that people are watching now is _____.
3 Once, I felt lightheaded when _____.

72

VOCABULARY IN CONTEXT

A ▶ **5.13** Play the video. If necessary, play it again.

B Explain that students should use their own ideas to show that they understand the meaning of the vocabulary expression. Have pairs share their sentences with the class.

⭐ **CHALLENGE** Have pairs write personalized sentences for the other vocabulary from **A**.

PRESENTATION SKILLS Explaining technical words

Sometimes speakers use technical terms and then immediately define them. Giving definitions can help your audience understand difficult words.

- Include technical terms only when they're essential to your message. Learn to distinguish between essential and non-essential terms.
- Explain technical terms as soon as you use them for the first time.

A ▶ **5.14** Watch part of David Blaine's TED Talk. Match each technical term to the definition he gives.

1 static apnea — holding your breath without moving
2 purging, hyperventilating — blowing in and out quickly
3 buoyant — floating
4 blood shunting — when the blood rushes away from your arms and legs
5 ischemia — when your heartbeat changes suddenly

B You are going to talk briefly on a topic of your choice. It could be a sport, a hobby, or something you learned in school. Make brief notes on what you want to say, and choose two or three technical terms that are essential to your message. Answers will vary.

C Work with a partner. Take turns giving your presentations, and explain the technical terms you chose in **B**.
Answers will vary.

David Blaine interacts with a passerby during *Drowned Alive*.

73

feedback about what they enjoyed about the presentation and what could be improved.

⭐ **CHALLENGE** Have students present to the class after presenting to their partners.

Language Note

When a person sets a *personal record,* it means they got the best score or time that they have ever gotten.

The *pearl divers* that Blaine mentions are individuals who make a living diving into the ocean to find pearls. They do this unassisted, without any breathing equipment. The sport of *free diving* is similar, in that divers stay underwater for as long as they can, and try to push themselves on deeper and longer dives.

To *hyperventilate* means to breathe at an overly rapid rate, which results in losing carbon dioxide in the body. A person's *lung capacity* refers to how much air they can hold in their lungs. A person's *resting heart rate* is the amount of times their heart beats per minute when they are not moving.

When someone is *under duress,* they are constrained or forced to do something. In Blaine's case, he is acting *under duress* even though it is a stunt that he planned himself. He has willingly created the environment of duress.

A person's *vital organs* refer to organs in our body that need to operate properly in order for us to stay alive.

PRESENTATION SKILLS

A Read the Presentation Skills paragraph **Explaining technical words** aloud. Explain that technical words often have the effect of disengaging an audience, so they must be explained clearly. Point out that the information in the box says to only use essential technical words in a presentation. This is because difficult language can alienate a speaker from his or her target audience.

▶ **5.14** Play the video. Check answers as a class. Note that while Blaine uses a lot of technical terms, he is skilled at keeping his audience engaged and interested. He not only explains the terms, but he uses them to add a sense of excitement and mystery to his story.

B Give students time to think about a topic that they want to talk about. Tell them to make sure to choose a topic that they know well and that requires technical words to explain. Ask them to outline the points that they want to present in linear notes or a mind map.

C Tell partners to take turns giving their presentations. Tell the listeners to ask follow-up questions, and then to give

Skill Note

TED speaker and communications expert Melissa Marshall, whose TED Talk is in **Level 3** of Keynote, gives the following advice about presentations that involve technical topics:

1. Avoid jargon.

2. Simplify ideas, but don't dumb them down.

3. Use more visuals and less text on slides.

4. Give demonstrations when possible.

LESSON OVERVIEW

Aims: Research and give a talk; write a comparative essay

COMMUNICATE

A Have students read the direction line and the questions. Encourage students to choose someone from their home country to introduce to the class. Ask students to have a person in mind before they start their research, and to use their time online to find out more information about that person. Tell them to use the questions provided to guide their research.

B Divide the class into groups of three or four. Explain that students are going to give a presentation about the person to a group. Model the example presentation. Remind students to use the presentation skills they've learned so far in the book, and encourage them to include technical explanations if possible in their presentations. Tell those who are listening to take notes during the presentations so they can ask better questions and remember the content for their discussion in **C**.

C Read the questions aloud. Ask groups to discuss the following questions: *Which person overcame the biggest challenges? Which person did you find most impressive? Which person did you connect to the most?* If time permits, have a class discussion about the questions. Ask students to share what they learned in their groups and which person's achievement they were most impressed with.

COMMUNICATE Talking about big achievements Answers will vary.

A Think of someone who has achieved something extraordinary in sports, science, the arts, or any other area. Do research and make notes. Consider the following questions.

What did the person achieve? _____

When did they achieve this? _____

How did they train or prepare for it? _____

B Work in groups of three or four. Talk about the person you researched.

> **Describing achievements**
> *He/She made history by ...*   *He/She made a significant contribution to ...*
> *He/She succeeded in ...*   *He/She set a record for being ...*

> In 1975, Junko Tabei became the first woman to reach the summit of Mount Everest. Her climbing team was made up of 15 women, including teachers and a computer programmer. To prepare for her climb, Tabei ...

C Of the people you talked about in **B**, which achievement do you think was the most difficult? Which achievement would you most like to emulate? Discuss with your group members.

WRITING Making a comparison Answers will vary.

Choose one of the people you discussed above, and compare and contrast their achievements with David Blaine's. Include details about how they prepared to reach their goals.

> Junko Tabei was a mountain climber, while David Blaine is a magician and endurance artist. These are two very different activities. However, both of them had a strong desire to achieve difficult goals and worked very hard to reach them. Tabei trained on higher and higher mountains, and ...

Junko Tabei was the first woman to reach the summit of Mount Everest.

WRITING

Note that students don't have to choose the person that they researched. They can also choose one of the people a group member talked about. Explain that students have gathered a lot of background knowledge about David Blaine during the unit that they can use in their writing. Read the model aloud. Point out that the writer goes into detail about differences and similarities between the two achievers. Have students write individually.

⭐ CHALLENGE Ask students to

compare their paragraphs with a partner's. Have them discuss the differences and similarities in their content in relation to David Blaine. Ask them to also compare their writing styles: Did they include the same information? Did they organize the information differently? Did they come to the same conclusion?

6 Money Matters

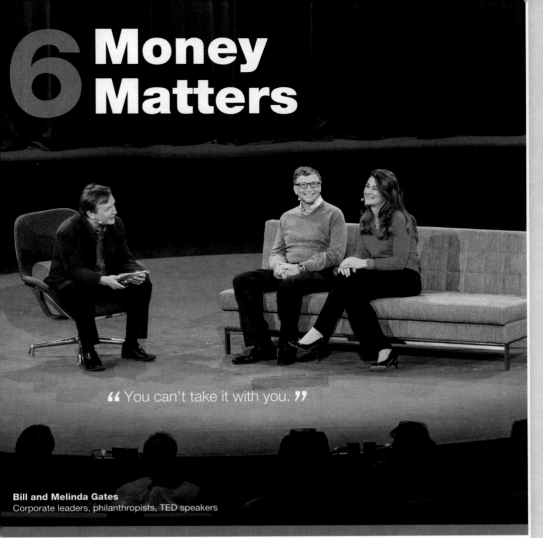

" You can't take it with you. **"**

Bill and Melinda Gates
Corporate leaders, philanthropists, TED speakers

UNIT GOALS

In this unit, you will …

- talk about crowdfunding and giving to charity.
- read about how wealthy people have used their money.
- watch a TED Talk about using wealth responsibly.

WARM UP

▶ **6.1** Watch part of Bill and Melinda Gates's TED Talk. Answer the questions with a partner.

1 What does Bill Gates think the wealthiest people should do with their money? Give it to the least wealthy

2 What is Melinda Gates trying to change in the U.S.? The education system

75

---

6 Money Matters

WARM UP

Have students look over the picture, caption, and quote on the page. Read the quote aloud. Ask students to guess the meaning of *it* before they watch the video.

▶ **6.1** Play the preview clip of the TED Talk. Elicit what *it* refers to in the quote on the page (*money, wealth*).

For question 1, Bill Gates explains in the clip that he believes wealthy people should give some of their riches to poor people in need, as this will help repair the wealth distribution imbalance. Remind students they learned about the imbalance in **Unit 3** and have them review if necessary.

For question 2, Melinda Gates says that their focus is on education. Ask students to discuss which aspect of education they think the Gates are most focused on improving.

➡ **EXTENSION ACTIVITY** Have students work in pairs. Ask them to go online to the site for the Bill & Melinda Gates Foundation (http://www.gatesfoundation.org) to find out more specifics about one issue that the charity is focused on improving. After pairs research, have them get together with a pair who researched a different issue to share what they learned.

Content Note

Although Bill Gates made his wealth as the head of Microsoft, he left the company in 2008 to focus on philanthropy. He now co-chairs the Gates Foundation with his wife, Melinda. The couple are committed to using their great wealth, and that of other billionaires, to make an important difference in the world. They focus on the areas of HIV/AIDS, education, vaccinations, agriculture, and disaster relief.

UNIT GOALS

In this unit, students will read, watch, and talk about money, focusing on charity and how to use money to make a difference in the lives of others. Students will practice talking about budgets and learn ways to raise money for projects, such as crowdfunding. Note that the topics discussed in this unit can be linked back to the issue of wealth distribution that students read about in Unit 3.

TED Speakers

Bill and Melinda Gates run the largest privately funded charity in the world.

TED Talk Summary

In an interview with the TED moderator, the Gates share their story about how raising a family with incredible wealth has given them a clear sense of responsibility toward their role as philanthropists. They also explain how they've gotten other billionaires to give away their wealth to help improve the lives of those who are less fortunate.

Idea Worth Spreading

Wealthy entrepreneurs can use their business acumen and success to help make the world a better place.

Money

VOCABULARY

A Have students work individually to complete the collocations. Check answers as a class, going over meaning when necessary. Elicit example sentences for each collocation.

B Have students work individually. Have them check answers in pairs first. Then elicit the meaning of each sentence. For example, for item 3, make sure students understand the meaning of *pension plan*.

C Read the questions aloud. For question 2, ask students to share what kind of charity they would donate to, and why. Tell students to also talk about any charity work they have done in the past. If time permits, elicit a class discussion to hear students' answers to the questions.

Language Note

Some additional collocations for talking about charity-related topics:

collect: *collect donations, collect money, collect contributions*

find: *find donors, find sponsors, find funding*

give: *give a donation, give to a charity, give to a cause*

contribute: *contribute to a cause, contribute time*

Bank officers count money at a shrine in Kyoto, Japan.

6A Money

VOCABULARY Money collocations

A Complete the collocations. Add the words in the box to the correct column.

interest	an investment	services	an income	to charity	a difference

make	earn	donate
a contribution	a living	money
an investment	interest	services
a difference	an income	to charity

B Complete the sentences using the correct form of the words in the chart above.

1 In 2016, Warren Buffett _____donated_____ nearly $2.9 billion to the Bill & Melinda Gates Foundation and other charities.

2 It can be difficult to earn _____a living_____ as a musician.

3 Many companies make ___a contribution___ to their employees' pension plan.

4 My mother often works overtime to earn extra _____income_____ .

5 My money earns a little _____interest_____ from the bank.

C Work with a partner. Discuss your answers to these questions. Answers will vary.

1 What are some things you can invest your money in?

2 Would you rather donate time or money to a charity? Why?

76

➡ **EXTENSION ACTIVITY** Have students work individually. Ask them to use each of the collocations in **Vocabulary** to write sentences about their own plans for how they want to make and spend their money. Then have students read the sentences to a partner and discuss some ideas they have for their financial futures.

LISTENING Crowdfunding

A ▶ **6.2** Watch entrepreneur Shree Bose talk about launching a crowdfunding campaign. How does it work?

   a by asking a few people to donate big sums of money

   ⓑ by asking many people to donate a small amount of money

B ▶ **6.2** Watch again. Check (✓) the benefits of crowdfunding Bose mentions.

   ☑ It can help demonstrate the demand for a new product.

   ☑ It's a great way to reach people from all over the world.

   ☐ It minimizes the financial risk to investors.

   ☑ It can help to create a loyal customer base.

C **CRITICAL THINKING** Answers will vary.

   Evaluating Can you think of any downsides to crowdfunding? Discuss with a partner.

Shree Bose started her company Piper through crowdfunding.

SPEAKING Talking about making a contribution

A ▶ **6.3** What is Speaker B's opinion about crowdfunding?
Speaker B has doubts about crowdfunding, and would prefer to donate money to charity.

   A: Would you make a crowdfunding contribution to Piper?

   B: I'm not sure. It sounds like a good idea, but I'd rather invest in it after I've seen and used the product.

   A: I see your point. But I think it's a great way to support a company—investing some money in it and helping it to develop its idea.

   B: I don't know. Shouldn't a business just get a bank loan or get investors to help them?

   A: Maybe. But with crowdfunding, you build a relationship with the company. You aren't just giving them your money; you're paying for a product you believe in, and you usually get rewards in exchange.

   B: OK, I guess some people enjoy feeling like they're part of the process. But personally, I'd prefer to donate money to a charity—to help wildlife or something like that, or to help people.

B Practice the conversation with a partner.

C Work with a partner. Look up the Kickstarter website and select a project. Would you donate money to support it? What would you want in return? Use the expressions in blue above to help you. Answers will vary.

> I'd support ... and invest money in it. It sounds like an interesting idea.

> I'd only invest in it if I get ... in return.

77

LISTENING

A Read **Listening for gist** aloud as students read along. Explain that gist is the general idea of a speech or text, and understanding gist can help them make predictions using common sense and background knowledge. Note that this is a useful skill in reading as well.

Have students preview the task. Note that students will listen to define *crowdfunding*, so it's OK if they don't understand the word in the direction line.

▶ **6.2** Play the video. Check answers as a class. Ask students if they've participated in a crowdfunding campaign before.

B Have students preview the task.

▶ **6.2** Play the video again. Have students check answers in pairs.

C **CRITICAL THINKING** Read the question aloud and give students time to consider their answers. Note that students should talk about the disadvantages of crowdfunding and why they might not want to invest in or start a crowdfunding project.

SPEAKING

A Ask students to read along as they watch. Read the question aloud and tell students to listen for the answer.

▶ **6.3** Play the audio/video. Check answers as a class. Ask students if they agree with the speaker's views. Elicit opinions about crowdfunding, both positive and negative. Point out the phrase *I see your point,* which is useful to communicate that you understand and respect someone's opinion, even if it is different from your own.

B Model the conversation aloud with a student. Then have students work in pairs to practice. Make sure they alternate between A and B roles.

C Read the task aloud. Model the example aloud with a volunteer. Give students time to go to the Kickstarter site. Note that there are hundreds of projects on the site and students can search based on their areas of interest. Encourage students to find one project that they'd support and one that they wouldn't.

Content Note

Kickstarter is a crowdfunding website known for bringing innovative projects to the public to find investors. In most projects, there are various levels of funding that an investor can choose. Usually, the more you invest, the better your return will be. Many investors receive a sample of the product that they are investing in.

6B What we're saving for

LESSON OVERVIEW

Aims: Read an infographic about how Australians use their savings; talk about planning a budget

Infographic Summary: Most Australians are saving to buy a home, but only by a slim margin of one percent. Coming in at a very close second is saving for a vacation.

LANGUAGE FOCUS

A Read the questions aloud.

▶ **6.4** Play the audio/video as students read along. Then give them additional time to look over the infographic. If necessary, elicit or explain the meaning of *emergency fund*. It is extra money to be used for expenses in case of an unexpected situation, such as losing your job or getting injured. Have students discuss their answers in pairs. Note that they should talk about anything that they are saving for right now. Encourage them to also talk about how they spend their money monthly. What are their biggest expenses? Are they able to save at the end of each month?

B Read the question aloud and tell students to listen for the answers.

▶ **6.5** Play the audio/video. Check answers as a class.

⭐ **CHALLENGE** Ask students to refer back to their answers to **A**. Encourage them to explain to the class one thing that they are saving for, in a way similar to how each speaker in the audio does—but without directly naming it. Then have the class guess what that student is saving for.

C Have students read over the language chart for **Using phrasal verbs**.

LANGUAGE FOCUS Talking about saving habits

A ▶ **6.4** Read about what Australians save money for. Do you save money regularly? What are you saving for? Answers will vary.

WHAT AUSTRALIANS SAVE MONEY FOR

EVERYONE SAVES MONEY FOR DIFFERENT REASONS. HERE'S WHAT MOST AUSTRALIANS SAVE FOR.

- A HOME — 48%
- A VACATION — 47%
- AN EMERGENCY FUND — 33%
- A CAR — 13%
- EDUCATION — 10%
- FURNITURE/APPLIANCES — 8%
- A WEDDING — 5%
- A NEW COMPUTER/TECHNOLOGY — 4%

B ▶ **6.5** Listen. What is each person saving for? Write the reasons from the infographic.

1 A wedding
2 An emergency fund
3 A home
4 A vacation
5 A car
6 Education

C ▶ **6.6** Watch and study the language in the chart.

Using phrasal verbs
Separable
We're putting aside some funds for our vacation.
We're putting a few thousand dollars aside for our house renovation.
We brought up our children to be polite.
We brought our children up well.
Not separable
The coach really believes in the team.
I need to save money in case I lose my job or my car breaks down.
Eric does without a car because he wants to protect the environment.

For more information on **phrasal verbs**, see Grammar Summary 6 on page 185.

78

▶ **6.6** Play the audio/video. Ask students to pay close attention to the difference between separable and non-separable phrasal verbs. Direct students to page 185 for more information.

Grammar Note

The language chart introduces phrasal verbs. Phrasal verbs combine a verb and a particle (adverb or preposition). Note that the meaning of a phrasal verb is often best understood by checking a dictionary, which is why most of the activities in this lesson suggest students use a dictionary. Explain that the meaning usually can't be inferred by looking at the verb and particle separately.

Only some phrasal verbs can be separated, or broken up, with the object coming between the verb and the particle. In phrasal verbs that can be separated, both separating and not separating are allowed. However, when the object is a pronoun, the pronoun must come between the verb and the particle.

D ▶ **6.5** Listen to the information in **B** again. Complete the sentences with the words you hear.

1 "We're _____putting aside_____ about two hundred dollars a month right now."

2 "We're _____bringing up_____ two kids, and we just have a small flat that we're renting."

3 "I haven't _____figured out_____ what I want to study, but I definitely want to go to university."

E Read the paragraph below. Match each **bold** verb to the phrasal verb that has the same meaning.

Household savings rates can be very different across different countries. *Global Finance* magazine **researched** how much families around the world save, and **discovered** that while richer countries generally have higher savings rates, not all wealthy countries save a lot. In 2015, the best savers in the world were the Swiss, who **saved** over 17 percent of their household income. However, Denmark's household savings in 2015 was very low, at about -4 percent. This could be due to the Danes' confidence in the economy, Denmark's well-developed social security system, and other factors that **create** more equal distribution of incomes in the country.

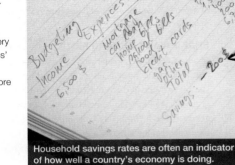

Household savings rates are often an indicator of how well a country's economy is doing.

1 researched ○   ○ found out
2 discovered ○   ○ result in
3 saved ○   ○ looked into
4 create ○   ○ put aside

F Put the words in the correct order to make sentences or questions.

1 off / We / loan / our / paid
   We paid off our loan. OR We paid our loan off.   .

2 think / Let's / options / our / over
   Let's think over our options.
   OR Let's think our options over.   .

3 payments / Can / the / we / out / spread
   Can we spread out the payments?
   OR Can we spread the payments out?   ?

4 set / you / Do / much / aside / money
   Do you set aside much money?
   OR Do you set much money aside?   ?

5 give / up / going to / I'm / restaurants / expensive
   I'm going to give up expensive restaurants.
   OR I'm going to give expensive restaurants up.   .

6 is / Bill Gates / away / giving / money / his / of / most
   Bill Gates is giving away most of his money.
   OR Bill Gates is giving most of his money away.   .

SPEAKING Planning a budget   Answers will vary.

A Work with a partner and plan a budget together. Look at the infographic on page 78. Which of these things would you save for? How much of your budget would you set aside?

I'd set aside ... for a vacation to Bali.

I don't think that's enough. We may have to give up ... to save more money.

B Share your budget with another pair. Discuss the similarities and differences.

79

D Have students preview the task.

▶ **6.5** Play the audio/video. Have students work individually to complete the activity. Check answers as a class. Elicit the meaning of each of the phrasal verbs. Note that *put aside* is used to talk about saving something, such as money. The verb suggests that something is put to the side now to be used at a later time.

E Have students work individually. Explain that they should infer the meaning of any verbs that they don't know by looking at how they are used

in the sentence. Encourage them to substitute the phrasal verbs to see which ones work. Have students check answers in pairs. Let them use a dictionary to double-check the meaning of each phrasal verb.

F Have students work individually. Tell them to use the information in the language chart to help them decide if a phrasal verb can be separated or not. Note that phrasal verbs that can be separated can also be left as is.

→ **EXTENSION ACTIVITY** Have students work alone to write a summary of the infographic. Tell them to look at the paragraph in **E** as an example. Tell students to use phrasal verbs in their summaries to explain what Australians save their money for. Let students use dictionaries, if necessary, to find more useful phrasal verbs. Have them read their paragraphs to a partner to compare how they used the phrasal verbs in their summaries.

SPEAKING

A Give students time to preview the task and review the infographic again. Have students work in pairs to plan a budget together. Tell them to plan their budget specifically saving up for items such as those suggested in the infographic. Model the example with a volunteer. Note that the speaker in the model uses the phrasal verb *set aside,* which has the same meaning as *put aside.* Elicit some other phrasal verbs to talk about saving. Write them on the board. Some possibilities include: *put aside, set aside, save up, keep for future use, keep in reserve, hang on to,* and *save for.*

B Have pairs work with another pair. Ask them to each present their budgets with details about how much money they are planning to save for each item. Tell groups to compare their budgets and to discuss which details and amounts are different. Ask pairs to explain to the other why they decided to save a certain amount for each item.

→ **EXTENSION ACTIVITY** Ask pairs to share their budgets from **Speaking** with the class. After each pair has presented their budget, have the class calculate the average for each category. Ask students to work in pairs or groups to then make an infographic that represents the whole class's habits in regard to saving money.

Giving something back

LESSON OVERVIEW

Aims: Read and comprehend an article about two famous couples who are heavily involved in charities; understand main ideas and details

Target Vocabulary: celebrity, foundation, pledge, poverty, take off

Reading Summary: Many celebrities give to charities, but some have made it their life's passion to give much of the wealth they've attained to those who are less fortunate. Two such couples are introduced in more detail: musician Shakira and soccer star Gerard Piqué, and TED speakers Melinda and Bill Gates. Shakira and Piqué focus especially on issues related to children in poorer countries, while the Gates are focused on healthcare, reducing poverty, and increasing access to education and technology worldwide.

PRE-READING

Read the question aloud. Tell students to read quickly to find the names of the world's largest donors. Check answers as a class, eliciting hints about how students found the names quickly. Note that the information can actually be quickly found in the sidebar, but is also in the main content in the first paragraph about Bill and Melinda Gates.

Point out the footnotes at the end of the reading. Remind students to refer to it before or while reading.

▶ **6.7** Play the audio/video as students read along. Go over any unfamiliar language. See **Language Note**.

PRE-READING Scanning

Scan the passage. Who's the world's biggest charity donor?   Bill Gates

▶ **6.7**

1 Whether they're donating to disaster relief funds, education, or healthcare, these **celebrity** couples have made a habit of giving their wealth away, and are inspiring many 5 others to do the same.

SHAKIRA AND GERARD PIQUÉ

She's a Colombian pop star who has sold over 70 million albums worldwide. He's a Spanish soccer star with a World Cup title to his name. They met 10 in 2010 when Piqué appeared in Shakira's music video for "Waka Waka (This Time for Africa)"—the official song of the 2010 FIFA World Cup—and have been together ever since. After three years together,

The world's biggest charity donors (2015)	
$28 billion	**Bill Gates** has donated $28 billion of his fortune to his own charity, the Bill & Melinda Gates Foundation.
$21.5 billion	**Warren Buffett**, one of the richest men in the world, has pledged to donate the bulk of his fortune to the Bill & Melinda Gates Foundation and four other charities.
£5.1 billion	Businessman and investor **George Soros** has donated his wealth to educational and healthcare institutes across the world.
$6.8 billion	**Gordon Moore**, technology pioneer and Intel founder, has donated $6.8 billion to the charity he founded with his wife—the Gordon and Betty Moore Foundation.
$498 million	Facebook CEO **Mark Zuckerberg** has donated to various causes such as public schools and the Silicon Valley Community Foundation.

80

the couple welcomed their first son, Milan, followed 15 by their second little boy, Sasha, in 2015.

The birth of both children prompted the couple to give back. They set up a World Baby Shower in the lead-up to each birth, and asked fans to send gifts to other babies around the world who were 20 in need of help. Both of these Baby Showers were huge successes, raising more than $200,000 for food, medicines, and blankets. Shakira said she hoped her two boys would appreciate what she'd done and be inspired themselves. "My hope is that 25 by the time my sons are adults, they can look back and see how even small efforts can have a big impact when multiplied," she wrote in her blog.

Shakira is also a Goodwill Ambassador for UNICEF (United Nations Children's Emergency Fund). 30 In fact, she has long been involved in promoting children's rights. When she was only 18, Shakira set up the Barefoot **Foundation**. This organization educates and feeds more than 6,000 children in Colombia and other countries. Her charities have 35 received donations as high as $200 million from Carlos Slim, Mexico's richest man, and Howard Buffett, son of American billionaire Warren Buffett.

BILL AND MELINDA GATES

With a net worth of $81 billion, they're the wealthiest 40 couple on the planet. And according to *Forbes* magazine, they're the world's most generous as well. Bill Gates amassed billions of dollars after Microsoft **took off** in 1980. Along with his wife Melinda—who was once a Microsoft employee 45 herself—Bill now works full-time as co-chair of the

➡ **EXTENSION ACTIVITY** Have students work in pairs. Tell them to research one of the people listed in the sidebar (other than Bill Gates). Ask them to find out more about the person and how they made their riches. Then elicit a class discussion to have students share what they learned.

Skill Note

Note that scanning involves reading quickly for specific information, whereas skimming is done to get a main idea. While scanning, students should stop when they come to information that they think is relevant to what they are searching for, and then read more carefully.

Shakira meets with local children on a visit to Bangladesh.

Bill & Melinda Gates Foundation. The foundation was set up in 1997 and works to improve healthcare, reduce **poverty**, and increase access to education and information technology worldwide. One of the
50 foundation's primary goals is to eradicate[1] polio worldwide by 2018. The couple practice what they preach,[2] and have traveled to hospitals and remote villages all over the world to help those in need.

In 2006, Warren Buffett joined the cause
55 when he **pledged** to give about $30 billion to the Gates Foundation—the largest donation to charity in history. And on December 9, 2010, Gates, Buffett, and Mark Zuckerberg—CEO of Facebook—signed the "Gates-Buffett Giving
60 Pledge": a promise to donate half of their wealth to charity, and also to try to get other wealthy people to do the same.

[1] **eradicate:** v. to remove completely
[2] **to practice what you preach:** v. to do what you advise other people to do

son last week. A baby shower (line 17) is a party held usually before the arrival of a newborn in which the mother or parents are given baby-related gifts. While it is a common event in some countries, such as the United States, it is not common in other countries, such as the U.K.

A lead-up (line 18) is an event or a series of events that happens before something else. For example, the lead-up to the first day of school may involve buying school supplies and new clothes, as well as visiting the campus.

The title Goodwill Ambassador (line 28) refers to someone, often someone famous, who becomes a figurehead to spread the word about a cause.

Someone's net worth (line 39) refers to how much money they have including cash, investments, and items of great value. To amass (line 42) something means to collect a great amount of it over a period of time.

To eradicate (line 50) means to make something disappear. It is often used to talk about putting an end to something negative, such as an illness; this is the case in the reading passage content, which refers to eradicating the disease polio.

Content Note

Shakira's Barefoot Foundation was founded in 1997 to improve the quality of life for children in her home country of Colombia. The organization provides better educational opportunities for vulnerable children by partnering with schools to improve learning environments and nutrition, as well as assist in the personal growth of students.

Shakira also continues to focus on improving the quality of life for children worldwide in her work with the ALAS foundation and UNICEF.

Language Note

The term disaster relief (line 1) refers to helping to support a community after a natural disaster strikes, such as an earthquake, hurricane, or tsunami.

To make a habit of (lines 3-4) something means to be committed to doing something. It usually refers to something that requires a conscious decision and effort.

The verb welcome (line 14) is often used to refer to the arrival of a new baby: The parents welcomed the birth of their new

UNDERSTANDING MAIN IDEAS

Have students work individually. If necessary, explain that the part of the overlapping circles in the Venn diagram is for information that is relevant for both couples. Check answers as a class.

UNDERSTANDING DETAILS

Have students complete the activity without referring to the passage. Then have them check their answers by checking the passage. Which organization or initiative resonated with them the most?

➡ **EXTENSION ACTIVITY** Have students work in pairs. Tell them to imagine that they are billionaires. What kinds of charities would they want to be involved with? Would they be more interested in starting their own foundation like the Gates's or in giving money to someone else who is already running a charity like some of the billionaires mentioned in the sidebar on page 80?

BUILDING VOCABULARY

A Have students work individually to complete the activity. Check answers as a class. Elicit additional example sentences using each word. Write them on the board. Point out that *take off* is a phrasal verb. When used to mean that something is beginning to gain success, it is not separable (*the business is taking off*). However, when used to mean removing something, such as an item of clothing, it is separable (*take my jacket off*).

B **CRITICAL THINKING** Read the questions aloud as students read along. Ask them to think of any charity they know, and whether celebrities are involved or not. Note that celebrities often add to the public exposure of a charity. Charities with a celebrity spokesperson are better known simply because the media picks up more stories about them due to the connection with the celebrity. Have pairs tell the class the name of one celebrity who they think is a good role model in regard to being involved with charities.

UNDERSTANDING MAIN IDEAS

Complete the Venn diagram using the information below.

a have ties to the Buffett family

b have a foundation named after themselves

c were inspired to give back after becoming parents

d have donated money for education

e are the wealthiest couple in the world

f use their fame from sports and entertainment to raise awareness of children's issues

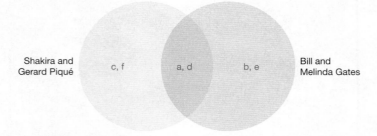

Shakira and Gerard Piqué — c, f | a, d | b, e — Bill and Melinda Gates

UNDERSTANDING DETAILS

Match each organization or initiative to its purpose.

1 World Baby Shower — to provide Colombian children with access to education
2 UNICEF — to eradicate poverty and polio globally
3 Barefoot Foundation — to give newborns a healthy start in life
4 Bill & Melinda Gates Foundation — to encourage wealthy individuals to donate to charity
5 Gates-Buffett Giving Pledge — to respond to emergencies in developing countries by providing aid for children

BUILDING VOCABULARY

A Complete the sentences with the words from the box.

| foundation | pledge | poverty | celebrities | take off |

1 Would you _____pledge_____ to give part of your wealth to help poor people?
2 They established a _____foundation_____ because they wanted to give away their money.
3 It often benefits charities to have _____celebrities_____ help spread their message.
4 George Soros's wealth is even more amazing given that he grew up in _____poverty_____.
5 He worked hard for many years before his business really began to _____take off_____.

B **CRITICAL THINKING** Answers will vary.

Reflecting Would you be more likely to donate to a charity if it is supported by a celebrity? Why or why not? Discuss with a partner.

➡ **EXTENSION ACTIVITY** Have students work in pairs to decide which charity mentioned in the reading they are most interested in learning more about. Have them go online to find out more about one of the charities, or another that a famous person is publicly involved in. Tell students to make a poster to explain the basic goals of the charity and what it is doing to accomplish those goals.

Why giving away our wealth has been the most satisfying thing we've done

TEDTALKS

BILL AND MELINDA GATES are the world's wealthiest couple and also two of its most generous philanthropists.

Bill and Melinda Gates's idea worth spreading is that entrepreneurs who have succeeded in business can use their wealth and knowledge to help deal with the world's biggest problems.

PREVIEWING

Read the paragraph below. Circle the correct meaning of each **bold** word. You will hear these words in the TED Talk.

Many of us dream of becoming wealthy, but the most **satisfying** thing Bill and Melinda Gates have done is to give their money away. Their **philosophy** for raising their children has been to teach them that **philanthropy** is more important than money. The Gates family believes that being wealthy is a great **responsibility**. Their mission is not only to give their own money away, but to encourage other wealthy people to do the same to help make the world a more **just** place.

1 Something that is **satisfying** gives you feelings of (**calmness** / (**pleasure**)).
2 The **philosophy** behind something refers to the ((**ideas and attitude**) / **uncertainty**) behind it.
3 **Philanthropy** refers to the effort you put in to (**distract** / (**help**)) other people.
4 If you have a great **responsibility**, you have a lot of ((**power**) / **common sense**).
5 A world that is more **just** is more ((**fair**) / **unfair**).

VIEWING

A ▶ **6.8** Watch Part 1 of the TED Talk. Check (✓) the ideas Bill and Melinda Gates would agree with.

☑ Giving children a good education is more important than giving them money.

☑ Children should be allowed to choose their own direction in life.

☑ Wealthy people should give something back to the world.

☐ Wealthy parents should limit their children's exposure to the outside world for safety reasons.

☐ Wealthy people should only invest money in profitable businesses.

83

LESSON OVERVIEW

Aims: Watch and understand an interview about charity work; observe and practice showing your authentic personality while presenting

Target Vocabulary: just, philanthropy, philosophy, responsibility, satisfying

TED Talk Summary: Guided by questions from the TED moderator, Bill and Melinda Gates share their philosophy as both philanthropists and parents. As parents, they explain that they've been upfront with their children about not passing on a large inheritance to them, and in doing so, hope it encourages them to find their own meaningful path in life. As philanthropists, they are trying to involve other billionaires to commit to giving up most of their fortune to help others as well, and believe that businesspeople are especially equipped to give back both with their skillset and with their wealth. Bill and Melinda Gates explain that giving away their money has been the most fulfilling thing they've ever done, and they encourage others to join in to make the world a better place.

6D

Why giving away our wealth has been the most satisfying thing we've done

PREVIEWING

Have students read the paragraphs that introduce the Gates first before moving on to the **Previewing** content. Tell them to pay attention to how each bold word is used in context in order to understand its meaning. Then have students work individually to complete each sentence before checking answers in pairs. Remind students of the **Warm Up** preview clip. Tell them to use all the language and information they have learned about philanthropy to support their viewing of the TED Talk.

VIEWING

A Have students preview the statements. Explain that students will infer what the Gates's stance would be on each statement based on what they will hear in Part 1. If necessary, elicit or explain the meaning of *profitable*.

▶ **6.8** Play Part 1 of the TED Talk. Check answers as a class or play the check-your-answers part of the video. Ask students to explain why the moderator refers to bringing up the Gates's children as "a social experiment." He is saying that it's so unusual to have as much money as they do, so raising children in that environment ends up being a kind of social experiment simply because it has never been done before. Elicit or explain the meaning of any unfamiliar language. Suggestions for Part 1 include *strike a balance, showered,* and *permission*.

B Have students preview the task. Note that the question format is similar to comprehension questions on exams such as TOEFL® and TOEIC®. Note that the answer choices paraphrase what students hear in the video, which will require an understanding of overall meaning.

▶ **6.9** Play Part 2 of the TED Talk. Check answers as a class or play the check-your-answers part of the video.

Elicit or explain the meaning of any unfamiliar language. Suggestions for Part 2 include *assets, homogenize, mind-blowing*, and *ingenuity*.

C Have students complete the activity without watching Part 3 first.

▶ **6.10** Play Part 3 of the TED Talk to have students check their answers.

D Have students preview the task. Encourage students to guess the answers based on their first viewing of Part 3.

▶ **6.10** Play Part 3 of the TED Talk again. Check answers as a class. If necessary, explain that a *pitch* is a sales pitch, which is a convincing argument to get someone to buy what you're selling, or in the Gates's case, to get someone to join the Giving Pledge.

Elicit or explain the meaning of any additional unfamiliar language. Suggestions for Part 3 include *shine some light* and *make a dent*.

E **CRITICAL THINKING** Read the questions aloud. For question 1, note that pairs will refer back to their answers in **D**. Ask them to summarize each point in Bill Gates's pitch. For question 2, remind students to think back to the budgets they planned together in **Lesson B**. If they had billions of dollars, how would this budget change?

B ▶ **6.9** Watch Part 2 of the TED Talk. Choose the correct options.

1 How much of their wealth have the Gates pledged to give away?
   a $95 billion
   (b) 95%

2 The Gates and Warren Buffett have been trying to persuade other billionaires to donate _____ of their assets for philanthropy.
   a a quarter
   (b) more than half

3 How many people have taken the Giving Pledge?
   a fewer than 100 people
   (b) over 100 people

4 The participants of the Giving Pledge meet every year to talk about _____.
   (a) different ways of doing good
   b how government policies can be improved

5 According to Bill Gates, one of the best things about philanthropy is its _____.
   (a) diversity
   b history

6 According to Melinda Gates, what must philanthropists have to inspire change?
   (a) creativity and drive
   b good speaking skills

C ▶ **6.10** Guess the answers to complete the sentences below. Circle the correct words. Then watch Part 3 of the TED Talk and check your answers.

1 According to Bill Gates, (**the U.S.** / Canada) has the strongest tradition of philanthropy in the world.

2 Bill Gates is (**doubtful** / **optimistic**) that philanthropy can help solve problems governments aren't good at working on.

3 The interviewer, Chris Anderson, believes that the world has a terrible (**inequality** / **debt**) problem.

4 Melinda Gates believes that the best way to address the (**inequality** / **debt**) problem is to change the (**financial** / **education**) system.

D ▶ **6.10** Watch Part 3 of the TED Talk again. Complete the sentences below summarizing Bill Gates's pitch to other billionaires.

1 It's the most fulfilling thing he's _____ever done_____.

2 You can't _____take it_____ with you.

3 It's _____not good_____ for your kids.

E **CRITICAL THINKING** Answers will vary.

Inferring/Reflecting Discuss these questions with a partner.

1 Look again at Bill Gates's pitch in **D**. How does he persuade other billionaires to donate their wealth?

> First, he explains that it gives him a great sense of satisfaction.

> Next, he points out that ...

2 Imagine you have $28 billion. What percentage of your wealth would you give away, and to what cause(s)?

84

Content Note

During the TED interview, Melinda Gates mentions Paul Farmer as the other person in the picture with the Gates's children. Dr. Paul Farmer is a famous philanthropist known for his efforts to provide better healthcare to people in poor countries throughout the world. He is co-founder of the organization Partners in Health, which focuses on healthcare issues in Haiti, and the Bill & Melinda Gates Foundation partners with that organization.

➡ **EXTENSION ACTIVITY** Have students work in groups to try to find some updated information about the Gates children. As they become young adults, what are they pursuing and does it involve philanthropy? Alternately, students can role-play an interview between a reporter and one of the Gates children, now age 20. Ask them to create a story about what he or she is planning to do as a young adult.

VOCABULARY IN CONTEXT

A ▶ **6.11** Watch the excerpts from the TED Talk. Choose the correct meaning of the words. 1.b; 2.c; 3.b; 4.c

B Work with a partner. Complete the sentences with your own ideas. Answers will vary.

1 It's important to strike a balance between _____ and _____.

2 I would like to be wealthy so I could shower money on _____.

3 We may not be able to end hunger or poverty worldwide by _____, but we can at least make a dent in the problem.

PRESENTATION SKILLS Being authentic

> The way you deliver your talk should reflect your personality. Whether you're naturally funny, serious, shy, or self-confident, you should be yourself. It's important to:
> • relax so that you move and gesture naturally;
> • wear clothes you feel comfortable in;
> • use words and expressions you normally use; and
> • not worry about being perfect. Audiences respond to speakers who are natural.

A ▶ **6.12** Watch part of Bill and Melinda Gates's TED Talk. How does Bill use the techniques from the box above? He's sitting on a comfortable sofa and wearing loose clothing. He uses colloquial expressions in his talk and his grammar isn't perfect, so he sounds more natural.

B Work with a partner. Discuss your answers to these questions. Answers will vary.

1 Is Bill Gates comfortable and relaxed? How can you tell?

2 What do you think your personal style is? Are you funny or serious, or something else?

3 If you had to give a TED Talk, what clothes would you choose to wear? Why?

4 Would you wear something different if you were just giving a presentation in class? Why or why not?

Bill Gates with One.org charity volunteers in Berlin, Germany

85

Language Note

Part 1

To *strike a balance* means to find a comfortable middle ground between two extremes. To be *showered* with something means to be given a lot of it. The term *permission* in regard to privacy refers to allowing others to see or know details about something or someone that are not public.

Part 2

The verb *homogenize* means to create a system that makes things similar to each other.

Part 3

To *shine some light* on something means to bring it to public attention or to explain something more clearly. The expression *make a dent* means to make a noticeable improvement in something or to make steps toward achieving a goal.

VOCABULARY IN CONTEXT

A ▶ **6.11** Play the video. If necessary, play it again.

B Explain that students are giving their own answers. Give students time to think about what they want to say first before sharing in pairs. Encourage partners to ask each other follow-up questions and to give each other reasons for their statements.

PRESENTATION SKILLS

A Read the Presentation Skills paragraph **Being authentic** aloud. Then elicit an explanation of what being *authentic* means. This speaking style shows your audience your real character, instead of a character created for the audience. Ask students to add ways to show your authentic self while presenting. Some possibilities are using natural body language and speaking in a relaxed and personal style. Have students preview the task. Ask them to make assumptions about Bill Gates's personality based on what they know so far. Then have them watch and see what kind of personality they see in his mannerisms, speaking style, and attitude.

▶ **6.12** Play the video. Check answers by eliciting a class discussion about cues students picked up throughout the unit and while watching the talk.

B Have students work in pairs. Read the discussion questions aloud. Note that students may have slightly different interpretations of Gates's body language depending on their own impressions. In general, Bill Gates is not known for being especially charismatic, but instead he is a fairly matter-of-fact speaker, which comes across in his discussion on the TED stage. After students discuss in pairs, ask for volunteers to share some points that they discussed together.

⭐ **CHALLENGE** Ask students to also share their impression of Melinda Gates's personality.

Creating a charity

COMMUNICATE

A Read the direction line aloud. Explain that the goal is to raise funding, but the project can be whatever students want it to be, from a charity to a new business idea. Have students work individually to write notes about the plan, the reasons for it, and the amount of funding they will need to make it happen. Give students enough time to brainstorm and think through their plans.

B Divide the class into groups of three or four students. Explain that each member will introduce their idea and try to get the group's support to fund the idea. Tell students to try to make a convincing pitch, like Gates did. Read the examples aloud. Elicit some positive and negative comments about the examples. For example, the first speaker doesn't give a good reason why they'd be a great actor; the second speaker raises a specific problem and succinctly explains a solution.

C Have groups discuss after each person has presented. Tell them to use the three questions as a guide for the discussion. Note that for question 2, not all presentations are going to have the goal of giving back to the world, but if an individual becomes wealthy, then that person may later give back somehow.

D Tell groups to think about what part of their pitch they want to improve. Encourage them to make changes before presenting to the class. Ask each group to get up in front of the class to present, with each group member having a say. Encourage students to stay as true to themselves as possible in speaking style, body language, and mannerisms. After each group has presented, have an anonymous vote where students write their favorite project idea on a piece of paper. Then tally the votes and announce the winner.

6E Creating a charity

COMMUNICATE Convincing people to give to your project or charity Answers will vary.

A Make some notes about a project you would like to raise money for. It could be a charitable project to make the world a better place, a business you want to start, or something just for yourself.

What I want to do	Why I want to do it	How much money I'll need

B Work in groups of three or four. Explain your project to your group members.

> I'd like to raise money to pay for acting lessons for myself. I think I could be a great actor. I'll probably need about $20,000.

> I'd like to help reduce pollution, so I want to raise money to buy electric buses for my city. I think I'll need about a million dollars.

C In your group, discuss these questions: Who might give money to fund each project? What could each project possibly give back to the world? Which project do you think is the most likely to be funded?

D After your group has chosen the project most likely to be funded, take turns explaining it and presenting your funding ideas to the class. Then vote for the best project or charity.

> **Presenting a proposal**
>
> *The ultimate goal of our project is ...*   *We estimate that it will cost ...*
>
> *This project will help ...*   *We intend to raise ... dollars by ...*

WRITING Promoting a charity initiative Answers will vary.

Find out more about a charity initiative you're interested in supporting. Explain its purpose and why people should contribute money to it.

> I would like to raise money to give out water rollers in developing countries. In some countries, people—usually women—have to walk a long way to reach clean water. Often, they carry it home in containers on their heads. Giving the women water rollers would allow them to carry seven or eight times more water in a single trip. This would …

The Hippo Water Roller makes it easier for rural communities in Africa to transport water.

86

WRITING

Tell students to choose a charity they're interested in supporting, either from **Communicate** above or from real life. Have them write a promotional pitch for funding. Read the model aloud as students read along. Encourage students to give basic information about the charity first, such as what its purpose is, followed by more specific information about how much money the charity needs to raise and why.

Presentation 2

MODEL PRESENTATION

A Complete the transcript of the presentation using the words in the box.

made up	fulfilling	had climbed	to climb
suffered	make it	draw on	might

"You'll die up there. You'll never [1] _____make it_____."

That's what everyone said when I told them I wanted [2] _____to climb_____ Mount Everest.
I'm happy to say I proved them wrong.

My name is Richard, and I've always loved the outdoors. By the time I turned 30, I
[3] _____had climbed_____ over 100 mountains. Last year, I joined an expedition to climb
Mount Everest. Many people doubted me and said that I wasn't ready for Everest
yet. But I had [4] _____made up_____ my mind, and nothing was going to change it.

I trained hard for the climb. But after the expedition began, I quickly realized that
nothing can prepare you for the conditions on Everest. It's easy for accidents to
happen when you're not getting enough oxygen to your muscles at high altitudes.
At one point, I slipped and dropped my goggles, which are safety glasses that
protect the eyes from harmful UV rays. I [5] _____suffered_____ from snow
blindness for a few days. Imagine you have something in your eye and your vision
is blurry. Your eyes [6] _____might_____ feel like they're burning. That's what it
felt like for me.

I had to [7] _____draw on_____ all my mental strength to reach the summit of Mount Everest. It was the
hardest thing I've ever done, but also the most [8] _____fulfilling_____. Thanks for listening.

B ▶ **P.2** Watch the presentation and check your answers.

C ▶ **P.2** Review the list of presentation skills from Units 1–6 below. Which does the speaker use?
Check (✓) them as you watch again. Then compare with a partner.

The speaker …
- ☐ asks the audience questions
- ☑ asks the audience to imagine themselves in a particular situation
- ☑ uses examples the audience is familiar with
- ☐ uses props
- ☑ begins with a strong statement
- ☑ explains technical words that the audience may not understand

87

B ▶ **P.2** Play the video to check answers.

C Have students preview the task.

▶ **P.2** Play the video again. Check answers as a class.

As a quick reminder, elicit the presentation skills from Units 1–3:

1. Involving the audience
2. Knowing your audience
3. Using props

Note that the speaker names a famous mountain that everyone in the audience is familiar with (Mount Everest), which is an example of keeping your audience in mind.

Then elicit the presentation skills from Units 4–6:

4. Beginning with a strong statement
5. Explaining technical words
6. Being authentic

Elicit the strong statement the speaker begins with. (*You'll die up there. You'll never make it.*)

Elicit the technical words that he explains. (*goggles* and *snow blindness*)

Elicit ideas about how the speaker showed that he was being authentic. (He talks candidly about how difficult the journey was.)

Review the presentation skills from Units 4–6 in more detail. Elicit the language options or techniques for each that students can use in **Your Turn**.

Presentation 2

LESSON OVERVIEW

Aim: Students give a short presentation to a partner about a significant achievement using each of the presentation skills they've learned in Units 4–6, and relevant ones from previous units.

MODEL PRESENTATION

A Have students work individually to complete the sentences. Elicit some basic points about the presentation:

1. Who is the speaker? (Richard)
2. What is the topic? (his achievement of climbing Mount Everest)
3. What challenge did the speaker face? (he had snow blindness)
4. What helped him most in making his achievement? (mental strength)

YOUR TURN

A Have students preview the presentation task. Point out that they can talk about a personal, school-related, sports-related, work-related or other achievement that was meaningful for them.

Explain that asking and answering questions about your topic is a useful technique for planning content. Note that the questions guide students to focus on relevant points of the story in order to communicate how and why the achievement was significant. Point out that students can use their answers as notes for the speech, or just write answers to brainstorm ideas.

Give students five or ten minutes to think of how to explain their achievement, including any technical terms that are involved. Tell students to also plan to start their presentations with a strong statement.

B Read aloud the useful phrases as students repeat. Give students more time to adjust their notes and decide what language they want to use in their presentation. Remind students of Bill and Melinda Gates's TED Talk in Unit 6 in which they talked about their achievements with their charity. Elicit a quick review on ways to be authentic while speaking: deliver your talk in a way that reflects your personality, use words you normally use, wear clothes you are comfortable in, and do not worry about being perfect.

C Tell students that they have two important roles in the activity: speaker and listener. Explain that they need to give their partner their full attention in order to evaluate in **C** and give effective feedback in **D**.

YOUR TURN Answers will vary.

A You are going to plan and give a short presentation about your most significant achievement. It can be school-related, or something from your personal life. Make notes in the chart below.

> What achievement are you most proud of?
>
> Who or what helped you achieve this goal?
>
> Why does this achievement mean so much to you?

B Look at the useful phrases in the box below. Think about which ones you will need in your presentation.

> **Useful phrases**
>
> | | |
> |---|---|
> | Using time expressions: | *When I was … years old, …*
Last year, … |
> | Talking about past goals: | *I wanted to …*
My goal was to … |
> | Describing an achievement: | *I managed to …*
… helped me achieve my goal of … |

C Work with a partner. Take turns giving your presentation using your notes. Use some of the presentation skills from Units 1–6 below. As you listen, check (✓) each skill your partner uses.

The speaker …
- ☐ asks the audience questions
- ☐ asks the audience to imagine themselves in a particular situation
- ☐ uses examples the audience is familiar with
- ☐ uses props
- ☐ begins with a strong statement
- ☐ explains technical words that the audience may not understand

D Give your partner some feedback on their talk. Include at least two things you liked and one thing that could be improved.

88

D Explain that when offering feedback after hearing a presentation, it's good to start with a short phrase of praise. Introduce some simple phrases for students to praise each other: *Well done; Wow, I really enjoyed that; What a story!*

Explain that after giving praise, students should next offer some positive feedback (*I felt you were really being authentic*), and then offer any points that need to be improved (*But you forgot to begin with a strong statement*).

After hearing about each other's achievements, students may have questions they want to ask. Give time for partners to ask and answer follow-up questions.

⭐ **CHALLENGE** Have students give their presentations to the entire class.

7 Medical Frontiers

" Disability in our age should not prevent anyone from living meaningful lives. "

David Sengeh
Biomechatronics engineer, TED speaker

UNIT GOALS

In this unit, you will ...

- talk about medical discoveries.
- read about the medical uses of 3-D printing.
- watch a TED Talk about a medical innovation.

WARM UP

▶ **7.1** Watch part of David Sengeh's TED Talk. Answer the questions with a partner.

1 What are some challenges that people with disabilities might face? Answers will vary.

2 How do you think David Sengeh is addressing these challenges? Answers will vary.

89

---

7 Medical Frontiers

WARM UP

Have students look over the picture, caption, and quote on the page. Read the quote aloud.

▶ **7.1** Play the preview clip of the TED Talk. Ask students to explain the concept of *meaningful lives*. Sengeh means lives that are not being hampered by the lack of a prosthetic.

For question 1, in Sengeh's TED Talk, he specifically addresses the issue of people who have lost limbs, and is mostly talking about challenges to movement and mobility. However, his overall message is about making strides toward creating technology that assists people with disabilities.

For question 2, students will guess their answers. Later on, they will see and hear in the full video that Sengeh designed technology to make prosthetic limbs more comfortable to wear, thereby encouraging more people to use them.

➡ **EXTENSION ACTIVITY** Have students work in pairs. Ask them to go online and learn more about the history of Sierra Leone to understand why the issue of prosthetic limbs is so important to the TED speaker.

Content Note

TED speaker David Sengeh lived through the civil war in Sierra Leone that lasted from 1991 to 2001. Over 50,000 people were killed during the war, and 450,000 were left with terrible injuries after being brutally attacked. Many victims of the war are now living with missing limbs, which is why Sengeh has chosen this cause in his research. There are so many amputees in Sierra Leone that the country has an entire soccer league for teams with players who are missing limbs.

UNIT GOALS

In this unit, students will read, watch, and talk about inventions and discoveries that are moving forward in healthcare and medicine. Students will learn and talk about innovations in these fields that are improving people's lives, and make predictions as to what to expect in the future. Students are asked to share their own ideas about possible inventions that might help others.

TED Speaker

David Sengeh is the head of the nonprofit Global Minimum, which works to effect change and empower local innovators in Sierra Leone.

TED Talk Summary

Sengeh shares his invention—prosthetic limbs that fit more comfortably for those who have lost an arm or a leg.

Idea Worth Spreading

Producing prosthetics that fit more comfortably has the power to transform the daily lives of people with disabilities worldwide.

7A

Innovation

Aims: Learn language for talking about innovations; listen to a biotech executive talk about drug invention; practice talking about better lives

Target Vocabulary: design, discover, innovate, invent

VOCABULARY

A Have students work individually to read the paragraph. Tell them to pay attention to how each word is used in the sentence before looking at the definition choices. Check answers as a class, eliciting example sentences for each word.

B Have students work individually before checking answers in pairs. Tell partners to identify both the noun and verb for each vocabulary word.

C Read the question aloud. Note that students can talk about inventors in any field, but encourage them to share ones especially connected to medicine or healthcare if possible. Tell students to tell their partner the inventor's name, country of origin, time period, and what they know about how the invention helped others. Ask for volunteers to introduce to the class any inventors and/or inventions they know about.

⬤ **EXTENSION ACTIVITY** Have pairs choose one of the inventors they spoke about in **C**. Give them time to search online for any additional information. Then ask them to make a poster with information about the person, the invention, and how the invention helped others. Students can hang their posters around the class. Give students time to walk around the class to read each other's posters.

A prosthetic leg helps its wearer get around more easily.

7A Innovation

VOCABULARY The language of discovery

A Read the paragraph below. Then match the base form of each **bold** word to its definition.

Many medical discoveries have made our lives better. Some have been drugs; others have been technologies. For example, Dr. Alexander Fleming saved millions of lives when he **discovered** penicillin, a drug that kills bacteria. In 1976, Dean Kamen **invented** the insulin pump. This modern **innovation** is **designed** to make life easier for people with diabetes by removing the need for daily insulin injections. The work of these scientists and inventors have contributed greatly to the area of science and medicine.

1 discover — to make changes or improvements to an existing product or idea

2 invent — to form a plan, sketch, or model of something

3 innovate — to create something that never existed before

4 design — to find something that exists, but that no one knew about before

B Complete the sentences. Circle the correct words.

1 Al-Zahrawi, a doctor who lived in Spain during the 10th and 11th centuries, (**invented** / discovered) many surgical instruments and procedures.

2 Architects (**design** / innovate) all kinds of buildings, including hotels and hospitals.

3 One of Galileo Galilei's contributions to science was his (innovation / **discovery**) of four of Jupiter's moons.

C Work with a partner. Can you think of any other famous scientists and inventors? Answers will vary.

90

Language Note

design (v.), *design* (n.)

discover (v.), *discovery* (n.)

invent (v.), *invention* (n.)

innovate (v.), *innovation* (n.)

Note that we often use the passive voice for verbs when speaking about inventions and discoveries because the actor (the discoverer) is usually not as important as the object (the discovery). The focus is on the discovery, and so that becomes the subject of the sentence. For example: *The device was invented to aid hearing loss.*

LISTENING Drug discovery and development

> **Detecting signpost language**
> Signpost words and phrases tell the listener what has just happened and what is going to happen next.
>
> *I'm going to focus on …*   *Let's turn to …*   *We've looked at …*

A ▶ **7.2** Watch biotech executive Michael Hanley talk about his research in diabetes. What is a "first in class" drug?

(**a**) a drug that uses a completely new approach to treat a condition

b a drug that is superior to existing treatments

B ▶ **7.3** Watch and circle **T** for true or **F** for false.

1 Symlin and Byetta treat different forms of diabetes. ⓣ F

2 Both Symlin and Byetta are based on a human hormone. T Ⓕ

3 The FDA decides whether to approve or reject a new drug. ⓣ F

C CRITICAL THINKING Answers will vary.

Analyzing What are some commercial advantages of developing a "first in class" drug? Discuss with a partner.

Dr. Michael Hanley has worked in the biotech sector for many years.

SPEAKING Improving lives

A ▶ **7.4** What is Speaker B's innovation for treating diabetes? Insulin patches

A: What made you decide to study medicine?

B: My sister, actually. She has diabetes, and I've seen how tough it is for her. I want to help people with diabetes live better lives.

A: I didn't know your sister has diabetes. Does she have to give herself insulin injections every day?

B: She used to. Now she uses an insulin pump. It's great because it's less painful and it delivers insulin more accurately than injections. Unfortunately, it's also pretty expensive.

A: Are there any other treatment options?

B: Yes, there are. In fact, my research focuses on designing insulin patches, which should make dealing with diabetes cheaper and safer.

A: Wow, that's great! I think that will be really useful for diabetics. I hope your research is successful.

B Practice the conversation with a partner.

C Work with a partner. Talk about the benefits of a drug or medical device. Use the expressions in blue above to help you. Answers will vary.

> I think asthma inhalers are great because …
>
> I agree. They're small and easy to carry, so they make dealing with asthma …

C CRITICAL THINKING Read the question aloud. Make sure students understand that *commercial* refers to selling the drug. Give students a little time to consider their answers before discussing in pairs. A drug that is "first in class" has the potential to sell well since it is a completely new and original product. Since there is no other drug like it out on the market, it would face less competition.

SPEAKING

A Before students watch the audio/video, elicit any background information they know about diabetes. Then ask students to read along as they watch.

▶ **7.4** Play the audio/video. Check the answer as a class. Ask students to raise their hands if they have heard of any of these medical innovations before. Point out the opening question *What made you decide to …?* Explain that this is a useful question for asking about someone's motivations behind doing something. It can be used when you want to find out more specific reasons or encourage a deeper discussion about personal motivations.

B Model the conversation aloud with a student. Then have students work in pairs to practice. Make sure they alternate between A and B roles.

C Read the task aloud. Give students time to go back over the words in blue in the conversation in **A**. Model the example aloud with a volunteer. Encourage students to talk about an area of medicine that they may have personal experience with, like in the conversation in which Speaker B's sister has diabetes.

LISTENING

A Read **Detecting signpost language** aloud as students read along. Explain that a signpost is specific language that tells a listener that the speaker is going to say something significant, or has said something significant.

Have students preview the task. Point out that they only need to listen for one piece of information.

▶ **7.2** Play the audio/video. Check answers as a class.

Elicit the signpost language the speaker uses in the clip (*I think I'm going to focus on …*).

B Have students preview the task.

▶ **7.3** Play the audio/video. Have students check answers in pairs.

⭐ **CHALLENGE** Elicit any other steps in the drug development process that were talked about or that students can infer from the audio/video.

LESSON OVERVIEW

Aims: Read an infographic about medical technology; talk about future technology

Infographic Summary: A timeline of future medical advances over a 100-year span is introduced. From using nanoparticles to fight cancer, to extending the human life span to 150 years, humankind is set to experience some amazing advances over the next century that will affect our bodies, health, and lives.

LANGUAGE FOCUS

A Read the question aloud. Note that answers will vary based on what students know, but that most students will likely have heard of wearable technology such as a smartwatch.

▶ **7.5** Play the audio/video as students read along. Then give them additional time to look over the infographic. Ask students to share any other devices or innovations similar to those in the infographic that they are familiar with, or to share any more background information that they have about one of the technologies mentioned in the infographic, other than nanoparticles. Note that students will learn more about nanotechnology in **B**.

B Read the question aloud and tell students to listen for the answers.

▶ **7.6** Play the audio/video. Check answers as a class. Elicit an explanation of what a nanoparticle is. Nanoparticles are very small particles that can be designed to go to specific parts of the body, which is why they may become a more efficient way of delivering medicine and vaccines.

⭐ **CHALLENGE** Have pairs get online and find out two or three more uses of nanoparticles. Then have each pair share with the class what they learned.

7B The future of medicine

LANGUAGE FOCUS Making predictions, expectations, and guesses

A ▶ **7.5** Study the timeline of future advances in medicine. Which technologies are you familiar with? Tell a partner. Answers will vary.

FUTURE MEDICAL TECHNOLOGIES
Enormous technological changes in medicine and healthcare are heading our way.

2022
Nanoparticles might be able to deliver medication directly to cancer cells to make cancer treatments less painful.

2024
Wearable devices could communicate information such as your heart rate and blood pressure directly to your doctor.

2045
Robots could replace nurses in hospitals; they will lift patients and help in surgery.

2122
Thanks to advances in medicine, people could start living to **age 150**.

150

2062
Contact lenses that give people superhuman eyesight may allow users to zoom in on objects and see in the dark.

B ▶ **7.6** Listen to an explanation of nanotechnology. What are some medical uses of nanoparticles? To treat cancer and diabetes, and to deliver vaccines.

C ▶ **7.7** Watch and study the language in the chart.

Making predictions
People will communicate with their doctors without leaving home in the future. Robots should be able to do nurses' jobs in the future.
People could live to age 150 by 2122, but I doubt it. I doubt that people will live to age 150 by 2122.
Do you think robots will replace nurses in the future? Yes, I think robots are likely to replace nurses in the future.

For more information on **modals of probability**, see Grammar Summary 7 on page 186.

92

C Have students read over the language chart for **Making predictions**.

▶ **7.7** Play the audio/video. Note the difference in the level of certainty for each prediction. Direct students to page 186 for more information.

Grammar Note

The language chart introduces language for predictions.

Both *will* and *going to* are used for future predictions when the speaker feels certain, although only *will* is introduced in the chart. The modal *should* is used for predictions that aren't as certain as *will*, but are possible. The adverb *likely* + infinitive is also used to express probability.

The modal *could* is used for lesser certainty than *should*. Note that *might*, which is in the activity but not the chart, can also work in this case. Students are also introduced to *I doubt that* + subject + *will* + verb, which is used when the speaker thinks something is not likely to happen.

D ▶ **7.6** Listen to the explanation in **B** again. Complete the sentences from the explanation.

1 "Researchers are also hopeful that nanoparticles _____ will _____ one day _____ be used _____ to treat diabetes by delivering insulin to targeted cells."

2 "In addition, nanoparticles _____ should be able _____ to deliver vaccines in the future."

3 "It _____ could _____ therefore _____ make _____ a big difference to public health, particularly in the developing world."

E Complete the conversation. Circle the correct words.

A: Technology allows us to treat a greater number of illnesses these days.

B: Yeah. I think advances in technology ¹(**will** / might) definitely enable us to live longer in the future.

A: How can you be so sure?

B: Well, my dad's a doctor and he says nanoparticles ²(**could** / should) be able to cure serious diseases. Also, in the future, scientists ³(doubt that they will /(**are likely to**)) grow organs in labs. In fact, some doctors have already done this.

A: Do you think people ⁴(**will**/ should) visit the doctor less often?

B: I'm not sure. It's possible. It's also possible that in a few years, nurses ⁵(**might**/ should) be replaced by robots. But I doubt it. I think nurses ⁶(may /(**will**)) always be around.

F Answer the questions. Then share your answers with a partner and explain why you are certain/uncertain about them. Answers will vary.

1 Do you think superhuman eyesight will be possible in the future?

_____

2 How likely do you think it is that people will live longer in the future?

_____

SPEAKING Talking about future technology
Answers will vary.

A Work in a small group. Look at the list of possible future technologies on the right. Brainstorm what problem each one might solve or what purpose it might have.

B Choose the innovation you think will be the most important. Explain the reasons for your choice to your group members.

> I think stem-cell technology is the most important because it could cure diseases like …

> I disagree. I think exoskeleton suits will be the most important innovation because they will …

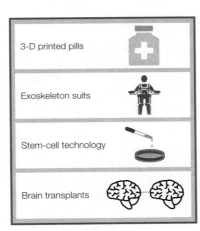

3-D printed pills

Exoskeleton suits

Stem-cell technology

Brain transplants

93

EXTENSION ACTIVITY Have students work alone to write a summary of another type of technology featured in the infographic (other than nanoparticles). Tell students to use the modals in the language chart to write their predictions, expectations, and guesses about that technology. Have them read their paragraphs to a partner and then discuss both their thoughts about the future of that technology.

SPEAKING

A Give students time to preview the task and look at the realia. Have students work in small groups. Ask them to go through each technology and discuss ideas about how each could be helpful in solving a challenge or problem. If necessary, give students some time to do some quick online research to find out more details about any technology listed that they are not familiar with.

B Give students a minute or so to gather their notes and thoughts, and form their opinions about which technology will be the most important. Ask them to tell their group members which innovation they think will be most valuable in the future and why.

Model the example with a volunteer. Note that both speakers in the example use the language "most important," but other options to introduce to students include: *most valuable, most significant,* and *most beneficial.*

EXTENSION ACTIVITY Have students work in groups to tell an imaginary story about how one of the technologies will help someone in the future. Explain that each group member will add a sentence to the story, and that this will continue until the story is completely told. Tell them to make sure they have characters, a plot, and a setting for their futuristic stories.

D Have students preview the task. Tell them to note the specific information to listen for and key phrases they might hear.

▶ **7.6** Play the audio/video. Have students work individually to complete the activity before checking answers in pairs.

E Have students work individually. Tell them to use the language chart for support. Have students check answers in pairs by taking parts and reading the conversation aloud.

F Read the questions aloud. Have students work individually before discussing answers in pairs. Then take a class poll to see what students think about each topic. If time permits, elicit a class discussion for students to share reasons for their ideas and opinions.

LESSON OVERVIEW

Aims: Read and comprehend an article about 3-D printing; understand main ideas and details

Target Vocabulary: customized, modified, synthetic, three-dimensional, traditional

Reading Summary: Three-dimensional (3-D) printers are changing the way we create. Industries from food to medicine are planning for a future with cheaper and easier ways to manufacture their goods. Because 3-D printing allows for easy changes to design plans, customized products can be made with greater ease and for less money, while also creating far less waste than traditional production methods. The health and medical industries in particular may be totally transformed by this technology as 3-D printers are already making skin cells, bones, and even prosthetic body parts.

PRE-READING

Read the question aloud. Explain that the author may not directly state a purpose, so students will have to infer it based on the content they skim. Give students a set time to skim the passage. Check answers as a class. Note that the author gives various examples of ways in which the technology is used, focusing on advantages instead of disadvantages. While the author's opinion toward 3-D printing can probably be inferred as being in favor of it, the opinion is not directly expressed and is not the main purpose of the passage.

Point out the glossary at the end of the reading. Remind students to refer to it before or while reading.

▶ **7.8** Play the audio/video as students read along. Go over any unfamiliar language. See **Language Note**.

7C Just press "print"

PRE-READING Skimming

Skim the passage. The main purpose of the passage is to _____.

(a) explain the uses of a technology

b express an opinion about a technology

c describe the advantages and disadvantages of a technology

▶ **7.8**

1 Imagine being able to print rocket engine parts, chocolate figurines, designer sunglasses, or even pizzas—just by pressing a single button. It may sound like something out of science fiction, but
5 it's increasingly becoming a reality.

Thanks to 3-D printing, companies are reimagining their long-term business plans. General Electric, for example, is already using 3-D printers to make some parts of jet engines. Airbus envisions
10 that by 2050, entire planes could be built out of 3-D printed parts. And this trend isn't just limited to corporate giants. Dutch architectural firm DUS is 3-D printing a house on the banks of Amsterdam's Buiksloter Canal.

15 **THE ADVANTAGES OF 3-D PRINTING**

Invented in the mid-1980s, 3-D printers create solid, **three-dimensional** objects from various materials such as plastic, wax, wood, gold, or titanium.[1] A major advantage of 3-D printing is that designs for
20 objects can be easily **customized** or changed. When designs change in **traditional** manufacturing, the machinery that makes the objects needs to be redesigned or upgraded, which can be very costly. But in the case of 3-D printers, only the software
25 needs to be **modified**.

3-D printing is also better than traditional manufacturing because there's no wasted material.

94

With traditional manufacturing, material is cut away to create an object, but 3-D printing uses only what
30 is necessary. Guided by software, a 3-D printer builds an object one layer at a time, placing material only where it needs to be. As a result, it can make complex objects less expensively.

MEDICAL USES OF 3-D PRINTING

35 This precision is making it possible to produce things that have never been made before. A team of Harvard University researchers recently printed human tissue, complete with blood vessels—a crucial step toward one day transplanting human
40 organs printed from a patient's own cells. "That's the ultimate goal of 3-D bio-printing," says Jennifer Lewis, who led the research. "We are many years away from achieving this goal."

⊙ **EXTENSION ACTIVITY** Have students work in pairs. Tell them to list the various ways that 3-D printers are used as they skim the reading material. Then ask them to add to the list based on their own knowledge or what they think might be possible. Tell students to use this discussion as background information to support their reading.

Skill Note

Skimming involves reading quickly for main ideas. The first step of skimming includes quickly reading the title, subheadings, and captions, as well as looking at the pictures. Then students should quickly read the entire first paragraph, then the first and last sentence of each paragraph, and finally the entire last paragraph. Explain that students should be reading very quickly, picking up on key words and phrases that can give them a general idea of what the passage is about.

A young boy with a hand malformation tries on his new 3-D printed hand.

3-D printers can create bones, organs,
45 **synthetic** skin, and prosthetic[2] body parts—such as hands and arms. In fact, 3-D printing saved a dying baby named Kaiba Gionfriddo, who was born with a condition that regularly caused the airways near his lungs to collapse. Using a 3-D printer, a
50 team of researchers in the United States printed a flexible tube, which they implanted[3] in Kaiba, and which enabled him to breathe on his own.

3-D printing also provided a nose for an Irish baby, Tessa Evans, who was born without one.
55 Over time, 3-D printed implants of increasing sizes will be surgically placed under her skin where her nose should be. The implants will gradually create a "nose" from her own skin, allowing her to look just like everyone else as she grows into
60 adulthood. If it weren't for 3-D printing, doctors would have had an extremely difficult time

modeling the implant and customizing it to suit Tessa's face.

THE FUTURE OF 3-D PRINTING

65 Clearly, 3-D printing has much potential for growth. While there is no doubt that this medical technology will continue to improve many people's lives, the challenge lies in developing software that is advanced or sophisticated enough to create the initial blueprints.
70 Designing the blueprint or a digital model for a vital organ—with all its cell types and structures—is an extremely complex process. Nevertheless, many are hopeful that this obstacle will soon be overcome, and that 3-D printing will change the face of medicine.

[1] **titanium:** *n.* a very hard metal
[2] **prosthetic:** *adj.* artificial
[3] **implanted:** *v.* inserted into the body

95

Language Note

The term *3-D* is hyphenated when used as a modifier throughout the passage. Note that it is also commonly written as *3D* with no hyphenation.

The term *corporate giants* (line 12) refers to large companies with financial power.

The expression *the banks of* (line 13) is used to talk about the land at the edge of a body of water.

Manufacturing (line 21) refers to producing items on a large scale with machines so that a lot are made at once.

The noun *precision* (line 35) describes the quality of being as accurate as possible.

The verb *transplanting* (line 39), when used in medicine, describes the action of putting a human or artificial organ into someone's body in order to replace an organ that is no longer functioning.

Another medical term, *airway* (line 48), describes the path of air to a person's lungs.

A *blueprint* (line 70) is a technical drawing that shows the design of something. The term can also be used more loosely to talk about a future plan.

A *vital organ* (lines 70–71) refers to the organs in our bodies that are necessary for us to stay alive. These include the lungs, liver, kidneys, heart, and brain.

Content Note

Blood vessels are too small for current 3-D printers to reproduce, which is why the technology needs to advance further in order for there to be widespread use in the medical industry. However, the technology is advancing and becoming especially useful in the educational arena as doctors and students can have access to actual 3-D models (instead of just printouts from scans) when diagnosing a patient and considering treatment options.

There are a range of TED and TEDx Talks on the topic of 3-D printing. Suggested ones include:

Print your own medicine by Lee Cronin

What if 3-D printing were 100 times faster? by Joseph DeSimone

The emergence of "4D printing" by Skylar Tibbits

Noteworthy TEDx Talk speakers on 3-D printing and medical applications include: Carsten Engel, Jan Torgersen, Michael Balzer, and Pamela Scott.

UNDERSTANDING MAIN IDEAS

Have students work individually. Point out that students will infer the answer based on what they read in the passage. Check answers as a class. Students should identify the author's attitude by recognizing that most of the content focuses on medical innovations rather than other applications of 3-D printing.

UNDERSTANDING DETAILS

Have students complete the activity without referring to the passage. Then have them check their answers by referring back to the passage. Elicit a class discussion about the areas where the two forms of production overlap.

● **EXTENSION ACTIVITY** Have students work in pairs. Ask them to predict additional possible applications of 3-D medical technology that are not discussed in the passage. Tell them to use the language they learned in **Lesson B** to discuss these predictions and guesses.

BUILDING VOCABULARY

A Have students work individually to complete the activity. Check answers as a class. Elicit additional example sentences using each word. Write them on the board. For item 3, make sure students understand that *modify* means to change something, while *customize* means to modify something in a very specific way.

B **CRITICAL THINKING** Read the question aloud as students read along. Elicit or explain the meaning of *ethical or moral issues*. Have students discuss in pairs first, and if time permits, have them also share their thoughts in small groups.

UNDERSTANDING MAIN IDEAS

Choose the sentence that best describes the author's attitude toward 3-D printing.

   a This technology will be of more benefit to corporate giants like General Electric than to smaller start-ups.

   (b) Medical uses of this technology will make life easier for many people.

   c Applications in engineering, such as manufacturing airplanes, are currently the most important use of this technology.

UNDERSTANDING DETAILS

Complete the Venn diagram using the information below.

   a cuts objects from material   **d** is easy to customize

   b runs on software   **e** makes three-dimensional objects

   c can be expensive to upgrade   **f** tends to create waste

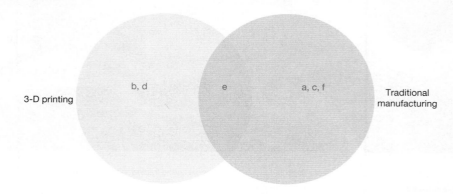

BUILDING VOCABULARY

A Complete the sentences. Circle the correct words from the passage.

   1 With 3-D printing technology, the process of making prosthetic devices is quicker and cheaper than with (**traditional** / **three-dimensional**) methods.

   2 The prosthetic arm was (**customized** / **synthetic**) to match the wearer's favorite color: purple.

   3 As more companies start to use 3-D printing, their business strategies will need to be (**customized** / **modified**).

   4 Playing (**synthetic** / **three-dimensional**) video games is fun because they are more realistic.

   5 Wigs made from human hair usually look more natural than wigs made from (**synthetic** / **customized**) hair.

B **CRITICAL THINKING**   Answers will vary.

Evaluating 3-D printing is making it possible to produce things that have never been made before, like replacement bones and organs. Do you think this could raise any ethical or moral issues? Discuss with a partner.

96

● **EXTENSION ACTIVITY** In the reading, students read two stories of young children who were helped by 3-D printing. Have students go online and find another story of a "medical miracle" that has happened due to 3-D printing. Ask them to work in pairs to summarize the story. Then have them present the anecdote to the class. Alternately, have them watch one of the TED Talks listed in the **Content Note** on page 95, summarize its content, and share what they learned with the class.

TEDTALKS

DAVID SENGEH grew up in Sierra Leone, where many people underwent **amputation** of their **limbs** during the country's civil war. Sengeh noticed that a lot of these people weren't wearing their prostheses. When he found out why, Sengeh realized that the **conventional** way of making artificial body parts wasn't working, and he decided to do something about it.

David Sengeh's idea worth spreading is that those who have a **disability** should have the opportunity to live active, enjoyable lives—beginning with more comfortable prosthetics.

PREVIEWING

Read the paragraphs above. Circle the correct meaning of each **bold** word. You will hear these words in the TED Talk.

1 In an **amputation**, a part of the body is (**cut off**/ replaced), either surgically or as the result of an accident or injury.

2 Your **limbs** are your (**fingers and toes** / **arms and legs**).

3 If something is **conventional**, it's based on an (**uncommon** /**accepted**) way of doing things.

4 **Disability** is a (**physical or mental condition**/ **side effect**) that limits a person's movements, senses, or activities.

VIEWING

A ▶ **7.9** Watch Part 1 of the TED Talk. Circle **T** for true, **F** for false, or **NG** for not given.

1 David Sengeh had to flee with his family during the war in Sierra Leone.   **(T)**   **F**   **NG**

2 One of Sengeh's family members is an amputee.   **T**   **F**   **(NG)**

3 After the war, David Sengeh was troubled when he saw how some amputees were using their prostheses incorrectly.   **T**   **(F)**   **NG**

4 Many amputees found their prosthetic limbs painful to wear because they didn't fit well.   **(T)**   **F**   **NG**

97

7D

The sore problem of prosthetic limbs

PREVIEWING

Have students work individually to read the paragraphs. Tell them to pay attention to how each bold word is used in context in order to understand its meaning. Then have students work individually to complete each sentence before checking answers in pairs. Note that while *amputation* usually refers to a surgical procedure, in the case of the civil war in Sierra Leone, many people had their limbs hacked by rebel soldiers, which is the main reason there are so many amputees in the population. Remind students of the **Warm Up** preview clip. Tell them to use all the language and information they have learned to support their viewing of the TED Talk.

VIEWING

A Have students preview the statements. Point out that NG is for information that is not given in the video.

▶ **7.9** Play Part 1 of the TED Talk. Check answers as a class or play the check-your-answers part of the video. For item 2, note that although Sengeh says that he has loved ones who are amputees, he does not specify if these are family members or close friends.

Elicit any background information students have about the country of Sierra Leone and the civil war that happened there. If students did the **Extension Activity** in **Warm Up**, they will already be prepared with information to contribute to a class discussion. See **Content Note** in **Warm Up** as well.

Elicit or explain the meaning of any unfamiliar language. Suggestions for Part 1 include *physical resources, ensure,* and *loved ones.*

LESSON OVERVIEW

Aims: Watch and understand a talk about improving on a medical device; observe and practice body movements and gestures

Target Vocabulary: amputation, conventional, disability, limbs

TED Talk Summary: David Sengeh was 12 years old when his family escaped from the brutal civil war in Sierra Leone, one in which amputation was used as a form of warfare. Sengeh says that after the war, he saw that many of the amputees were not using their prostheses, and he found out the reason was that the sockets did not fit well enough. As a student at MIT, Sengeh decided to focus his research in bionics on creating a better-fitting socket that would allow people worldwide to use prosthetics with more ease. In his talk, he explains his design and how it can help many people live a more meaningful life.

B Have students preview the pictures and headings in the activity. If necessary, pronounce each heading so that students are already familiar with hearing each of the technical terms before watching the video.

▶ **7.10** Play Part 2 of the TED Talk. Check answers as a class or play the check-your-answers part of the video. Elicit an explanation of what a socket is based on what Sengeh describes in his talk. Then elicit or explain the meaning of any other unfamiliar language. Suggestions for Part 2 include *residual, sores and blisters,* and *our age.*

C Have students work individually. Tell them to use the information they learned while watching Part 2. Then check answers as a class.

D Have students preview the task. Note that the question format is similar to comprehension questions on exams such as TOEFL® and TOEIC®. Note that the answer choices paraphrase what students hear in the video, which will require an understanding of overall meaning.

▶ **7.11** Play Part 3 of the TED Talk. Check answers as a class. Elicit or explain the meaning of any additional unfamiliar language. Suggestions for Part 3 include *highly functional* and *souls.*

E CRITICAL THINKING Read the question aloud. Have students discuss in pairs before eliciting a class discussion. Ask each pair to share at least one idea that they discussed. Sengeh talks about healing souls by making amputees highly functional again physically, with comfortable prostheses. His wish is that the disabilities that amputees face are not keeping these individuals from having meaningful and happy lives.

B ▶ **7.10** Watch Part 2 of the TED Talk. Match the labels to the images that show how David Sengeh creates custom prosthetic sockets.

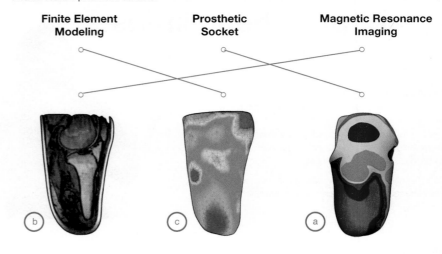

Finite Element Modeling — Prosthetic Socket — Magnetic Resonance Imaging

C Match the descriptions (**a–c**) to the images in **B**.

a Sengeh creates a customized, multi-material prosthesis using a 3-D printer.

b Sengeh captures the actual shape of the patient's anatomy.

c Sengeh predicts where pressure points on the socket will be.

D ▶ **7.11** Watch Part 3 of the TED Talk. Choose the correct options.

1 Which of the following is NOT mentioned by Sengeh?

ⓐ We need to remove the negative stereotype associated with wearing prostheses.

b We need to create comfortable and affordable prostheses.

c We need to make functional prostheses more readily available around the world.

2 Which sentence best paraphrases the following quote from the talk?

"Whether it's in Sierra Leone or in Boston, I hope this not only restores but indeed transforms their sense of human potential."

a Sengeh hopes that the work he's doing will make people more interested in helping others.

ⓑ Sengeh hopes his work will help people become the best versions of themselves.

c Sengeh feels that people in poor countries need his work more than people in wealthy countries.

E CRITICAL THINKING Answers will vary.

Evaluating How do you think Sengeh's prostheses can help amputees heal psychologically? Discuss with a partner.

98

Content Note

In his TED Talk, Sengeh mentions both Professor Hugh Herr and the MIT Media Lab. The Media Lab at MIT (Massachusetts Institute of Technology) is a place for research involving more than one department. Hugh

Herr is an engineer and head of the biomechatronics group at MIT.

Biomechatronics focuses on combining electromechanics with the human body. As a result of his groundbreaking work in the lab, Herr is considered an important leader in the field of bionics. As a grad student at MIT, Sengeh worked with Herr. Sengeh says in his talk that Herr encouraged him to focus on the prosthetic socket in his research.

Language Note

Part 1
When Sengeh uses the term *physical resources*, he is referring to natural resources of Sierra Leone. The country has mines that produce gold, diamonds, and other minerals.

To *ensure* means to make certain that something will happen.

Your *loved ones* are the people in your life who you are emotionally close with, such as family and good friends.

VOCABULARY IN CONTEXT

A ▶ **7.12** Watch the excerpts from the TED Talk. Choose the correct meaning of the words.

1.c; 2.b; 3.a; 4.b

B Complete the sentences with the words from the box.

infamous	go through	intolerable	interface

1 That restaurant is _____infamous_____ for its poor service.

2 The heat and humidity in the summer can be _____intolerable_____.

3 In order to get a job, you have to _____go through_____ an interview selection process.

4 The well-designed _____interface_____ of this app makes searching for information easy.

PRESENTATION SKILLS Body movement and gestures

> Your body language and gestures can reinforce your listeners' understanding of your message, or they can distract.
> • Try to keep calm. Avoid nervous body language like swaying.
> • Gesture with your palms out and open.
> • Use arm and hand movements that help to illustrate your message.

A ▶ **7.13** Watch part of David Sengeh's TED Talk. Check (✓) the gestures he makes with his hands.

☐ He claps his hands.

☐ He puts his hands in his pockets.

☑ He gestures with his palms open.

☑ He points to a slide in his presentation.

B Work with a partner. Brainstorm other positive body movements and gestures.

Answers will vary.

99

Part 2
Something that is *residual* is left over; in the case of amputees, this means the part of the physical limb that is still attached to the body. *Sores and blisters* are painful spots that often result from something rubbing against the skin. Sores are usually red and raw looking, while blisters can fill with water and bubble up. Both are painful. Amputees often get sores and blisters on their residual limbs when wearing a prosthetic for the first time. When Sengeh uses the expression *our age,* he means modern times.

Part 3
Souls is used by Sengeh to refer to people in order to highlight the emotional and immaterial part of being a human.

VOCABULARY IN CONTEXT

A ▶ **7.12** Play the video. If necessary, play it again.

B Have students work individually. Check answers as a class, eliciting additional example sentences for each vocabulary word.

PRESENTATION SKILLS

A Read the Presentation Skills paragraph **Body movement and gestures** aloud. Remind students that the presentation skill in **Unit 6** was about being authentic. Using natural body language is one way to show that you are being authentic during your presentation. Have students preview the task. Ask them to make guesses about Sengeh's body language.

▶ **7.13** Play the video. Check answers as a class. Ask students to raise their hands if Sengeh's natural body language is similar to theirs. Point out that we all have natural body language, and everyone's differs, so what is comfortable for Sengeh might not be for others.

B Have students work in pairs. Ask them to make a list of some positive gestures and body language that are common or that they use personally. After students discuss in pairs, elicit a class discussion to brainstorm a list of positive body movements and gestures.

⊙ **EXTENSION ACTIVITY** Ask students to keep a journal of their own body language over a one-day period. Tell them to be aware of the gestures they use while communicating with others, especially when they are comfortable and relaxed. Tell students to use the information that they gathered about their own body language to help them during their next presentations.

Inventing solutions

LESSON OVERVIEW

Aims: Design and present a plan for a new technology; write a persuasive letter

COMMUNICATE

A Read the direction line aloud. Tell students to use the knowledge they've gathered in the unit, including in their discussions with each other, to imagine a technology that would be helpful to a group in need. Encourage students to focus on a medical issue that they are familiar with. Have students work in pairs to discuss and brainstorm ideas. Tell them to use the questions as a guide in their discussion. Point out that they can take notes individually before writing their decisions in the student book. Give them enough time to brainstorm and consider their plans.

B Tell partners that their goal is to introduce their idea, explain how it will help, and try to get the class to support it. Remind them to think about what kind of body language will be effective when presenting.

Read the phrases aloud for **Using persuasive language**. Have students also review the language in **Lesson B** for making predictions, expectations, and guesses, as they can be used with these phrases.

C After pairs present, have the class discuss their impressions and opinions. Encourage them to ask additional questions. For the class vote, have students write their favorite invention on a piece of paper. Then tally the votes and announce the winner.

7E Inventing solutions

COMMUNICATE Pitching an invention Answers will vary.

A Work with a partner. "Invent" a technology that would make life easier, more enjoyable, or more comfortable for a disabled person or a person with a particular illness. Consider the following questions.

What is your invention?	What problem does it solve?	How does it work?
Who is it designed for?	What does it look like?	How much does it cost?

B With your partner, pitch your invention to the class. You may want to use visuals like posters.

> **Using persuasive language**
> *Without a doubt, …*   *It's certain that …*
> *For these reasons, …*   *Not only is it able to … , it also …*

C As a class, vote on the best pitch.

WRITING A persuasive letter Answers will vary.

Choose either your own invention or one of the inventions that the other pairs in your class presented. Write a letter to a potential investor describing what it does and why it is worth investing in.

> Dear Mr. Smith,
> My name is _____ . I am writing to inform you of my latest invention. I have invented a new kind of wheelchair that can climb stairs. When the user pushes a button, …

100

The iBot, a special wheelchair created by Dean Kamen

WRITING

Tell students to put the content of either their own presentation or one of their classmates' presentations to make a written pitch for funding. Explain that they can use the same persuasive phrases from their presentations in their letters. Read the model aloud as students read along. Encourage students to provide basic information about the invention, such as what kind of problem it fixes or how it can help someone, and then more specific information about how much money they need and why.

⭐ CHALLENGE
Have students share their persuasive letters with a partner. Encourage partners to ask follow-up questions before giving their opinions about whether they think the pitch is persuasive enough. Then have students revisit their writing individually to make improvements based on their discussions.

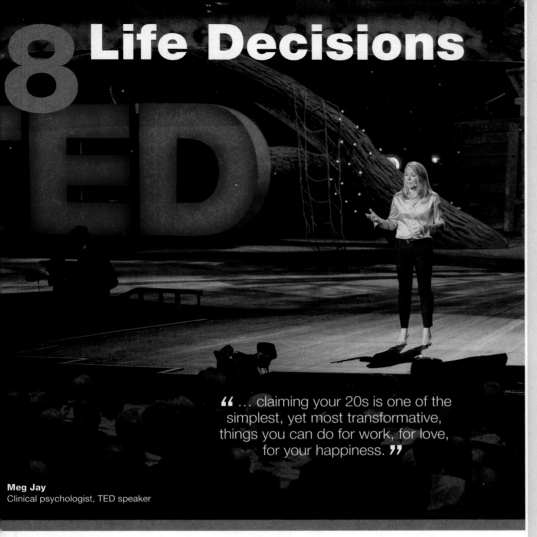

8 Life Decisions

" … claiming your 20s is one of the simplest, yet most transformative, things you can do for work, for love, for your happiness. "

Meg Jay
Clinical psychologist, TED speaker

UNIT GOALS

In this unit, you will …

- talk about important life events.
- read about decisions that define your life.
- watch a TED Talk about the importance of your 20s.

WARM UP

▶ 8.1 Watch part of Meg Jay's TED Talk. Answer the questions with a partner.

1 What do you think Meg Jay means by "claiming your 20s"? Answers will vary.

2 When do you think is the best time in life to get married or have children? Answers will vary.

---

8 Life Decisions

UNIT GOALS

In this unit, students will read, watch, and talk about defining life events. Discussions will be focused on decisions we make in our 20s, and how these decisions affect the rest of our lives. Students will share their own aspirations and plans throughout the unit.

TED Speaker

Meg Jay is a clinical psychologist who specializes in working with patients in their 20s.

TED Talk Summary

Meg Jay says that our 20s should be seen as a significant time in our lives. She aims to reverse the mentality that this period is a throwaway decade before getting serious about work and love in our 30s. Instead, she says that our 20s should be a decade of learning and development, when we begin to make the choices that set us in the direction of goals and relationships to ultimately define the rest of our lives.

Idea Worth Spreading

Our 20s are the defining decade of adulthood.

WARM UP

Have students look over the picture, caption, and quote on the page. Read the quote aloud. Note that students will hear the quote in the video clip. Elicit the meaning of *transformative*.

▶ 8.1 Play the preview clip of the TED Talk. After students watch, elicit the meaning of *20-somethings*. Students should understand that it refers to people aged 20 to 29.

For question 1, note that *claims* in this case is a synonym for *owns*. To own or claim your 20s means to be in control of your life, instead of wandering aimlessly. Note that in the clip, Jay lists experts in various stages of personal development, which should be a clue to students. She is saying that 20-somethings should make this a more fruitful time of their lives.

For question 2, note that students' answers will likely vary, as well as be influenced by culture and background. Encourage an open class discussion about what is typical in their home countries, as well as what is typical in generations past versus now.

➡ **EXTENSION ACTIVITY** Have students work individually to make a timeline of their 20s and 30s. Ask them to predict when big life events will happen to them over these two decades. Have students then share and compare their timeline with a partner. Explain that students can refer back to these timelines during the unit. Note that it is likely that students' ideas and understanding about their 20s will change during the unit. Have them come back and make changes to the timeline as they gather more useful information throughout the unit.

Entering adulthood

VOCABULARY

A Have students work individually to read the paragraph and complete the activity. Tell them to pay attention to how each phrase is used in context in the sentences before choosing the definition. Remind students that they read about Millennials in **Unit 1**. Check answers as a class, going over the meaning when necessary.

B Have students work individually. Note that answers will vary based on students' personal goals.

C Have students share their answers in **B** in pairs. Encourage them to give specific ages for when they hope to experience each milestone. Ask them to give reasons for these predictions. If students did the **Extension Activity** in **Warm Up**, have them share and refer to their timelines during the discussion.

⭐ **CHALLENGE** Ask students to talk about which of the actions listed they don't want to do, and why.

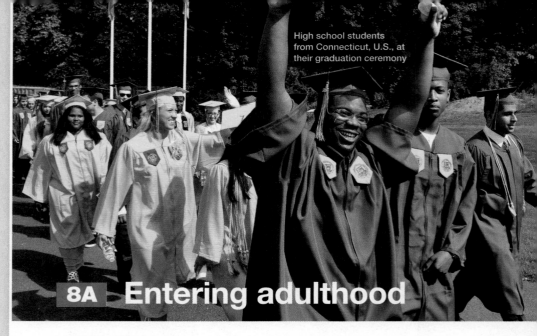

High school students from Connecticut, U.S., at their graduation ceremony

8A Entering adulthood

VOCABULARY Describing milestones in life

A Read the paragraph below. Then match each **bold** phrase to its definition.

A Pew Research Center study in the United States compared Millennials (people born between 1981–1996) with the Silent Generation (people born between 1928–1945). The study showed that many more Millennial women are **getting degrees** and **pursuing careers** than Silent Generation women did in their young adult years. In 1963—when they were aged 18 to 33—only 38 percent of Silent Generation women were employed; today, 63 percent of Millennial women are employed. Furthermore, fewer young adults today are **settling down** compared to their Silent Generation counterparts. According to the study, financial concerns are causing many young people to **put off** owning a home and **raising a family**.

1 getting a degree   working hard in a profession

2 pursuing a career   getting married or finding a permanent place to live

3 settling down   taking care of children while they are growing up

4 put off   completing a college or university course

5 raising a family   delay

B Which of the following would you like to do in the future? Check (✓) your answers. Answers will vary.

☐ get married   ☐ get a job   ☐ live overseas

☐ buy a house   ☐ have children   ☐ get a degree

C Compare your answers in **B** with a partner. Give reasons for your choices. Answers will vary.

102

Content Note

Giving nicknames to generations became a popular trend in the United States in the 1900s. The nicknames are often first given by academics or writers, and then catch on and become popularized in the media. The trend is said to have started when a writer, Gertrude Stein, referred to the generation of people born between 1880 and 1900 as the Lost Generation. The generations that followed are known as the Greatest Generation, the Silent Generation, Baby Boomers, Generation X, and Millennials.

LISTENING Comparing generations

A ▶ **8.2** Watch Professor Laurence Steinberg talk about adolescence. Check (✓) the milestones he reached by the time he turned 25.

☑ finished his formal education   ☑ was financially independent

☑ got a job   ☑ got engaged

☐ started his own business   ☐ became a parent

Dr. Laurence Steinberg, author of the best-selling book *Age of Opportunity*

B ▶ **8.3** Watch the rest of the interview. Is Dr. Steinberg worried about today's young people? Why or why not?
No, because he thinks delayed adulthood is a rational response to today's competitive world.

C CRITICAL THINKING
Answers will vary.
Reflecting Look at your answers in **A**. Do you think 25 is an appropriate age to reach these milestones? Discuss with a partner.

SPEAKING Talking about adult responsibilities

A ▶ **8.4** Do you agree with Speaker A or Speaker B? Why? Answers will vary.

A: Did you hear Anne's brother is about to become a father?

B: Yeah, I heard. Exciting, right?

A: Don't you think he's kind of young to be a parent?

B: Well, he's 27 already. I think that's a good age to start raising a family.

A: Really? Do you think you'll be ready to be a parent at 27?

B: I think so. I love children, and I can't wait to have one of my own. What about you?

A: For me, 27 is way too young.

B: Why?

A: Because I'll have just started my career at that age, and I'll still be paying off my school loans, too. I want to be more financially secure before I have any kids.

B Practice the conversation with a partner.

C Work with a partner. What do you think is a good age to start living on your own? Use the expressions in blue above to help you. Answers will vary.

> I think 20 is a good age to start living on your own.

> I disagree. I think you should … before you start living on your own.

103

SPEAKING

A Ask students to read along as they watch. Explain that students will listen in order to form an opinion about which speaker they agree with.

▶ **8.4** Play the audio/video. Elicit opinions with reasoning from students. Note that Speaker A says that being *financially secure* is important. Elicit what it means to have financial security based on what the speaker says. Then ask students to guess or explain the meaning of *job security*.

Point out the adverb *way* in the conversation. Explain that *way* adds emphasis to *too* in order to show excessiveness. While the word is often associated with casual language for young people (*way cool*), it is in fact an acceptable and commonly used adverb of emphasis. However, it is not typically used in formal situations. For example: *I am way behind on my homework*.

B Model the conversation aloud with a student. Then have students work in pairs to practice. Make sure they alternate between A and B roles.

C Read the task aloud. Go over the meaning and use of the expressions in blue in the conversation. Also, review language for expressing opinions. Read the model aloud with a volunteer. Elicit the meaning of *live on your own*.

➕ **SUPPORT** Play the audio/video again, pausing after each expression in blue so students can repeat.

LISTENING

A Read **Listening for opinions** aloud as students read along. Elicit any other words that students know for sharing opinions (*agree, disagree*, etc.).

▶ **8.2** Play the video. Check answers as a class.

B Have students preview the task.

▶ **8.3** Play the video. Check answers as a class by eliciting some examples of how the generations are different. Ask students to comment on whether they also see these differences between themselves and their parents.

C CRITICAL THINKING Read the question aloud. Give students a little time to consider their answers. Note that students' reactions will vary widely depending on their own experiences, backgrounds, and cultures. How do students think the world has changed for young adults since their parents were their age? After students discuss in pairs, elicit a class discussion, encouraging students to share their opinions.

8B

Plans and aspirations

LESSON OVERVIEW

Aims: Read an infographic about what college students hope for after graduation; talk about aspirations

Infographic Summary: The infographic shows the aspirations of college students. At first glance, the data shows that most are concerned about attaining financial security after graduation, so stability seems to be a big aspiration. However, the percentage of students who want to go to grad school matches the percentage that want to get married right after graduating— and that's higher than the percentage of students who want to pay back their student loans, so maybe financial security is not everyone's first priority after all.

LANGUAGE FOCUS

A Read the question aloud.

▶ **8.5** Play the audio/video as students read along. Then give them additional time to look over the infographic. Point out that students may have goals that are not found on the infographic. Ask students to think about their immediate plans upon graduating, and then one year down the line. Have them share both with a partner.

B Read the question aloud and tell students to listen for the answers.

▶ **8.6** Play the audio/video. Check answers as a class. Note that Ian mentions two aspirations: getting a job in banking and paying off loans. Elicit more details about the conversation. Ask:

What does Julia want to do after college? (travel)

How long has she been studying Mandarin? (six years)

LANGUAGE FOCUS Making plans for the future

A ▶ **8.5** Read about aspirations of young adults after they finish college. Do any of the aspirations below match your own? Tell a partner. Answers will vary.

ASPIRATIONS OF COLLEGE STUDENTS

Here's what most young adults would like to do after they finish college.

- **31%** Become financially stable
- **28%** Secure a dream job
- **10%** Get married
- **10%** Go to graduate school
- **2%** Become a business owner
- **2%** Buy a house
- **4%** Start a family
- **6%** Travel
- **8%** Pay off student loans

B ▶ **8.6** Listen to the conversation. What aspirations does Ian have? To get a good job in banking and pay off his student loans

C ▶ **8.7** Watch and study the language in the chart.

Talking about milestones

By this time next year, Ian will have paid off his loan.
I'll have gone to graduate school by then.
By the time they turn 20, the twins will have moved out of their parents' house.

Next year, I'll have been working here for five years.
When Dave turns 30, he'll have been living on his own for ten years.
When Jack and Kate get married, they will have been dating for four years.

Won't Emma have graduated from college by then?
How long will you have been studying when you graduate?

For more information on the **future perfect** and **future perfect progressive**, see Grammar Summary 8 on page 186.

104

C Elicit or explain the meaning of *milestone*, which is another way to say *defining life moment*. Have students read over the language chart for **Talking about milestones**.

▶ **8.7** Play the audio/video. Go over the formation and use of the future perfect and future perfect progressive. Direct students to page 186 for more information.

Grammar Note

The future perfect tense is used for talking about important events that will be completed by a certain point in the future.

The future perfect tense is formed with *will have* + past participle.

This tense is useful for talking about aspirations as it allows you to say what you will have accomplished in the future, which also allows you to talk about what you plan to do after that or as a result of that: *Since I will have lived in London for five years this May, I plan to apply for a permanent resident visa.*

D ▶ **8.6** Listen to the conversation in **B** again. Complete the sentences from the conversation.

1 "When do you think _____you'll have paid off_____ your loans?"

2 "Hopefully, _____I'll have saved_____ enough money by the time I start my trip."

3 "By the time I graduate, _____I'll have been learning_____ Mandarin for six years."

E ▶ **8.8** Complete the information using the correct form of the words in parentheses. Then listen and check your answers.

By the time they reach retirement age, most of today's American Millennials ¹ _____will have been working_____ (**work**) for over 40 years. But ² _____will_____ they _____have saved_____ (**save**) enough money by then? According to Alexandra Mondalek, writing in *Time* magazine, Millennials are saving more money than any other generation. Even so, the majority of Americans still ³ _____won't have saved_____ (**will not save**) enough to retire comfortably. This explains why more and more Millennials think they will be forced to put off retirement. Many young homeowners are planning to work well into their 70s, as they expect that they ⁴ _____won't have paid off_____ (**will not pay off**) their mortgages before then.

The office of the Society of Grownups, a company that provides financial advice to Millennials

SPEAKING When will you ...? Answers will vary.

A Complete your plans and aspirations in the timeline below.

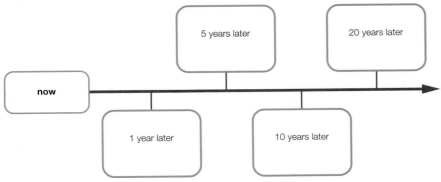

now

5 years later

20 years later

1 year later

10 years later

B Share your timeline with a partner. Compare your partner's plans and aspirations with your own. Discuss any similarities or differences that you notice.

By this time next year, I'll have ...

Really? That's too soon for me. I don't plan to ... for another five years or so.

105

The defining decade

Aims: Read and comprehend an article about how the 20s influence adulthood; understand details and scan for facts

Target Vocabulary: coast, defining moment, extend, peak, trivialize

Reading Summary: Being a *kidult* has become a recent trend in the United States that the media has now begun to romanticize. Instead of jumping into adulthood, 20-somethings are instead being given more leeway to continue to live like teenagers, at home with their parents, with part-time jobs, hanging out with their friends. Psychologist Meg Jay feels that this trend has to stop, as a generation of young adults is missing the most defining decade of their lives. She points to research that supports why the decisions we make in our 20s affect the rest of our lives, which is why 20-somethings need to get out of dead-end jobs and unhealthy relationships, and start making decisions to put themselves on the right path for their futures. Before the age of 35, the majority of our life-defining moments will have taken place, which tells us that the 20s cannot be wasted or spent coasting, but have to be claimed and used as a decade for personal growth.

PRE-READING

Read the question aloud. Give students time to look over the photo and think about their answers. Tell them to also take into consideration the discussions they've had about aspirations and milestones in the unit so far. Check answers by eliciting a class discussion about what decade students think is most important. Ask students to share their opinions and give reasons.

Point out the glossary at the end of the reading. Remind students to refer to it before or while reading.

8C **The defining decade**

PRE-READING Predicting Answers will vary.

Look at the photo. What decade of your life do you think is the most important?

▶ 8.9

1   For the longest time, adulthood—and the responsibilities that come with it—was thought to begin in your 20s. After finishing school, 20-something-year-olds were expected to
5   be independent, start careers, and raise families. Many of today's youth, however, are now delaying marriage, careers, children, and other milestones of adulthood. In the last few years, the media has romanticized this phenomena, coining phrases like
10   "30 is the new 20" and "kidulthood." As society has begun to believe that it's OK for young adults to put off commitments, it's now increasingly acceptable for today's 20-somethings to work at low-level jobs and to live with their parents. Many "kidults" are leaving
15   serious decisions about work, marriage, and family until later, when they're in their 30s.

Psychologist and TED speaker Meg Jay felt this way about her 20s, too, until she had what she calls an "aha" moment.[1] What changed her mind?
20   A 26-year-old woman named Alex. A 20-something herself, Jay was just starting her career as a counselor when Alex came to see her. Alex wanted advice on how to deal with her "knucklehead" boyfriend. Jay didn't consider Alex's problem to be
25   serious; however, her supervisor pointed out that maybe Alex had a more complex problem. Perhaps Alex wasn't taking her relationships seriously enough. In other words, even though Alex knew she was with a person who wasn't good enough for
30   her, she might still end up marrying him or someone similar. "The best time to work on Alex's marriage," the supervisor said, "is before she has one."

Jay realized at that moment that the 20s aren't a time for **coasting**, but rather, the best
35   time to be making serious choices about the future and preparing for adulthood. She points out that 80 percent of life's most **defining moments** take place by age 35. This means that eight out of ten of life's important decisions and experiences
40   will have happened by your mid-30s. Jay refers to research that backs this up:[2]
• Female fertility **peaks** at age 28.
• More than half of Americans are married to or dating their future partners by the age of 30.
45   • Approximately 70 percent of lifetime wage growth happens in the first ten years of a career.

▶ 8.9 Play the audio/video as students read along. Go over any unfamiliar language. See **Language Note**.

➡ **EXTENSION ACTIVITY** Have students skim the passage before reading. Have them work individually to write a summary of the passage based only on the content that they skimmed. After students read the entire passage properly, have them come back to their summaries to see if their summaries were accurate. Tell them to change or add any content as necessary.

Skill Note

Skimming involves reading quickly for main ideas. The first step of skimming includes quickly reading the title, subheadings, and captions, as well as looking at pictures. Then students should quickly read the entire first paragraph, then the first and last sentence of each paragraph, and finally the entire last paragraph. Explain that students should be reading very quickly, picking up on key words and phrases that can give them a general idea of what the passage is about.

A couple in Pankisi Gorge, Georgia, cuts their wedding cake.

- The brain ends its final growth spurt[3] in the 20s,
  as it begins to rewire[4] itself for adulthood. This
  means that if you want to change something
50 about yourself, your 20s is a good time to do it.
  According to Jay, "[American] culture has
  '**trivialized**' young adulthood," reinforcing the
  message that it's OK to **extend** adolescence. In
  an interview with National Public Radio, Jay said
55 that more and more people these days suffer from
  "present bias." In other words, they place more value
  on immediate rewards than on achieving long-term
  goals. But Jay is hopeful that more 20-somethings
  will start thinking ahead. A lot of what she does with
60 her 20-something clients is to ask them specific

questions about the future, such as where they hope
they will be in five or ten years, if they want children,
or what type of job they hope to get. She believes
that in order to pursue a happier, more fulfilling future,
65 what's important is not only thinking about these
things, but thinking about them at the right stage of
your life. And in Jay's opinion, the critical period for
adult development is actually in your 20s.

[1] **an "aha" moment:** *n.* a situation in which a person has an
  important realization
[2] **back something up:** *v.* to support it
[3] **growth spurt:** *n.* a period when a thing or a person grows a lot
  in a short period of time
[4] **rewire:** *v.* to change the connections between neurons in the brain

107

Content Note

The author gives the example of the
brain's growth spurt as one reason
why the 20s is the right decade to
make changes and develop yourself
further as an individual. While it was
formerly believed that our brains
stopped developing in our teen years
after puberty, it is now widely accepted
that the brain continues to develop in
our 20s. During our 20s, connections
between certain areas of our brains get
strengthened, and the prefrontal cortex,
which is the control center for our more
complex thinking, grows more efficient in
its operations. Some experts use these
new discoveries to argue that we're not
physiologically ready to make important
decisions until our late 20s. However,
others argue that the changes are not so
dramatic that we can't make significant
decisions that are rational and useful for
our futures.

UNDERSTANDING MAIN IDEAS

Have students work individually. Check answers as a class.

UNDERSTANDING DETAILS

Have students complete the activity without referring to the passage. Then have them check their answers by checking the passage.

SCANNING FOR FACTS

Explain that students should scan the passage to look for the specific piece of information that they need to complete each sentence. Have students work individually. Give students a short time limit for each, checking answers as a class after each sentence.

Skill Note

Scanning involves reading quickly for specific information, whereas skimming is done to get a main idea. While scanning, students should stop when they come to information that they think is relevant for what they are searching, and then read more carefully.

BUILDING VOCABULARY

A Have students work individually to complete the sentences. Check answers as a class. Elicit additional example sentences using each word. Write them on the board.

B **CRITICAL THINKING** Read the questions aloud as students read along. Point out that it is OK for students' opinions and answers to be very different from each other.

Remind students of useful phrases for discussing opinions, such as *I think …; I disagree; I agree, but …,* as well as useful phrases for talking about personal decisions, such as *In my case, …; For me, …*

UNDERSTANDING MAIN IDEAS

Which sentence best summarizes the main idea of the passage?

a Many people in their 20s are unable to handle the responsibilities that come with adulthood.

(b) The 20s are an important time to make decisions about the future because many important social and biological milestones occur during that period.

c We are currently experiencing serious social problems because the media has convinced young people that their 20s aren't important.

UNDERSTANDING DETAILS

Match each expression to the point it is used to describe.

1 "Thirty is the new 20." ○——○ People in their 20s should take their current relationships more seriously.

2 "The best time to work on Alex's marriage is before she has one." ○——○ It's OK for people in their 20s to put off serious commitments until later in life.

3 "Present bias" ○——○ Most people in their 20s don't have enough discipline or patience to plan ahead and wait for future rewards.

SCANNING FOR FACTS

Scan the passage to complete the facts below.

1 About 80 percent of major life decisions are made by age _____35_____ .

2 Over _____50_____ percent of Americans will have met their future partners by the time they turn 30.

3 In your _____20s_____ , your brain starts preparing you for adulthood.

BUILDING VOCABULARY

A Complete the sentences using the correct form of the words in blue from the passage.

1 Graduating from college is a(n) __defining moment__ for many people.

2 Neuroscientists now believe that intelligence can _____peak_____ at any time up to age 40.

3 Experts say that if you're just _____coasting_____ at work, it's probably time to get a new job.

4 Some sociologists worry that reality TV shows such as *The Bachelor* _____trivialize_____ important life milestones, such as marriage.

5 I had to _____extend_____ my medical leave because I still wasn't feeling well enough for work.

B **CRITICAL THINKING** Answers will vary.

Reflecting Jay asks her 20-something clients the following questions to help them think about the future. How would you answer these questions? Discuss with a partner.

1 Do you want children? If so, what do you hope to accomplish before you have children?

2 What type of job do you hope to get?

EXTENSION ACTIVITY Ask students to work in small groups to talk about whether the information about *kidulthood* in the passage is relevant for young people in their home countries. Note that in general, this phenomenon is associated with people in their 20s in developed countries, but not necessarily in other parts of the world. After students discuss in groups, elicit a class discussion on how the attitudes of 20-somethings vary around the world, and what may influence these attitudes.

8D Why 30 is not the new 20

TEDTALKS

MEG JAY believes that young adults should be planning their lives more **consciously** than many of them are doing today. Exploration is OK in the 20s, she says, but unless it has a real focus, Jay considers it **procrastination**. To avoid having an **identity crisis** in your 20s, Jay recommends using the time to make an **investment** in yourself instead. She believes that new opportunities are more likely to come from people we don't know, rather than our **peers**.

Meg Jay's idea worth spreading is that the 20s are the defining decade of adulthood.

PREVIEWING

Read the paragraphs above. Circle the correct meaning of each **bold** word. You will hear these words in the TED Talk.

1 If you do something **consciously**, you do it (**with intention** / carelessly).

2 **Procrastination** is the act of (forgetting / **delaying**) something.

3 If you are having an **identity crisis**, you are unsure of (**your purpose in life** / what to call someone).

4 An **investment** refers to the (**time or effort** / thought) that you put into something.

5 Your **peers** are people who are (**similar to** / different from) you in age, rank, or ability.

VIEWING

A ▶ 8.10 Watch Part 1 of the TED Talk. Check (✓) the statements that are true about Emma.

- ☑ She was underemployed.
- ☐ She had a well-paying job.
- ☑ Her boyfriend didn't always treat her well.
- ☐ Her boyfriend was very ambitious.
- ☑ She had an unhappy childhood.
- ☑ She had negative feelings about her family.
- ☐ She had a serious health problem.
- ☑ She had nobody to rely on in a crisis.

109

LESSON OVERVIEW

Aims: Watch and understand a talk about the overlooked importance of the 20s; observe and practice using a case study

Target Vocabulary: consciously, identity crisis, investment, peer, procrastination

TED Talk Summary: Psychologist Meg Jay shares an important "aha" moment she had while working with a patient as a young counselor, which convinced her that the 20s is a much more significant decade in our lives than many young people today think. Instead of wasting that decade with aimless exploration and unhelpful relationships, she says it should be used for more focused personal growth and development that will put us on the right path to the defining moments that wait just around the corner. Our 20s influence our lives much more than many people think, which is why that decade, and not the 30s, needs to be used for finding a way to get yourself on the general path that you want to be on as you head into the rest of your life.

PREVIEWING

Have students read the paragraphs. Tell them to pay attention to how each word is

---

8D

Why 30 is not the new 20

used in context in order to understand its meaning. Have students work individually before checking answers in pairs. Make sure students understand that an *identity crisis* describes a time in someone's life when they are confused about the direction that they want to go next. An *identity crisis* can happen at any age, but it's often referred to as happening in one's mid-20s and mid-40s.

Remind students of the **Warm Up** preview clip. Tell them to use the language and information they have learned to support their viewing of the TED Talk.

VIEWING

A Have students preview the task. Explain that students will infer some points about Emma based on how the speaker describes her life situation.

▶ 8.10 Play Part 1 of the TED Talk. Check answers as a class. Elicit a summary of the event that prompted Emma's breakdown in Jay's office. Jay explains that Emma bought a new address book for writing her contacts in, and when she came to a part that asked for a contact in case of an emergency (if something bad happened to Emma), it triggered a realization. When Emma realized she had no one's name to write in that space, she had a breakdown that made her realize that she needed to make changes.

Write on the board the expression that Jay uses to describe Emma's boyfriend: that he *displayed his temper more than his ambition*. Ask students to explain how they were able to infer from this comment that he didn't treat her well. Jay is saying that he was either verbally or physically abusive to Emma, and that he was not very ambitious. Elicit or explain the meaning of any unfamiliar language. Suggestions for Part 1 include *wait tables, hangs her head in her lap,* and *address book.*

B Have students preview the expressions and answer choices. Note that students are being asked to paraphrase the meaning of each expression that Jay uses. Explain that they should listen for how the phrase is used in the context of the talk.

▶ **8.11** Play Part 2 of the TED Talk. Check answers as a class or play the check-your-answers part of the video. Write on the board the term *urban tribe*. Elicit a definition based on what students heard in the video. The urban tribe refers to a group of friends that take on family-like roles for each other in their young adult lives. These groups of young people tend to exclusively spend time with each other, which Jay explains can be detrimental to their futures because they are not meeting many new people outside of their immediate group of friends.

C Have students work individually before checking answers as a class. Elicit or explain the meaning of any unfamiliar language. Suggestions for Part 2 include *begets, internship, start-up,* and *walking down the aisle*.

D Have students preview the task and guess the answers before watching the video. Have students also preview the task in **E** before watching.

▶ **8.12** Play Part 3 of the TED Talk. Check answers as a class.

E Note that both answer choices are logical possibilities, so students will have to listen closely to understand what Jay means when she uses the analogy of an airplane. Elicit or explain the meaning of any additional unfamiliar language. Suggestions for Part 3 include *live-in* and *LAX*.

F **CRITICAL THINKING** Read the direction line and questions aloud. For question 1, ask students to think about who Jay's message is for. Note that it's likely that Jay's physical audience at the time when she gave her talk probably did not have a lot of 20-somethings in it since the TED audience is usually made up of other TED speakers. However, her TED Talk has been viewed over eight million times online since she gave it in 2013.

B ▶ **8.11** Watch Part 2 of the TED Talk. Choose the correct paraphrase for each piece of advice Meg Jay gave to Emma.

1 "Get identity capital."

ⓐ Develop your qualities and skills by getting some experience.

b Become wealthier by putting your money into reliable investments.

2 "Explore work and make it count."

ⓐ Try new things, but get a job that you're genuinely interested in.

b Try new things, but only take jobs that pay well.

3 Connect with "weak ties."

a Build close relationships with everyone you know.

ⓑ Get in touch with people who aren't close to you, such as friends of friends.

4 "Pick your family."

a Change your attitude toward the family you were born into.

ⓑ Create your own family by choosing a partner and having children.

C Which of these pieces of advice is Meg Jay most likely to agree with?

a Try your best to stay positive and be happy with your current situation.

ⓑ Be honest with yourself and use all the information available to you to make decisions.

c Don't take love and work too seriously—it will all work out in the end.

D ▶ **8.12** Watch Part 3 of the TED Talk. How did Emma follow Meg Jay's advice and turn her life around? Order the events from 1 to 4.

__3__ She left her live-in boyfriend.

__2__ She found a job at an art museum in another state.

__4__ She found a suitable partner and got married.

__1__ She found a distant contact in her address book.

E Meg Jay compares 20-somethings to airplanes taking off. What does she mean by this analogy?

ⓐ Small actions and events can help transform and shape the lives of 20-somethings.

b 20-somethings must be clear where they want to go in life and learn how to stay the course.

F **CRITICAL THINKING** Answers will vary.

Evaluating/Reflecting **Discuss these questions with a partner.**

1 Who is Meg Jay's intended audience? Who does she want to convince that "30 is not the new 20"?

2 After watching Meg Jay's TED Talk, do you feel differently about your 20s or 30s? Which pieces of Jay's advice might apply to you or someone you know?

I think my cousin would really benefit from watching Meg Jay's TED Talk.

How so?

For question 2, elicit a class discussion after students discuss in pairs. Ask students to share what insights they have learned, and if they might make any slight adjustments on their own "airplane" course as a result of what they learned.

➲ **EXTENSION ACTIVITY** Ask students to work individually to make a chart similar to a family tree, but instead to map out their personal connections to weak ties. Tell them to think about people they know and the people that those people know. Let them complete the chart as homework so they can talk to friends and family members to see what connections they have. Tell students to make the chart with one of their life goals in mind in order to find ways in which weak ties can help them move closer to attaining that goal.

VOCABULARY IN CONTEXT

A ▶ **8.13** Watch the excerpts from the TED Talk. Choose the correct meaning of the words.

1.c; 2.b; 3.a; 4.c

B Complete the sentences with the words from the box.

collect	like-minded	inner circles	kill time

1 I often _____kill time_____ by reading magazines and listening to music.

2 After hearing the bad news, she paused for a moment to _____collect_____ herself.

3 Meg Jay encourages 20-somethings to form relationships beyond their _____inner circles_____ and broaden their life experiences.

4 A study by two colleges found that we are often more attracted to _____like-minded_____ people.

PRESENTATION SKILLS Using a case study

> Using a case study—describing a particular person or situation—is a memorable way to support your ideas. Here are some ways to do this.
> • Present the case study like a story, with a beginning, a middle, and an end.
> • Give specific details. For example, give a clear picture of the people involved. Describe when and where the situation took place.
> • Ask the audience questions.
> • Include a quote.

A ▶ **8.14** Watch part of Meg Jay's TED Talk. Which of the techniques above does she use?
She presents the case study like a story, gives specific details, and includes a quote.

B Work with a partner. Why might giving a case study be better than presenting facts to support an argument? To help your discussion, think about the following questions. Answers will vary.

1 What would Meg Jay's TED Talk be like if she only used study results or statistics instead of a case history?

2 What topics or arguments might be better supported by case studies than by facts, and vice versa?

111

Language Note

Part 1

To *wait tables* means to work as a server or waiter at a restaurant. When Jay describes Emma as *hanging her head in her lap*, she means that Emma was overly sad about something. The expression *hangs his/her head* is used to describe someone in a despondent emotional state, especially one of shame. An *address book* is a small book in which a person writes all their contacts' information, such as addresses and phone numbers.

Part 2

To *beget* something means to cause it to happen. An *internship* is a temporary job, often unpaid, that a young adult has as a form of training or in order to learn about an industry. A *start-up* is a new business. The expression *walking down the aisle* refers to getting married.

Part 3

A *live-in partner* is someone who you live with, and are usually involved with romantically. *LAX* refers to Los Angeles International Airport in California.

VOCABULARY IN CONTEXT

A ▶ **8.13** Play the video. If necessary, play it again.

B Have students work individually to complete the sentences. Check answers as a class. If necessary, explain that a person's *inner circle* is made up of the individuals they are closest with. Jay uses this term when discussing the *urban tribe*.

PRESENTATION SKILLS

A Read the Presentation Skills paragraph **Using a case study** aloud. Explain that a case study is a real-life anecdote from someone's research that is used to give a specific and lengthy example to support a point or idea. Presenting a case study as a story means introducing the characters and the setting, and explaining the plot. Additionally, other supporting details, such as a quote, can be added to make the story even stronger. Point out that a case study should be interesting, so it's important that a speaker thinks about how to engage the audience without exaggerating details or results. Have students preview the task.

▶ **8.14** Play the video. Check answers as a class.

B Read the questions aloud. Have students work in pairs before eliciting a class discussion. Note that students' answers will vary based on opinions, but they should recognize that a case study humanizes an argument and is easier for an audience to connect with.

⊙ **EXTENSION ACTIVITY** Have students work in pairs to make up another case study that would support Jay's talk. Tell them to perform a role play where one person is Jay and the other is the person she is helping.

Hard choices

Aims: Give advice to 20-somethings; write an advice column

COMMUNICATE

A Give students enough time to work individually to read each person's situation before dividing them into groups. Encourage them to take notes about advice they think would be useful for each case study. Tell groups to go through each case study and offer their advice. If necessary, elicit the pieces of advice that Meg Jay gave in her talk for students to use as a guide in their discussions. As they discuss, ask students to think about whether any of the case studies resemble themselves or someone they know. Encourage them to share any other case studies they might know that are related.

Read the box **Expressing opinions** aloud. Remind students of the verbs and expressions for expressing opinions that they already know from earlier in the unit (*think, feel, believe, agree, disagree, In my opinion*).

B Have groups get together with another group. Tell them to go through each case study again, sharing a summary of what advice the group decided on. Ask a different group member to speak for each case study. If time permits, elicit a class discussion so each group can share their advice and the reasons for their ideas.

8E **Hard choices**

COMMUNICATE Giving advice Answers will vary.

A Work in a group. Discuss what advice you think Meg Jay would give to the following people.

Matt, 23: Matt works at entry level in a good company, but he doesn't love his job. He doesn't know whether he'll grow in this career. Matt lives with a group of friends who are unemployed. They spend most of their time playing video games, so they can't give good career advice. They often tease Matt for worrying about his job.

Rachel, 25: Rachel has been going out with Aaron, a boy she met in high school, for ten years. Neither Rachel nor Aaron has dated anyone else. They don't have much in common anymore, but Rachel doesn't have any reason to dislike Aaron. Aaron recently proposed to her, but she thinks she's too young to get married. She's not sure what to do.

Elena, 28: Elena works over 60 hours a week at a high-paying, high-pressure job. She loves her job, and the company loves her. She's pretty certain she'll get a promotion soon. Elena doesn't have time for dating. She's OK with the idea of getting married, but she's not sure if marriage is really for her. All her friends are getting married, and she's starting to feel the pressure.

> **Expressing opinions**
> I think she'd suggest ...   She might say it's better to ...
> She'd probably recommend ...   I guess she'd advise him/her to ...

B Compare your ideas with another group's.

WRITING An advice column Answers will vary.

Imagine you write an advice column for a newspaper. Choose one of the three people above, and write a piece for your column giving your advice.

> Dear Matt,
> I'm sorry to hear that your friends aren't very supportive of your goals and ambitions. I think you should find a new place to live and try to look elsewhere for new job opportunities. Moving out would help you because …

112

WRITING

Tell students that they are now going to pretend that they write an advice column for a living, which means that people write in to ask for help with a problem, and they give those people suggestions on how to handle it. Explain that students are going to use the same case studies from **Communicate**, but they can use their group's ideas, another group's ideas, or their own ideas when writing the advice.

Read the example aloud. Point out that it's written as a personal letter, even though it will be published in a newspaper.

 EXTENSION ACTIVITY Have students write a private letter of advice to themselves. Tell them to use everything they have learned in the unit about making their 20s meaningful, and write themselves a private letter about their aspirations and what changes they should make in order to adjust their direction somewhat to make their 20s more fruitful. Encourage them to include an action plan in the letter to turn this advice into a reality.

9 Technology and Innovation

❝ I'd like to tell you a little bit about the challenges in building these, and some of the terrific opportunities for applying this technology. **❞**

Vijay Kumar
Roboticist, TED speaker

UNIT GOALS

In this unit, you will ...

- talk about robots and other innovative technologies.
- read about the advantages and disadvantages of drones.
- watch a TED Talk about the applications of tiny flying robots.

WARM UP

▶ 9.1 Watch part of Vijay Kumar's TED Talk. Answer the questions with a partner.

1 What do robots help us with today? Have you ever seen a robot at work? Answers will vary.

2 What advantages do you think small robots have over large robots? Answers will vary.

113

---

9 Technology and Innovation

Idea Worth Spreading
Lightweight drones that function autonomously can be of great assistance to humans in dangerous and physically difficult situations.

WARM UP
Have students look over the picture, caption, and quote on the page. Read the quote aloud.

▶ 9.1 Play the preview clip of the TED Talk.

For question 1, ask students to share any personal stories they have about experiences with robots or robotic technology. If students have no firsthand experience with robots, ask them to share any background knowledge they have about robots.

For question 2, ask pairs to brainstorm some ideas. Then elicit a class discussion for possible uses and advantages of smaller robots. Advantages may include that they're easier to maneuver, easier to make, cost less money to make, and can get in small spaces, and therefore have more uses.

➡ **EXTENSION ACTIVITY** Have students work individually to write a short story about having a small robot in their daily lives. Tell them to describe one entire day from morning to night with the robot by their side. Tell them to explain how the robot helps them and describe what the small robot looks like.

UNIT GOALS

In this unit, students will read, watch, and talk about innovative robotic technology that may change our lives in the near future. Students will learn about microrobotics, driverless cars, and drone technology. They will debate the advantages and disadvantages of this technology, and use conditionals to discuss whether or not it's safe to introduce it into civilian life.

TED Speaker
Roboticist Vijay Kumar was assistant director of robotics at the Office of Science and Technology Policy, which advises the President of the United States.

TED Talk Summary
Vijay Kumar introduces some useful applications of drones, sharing how the technology is changing the way we operate rescue missions after natural disasters, how we build things, and how we transport cargo. He then goes into more detail about how drones can fly in formation and work cooperatively.

Technologies that make a difference

VOCABULARY

A Have students work individually to read the paragraph and choose the correct definition for each word. Tell them to pay attention to how each word is used in context in the sentences before choosing the definition. Check answers as a class.

B Have students work individually and then check answers in pairs. Ask them to write one more sentence for each vocabulary word. Elicit one sentence from each pair.

C Read the questions aloud. Give students time to think of reasons for their opinions before discussing. Then have students work in pairs to share their thoughts with each other. Tell them to be specific about what kinds of surgery they would be comfortable with and what kinds they wouldn't. For example, would they feel differently about hand surgery versus heart surgery? Ask volunteers to share with the class what they discussed in pairs.

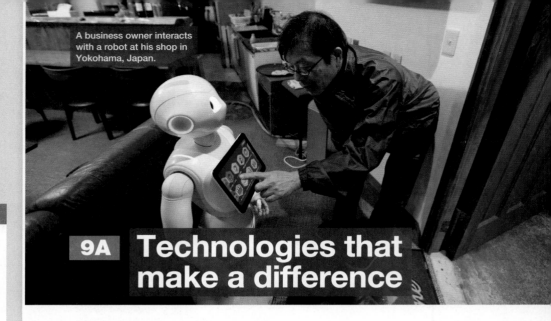

A business owner interacts with a robot at his shop in Yokohama, Japan.

9A Technologies that make a difference

VOCABULARY What can robots do?

A Read the paragraph below. Then match each **bold** word to its definition.

Robots are machines that we can **program** to handle repetitive or dangerous **functions**. For example, we use robots to **assemble** cars because they can do it more quickly and less expensively than humans. Also, because we can control them from a distance, **remote-controlled** robots can gather data and images from inaccessible places. For example, scientists can **operate** robots safely from dry land while they explore the ocean floor. Robots can also perform delicate tasks such as surgery. Using robots for surgery can sometimes be better than using human hands because robots can make tinier, more precise movements.

1 program — to write a set of instructions for a computer
2 functions — uses
3 assemble — to put together
4 remote-controlled — managed from far away
5 operate — to make something work

B Complete the sentences using the words in **A**. One word is extra.

1 Robots often work in factories, where they ___assemble___ objects like cell phones.
2 Because a robot is a machine, it only does what we ___program___ it to do.
3 Robots can have many ___functions___, such as cleaning and doing industrial tasks.
4 ___Remote-controlled___ robots can go into areas that are dangerous for humans.

C Work with a partner. Would you trust a robot to perform surgery on you? Why or why not? Answers will vary.

114

Content Note

Robert Wood (on page 115) is the founder of Harvard's Microrobotics Lab. In the video, he refers to small-scale robots. Wood also focuses his research on soft robotics, which use flexible materials such as fiber, paper, or cloth. Wood was named a National Geographic Emerging Explorer in 2014. Wood said that he believes robotics is the next Internet, and that in coming years it will affect all aspects of our lives and transform our daily lives tremendously, similar to how the Internet did.

LISTENING Robobees

> **Drawing clues from context**
> Scientists often use jargon—technical terms used in specific areas of work or study—in presentations. When you hear scientific or technical jargon that you don't understand, try to work out the meaning from the context.

A ▶ **9.2** Watch roboticist Robert Wood talk about the types of robots he builds. Check (✓) the ways his robots are different from traditional robots.

- ☑ His robots are smaller.
- ☐ His robots are heavier.
- ☑ His robots move faster.
- ☐ His robots are easier to build and design.

B ▶ **9.2** Watch again. Discuss these questions.

1 Where does Wood get his ideas for his robots? *From nature*

2 What kinds of applications might Wood's robots have in 20 years? *Search-and-rescue operations*

C **CRITICAL THINKING** *Answers will vary.*

Reflecting If you could build a robot, what kind of robot would you want to build? Discuss with a partner.

Robert Wood builds robots that can work together.

SPEAKING Talking about technological devices

A ▶ **9.3** In what ways is Speaker B's device useful? *It can be controlled remotely, so the house will be cool when Speaker B gets home, and it can help reduce the electricity bill.*

A: It's so hot today. I can't wait to go home and turn on the air conditioning.

B: Why don't you get a smart air conditioner? I got mine installed a few months ago.

A: A smart air conditioner? What's that?

B: It's an air conditioner that's connected to the Internet, so it can be controlled remotely. I usually turn it on using my smartphone while I'm out, so my house will be cool when I get home. It's great for hot days like today.

A: Sounds perfect! Is it easy to operate?

B: Yeah, it's really simple. It automatically turns off when I'm out. What I like most about it is that it can track usage over time and adjust its behavior. It's helped me reduce my electricity bill!

A: That sounds pretty cool. Can we go to your house now? I want to check it out!

B Practice the conversation with a partner.

C Work with a partner. Talk about your favorite device or technology and why it's useful. Use the expressions in blue above to help you. *Answers will vary.*

> My favorite tech device is my smart TV.

> What does it do?

115

LISTENING

A Read **Drawing clues from context** aloud as students read along. Explain that understanding meaning based on context means paying attention to the words before and after the unknown word, and then using these, and the situation being discussed, as clues to understanding the meaning. Note that even native speakers don't always understand technical jargon, so they also have to make guesses by drawing clues from context.

▶ **9.2** Play the video. Check answers as a class. Elicit any examples of microrobots that students already know or saw in the video.

B Read the questions aloud. Tell students to take notes on the topics while watching.

▶ **9.2** Play the video again. Check answers as a class.

C **CRITICAL THINKING** Read the question aloud. If students did the **Extension Activity** in **Warm Up**, let them use these small robots in their discussion. Otherwise, give students time to decide what kind of robot they'd like to build. Tell them to think about the robot's purpose and how it will help people.

SPEAKING

A Read the question aloud. Ask students to read along with the conversation as they watch.

▶ **9.3** Play the audio/video. Check answers as a class. Point out the phrase *Sounds perfect!* in the conversation. Explain that this is a common way to say that you really like an idea or a thing that someone is describing to you. The phrase is also often used to tell someone that you agree with their idea for a plan.

B Model the conversation aloud with a student. Then have students work in pairs to practice. Make sure they alternate between A and B roles.

➕ **SUPPORT** Play the audio/video again, pausing after each sentence so students can repeat.

C Read the task aloud. Point out that students should talk about devices they currently use in their daily lives. Go over the meaning and use of the expressions in blue in the conversation. Model the example aloud with a volunteer. Elicit the meaning of a *smart appliance*.

LESSON OVERVIEW

Aims: Read an infographic about driverless cars; talk about how technology impacts us

Infographic Summary: The infographic explains some of the key technologies being developed for the driverless car, from how it stays in lanes, to how it drives at night, to how it avoids accidents.

LANGUAGE FOCUS

A Read the questions aloud. Tell students to think about their answers as they look over the infographic.

▶ **9.4** Play the audio/video as students read along. Then give them additional time to look over the infographic. Encourage a class discussion by eliciting some possible applications as well as students' opinions about driverless cars. Tell students to give reasons for their opinions.

⭐ **CHALLENGE** Ask students to comment on whether their opinions about driverless cars are the same as or different from their opinions about robotic surgery, and why.

B Have students preview the task.

▶ **9.5** Play the audio/video. Check answers as a class.

C Elicit or explain the meaning of *conditions*. Make sure students understand that it refers to how one circumstance is needed for another to happen. Have students read over the language chart.

▶ **9.6** Play the audio/video. Go over the formation and use of the first and second conditionals. Direct students to page 187 for more information.

LANGUAGE FOCUS Talking about advantages and disadvantages

A ▶ **9.4** Read about how driverless cars work. Would you like a driverless car? Why or why not?

Answers will vary.

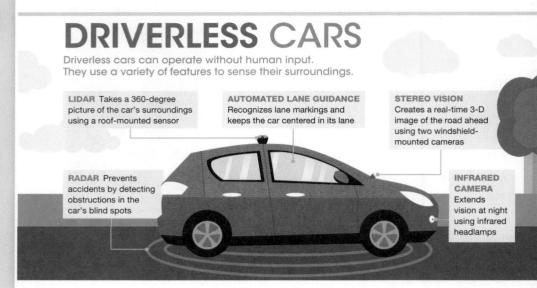

DRIVERLESS CARS

Driverless cars can operate without human input.
They use a variety of features to sense their surroundings.

LIDAR Takes a 360-degree picture of the car's surroundings using a roof-mounted sensor

AUTOMATED LANE GUIDANCE Recognizes lane markings and keeps the car centered in its lane

STEREO VISION Creates a real-time 3-D image of the road ahead using two windshield-mounted cameras

RADAR Prevents accidents by detecting obstructions in the car's blind spots

INFRARED CAMERA Extends vision at night using infrared headlamps

B ▶ **9.5** Listen to the conversation. Complete the sentences. Circle the correct words.

1 According to Jason, driverless cars will (**increase** / **reduce**) the likelihood of traffic jams.

2 Elizabeth is worried that the software in driverless cars might (**fail** / **collect personal information**).

C ▶ **9.6** Watch and study the language in the chart.

Talking about conditions

If you keep your eyes on the road, you'll be less likely to have an accident.
If you like to be in control, you won't like driverless cars.
Do you think more people will buy driverless cars if they become more affordable?

If I had a driverless car, I'd save money on insurance.
I'd buy a driverless car if there was no risk of malfunction.
If you had a driverless car, would you feel safe?

For more information on **first conditional** and **second conditional**, see Grammar Summary 9 on page 187.

116

Grammar Note

A conditional sentence shows that one action results from another. So if or when the condition is met, then the result occurs:

if/when + conditional clause + result clause

The first conditional is used in "real" situations—ones that are likely to happen. For the first conditional, the present tense is used in the *if*-clause, and the future tense is used in the result clause. The first conditional shows a situation that will likely result from an action:

If I eat, I will be full.

If she wins, she will be happy.

When an unreal, unlikely, impossible, or imaginary situation is being described, the second conditional is used. For the second conditional, the *if*-clause has a past-tense verb and the main clause uses *would* + verb:

If I were taller, I would play basketball.

Note that in conditional sentences, either clause can come first, but a comma must separate the clauses when the *If*-clause comes first.

D ▶ **9.5** Listen to the conversation in **B** again. Complete the sentences from the conversation.

1 "If I ___had___ a driverless car, ___I'd feel___ a lot more relaxed because I ___wouldn't have___ to worry about parking."

2 "Also, if everyone ___had___ a driverless car, ___there'd be___ less traffic."

3 "If the software ___fails___, ___it'll / it will___ probably ___cause___ a car crash."

E Match the two parts of the sentences.

1 If more people had driverless cars, — if they were equipped with better sensors.

2 If driverless cars become more popular, — cities will need to be redesigned.

3 People will be more likely to buy driverless cars — there would be fewer traffic accidents.

4 Driverless cars would be safer — if costs come down.

F ▶ **9.7** Complete the information using the correct form of the words in parentheses. Then listen and check your answers.

A driverless pod from a transportation company in the U.K.

Lyft—a private driving service—is planning to have an all-driverless car fleet by 2020. If it ¹ ___achieves___ (**achieve**) this goal, it may be one of the first companies to have driverless taxis. Lyft is working with General Motors, which is currently developing driverless cars. If driverless car technology ² ___is___ (**be**) successful, taxi companies like Lyft ³ ___will be___ (**be**) able to reduce their operating costs significantly. Lyft will first test its vehicles in the United States. If customers use the service during the test period, they ⁴ ___will be___ (**be**) offered a choice of either a driverless car or a car with a human driver. However, for safety reasons, Lyft ⁵ ___will have___ (**have**) human drivers on board to take over if something goes wrong with the driverless vehicle.

SPEAKING Discussing the impact of driverless cars   Answers will vary.

Work with a partner. How would cities be redesigned if everyone drove driverless cars? To help your discussion, consider the impact of driverless cars on the following.

| traffic lights | road signs | parking lots |

If everyone drove driverless cars, there would probably be ... because ...

F Have students work individually to complete the paragraph. Explain that they will need to recognize what kind of conditional it is (real or unreal) in order to decide the tense of the verb.

▶ **9.7** Play the audio/video to check answers. Ask students if they'd like to try a driverless taxi or not.

SPEAKING

Read the question aloud. Give students time to think about their ideas and arguments. Tell them to use conditional clauses in discussing points of concern or support. Have students work in pairs using the three topics as a guide in their discussion.

⭐ **CHALLENGE** Have pairs meet with another pair to share and discuss ideas, and to debate what decisions are most practical and efficient for a city planning to have driverless cars.

➡ **EXTENSION ACTIVITY** Have students work in small groups to design a city plan based on their discussion in **Speaking**. Tell them to draw a map of the city with notes about how to make it safe for driverless cars. Have each group present their city plans to the class. Tell them to use conditional clauses in their presentations.

D Have students preview the task. Encourage them to guess the answers based on the content they heard in the first listening as well as the grammar in the language chart.

▶ **9.5** Play the audio/video. Have students work individually. Check answers as a class.

E Have students work individually. Tell them to use the information in the language chart to help them complete the sentences. Have them check answers in pairs. Ask students to identify whether the sentence uses the first (real) or second (unreal) conditional.

9C
Drones are here to stay

LESSON OVERVIEW

Aims: Read and comprehend an article about drones; understand main ideas and details

Target Vocabulary: carry out, civilian, drawback, humanitarian, pose a hazard, surveillance

Reading Summary: Drones are slowly becoming part of our everyday lives, but many have concerns about this technology. Once used only by the military for missions which would be too dangerous for humans, drones can now be used to help in humanitarian disasters as well as for gathering data for weather forecasts, mapping, and conservation, and to assist the work of farmers and law enforcement agencies. While drones have many useful applications, there is concern that drones may be used to spy on civilians, and that potential accidents make them too dangerous to use in everyday life.

PRE-READING

Read the question aloud. Give students time to skim the content to find the answers. Have students check answers in pairs. Tell them to also point out where in the passage they found the information.

Point out the glossary at the end of the reading. Remind students to refer to it before or while reading.

▶ 9.8 Play the audio/video as students read along. Go over any unfamiliar language. See **Language Note**.

9C Drones are here to stay

PRE-READING Skimming   Answers will vary.

Skim the passage. What are some benefits of drones? Check your answers with a partner.

▶ 9.8

1 Until recently, drones have generally been associated with military **surveillance**. Now, however, they are becoming easier for the average person to obtain; we may soon see them
5 replacing human labor in a variety of tasks. But are drones an important tool, or a danger to private citizens?

DRONES IN THE MILITARY

Drones, also known as unmanned aerial vehicles
10 (UAVs), are remotely controlled flying robots. Some drones are as small as birds, while others are the size of airplanes. Drones can carry instruments such as cameras and global positioning systems (GPS), and are used in situations where manned
15 flight is considered too risky or difficult. For example, they are commonly used by the military for intelligence-gathering, surveillance, and identifying targets.

OTHER DRONE USES

20 Apart from benefiting the military and law enforcement agencies, drones can help people perform **humanitarian** tasks. For instance, they can be used in disaster relief efforts to deliver blankets, clothing, and medical supplies to hard-to-reach
25 places. Furthermore, drones can be programmed to fly into the heart of storms—without any risk to human life—and gather important weather data. This information can help scientists predict natural disasters like hurricanes or tornadoes, and hopefully
30 save many lives in the process.

Camera-equipped drones can also produce maps that are much more detailed and accurate than those produced from satellite imagery. This will be a big help to conservation experts in mapping land use
35 changes such as deforestation, which is threatening an untold number of species. The U.S. government already uses drones to protect its lands and the species that inhabit them.

In addition, farmers can use drones to drop
40 fertilizers and pesticides[1] on crops. This not only saves money, but keeps farm workers safer by limiting their exposure to dangerous chemicals. Drone technology can also be used by farmers to monitor fields and find lost cattle. According to the Association
45 for Unmanned Vehicle Systems International (AUVSI), "Agriculture, far and away, is going to be the dominant market for UAV operations."

PRIVACY AND SAFETY ISSUES

Drones can be equipped with infrared sensors
50 which use temperature variations to "see" things

118

Skill Note

Skimming involves reading quickly for main ideas. The first step of skimming includes quickly reading the title, sub-headings, and captions, as well as looking at pictures. Students should then read the entire first paragraph quickly, then the first and last sentence of each paragraph, and finally the entire last paragraph. Explain that students should be reading very quickly, picking up on key words and phrases that can give them a general idea of what the passage is about.

A drone flying over Dallas, Texas

the naked eye cannot detect. While this is helpful for getting a bird's eye view of a disaster or conflict zone, it could also be used by law enforcement agencies to spy on **civilians**. With thousands of
55 remote-controlled drones set to take to the skies over the United States, many people are concerned about privacy. The American Civil Liberties Union (ACLU) is worried that drones may be linked with cell phone tracking software[2] in the future, which
60 would enable law enforcement agencies to **carry out** surveillance on U.S. citizens and monitor people's movements.

Safety is another major concern. Anyone— from terrorists to criminals—can get their hands
65 on a drone. And even when controlled by skilled operators with good intentions, drones **pose a hazard**. Since 2001, there have been hundreds of military drone accidents worldwide. Even people in favor of drones feel that lack of safety is one of their
70 biggest **drawbacks**. Think of drones accidentally landing in backyards or, worse, crashing into commercial planes. In April 2016, a British Airways aircraft was just about to land at Heathrow Airport when it collided with a drone. There have been
75 several similar instances already.

DRONES AND REGULATION

The ongoing debate over drones suggests that we are in the midst of a "drone fever." The most important question going forward is how
80 governments and agencies will regulate this technology to make sure it benefits, rather than harms, individuals and societies. As drones become more common, the importance of ensuring safe and responsible use will no doubt
85 become greater.

---

[1] **fertilizers and pesticides:** *n.* chemicals used in farming; fertilizers help plants grow, and pesticides kill insects
[2] **cell phone tracking software:** *n.* software installed on a cell phone that indicates the phone's location

119

Content Note

Drones are useful in conservation efforts because they keep costs down, don't require a human pilot, and are able to gather information over large territories without bothering wildlife or negatively impacting natural habitats.

Drones are presently used in conservation in order to gather information about wildlife and to map out ecosystems, as they can take high-quality photos and videos from high above. Additionally, they are used to monitor the borders of nature reserves.

Students can learn more by watching the TED Talk "A drone's-eye view of conservation" by Lian Pin Koh.

Language Note

The average person (lines 3–4) refers to a regular civilian.

A machine that is *unmanned* (line 9) does not have a person in it, versus a *manned* (line 14) machine, which does. The adjectives are usually used in regard to aircraft and spacecraft.

A *global positioning system (GPS)* (lines 13–14) is a satellite-based mapping system that is used worldwide to assist navigation in machines from cars to airplanes.

An example of *law enforcement* (lines 20–21) is the police department.

Deforestation (line 35) refers to the loss of forest areas due to trees being cut down for human development. It has become a major environmental issue in places where precious natural habitats are being destroyed, causing species of plants and animals to go extinct.

In regard to a product, the term *dominant market* (line 47) refers to the main buyers and users of that product. The expert mentioned in the passage says that agriculture is going to be the dominant market for drones, as the machines will have a major effect on how farming is done.

A *bird's eye view* (line 52) refers to a view from high above ground, similar to what a bird would see.

UNDERSTANDING MAIN IDEAS

Have students work individually. Check answers as a class. Elicit a few different ways to paraphrase the main idea in students' own words.

UNDERSTANDING DETAILS

Elicit synonyms for the terms *pros* (advantages, positive points) and *cons* (disadvantages, negative points). Have students complete the activity without referring to the passage. Then have them check their answers by checking the passage. Elicit the meaning of *natural disaster* by asking for examples of one (typhoon, earthquake, etc.).

BUILDING VOCABULARY

A Have students work individually. Tell students to go back to the passage to find the word and see how it is used in context. Check answers as a class. Elicit example sentences using each word. Write them on the board.

B **CRITICAL THINKING** Read the question aloud as students read along. Point out that it is OK for students' opinions and answers to differ. Remind students of useful phrases for discussing opinions: *In my opinion, …; I think …; I disagree; I agree, but …*

Model the example aloud with a volunteer. Explain that partners will be having a light debate in the form of a discussion, so their language will continue to be somewhat informal. Note that later in the unit, students will be introduced to more formal language for expressing opinions in a more serious debate format.

○ **EXTENSION ACTIVITY** Have students work in pairs. Ask them to choose one application for drones mentioned in the passage and find out more information about it. Alternately, have them find out about another application for drones that was not mentioned in the passage. Have them search online for additional background information and more

examples. Ask pairs to report what they learned back to the class. Note that this additional background information will help in their viewing of the TED Talk in **Lesson D** as well as in their class debate in **Lesson E**.

UNDERSTANDING MAIN IDEAS

Which of the following sentences would the author agree with?

   a Although drones can be useful, the disadvantages far outweigh the advantages.

   ⓑ Drones may be able to improve our lives, but there are issues that need to be addressed first.

   c Due to safety reasons, only governments and agencies should be allowed to operate drones.

UNDERSTANDING DETAILS

Complete the chart showing the pros and cons of drones.

Pros	Cons
1 Can help the _____military_____ gather intelligence and identify targets	1 Could be used to spy on civilians by connecting with _____cell phone tracking software_____
2 Can be used to _____deliver_____ disaster relief items to victims of natural disasters	2 Easy access to drones means that dangerous people like _____terrorists_____ or _____criminals_____ can get one
3 Able to use weather data to _____predict_____ natural disasters	3 Drones have caused many _____accidents_____
4 Can track wildlife and map changes in _____land use_____	
5 Can make farm jobs _____safer_____ by reducing workers' contact with harmful chemicals	

BUILDING VOCABULARY

A Match the words in blue from the passage to their definitions.

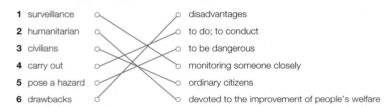

   1 surveillance   disadvantages

   2 humanitarian   to do; to conduct

   3 civilians   to be dangerous

   4 carry out   monitoring someone closely

   5 pose a hazard   ordinary citizens

   6 drawbacks   devoted to the improvement of people's welfare

B **CRITICAL THINKING**   Answers will vary.

   Evaluating In your opinion, is widespread civilian use of drones unavoidable? Discuss with a partner.

     In my opinion, it'll be difficult to stop people from using drones. They're already quite common.

     Yeah, but I think there needs to be stricter rules on ...

120

9D Robots that fly ... and cooperate

TEDTALKS

VIJAY KUMAR's robots can do jobs that are too difficult or dangerous for humans. For example, they can act as **first responders** in disaster situations; they can **assess** dangerous situations before humans get involved. Several of Kumar's robots can work **cooperatively**, allowing them to increase their strength and abilities. They can also be fitted with cameras that show them where **obstacles** are.

Vijay Kumar's idea worth spreading is that agile, **autonomous** robots can help humans respond to disasters, perform difficult physical tasks, and much more.

PREVIEWING

Read the paragraphs above. Match each **bold** word to its meaning. You will hear these words in the TED Talk.

1	evaluate	assess
2	done in a manner that involves working together	cooperatively
3	independent; self-controlling	autonomous
4	things that get in the way	obstacles
5	people trained to provide immediate assistance in an emergency	first responders

VIEWING

A ▶ **9.9** Watch Part 1 of the TED Talk. Check (✓) the ways Kumar's robots can be used.

☐ They can design buildings.

☑ They can look for dangerous leaks.

☑ They can be used to transport goods.

☑ They can work together to carry heavy objects.

☐ They can be used to prevent natural disasters.

☑ They can assess the damage after natural disasters.

121

9D

Robots that fly ... and cooperate

PREVIEWING

Have students read the paragraphs. Tell them to pay attention to how each word is used in context in order to understand its meaning. Have students work individually before checking answers in pairs. Note that Kumar's TED Talk contains a lot of technical information about drones. Tell students to rely on all the background information that they've learned so far in the unit to support their viewing of the talk.

VIEWING

A Have students preview the task. Explain that students will hear each of the applications described in slightly more complex language. Tell them to listen for key phrases.

▶ **9.9** Play Part 1 of the TED Talk. Check answers as a class. Elicit the meaning of *leak* and the examples given in the TED Talk of two types of dangerous leaks (biochemical, gaseous).

Elicit the applications of drones that Kumar talked about but students have not heard about so far in the unit (building items, cooperative work), as well as the applications they already know about but Kumar did not talk about (conservation, agriculture).

Elicit or explain the meaning of any unfamiliar language. Suggestions for Part 1 include *tenth of a pound, intruder, payload-carrying capacity,* and *reactor*.

LESSON OVERVIEW

Aims: Watch and understand a talk about drone technology; observe and practice referring to visuals

Target Vocabulary: assess, autonomous, cooperatively, first responders, obstacles

TED Talk Summary: Roboticist Vijay Kumar begins his talk by introducing some useful applications of drones, showing visuals of how the technology is changing many things, including the way we operate rescue missions after natural disasters, how we build things, and how we transport things. Kumar then goes into more detail about how drones are programmed to move, including how they can be programmed to fly in formation and as a result work cooperatively, much like ants do. He then shows how drone technology has developed to the point where a drone is able to intuitively make adjustments to its navigation path based on the mapping it creates through its real-time movements through a space.

B Tell students to look closely at the diagram. Check answers as a class. Note that Kumar uses various technical terms in his talk, so it is important that students have a grasp of the key phrases and terminology. Give students a demonstration of each stage by using an item that you hold in the air.

C ▶ **9.10** Play Part 2 of the TED Talk. Have students look at the picture on page 123.

Read the questions aloud that students will discuss. Ask pairs to first summarize together what Kumar explains about ant behavior in his talk and why this behavior is something he wants to mimic in drones. Ask students to also think of some situations where this type of behavior could be useful. Then ask volunteers to share with the class their answers to the questions.

Elicit or explain the meaning of any unfamiliar language. Suggestions for Part 2 include *change gears, sense, planar,* and *figure-eight*.

⭐ **CHALLENGE** Ask pairs to also think of any other behaviors from animals in nature that might be useful for drones to mimic, and why. Have them share their ideas with the class.

D Have students preview the task.

▶ **9.11** Play Part 3 of the TED Talk. Check answers as a class.

Elicit a summary of what students saw the drone do in the video that Kumar shows. The drone enters an unknown location and adjusts its movements based on its own measurements of the environment instead of relying completely on programming or GPS technology. The drone is actually able to create a map of the building and continue to explore it by applying the information it is gathering while moving.

Ask students to share their ideas about why Kumar ended his TED Talk with a music video. Note that after a rather technical talk, Kumar decided it was time to entertain his audience by showing a lighter side of applications for drones. This lighthearted end to the talk was a nice way for his audience to relax a bit and enjoy watching drones in action.

B The diagram below illustrates the robots' motions—how they move. Match each description to the correct stage in the diagram. Write **a, b,** or **c**.

  a The robot changes its orientation.

  b The robot builds up momentum to start moving.

  c The robot recovers and hovers in the air.

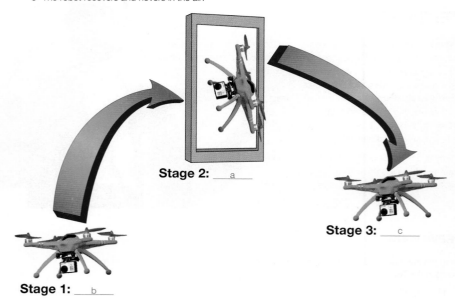

Stage 2: _a_

Stage 3: _c_

Stage 1: _b_

C ▶ **9.10** Watch Part 2 of the TED Talk. Then look at the picture on page 123. Discuss the questions below with a partner.

  1 What are the ants in the picture doing? Working together to carry a heavy leaf

  2 What aspect of ant behavior does Kumar want his robots to have? Coordination

D ▶ **9.11** Watch Part 3 of the TED Talk. If a drone is entering a building for the first time, can it complete its mission under the following conditions? Circle **Y** for yes or **N** for no.

1 The drone is not connected to GPS but has a map of the building.	Ⓨ	N
2 The drone is not connected to GPS and doesn't have a map of the building.	Ⓨ	N
3 The drone doesn't have a camera.	Y	Ⓝ
4 The drone is remotely controlled by someone.	Ⓨ	N
5 The drone is not controlled by anyone.	Ⓨ	N

E **CRITICAL THINKING** Answers will vary.

  Applying Vijay Kumar says, "Robots like this can really change the way we do K-12 education." How do you think drones could be used in K-12 education? Discuss with a partner.

122

Elicit or explain the meaning of any additional unfamiliar language. Suggestions for Part 3 include *motion-capture systems* and *algorithms*.

E **CRITICAL THINKING** Read the quote and question aloud. Elicit the meaning of *K-12 education*. Make sure students understand that it refers to education up through the end of high school. The *K* refers to kindergarten, which in the United States refers to a year of schooling before students start their first year of elementary school.

Ask partners to brainstorm some ideas of how drones can be used in education. Have each pair present one or two ideas to the class. Tell them to explain how the idea will be an improvement to the current education practices.

➡ **EXTENSION ACTIVITY** Ask students to work in pairs to describe their ideal school day with a drone. If students could get access to a drone for one day at school, and use it any way that they want to, what would they do? How would they use the drone to help them in their education? Have students role-play how they would use the drone in their day at school.

VOCABULARY IN CONTEXT

A ▶ **9.12** Watch the excerpts from the TED Talk. Choose the correct meaning of the words.

1.a; 2.b; 3.c; 4.a

B Complete the sentences with the words from the box.

figure out	jump through hoops	on the fly	team with

1 It's not easy to deliver a speech _____on the fly_____; you usually need to prepare for it.

2 You may need to _jump through hoops_ if you want to borrow a large sum of money from the bank.

3 If we could _____figure out_____ what animals are saying, we'd be able to learn a lot more about them.

4 In my final year in college, I had to _____team with_____ a classmate to build a robot.

PRESENTATION SKILLS Referring to visuals

> If you use visuals, let the audience know when you are referring to them. There are various expressions you can use to do this. For example:
>
> *As you can see (here), …*   *Take a look at …*
>
> *Here you see/you'll see …*   *Please turn your attention to …*
>
> *Here we have …*   *If you'll look at …*

A ▶ **9.13** Watch part of Vijay Kumar's TED Talk. Complete the sentences with the expressions he uses.

1 "And _____here_____, _____you'll see_____ Daniel throw this hoop into the air, while the robot is calculating the position of the hoop, and trying to figure out how to best go through the hoop."

2 "_____As you can see here_____, they collapse from a three-dimensional formation into planar formation."

3 "_____As you can see_____ in this figure-eight flight, they come within inches of each other."

B Work with a partner. Brainstorm more phrases you could use to draw attention to visuals in a presentation.

Answers will vary.

Leafcutter ants (*Atta colombica*) in Costa Rica

123

Language Note

Part 1

A *tenth of a pound* is approximately 45 grams. An *intruder* refers to a criminal or other person in a building who is not supposed to be there. In military circumstances, it refers to the enemy. When Kumar refers to the *payload-carrying capacity* of the drones, he means how much weight and bulk a drone can carry on its own. The *reactor* that Kumar refers to is a nuclear power plant.

Part 2

The expression *change gears* is colloquial and used to introduce a new,

somewhat related topic. To *sense* something means to feel its presence. A *planar* shape refers to a flat shape formed by lines, while a *figure-eight* shape has two connected circles, like the number eight. Examples of each of the shapes are shown in the videos.

Part 3

In the lab where Kumar works, a *motion-capture system* films the movements of drones in order to gather data for their programming and mapping in the experiments. An *algorithm* is the pattern that a computer program follows in order to complete a task.

VOCABULARY IN CONTEXT

A ▶ **9.12** Play the video. If necessary, play it again.

B Have students work individually to complete the sentences. Check answers as a class, eliciting additional example sentences for each term. If necessary, explain that *jumping through hoops* uses a literal image to describe a figurative situation of having to go through difficult, and somewhat unnecessary, steps and deal with obstacles to get to an end goal. Note that in the talk, Kumar shows the drone flying through hoops and then makes a joke about finding funding for research by using the expression *jump through hoops*.

PRESENTATION SKILLS

A Read the Presentation Skills paragraph **Referring to visuals** aloud. Elicit examples of types of visuals (pictures, infographics, slides, videos, etc.). Explain that visuals aid the audience's understanding of the speaker's message, and are especially useful in technical talks. Read the phrases aloud and have students repeat.

Have students preview the task.

▶ **9.13** Play the video. Check answers as a class.

B Read the task aloud. Have students work in pairs. Give students time to brainstorm a list of useful phrases for introducing all kinds of visuals. Elicit answers by having each pair share one or two expressions. Write them on the board so students have a mind map of useful expressions for referring to visuals. Some possible phrases include: *Here you can see that …; You'll see next that …; Can you see …?*

⮕ **EXTENSION ACTIVITY** Have students work in groups to make a public service announcement to explain one kind of drone technology. Tell them to choose one application of a drone that they've learned about in the unit and try to explain it to the public. Explain that groups should introduce the drone application, show it in a visual, and explain the benefits that this kind of application will have for the general public.

LESSON OVERVIEW

Aims: Debate drone technology; write an essay

COMMUNICATE

A Explain that students are going to have a debate. Read the main debate question aloud and then the two sides of the argument. Then let students divide themselves into groups based on their opinions. Alternately, divide the class evenly so each side is fairly represented and ask students to support that argument for the activity. Remind students that they have gathered a lot of background information about drones in the unit. Tell them to use this information, as well as any other background information or anecdotes they have.

B Give groups time to brainstorm a list of arguments. Point out that obvious arguments, the ones that students have come across in the unit so far, will be useful, but encourage students to also think of some not-so-obvious arguments. Tell them to discuss their ideas first before deciding which three to write in the chart.

Make sure students understand that counter arguments are what the other side might say. Explain that after students think of possible counter arguments, they should also think about their responses to such arguments. Note that students can also provide real-life examples or anecdotes to support their arguments.

C Read the box **Expressing disagreement** aloud. Explain that these expressions are slightly formal, as a class debate requires more formal language than what students will generally use with their peers. However, note that the expressions can also be used in regular conversation when

COMMUNICATE Debating Answers will vary.

A Work in groups. You are going to have a debate on the topic: Should we continue to develop drone technology? **Group A:** You think drones are useful and we should continue to develop them. **Group B:** You think drones are harmful. You are against developing them.

B In your group, think of at least three arguments and examples that support your position. Also, think about possible counter arguments and how you would respond. Make notes in the chart below.

Arguments supporting your position	Possible counter arguments

C Have a debate on the topic. Take turns explaining why your group's position is better.

Expressing disagreement

I don't think that's quite true. *Actually, I'd say that …*
I'm afraid I disagree with that. *I see your point, but we think …*

WRITING Discussing the applications of a technology Answers will vary.

Write a short essay. What applications of drone technology would you like to see? How would that change the way we do things?

Personally, I would like to see drones being used to help people who have difficulty getting around. Drones can help deliver groceries to them or allow them to …

A delivery drone from online shopping company Rakuten

someone disagrees with something strongly and wants to emphasize this disagreement. Have the two teams take turns presenting arguments and then counter arguments. If necessary, give teams a minute or so in between each argument to present a counter argument. After both teams have finished, take a written anonymous vote in which students decide their true opinions for or against drones. Tally the votes and announce the winner.

WRITING

Ask students to think of some possible applications for drones that they believe will be beneficial and will improve the lives of others. Tell them to choose an idea and write about that in their essay. Read the example essay aloud. Tell students that their essays should include an explanation or description of the technology and their ideas about how it will benefit others.

⭐ **CHALLENGE** Have students present the ideas in their essays to the class.

Presentation 3

MODEL PRESENTATION

A Complete the transcript of the presentation using the words in the box.

has employed	discover	invest	will create
passionate	innovations	could	prosthetic

Hi. My name is Joel. I'm so pleased to be here. Today, I'll be discussing something that I am very ¹_____passionate_____ about: space exploration.

I'm sure you've all heard of the space agency NASA. Some people claim that its space program is a waste of money. How many of you agree? Well, I personally believe it's money well spent. For one thing, many medical ²_____innovations_____ have been developed as a direct effect of space exploration. For example, when NASA was designing robots for space exploration, it developed shock-absorbing materials that are used today to help make ³_____prosthetic_____ limbs more comfortable.

Also, space exploration creates jobs. Since its beginnings, NASA ⁴_____has employed_____ thousands of engineers, scientists, and support staff. And a recent study shows that commercial space exploration ⁵_____will create_____ an average of 11,800 jobs per year over the next five years.

Finally, space exploration ⁶_____could_____ help save the human race. Pretend you live in a world destroyed by global warming. Space exploration gives us the opportunity to ⁷_____discover_____ new planets to live on. Even Stephen Hawking says that we may need to escape "our fragile planet" one day. We must therefore continue to ⁸_____invest_____ in the space program. Thank you very much.

B ▶ **P.3** Watch the presentation and check your answers.

C ▶ **P.3** Review the list of presentation skills from Units 1–9 below. Which does the speaker use? Check (✓) them as you watch again. Then compare with a partner.

The speaker …
- ✓ asks the audience questions
- ✓ asks the audience to imagine themselves in a particular situation
- ✓ uses examples the audience is familiar with
- ☐ uses props
- ☐ begins with a strong statement
- ☐ explains technical words that the audience may not understand
- ☐ raises their hand above their head
- ✓ includes a quote

125

B ▶ **P.3** Play the video to check answers.

C Have students preview the task.

▶ **P.3** Play the video again. Check answers as a class.

As a quick reminder, elicit the presentation skills from Units 1–6:

1. Involving the audience
2. Knowing your audience
3. Using props
4. Beginning with a strong statement
5. Explaining technical words
6. Being authentic

Then elicit the presentation skills for Units 7–9:

7. Using body movements and gestures
8. Using a case study
9. Referring to visuals

Ask students to comment on the body movements and gestures they saw in the video. Did they feel that the speaker was being authentic? Why?

Elicit any of the skills from the units so far that students saw in use in the presentation. For example, the speaker shows that he knows his audience by talking about the space agency NASA, which he knows everyone in the audience has heard of. Review the presentation skills from Units 7–9 in more detail. Elicit the language options or techniques for each that students can use in **Your Turn**.

Presentation 3

LESSON OVERVIEW

Aim: Students give a short presentation to a partner to make an argument for or against robotic surgery, using presentation skills they learned in Units 7–9 as well as relevant ones from previous units.

MODEL PRESENTATION

A Have students work individually to complete the sentences. Elicit points about the presentation:

1. What is the topic? (space exploration)
2. Is the speaker for or against it? (for)
3. What arguments against the topic does he present? (It's a waste of money.)
4. And what are his counter-arguments? (The technology that results from space exploration, such as medical devices, is important. Space exploration creates jobs, and it may save the human race.)

YOUR TURN

A Have students preview the task. Explain that they will all be presenting on the same topic, but that they can choose either side of the issue.

Give students five or ten minutes to brainstorm topics and write down notes about their arguments. Although it is not a topic in the box, remind students to also consider possible counter-arguments and their responses to those. Note that students will mostly be focusing on language and expressions learned in Unit 9 for this presentation. If time permits, have students do a quick page-by-page look at the unit to review the content.

B Read the useful phrases aloud as students repeat. Tell students to think about which ones would work best for their presentation content. Explain that they can also use other phrases that they learned in the units. Give students additional time to revise their notes and decide what language to use in their presentations.

C Tell students that they have two important roles in the activity: speaker and listener. Explain that they need to give their partner their full attention in order to evaluate in **C** and give effective feedback in **D**. Encourage listeners to ask questions during and after presentations.

YOUR TURN Answers will vary.

A You are going to plan and give a short presentation that argues for or against robotic surgery. Give some background information on the topic, think about what your position is, and explain your reasons. Make notes in the chart below.

> Background information (e.g. recent trends or statistics)
>
> Your position (for or against)
>
> Reasons for your position

B Look at the useful phrases in the box below. Think about which ones you will need in your presentation.

> **Useful phrases**
>
> Stating your position: *I'm convinced that …*
> *Personally, I believe …*
>
> Listing points: *For one thing, …*
> *Another reason I'm for / against …*
>
> Giving examples: *For instance, …*
> *As proof of that, …*

C Work with a partner. Take turns giving your presentation using your notes. Use some of the presentation skills from Units 1–9 below. As you listen, check (✓) each skill your partner uses.

> The speaker …
> ☐ asks the audience questions
> ☐ asks the audience to imagine themselves in a particular situation
> ☐ uses examples the audience is familiar with
> ☐ uses props
> ☐ begins with a strong statement
> ☐ explains technical words that the audience may not understand
> ☐ raises their hand above their head
> ☐ includes a quote

D Give your partner some feedback on their talk. Include at least two things you liked and one thing that could be improved.

126

D Remind students that when offering feedback, it's good to start with some praise. Elicit some simple phrases for students to praise each other: *That was really interesting; Great job; I enjoyed listening to that.*

Explain that after giving praise, students should offer some positive feedback (*You made a strong argument; You brought up a lot of good points*), and then offer any points that need to be improved (*I think a case study would have helped support your argument even more*).

⭐ **CHALLENGE** Have students take the feedback from their partners into account and then give their presentation again to a group or the entire class.

10 Connections

> **"** We spend roughly 60 percent of our communication time listening, but we're not very good at it. **"**

Julian Treasure
Author and blogger, TED speaker

UNIT GOALS

In this unit, you will ...

- talk about how to be a good listener.
- read about why we are not good at listening.
- watch a TED Talk about "conscious listening."

WARM UP

▶ **10.1** Watch part of Julian Treasure's TED Talk. Answer the questions with a partner.

1 Treasure says, "We retain just 25 percent of what we hear." Do you agree with him? Answers will vary.

2 Do you know anyone who is a good listener? What makes them a good listener? Answers will vary.

127

---

10 Connections

Idea Worth Spreading

Learning to listen consciously will lead to more meaningful relationships and connections in today's world.

WARM UP

Have students look over the picture, caption, and quote on the page. Read the quote aloud.

▶ **10.1** Play the preview clip of the TED Talk. Ask students to explain what they think the speaker means when he says we are *losing our listening*. He means that our listening skills have decreased.

For question 1, elicit the meaning of *retain*. Then ask students to think about how much they retain from their classes every day. Is it more than 25 percent? What about in conversations with friends?

For question 2, ask students to describe a person they know who is a good listener and what character traits that person has that make them a good listener. Do students observe that person do anything differently than others while listening?

● **EXTENSION ACTIVITY** Have students work in pairs. Ask them to go to the blog on Julian Treasure's website (juliantreasure.com) and find one post about communication that sounds interesting to them. Ask them to read the post and write a short summary of what Treasure says. Then have them present the main points of the post to the class.

UNIT GOALS

In this unit, students will read, watch, and talk about communicating with others, especially in regard to listening skills. They will learn why many people aren't good at listening, and analyze and learn tips on how to improve their own behavior. Students will use reporting verbs to talk about what they hear and watch, and they will be asked to analyze and evaluate their own listening skills. Note that the skills taught in the unit are not just relevant for English language learning, but for communicating and connecting with people in any language.

TED Speaker

Julian Treasure is a sound and communications expert who has given several TED Talks.

TED Talk Summary

We have increasingly poor skills when it comes to listening and retaining information. Treasure says the mental process of listening is being lost in modern times, and this is a major concern because listening is our path to understanding. He ends his talk with a series of exercises to help us relearn how to listen consciously.

10A

Our listening

VOCABULARY

A Have students work individually to complete the sentences. Tell them to pay careful attention to the situation being described when choosing a modifier for the verb *listen* in each case.

▶ **10.2** Play the audio/video and check answers as a class. Elicit or explain the meaning of each collocation by demonstrating each style of listening through a simple role play.

B Have students work individually to read each of the situations before getting into pairs. Explain that their choice of listening styles in each situation may differ depending on the person. Model the example aloud. Explain that partners should ask each other conditional questions like the question in the example.

○ **EXTENSION ACTIVITY** Have students work in pairs. Tell them to act out for the class one of the collocations in the vocabulary. Students perform a short role play between two people that demonstrates one kind of listening. Tell the class to shout out the answer when they know it.

A group of children listen intently to a story.

10A Our listening

VOCABULARY Collocations with *listen*

A ▶ **10.2** Complete the sentences. Circle the correct words. Then listen and check your answers.

1 The students all listened (**carefully** / **sympathetically**) as the teacher explained what to do.

2 All the voters listened (**anxiously** / **politely**) as the winner of the election was announced.

3 Despite the fact that the speech was much too long, everyone listened (**patiently** / **anxiously**).

4 The children listened (**effectively** / **with great interest**) to the storyteller.

5 A good doctor should listen (**sympathetically** / **with half an ear**) to patients' complaints.

6 We are often told to respect our elders and to listen (**politely** / **reluctantly**) to what they have to say.

B Work with a partner. Take turns asking how you would listen in the following situations. Choose from the collocations in **A**, and give reasons for your choices. Answers will vary.

1 You are at an airport and there is an announcement about a delay to your flight.

2 You are at a soccer match and the national anthem is being played.

3 A close friend is giving you relationship advice even though you didn't ask for it.

4 You are at a conference and the speaker is using technical jargon that you don't understand.

If you're at an airport and there's an announcement about a delay, how would you listen?

I'd listen really ..., because ...

128

Language Note

To *listen with half an ear* means to not listen attentively. The expression *listen with one ear* means the same. Some other idioms about listening that mention *ears* include:

When you say you're *all ears*, it means that you're listening carefully.

When you *lend an ear* to someone, you listen sympathetically.

If what you're saying *falls on deaf ears*, it means that the other person isn't listening at all.

LISTENING Mediation

> **Paraphrasing details**
>
> It's a good idea to repeat in your own words what someone has said so that you can be sure your understanding is correct.
>
> *It sounds like …*   *So you're saying that …*   *So you mean …*

A ▶ **10.3** Watch David Walker talk about the kinds of issues he deals with as a mediator. What specific example does he give? How did he resolve the dispute? A neighborly dispute involving a child with autism; by listening carefully to everyone's side of the story

B ▶ **10.4** Watch and list three tips Walker gives to improve our listening skills.

1 _____ Don't interrupt. _____

2 _____ Remove all distractions. _____

3 _____ Observe the emotions behind the words. _____

C **CRITICAL THINKING** Answers will vary.

Reflecting Do you think you would be a good mediator? Why or why not? Discuss with a partner.

David Walker is an experienced mediator.

SPEAKING Staying focused

A ▶ **10.5** How does Speaker B stay focused in meetings?
By turning the cell phone on "silent" and putting it out of sight, and by asking questions

A: Can I borrow your notes from today's meeting?

B: Sure. But why do you need them? Weren't you there too?

A: Yeah, but I was a bit distracted. I find it very difficult to concentrate in long meetings like that. My mind's always wandering.

B: Well, it's not always easy to stay focused. When I'm in a meeting, I find it helpful to turn my cell phone on "silent" and then put it somewhere I can't see it.

A: I tried that, but it didn't work. I still got sidetracked thinking about other things.

B: Hmm. Maybe you should join in the discussions more. Whenever I find myself getting distracted, I try to stay engaged by asking questions. You were pretty quiet in today's meeting.

A: You're right. I'll try to speak up more in tomorrow's session. Hopefully that'll help me stay focused and listen carefully.

B Practice the conversation with a partner.

C Work with a partner. How do you stay focused when listening to your teacher in class? Use the expressions in blue above to help you. Answers will vary.

> Whenever I get distracted in class, I look at the teacher and try to make eye contact with her.

> That's a good idea. I find it helpful to …

129

LISTENING

A Read **Paraphrasing details** aloud as students read along. Explain that paraphrasing is an important part of listening actively or consciously. When you paraphrase what someone has said to you, it shows that person that you were listening attentively. And it also lets you check your comprehension as they can correct you if you paraphrase incorrectly.

Have students preview the task. Elicit the meaning of the job *mediator* before students watch. Note that there are different types of mediators, but the overall responsibility of a mediator is to help solve a conflict between two people or two groups.

▶ **10.3** Play the video. Check answers as a class. Ask students to think about whether they have ever had a conflict that could have been better resolved with a mediator.

B Have students preview the task. Explain that students will now watch the rest of the interview.

▶ **10.4** Play the video. Check answers as a class. Write on the board: *Observe the emotions behind the words.* Ask students to paraphrase what this means. Ask students if they can recall a situation where they spoke too harshly during a conflict because they were feeling emotional at the moment.

C **CRITICAL THINKING** Read the questions aloud. Give students a little time to consider their answers. Ask partners to brainstorm together a list of characteristics that a good mediator has, before they decide if they would be a good one. Tell students to support their answers with reasons. If students don't think that they would be good mediators, ask them to name someone they know who would make a good mediator, and why.

SPEAKING

A Read the question aloud. Ask students to also think about what they do to stay focused in meetings.

▶ **10.5** Play the audio/video. Check answers as a class. Ask students if they think Speaker B's advice is useful or not. Elicit some other tips for how to stay focused in a long meeting. Point out the expression *You're right*. Explain that this is a useful phrase for telling someone that you think they've given you good advice.

B Model the conversation aloud with a student. Then have students work in pairs to practice. Make sure they alternate between A and B roles.

C Read the task aloud. Give students time to go back over the words in blue in the conversation in **A**. Model the example aloud with a volunteer. Elicit or explain the meaning of *distracted*. After students discuss in pairs, elicit ideas from each pair. Write them on the board in a mind map. Encourage students to use the ideas to help them become better listeners in their classes.

10B Sound facts

LESSON OVERVIEW

Aims: Read an infographic about sound and listening; talk about the results of a survey

Infographic Summary: Six fascinating facts about the things we hear and how we listen are introduced in the infographic. While 85 percent of what we learn is through listening, we only remember 20 percent of what we heard an hour later. However, some good news is that 55 percent of the meaning of a spoken message is actually communicated nonverbally and 38 percent through tone of voice, so perhaps picking up on other cues can help us improve our listening skills even more than learning to pay closer attention to what is being said.

LANGUAGE FOCUS

A Read the question aloud.

▶ **10.6** Play the audio/video as students read along. Then give them additional time to look over the infographic. Elicit opinions about which piece of information is the most surprising and why.

B Read the questions aloud and tell students to listen for the answers.

▶ **10.7** Play the audio/video. Check answers as a class.

⭐ **CHALLENGE** Test the students' listening skills. Have students write and read a list of 13 grocery items to a partner, who then must repeat them all back after hearing the list once.

C Have students read over the language chart for **Reporting what someone said**.

▶ **10.8** Play the audio/video. Direct students to page 188 for more information.

LANGUAGE FOCUS Learning to listen

A ▶ **10.6** Read the information. Which fact do you find most surprising? Answers will vary.

INTERESTING FACTS ABOUT SOUND

The next time you get ready to have a conversation with someone, consider these facts about sound and listening.

- **85%** of what we learn is through listening (not talking or reading).
- Less than **2%** of the population has had formal training on how to listen.
- After listening to someone talk, we can immediately recall about **50%** of what was said. One hour later, we remember less than **20%** of what we heard.
- We think at least **four** times faster than we speak.
- In a spoken message, only **7%** is conveyed by the words used. **55%** of the meaning is derived from facial expressions, and **38%** is indicated by the tone of voice.
- **Words** are processed by our short-term memory. **Images** go directly into long-term memory.

B ▶ **10.7** Listen to the conversation. What was Tom's problem? What does Jane suggest?
A lot of people found Tom's presentation boring. Jane suggests that he use more visuals.

C ▶ **10.8** Watch and study the language in the chart.

Reporting what someone said

"Listening is a learned process."	He said / told me	(that) listening was a learned process.
"You'll have to bring your notes tomorrow."	She said (that) I would have to bring my notes the next day.	
"Don't interrupt."	He told me not to interrupt.	
"How did your test go?"	She asked him how his test had gone.	
"You should use audio-visuals."	She suggested that I use audio-visuals.	
"I'll buy you lunch today."	He promised to buy her lunch that day.	
According to experts, multitasking is often a barrier to effective listening.		

For more information on **reported speech**, see Grammar Summary 10 on page 188.

130

Grammar Note

The language chart introduces language for reported speech. While a quote is considered *direct speech*, saying what someone else has said is called *reported* (or *indirect*) *speech*.

Reported speech uses verbs like *say, ask, told, promise*, and *believe*. Pronouns are used to introduce the speaker, and the past tense is used to match the reporting verb—since information is being relayed that has already been said.

When the direct quote is a request, promise, or advice, the infinitive follows the reporting verb: *She promised to be in touch after the interview. He asked me to call back next week.*

Note that for questions, the question word is inserted in the reported sentence, such as in the example of *how* in the language chart. In cases of *yes/no* questions (*Do …? Is …?*), *if* or *whether* is usually inserted in the reported sentence.

D ▶ **10.7** Listen to the conversation in **B** again. Using reported speech, write what the speakers said.

1 "How did your presentation go this morning?"
She asked him ___how his presentation had gone that morning.___

2 "I'll try to use more visual aids and slides tomorrow."
He said that ___he would try to use more visual aids and slides the next day.___

3 "Don't worry."
She told him _____ ___not to worry.___

E Complete the information with the words from the box. Two options are extra.

suggested	explained	according to	were
promised	called	said	are

¹ ___According to___ Richard Branson—the founder of Virgin Group—the best leaders ² ___are___ great listeners. In an interview with *Forbes*, he ³ ___explained___ why listening was important for good leadership, and shared anecdotes from his own business dealings. He ⁴ ___said___ that business leaders need to listen carefully to feedback from staff and customers, which requires effort and focus. Unfortunately, many people think of listening as a passive activity; Branson even ⁵ ___called___ it a "dying art." In order to improve people's active listening, he ⁶ ___suggested___ that we pay close attention not just to what someone says, but the way in which they say it—their body language and facial expressions.

SPEAKING A survey   Answers will vary.

A Work in pairs. The graph below shows the results of a survey. Tell your partner about it. Take turns reporting each statement.

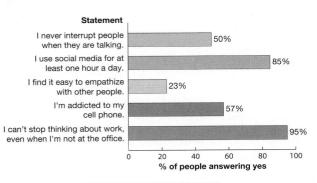

Statement

- I never interrupt people when they are talking. 50%
- I use social media for at least one hour a day. 85%
- I find it easy to empathize with other people. 23%
- I'm addicted to my cell phone. 57%
- I can't stop thinking about work, even when I'm not at the office. 95%

0 20 40 60 80 100
% of people answering yes

Fifty percent of people said that …

According to the survey, 85 percent of people …

B With your partner, discuss whether each statement in the graph helps or prevents effective listening. Give reasons for your conclusions.

131

SPEAKING

A Give students time to look over the graph in detail. Explain that students are going to explain pieces of information in the graph to their partners. This is a good opportunity to point out the difference between reported sentences with *According to …,* which use the present tense, and those with reporting verbs like *said*, which require the past tense. Model the examples aloud. Point out that the first speaker uses the subject of *Fifty percent of people* based on the information in the graph.

B Tell partners to go through each statement and discuss it in relation to good listening skills. Ask students to also discuss whether they agree or disagree with each statement.

⊙ **EXTENSION ACTIVITY** Take the survey in **Speaking** as a class and record the results on the board. Encourage some students to take leadership in organizing this survey. After the survey has been taken, ask another group of students to calculate the results to draw a graph on the board. Finally, have the remaining students explain the results using reported speech.

D Have students preview the task. Note that the reporting verb is already chosen, and that students only have to change the tense of the second verb.

▶ **10.7** Play the audio/video. Have students work individually to complete the activity before checking answers as a class.

E Have students work individually. Tell them to use the language chart for support. Have them check answers in pairs by taking turns to read the paragraph aloud to each other.

⊙ **EXTENSION ACTIVITY** Have students work in pairs. Ask them to think of two pieces of advice that someone has given them recently. Tell them to explain the situation to their partner and then use reported speech to share the advice they received.

Unit 10   **131**

LESSON OVERVIEW

Aims: Read and comprehend an article about why we are generally not good at listening; understand main ideas and identify cause and effect

Target Vocabulary: disruptive, enhance, pioneer, overestimate, rapport

Reading Summary: Our listening skills are on the decline. We may think that as we get older and our brains become more fully developed, we become better listeners; however, research shows the opposite. We tend to think about too many things at once, which makes us poor listeners. Younger children aren't as easily distracted as teenagers and adults, so they actually retain more information. In addition, modern technology has shortened our attention spans by creating even more distractions and interruptions.

PRE-READING

A Read the question aloud. Give students time to think alone before having them work in pairs to share their predictions. Tell them to give reasons for their ideas.

B Give students time to skim the two paragraphs individually and then compare what they learned with their partner. Elicit a class discussion to hear about students' predictions and reactions to the actual information.

▶ **10.9** Play the audio/video as students read along. Go over any unfamiliar language. See **Language Note**.

10C The lost art of listening?

PRE-READING Predicting/Skimming   Answers will vary.

A Who do you think are generally better listeners: high school students or younger kids? Predict and discuss with a partner.

B Skim the first two paragraphs. Check your prediction.

▶ **10.9**

1 Do you think you're a good listener? Chances are you do. But studies show that most people seriously **overestimate** their ability to listen. The truth is we are generally not
5 good at listening, and our listening comprehension declines as we age.

   This was proven by Dr. Ralph Nichols, a **pioneer** in the scientific study of listening behavior. With the help of school teachers in Minnesota, he conducted
10 a simple experiment to test students' listening skills. He had teachers stop what they were doing mid-class, and then asked students to describe what their teachers had been talking about. You might assume that older kids, with more developed
15 brains, would be better listeners. The results, however, showed otherwise: While 90 percent of first- and second-graders gave correct responses, this percentage dropped rapidly as the students got older. A little under half of junior high students could
20 remember correctly, and only 25 percent of high school students got the answers right.

   So why aren't we good at listening? One reason concerns the speed at which we think. The adult brain can process up to around 400 words per
25 minute, more than three times faster than the speed an average person speaks. This means that we can easily think about something else while someone is talking to us, allowing our mind to wander or get sidetracked. Thinking about how you will reply while
30 someone is still talking is one of the most common

132

barriers to effective listening. The younger students in Dr. Nichols's experiment were better listeners partly because their brains were less developed—they lacked the extra brain power to be distracted.
35   Another factor that contributes to our poor listening is our ever-decreasing attention span. According to a study conducted by Microsoft, the age of smartphones has had a negative impact here. In 2000—around the time the mobile
40 revolution began—the average human attention span was 12 seconds; by 2013, it had fallen to 8 seconds. Even a goldfish—with an average attention span of 9 seconds—can hold a thought for longer!
45   Our mobile devices also provide constant distractions, which can be very **disruptive** to listening.

➡ **EXTENSION ACTIVITY** Have students work individually to write down everything that they remember so far from today's class. Tell them to list every detail that they can remember. Go around the class and elicit one detail from every student; correct any mistaken information. Ask students to tally what percentage of the accurate details mentioned were on their list. Were they able to remember everything correctly?

Skill Note

Skimming involves reading quickly for main ideas. When skimming a paragraph, students should read the first and last sentence of the paragraph, and then quickly skim over the sentences in between to get general meaning. Explain that students should be reading very quickly, picking up on key words and phrases that can give them a general idea of what the text is about.

Mobile devices are changing the way people interact, and can negatively affect our listening ability.

To be *sidetracked* (line 29) means to be distracted, usually from something important.

A person's *attention span* (line 36) is the amount of time they are able to concentrate on one task.

Test results have shown that being interrupted by a cell phone message (or even just expecting a message) lowers listening comprehension by 20 percent. Similar results were observed even before the age of digital technology. According to a 1987 study, people could remember only about 10 percent of a face-to-face conversation following a brief distraction.

Interruptions and other distractions, whether digital or more traditional, can cause a dramatic decline in listening ability—but they don't have to. More and more people now realize that listening is a skill that can be developed through practice. Learning to observe a speaker's body language and emotions, for example, can improve our active listening. Even the simple act of note-taking or making eye contact can help us stay focused while listening.

Many schools and businesses now provide courses in effective listening, as it has been proven to **enhance** teamwork and build **rapport**. Research also suggests that people who are good listeners make better leaders. A study in the *Academy of Management Journal* indicated that employees who don't believe their bosses are listening to them are less likely to offer helpful suggestions and new ideas.

The fact is that listening plays a central role in everything we do—both socially and professionally—so the rewards of effective listening are many. As Dr. Ralph Nichols once said, "The most basic of all human needs is the need to understand and be understood. The best way to understand people is to listen to them."

133

Content Note

The author mentions Dr. Ralph Nichols twice in the passage as an expert and pioneer in listening communication. Nichols is considered to be one of the first scientists to bring attention to the field of listening and its importance in human development. He was a professor at the University of Minnesota, and through his research and writing, an entire field was developed with the understanding that listening is a skill that can be taught, and that learning to be an effective listener can change a person's life. This is why Nichols is considered a pioneer and has been called the "father of the field of listening."

Language Note

To *conduct* (line 9) a study or research simply means to do it. The verb implies that something needs to be organized in order to be carried out.

An interruption that happens *mid-class* (line 12) happens while that class is in session. It does not necessarily mean exactly halfway through the class, but simply an interruption during the class.

First- and second-graders (line 17) are in the first two years of elementary school. Usually, a child becomes a first-grader the year they turn six and a second-grader the year they turn seven.

UNDERSTANDING MAIN IDEAS

Have students work individually. Check answers as a class. Note that item **a** may at first seem accurate to some students; however, the author does not specifically say that limiting modern technology is the best way to become a better listener, but it is one way.

IDENTIFYING CAUSE AND EFFECT

Have students preview the task. Note that they will have to go back to the passage to look at the supporting evidence in detail. Remind students that cause and effect are the same as reason and result. Check answers as a class. Ask students to raise their hands if they've ever attended a lesson or seminar on how to listen effectively. Elicit some suggestions that the students learned about how to listen better.

➡ **EXTENSION ACTIVITY** Have students work in small groups. Tell them to take one of the cause-and-effect relationships in **Identifying Cause and Effect** and create a commercial or public service announcement to show others the relationship between the two. Tell groups to make informative commercials that aim to change people's thinking or habits about the point that they choose from the list. Have students perform their commercials for the class.

BUILDING VOCABULARY

A Have students work individually to complete the activity. Check answers as a class. Elicit example sentences using each word. Write them on the board.

B **CRITICAL THINKING** Read the questions aloud as students read along. Elicit or explain the meaning of *guilty of*. Have students discuss in pairs first, and if time permits, have them share their thoughts in small groups.

UNDERSTANDING MAIN IDEAS

Which sentence is the author most likely to agree with?

a There are many techniques we can use to help us stay focused while listening, but the best way to improve our listening skills is to limit our use of modern technology.

b Effective listening is something we all do automatically, although most of us need to be taught the proper tools and techniques in order to be good at it.

c The mobile revolution has had a negative impact on our ability to listen, but there are various techniques we can use to improve our listening skills.

IDENTIFYING CAUSE AND EFFECT

Complete the diagram showing causes and effects.

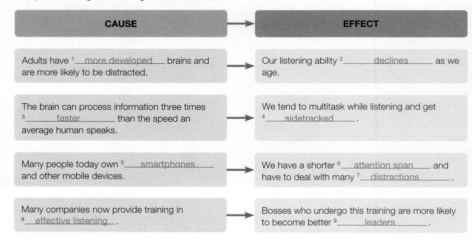

CAUSE	EFFECT
Adults have ¹ _more developed_ brains and are more likely to be distracted.	Our listening ability ² _declines_ as we age.
The brain can process information three times ³ _faster_ than the speed an average human speaks.	We tend to multitask while listening and get ⁴ _sidetracked_ .
Many people today own ⁵ _smartphones_ and other mobile devices.	We have a shorter ⁶ _attention span_ and have to deal with many ⁷ _distractions_ .
Many companies now provide training in ⁸ _effective listening_ .	Bosses who undergo this training are more likely to become better ⁹ _leaders_ .

BUILDING VOCABULARY

A Match the words in blue from the passage to their definitions.

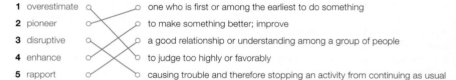

1 overestimate — one who is first or among the earliest to do something
2 pioneer — to make something better; improve
3 disruptive — a good relationship or understanding among a group of people
4 enhance — to judge too highly or favorably
5 rapport — causing trouble and therefore stopping an activity from continuing as usual

B **CRITICAL THINKING** Answers will vary.

Reflecting What behavior mentioned in the passage are you most guilty of? What can you do to change this? Discuss with a partner.

134

➡ **EXTENSION ACTIVITY** Ask students to keep a journal for the rest of the unit to note any time they get distracted during class. Ask them to write down when it happens and what distracted them. Were they thinking about something unrelated to the class content? Were they distracted by a noise? Were they thinking about their email inbox or a text message they wanted to send? Note that this journal will help students in **Lesson E** as they evaluate their listening skills, because they will already have a record of what keeps them from listening effectively.

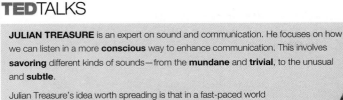

10D Five ways to listen better

TEDTALKS

JULIAN TREASURE is an expert on sound and communication. He focuses on how we can listen in a more **conscious** way to enhance communication. This involves **savoring** different kinds of sounds—from the **mundane** and **trivial**, to the unusual and **subtle**.

Julian Treasure's idea worth spreading is that in a fast-paced world where everyone is competing for attention, "conscious listening" may be the only way we can truly understand one another and maintain meaningful relationships.

PREVIEWING

Read the paragraphs above. Match each **bold** word to its meaning. You will hear these words in the TED Talk.

1 everyday; normal — mundane
2 enjoying — savoring
3 having qualities not easy to notice — subtle
4 not important — trivial
5 aware of one's surroundings and knowing what is happening — conscious

VIEWING

A ▶ **10.10** Read the scenarios below. Then watch Part 1 of the TED Talk. Match the listening techniques in the box to the correct scenario. Write **a**, **b**, or **c**.

a pattern recognition	b differencing	c filtering

Scenario 1
You move from the countryside to the city. At first, you find it hard to sleep because of all the traffic and general noise. After a few weeks, you get used to it and hardly notice the noise.

Scenario 2
You are listening to a lecture. You are only interested in some key facts and figures. You are not paying attention to anything else the speaker is saying.

Scenario 3
You are at a party, surrounded by lots of people talking. A friend arrives and calls out your name. You hear him, even though it is noisy and he is several meters away.

Listening technique: __b__

Listening technique: __c__

Listening technique: __a__

135

10D

Five ways to listen better

PREVIEWING

Have students work individually to read the paragraphs. Tell them to pay attention to how each bold word is used in context in order to understand its meaning. Then have students work individually to match the words and definitions before checking answers in pairs. Remind students of the **Warm Up** preview clip. Tell them to use all the language and information they have learned to support their viewing of the TED Talk.

VIEWING

A Have students preview the task. Tell them to familiarize themselves with the words in the box so they can listen selectively if necessary.

   ▶ **10.10** Play Part 1 of the TED Talk. Check answers as a class or play the check-your-answers part of the video. Elicit or explain the meaning of any unfamiliar language. Suggestions for Part 1 include *pink noise, discount, unconscious,* and *intention*.

⭐ **CHALLENGE** Elicit new example scenarios for each listening technique that Treasure describes. Note that these techniques mostly occur naturally, and are not consciously done on our part.

LESSON OVERVIEW

Aims: Watch and understand a talk about improving our listening skills; observe and practice using acronyms

Target Vocabulary: conscious, mundane, savor, subtle, trivial

TED Talk Summary: Communications expert Julian Treasure begins his talk by explaining three techniques we use to filter through all the sounds around us. He also says outright that our listening skills as a species are in trouble. Part of the reason for this is that modern technology causes constant interruptions and has shortened the average attention span and made us impatient listeners. Additionally, the world today is simply noisier than in times past, and we have to filter out more sounds in order to listen consciously. Treasure laments that we are heading down a dangerous path; he says that losing our listening skills is causing us to develop into less empathetic people, which is not a positive situation for the world. He ends by introducing a series of exercises on how to be a better listener. The exercises include learning to enjoy both silence and sounds in a new way, as well as specific steps on how to be an active listener.

B Have students preview the task. Explain that students will have to infer which point Treasure would agree with based on what they will hear in the video.

▶ **10.11** Play Part 2 of the TED Talk. Check answers as a class or play the check-your-answers part of the video. Write on the board: *Oratory versus Sound Bites*. Elicit the meaning of what Treasure meant when he said that we prefer sound bites to oratory these days. He means that the public generally doesn't want to listen to long speeches or explanations. Instead, we want quick one-line summaries. Elicit or explain the meaning of any additional unfamiliar language. Suggestions for Part 2 include *reverberation, micro-noises, cacophony,* and *desensitized*.

C Have students preview the task. Write on the board *conscious listening*. Elicit an explanation of its meaning after students watch.

▶ **10.12** Play Part 3 of the TED Talk. Check answers as a class.

D Have students preview the task. Encourage them to try to write the one-word answers before watching again. Were they listening consciously enough the first time to remember?

▶ **10.12** Play Part 3 of the TED Talk again. Check answers as a class, eliciting a summary for the step that each word in the acronym stands for. Elicit or explain the meaning of any additional unfamiliar language. Suggestions for Part 3 include *recalibrate, mundane,* and *Sanskrit*.

E **CRITICAL THINKING** Read the task and statements aloud. Note that these are three different ways in which the techniques that Treasure teaches can be applied. Have students share the technique they think is the most effective to build their own conscious listening skills. Tell them to give specific examples from their everyday lives as to how they can apply this technique.

VOCABULARY IN CONTEXT

▶ **10.13** Play the video. If necessary, play it again.

B ▶ **10.11** Watch Part 2 of the TED Talk. Would Julian Treasure agree with the following statements? Circle **Y** for yes or **N** for no.

1 Sounds help define our surroundings. (Y) N

2 Listening is difficult and tiring because the world is now so noisy. (Y) N

3 Many people nowadays prefer quick sound bites to actual conversations. (Y) N

4 We are becoming more sensitive to noise and what's being said in the media. Y (N)

5 It's less important for us to practice conscious listening now because of modern technology. Y (N)

C ▶ **10.12** Watch Part 3 of the TED Talk. Match each tool for conscious listening in the box to its corresponding exercise.

silence	the mixer	savoring

1 Listen closely to the ticking of a clock. Nod your head in time with the "beat" of the clock, as if you are listening to music on headphones.
Tool: _____savoring_____

2 Find a quiet area in your house, and sit on the floor in a cross-legged position. Close your eyes, clear your mind, and meditate for a few minutes.
Tool: _____silence_____

3 Listen to a song and identify the different instruments and voices you hear. Practice differentiating one sound from another.
Tool: _____the mixer_____

D ▶ **10.12** Watch Part 3 of the TED Talk again. What does the acronym RASA mean? Fill out the acronym in the space provided on the right.

(R) _____Receive_____
(A) _____Appreciate_____
(S) _____Summarize_____
(A) _____Ask_____

E **CRITICAL THINKING** Answers will vary.

Applying Which statement below do you personally agree with the most? Explain your reasoning to a partner and give examples. As you discuss, take turns applying the RASA techniques.

a I want to make a list of mundane sounds and practice savoring each of them.

b I think conscious listening is an important skill and should be taught in schools.

c I need to limit my use of social media and have more meaningful face-to-face conversations with my friends.

VOCABULARY IN CONTEXT

▶ **10.13** Watch the excerpts from the TED Talk. Choose the correct meaning of the words.
1.b; 2.c; 3.a

Language Note

Part 1

Different types of noise are categorized by color. The term *pink noise* refers to random sounds that include some low octaves. To *discount* something means it's not worth paying attention to. In the case of listening, Treasure means that we filter out those sounds. When we are *unconscious* of something, we are not aware that we are doing it. To listen with *intention* means to be aware of what you are doing—to listen consciously with purpose.

Part 2

A *reverberation* is a sound effect that continues. *Micro-noises* refer to almost unnoticeable sounds, and a *cacophony* is many sounds happening at once. When you are *desensitized* to something, you have stopped being shocked or surprised by it.

Part 3

To *recalibrate* something means to reset it. Something that is *mundane* is usually not considered interesting or unique. The language *Sanskrit*, which the word *rasa* comes from, is an ancient language from India.

PRESENTATION SKILLS Using acronyms to summarize

Using acronyms is an effective way to help your audience remember and understand key points or steps. To form an acronym, take the first letter of each word you are trying to remember. Next, arrange the letters into a word that is easy to pronounce. You can add vowels if necessary.

When using an acronym for the first time in a presentation, make sure you explain its meaning properly.

A ▶ **10.14** Watch part of Julian Treasure's TED Talk. How does he introduce the acronym RASA and explain its meaning? Complete the excerpt below with the phrase he uses.

"And finally, an acronym … the acronym is RASA, which is the Sanskrit word for juice or essence. And RASA ___stands for___ *Receive*, which means pay attention to the person; *Appreciate*, making little noises like 'hmm,' 'oh,' 'OK'; *Summarize*, the word 'so' is very important in communication; and *Ask*, ask questions afterwards."

B Below are two common acronyms. Fill out each of them in the space provided. You may look them up if you're not sure what they mean.

(N) ___National___   (P) ___President___

(A) ___Aeronautics and___   (O) ___of___

(S) ___Space___   (T) ___the___

(A) ___Administration___   (U) ___United___

                            (S) ___States___

C Work with a partner. What other acronyms can you think of? What do they mean? Answers will vary.

137

meanings with the class. Note that acronyms don't have to be words that already exist. Instead, they can become words when they are read as acronyms, such as *POTUS* (President of the United States). Note that these days, acronyms are commonly used in messaging or texting in order to shorten words. They are also traditionally used for military terms as well as for language specific to certain industries. Some commonly known acronyms include *ASAP* (as soon as possible), *MIA* (missing in action), *PM* (private message), *BTW* (by the way), *AWOL* (absent without leave), *BFF* (best friend forever), and *FYI* (for your information).

⭐ **CHALLENGE** Ask students to share their impression of the TED Talk with a partner. Tell partners to practice using RASA as they listen.

➡ **EXTENSION ACTIVITY** Tell students to use their names to make an acronym about themselves. Explain that they should tell the class some interesting information about themselves by using the letters of their names. Have each student present their acronym to the class.

PRESENTATION SKILLS

A Read the Presentation Skills paragraph **Using acronyms to summarize** aloud. Note that this is a new skill that students haven't seen in other TED Talks. Acronyms are considered a useful tool in helping to remember information. By creating an acronym for his audience, Treasure is giving them an easy way to recall the information he told them, which is his way of helping them listen more effectively. Have students preview the task.

▶ **10.14** Play the video. Check answers as a class. Ask students to comment on whether they think the acronym RASA will help them remember the steps that Treasure is teaching. Also ask students to share any tricks they know for remembering information more effectively.

B Have students work individually or in pairs. Check answers as a class.

C Elicit any other popular acronyms that students are familiar with. Ask them to share the acronyms and their

Conscious listening

LESSON OVERVIEW

Aims: Take a survey on listening skills and discuss; write a personal evaluation

COMMUNICATE

A Have students work individually to complete the survey or read each question aloud to the class, eliciting a paraphrase to check meaning. Then have students mark their answers.

B Have students work in pairs to then go through the survey to share their answers. Have students work with a partner whom they have worked with often in this unit so that they are knowledgeable about each other's listening styles.

C Model the example with a volunteer. Point out that students should talk about what kind of listener they think they are, and that partners are expected to agree or disagree based on what they know about the person, what they've experienced in communicating with them, and what information they shared in **B**. Encourage partners to ask follow-up questions to get more details about each point. Tell them to also share personal stories to give examples of how they typically listen. Read the questions aloud for **Asking follow-up questions**.

WRITING

Read the task aloud. Explain that students should write about their own listening skills first, based on their answers in the survey and the discussion with their partners.

Read the model aloud as students read along. Point out that the writer starts with an overall evaluation and then goes into detail about specific areas, and especially focuses on improvements that he or she hopes to make. If time permits, have students read their paragraphs to their partners. Do the two agree on the evaluations? If not, in what areas do they disagree?

COMMUNICATE How good are your listening skills? Answers will vary.

A Are you a good listener? Read the questions below and check (✓) your answers.

When someone is talking to you, do you …	Not usually	Sometimes	Yes, I usually do
1 keep an eye on the clock?	☐	☐	☐
2 make eye contact with the speaker?	☐	☐	☐
3 pay attention to the speaker's body language?	☐	☐	☐
4 check your cell phone for messages as you listen?	☐	☐	☐
5 interrupt the speaker if they say something you disagree with?	☐	☐	☐
6 think about how you'll reply as you listen?	☐	☐	☐
7 listen more for facts than for feelings?	☐	☐	☐
8 take notes about important information you've heard?	☐	☐	☐
9 wait for the speaker to finish before forming an opinion?	☐	☐	☐
10 make physical gestures (like nodding) to show that you're listening?	☐	☐	☐

B Work with a partner. Take turns asking and answering the questions. Circle your partner's answers.

C Look back at the answers. With your partner, discuss whether you are each good at conscious listening, and give reasons for your conclusions. You may ask follow-up questions to get more information if necessary.

> I think I'm a good listener because I …

> That's true. But you also sometimes …

Asking follow-up questions
Can you elaborate on that, please?   *Can you give an example?*

WRITING A survey report Answers will vary.

Look at the results above. Write one or two paragraphs summarizing the results of the survey, and include details about what makes a good listener.

> The survey showed that while I'm generally a pretty good listener, there are still some things I can work on to improve my listening skills. In particular, I tend to keep an eye on the clock during conversations. This is a bad habit because …
>
> According to the survey, David is good at conscious listening because …

⭐ **CHALLENGE** Have students instead write an essay that compares and contrasts their style of listening with their partner's.

➡ **EXTENSION ACTIVITY** Have students take the survey home and give it to someone they know well, such as a parent, sibling, or roommate. Tell them to first write a paragraph that evaluates the person's listening skills based only on their experiences with that person. Then after the person takes the survey, have students write about whether there is a gap between what the person thinks their listening style is and what the student's experience is with that person. Have students report the results of the exercise by giving a brief presentation to the class. Ask the class to conclude if most people know their own listening skill level or not.

11 Life in the Slow Lane

> **"** [Cloudspotting] is a pointless activity, which is precisely why it's so important. **"**

Gavin Pretor-Pinney
Science writer, TED speaker

UNIT GOALS

In this unit, you will ...

- talk about slowing down and monotasking.
- read about how nature affects the brain.
- watch a TED Talk about clouds and how we can benefit from appreciating them.

WARM UP

▶ **11.1** Watch part of Gavin Pretor-Pinney's TED Talk. Answer the questions with a partner.

1 Did you enjoy looking up at the clouds when you were a child? Why or why not? Answers will vary.

2 Can you think of any English expressions that mention clouds? Are these expressions positive or negative?
Answers will vary.

139

---

11 Life in the Slow Lane

kinds of clouds while explaining the benefits to our lives of stopping to notice clouds more often.

Idea Worth Spreading

We can all benefit from looking up and enjoying the clouds more often.

WARM UP

Have students look over the picture, caption, and quote on the page. Read the quote aloud. Elicit the meaning of *cloudspotting*.

▶ **11.1** Play the preview clip of the TED Talk. Point out the unit title: *Life in the Slow Lane*. Elicit ideas about what the expression means. The "slow lane" refers to the lane on a highway that the slow drivers use. The idiom "life in the slow lane" is used to describe someone who is generally more contemplative about decisions, and not rushing through life to get to the next step. The idiom "living in the fast lane" describes a lifestyle that is more typical in modern times.

For question 1, tell students to share any childhood memories they have of cloudspotting. Ask them to also talk about whether they do it these days. Tell students to also share other ways they connected with nature when they were young.

For question 2, if necessary, let students go online to find some expressions about clouds. Then have each pair introduce one expression and its meaning. In English idioms and expressions, clouds are often used as a symbol of something negative. Some examples of cloud idioms include: *cloud of suspicion, under a cloud, head in the clouds, behind every cloud there's a silver lining*. Ask students to also share how clouds are used in expressions in their native language. Are clouds considered a negative or positive symbol?

UNIT GOALS

In this unit, students will read, watch, and talk about slowing down in this fast-paced world. Students will learn language to discuss ideas about how to slow down and get more in touch with nature. As the unit theme is focused on getting us to slow down, encourage an environment of "slow learning" and monotasking for this unit to see if it has an effect on students' learning and ability to retain information.

TED Speaker

Gavin Pretor-Pinney has written two books about clouds and is the founder of the Cloud Appreciation Society.

TED Talk Summary

Pretor-Pinney tells us that it's time to slow down and pay more attention to the clouds. Not only are clouds overlooked, but they've been given so many negative associations in our language and culture that we see them as something undesirable. In fact, clouds are beautiful and fascinating, and looking at them gives us an excuse to slow down. Pretor-Pinney teaches his audience about the various

The slow movement

VOCABULARY

A Have students work individually to read the paragraph and match the words and definitions. Tell them to pay attention to how each word is used in context before choosing the definition. Check answers as a class, going over meaning when necessary. Elicit additional example sentences for each vocabulary word.

B Have students work individually. Then have them check answers in pairs. Tell them to make a sentence with each collocation to see if it sounds natural. Check answers as a class.

C Preview the task as a class. Read each of the categories aloud. Ask students to brainstorm possible activities for each that would represent the Slow Movement well.

⭐ **CHALLENGE** Ask students to talk about which of the slow activities in **C** they'd like to try and why.

➡ **EXTENSION ACTIVITY** Have students work individually. Tell them to use what they discussed in **C** to think about how they can slow down one activity they do regularly now. Ask students to choose an activity that they do on a daily or weekly basis. Then tell them to think about how they could change this one activity to better represent the ideals of the Slow Movement. Have students write a description of their new, slow activity.

A cheese stand at a Slow Food event in Turin, Italy

11A The slow movement

VOCABULARY Slowing down

A Read the paragraph below. Then match each **bold** word to its definition.

Today, people are living increasingly stressful lives trying to **juggle** work, family, and friends. There never seems to be enough time to do everything. As a result, many of us feel a need to rush through life. We now have faster cars, faster Internet, even "fast food." In response to the rush of modern life, a growing number of people have embraced the "Slow Movement." This began in 1986, when Carlo Petrini founded Slow Food to protest against the opening of the first McDonald's in Italy. He wanted to **restore** an **appreciation** for local food cultures and traditions, and promote quality over convenience. The Slow Movement encourages us to do things like eating and exercising in a more **leisurely** way, and to be more aware of our surroundings. This way, we can develop more **meaningful** ties with other people.

1 juggle — to balance or keep several activities in progress
2 restore — to bring back
3 appreciation — assessment of the true value of something
4 leisurely — relaxed; without hurry
5 meaningful — worthwhile; significant

B Cross out the word that does NOT collocate with each **bold** word.

1 **juggle**	projects	responsibilities	~~experiences~~	jobs
2 **restore**	balance	~~effort~~	order	confidence
3 **leisurely**	walk	meal	pace	~~hotel~~
4 **meaningful**	conversation	~~expert~~	relationship	life

C Work with a partner. Below are some branches of the Slow Movement. What kinds of activities do you think each one does? Answers will vary.

Slow Exercise	Slow Reading	Slow Travel	Slow Fashion

140

Content Note

Cittaslow is an organization founded in Italy that works to spread the philosophy of Carlo Petrini's Slow Movement across Italy and the world. Cities that want to participate register to become "slow cities" that focus on high-quality, local food production and celebrate a slower quality of life. Since 1999, Cittaslow's registry has expanded from Italy to an international network of small cities in 30 countries around the world.

LISTENING Living in the present

> **Repeating main ideas**
> Speakers sometimes repeat key points from their talk for emphasis or to make their main ideas clearer.
>
> *Again, ...*   *Like I said before, ...*   *As mentioned earlier, ...*

A ▶ **11.2** Watch author Carl Honoré talk about the importance of slowing down. Who helped him realize he was living life too fast?
His son

B ▶ **11.2** Watch again. What is Honoré's main message?

   a By doing things slowly, we can make sure we do them correctly.

   (b) We need to do things at the right speed for ourselves—faster isn't always better.

   c Leading a slower-paced life gives us more freedom to explore and try new things.

C **CRITICAL THINKING**   Answers will vary.

   Reflecting Are there aspects of your own life you would like to slow down? Discuss with a partner.

Carl Honoré, author of the best-selling book *In Praise of Slowness*

SPEAKING Leading a slower-paced life

A ▶ **11.3** How will the camping retreat help Speaker A unwind?
By providing a break from technology, and through activities like hiking, kayaking, and yoga

A: It's Friday. Finally!

B: Yeah, it's been a long week. Do you have any plans for the weekend?

A: I'm going on a camping retreat with David.

B: Oh, that's right. He was telling me about it. It's the one where you aren't allowed to bring your cell phones or laptops, right?

A: Yeah. I'm really looking forward to it. Things at work have been so hectic lately that I've barely had time to sleep. I seriously need to get away from work for a while.

B: What kind of activities will you be doing there?

A: Hiking mostly, maybe some kayaking. And we'll probably do a bit of yoga as well. It'll be good to slow down and take things easy for a change.

B: I've never been to a retreat before, but I've always found that hiking makes me feel happier. It's a great way to unwind. You're going to have a great weekend.

B Practice the conversation with a partner.

C Work with a partner. Talk about how you could slow down and enjoy life more. Use the expressions in blue above to help you.   Answers will vary.

> I think that cycling instead of driving is a great way to slow down and unwind.

> I'd like to go on vacation to a remote village in the countryside because ...

141

LISTENING

A Read **Repeating main ideas** aloud as students read along. Point out that in this case the speaker is repeating the main point, and the listener needs to catch this repetition in order to recognize that the point is an important one. Remind students that they also learned in **Unit 10** that repeating what a speaker says back to them is part of conscious listening. Explain that repetition is a useful tool for communication. Read the question aloud.

▶ **11.2** Play the video. Check answers as a class.

B Have students preview the task. Tell students to listen for what the speaker repeats.

▶ **11.2** Play the video. Check answers as a class. Elicit the phrase that the speaker used to indicate that he was going to repeat himself (*Like I said before, ...*).

C **CRITICAL THINKING** Read the question aloud. If students did the **Extension Activity** in **Vocabulary**, they can use what they wrote to support their conversation. Otherwise, give students time to think about how their daily lifestyle could benefit from being slowed down. Tell students to practice listening consciously to what their partners say so they can offer advice or suggestions.

SPEAKING

A Read the question aloud. Ask students to read along as they watch.

▶ **11.3** Play the audio/video. Check answers as a class. Elicit students' opinions about the event in the conversation. Ask students if they think a retreat like this where everyone unplugs and goes offline sounds interesting to them or not. What activities would they enjoy the most during such a weekend? If they're not interested in joining, why not?

Point out the expression *Oh, that's right*. Explain that we often use this expression when someone tells us information that we already know but had forgotten. In the conversation, Speaker B uses this expression to communicate that David had mentioned it, but Speaker B had forgotten.

B Model the conversation aloud with a student. Then have students work in pairs to practice. Make sure they alternate between A and B roles.

✚ **SUPPORT** Play the audio/video again, pausing after each sentence so students can repeat.

C Read the task aloud. Have students work with a different partner than in **Critical Thinking**. Ask students to share what part of their lives they want to slow down, and some ideas on how to do it. Then ask their partners to offer suggestions as well. Model the example with a volunteer.

Time to monotask

LESSON OVERVIEW

Aims: Read an infographic about multitasking; discuss multitasking versus monotasking

Infographic Summary: The infographic shows how multitasking affects us negatively in various ways, from reducing our IQs to decreasing our brain's ability to focus. Those who think they are good multitaskers are usually not, as only 2 percent of the population actually thrive as multitaskers.

LANGUAGE FOCUS

A Read the question aloud.

▶ **11.4** Play the audio/video as students read along. Then give them additional time to look over the infographic. Note that the infographic says that it's very rare for someone to actually be good at multitasking; many people think they are good at it, even though they are not. Ask students to also comment on any statistic in the infographic that surprised them.

B Read the questions aloud and tell students to listen for the answers.

▶ **11.5** Play the audio/video. Check answers as a class. Elicit the information in the infographic about multitasking while driving. Ask students to share if they've ever had a similar experience to Nicholas's.

C Draw students' attention to the box **Talking about quantity**. Encourage students to practice *slow learning* here by giving students enough time to read over the language chart in a careful (not rushed) fashion.

▶ **11.6** Play the audio/video. Go over the use of the articles and quantifiers. Direct students to page 189 for more information.

11B **Time to monotask**

LANGUAGE FOCUS Multitasking versus monotasking

A ▶ **11.4** Read the information. Do you think you are a true multitasker? Answers will vary.

THE TRUTH ABOUT MULTITASKING

People who multitask might feel like they're accomplishing more, but they're actually getting less done in the process.

Our brains are designed to focus on **one** thing at a time. When people think they're multitasking, they're really only changing from one task to another very rapidly.

People who think they're the best at multitasking are almost always **the worst**.

Just knowing about an unread email or message can keep us distracted and reduce a person's effective IQ by **10 points**.

Listening to a cell phone while driving can reduce a driver's concentration by about **37%**.

Multitasking **reduces** the efficiency and quality of our work. Each time we switch tasks, it takes time and effort to refocus.

Only about **2%** of the population are true multitaskers. These people can multitask without losing efficiency or quality.

B ▶ **11.5** Listen to the conversation. Why was Nicholas distracted while driving? What is Sarah's advice?
Because he was listening to his cell phone while driving; Sarah's advice is to not multitask while driving.

C ▶ **11.6** Watch and study the language in the chart.

Talking about quantity

Articles: *a*, *an*, *the*, zero article
Multitasking takes a toll on the brain.
Experts say that social media can become an addiction.
A new poll shows that the average U.S. employee spends 6.3 hours checking email every day.
Young people often prefer texting to talking on the phone.

Quantifiers
Every time we switch tasks, the brain uses a little bit of energy to refocus.
Information overload can cause a lot of stress over time.
It's important to prioritize when you have to juggle a large number of projects.
A huge amount of data flows through the Internet each second.

For more information on **articles and quantifiers**, see Grammar Summary 11 on page 189.

142

Grammar Note

The language chart introduces articles and quantifiers as modifiers (or markers) to nouns.

Articles (*a, an, the*) can be used to refer to general versus specific things (*a book* versus *the book*). *The* is also used for a noun that has already been mentioned, as well as to mark unique nouns, such as *the world*. The article *a* (or *an*) is used to mark a general noun as well as a single noun.

Zero article refers to cases when no article is needed. Some nouns simply don't take articles at all, while others don't need articles in certain situations.

Quantifiers express how many or how much. Some quantifiers can be used with both countable and uncountable nouns (*a lot of, every*), while some can only be used with countable nouns (*many, several*) or some only with uncountable nouns (*a little, a little bit of*).

D ▶ **11.5** Listen to the conversation in **B** again. Complete the sentences from the conversation.

1 "I had to stop _____the_____ car _____a couple of_____ times to check _____the_____ directions."

2 "No, _____the_____ address was correct. It was my fault. I had to take _____a_____ work call while I was driving."

3 "_____A lot of_____ accidents happen because people try to multitask while driving."

E ▶ **11.7** Complete the information. Circle the correct words. If no article is necessary, circle **x**. Then listen and check your answers.

Earl Miller is ¹(**the** /**a**) famous scientist and ²(**the** /**an**) expert on multitasking and ³(**the** / **x**) brain. He says that ⁴(**a** /**x**) multitasking can be addictive because every time we complete a small task—like sending ⁵(**an**/ **the**) email or answering ⁶(**a**/ **the**) text message—the brain releases ⁷(**x** /**the**) pleasure chemical dopamine. Over time, however, this constant task-switching leads to anxiety and stress. In fact, multitasking has been found to increase production of ⁸(**x** /**the**) stress hormone cortisol in the brain, which can lead to health problems like diabetes, heart disease, and even ⁹(**a** /**x**) depression.

Earl Miller, brain expert

F Complete the sentences with the words from the box. One option is extra.

each	very few	too much	many	a little bit of

1 Employees can become overwhelmed and make mistakes when they have to deal with _____too much_____ information.

2 _____Very few_____ people are truly able to multitask.

3 _____Many_____ people now believe that multitasking is a bad habit.

4 We should stop multitasking and instead, do _____each_____ task separately.

SPEAKING A multitasking test   Answers will vary.

A Work in pairs. Take turns doing the following tasks, and time yourselves. Compare your results with your partner. What do you find?

1 On a separate piece of paper, write your full name. As you do so, spell aloud the sentence, "I am multitasking."

2 On a separate piece of paper, write your full name. As soon as you are finished, spell aloud the sentence, "I am multitasking."

B Share your results with the class. Are they similar? How many students performed faster when multitasking? What does this suggest?

I was quicker when I did the two tasks separately.

I made more mistakes when I …

143

→ **EXTENSION ACTIVITY** Have students go online to learn more about Earl Miller's thoughts on modern technology and multitasking. Ask them to search for his interview on today.com titled "How to do one thing at a time." Tell them to summarize what they learn in the interview and discuss in groups how they can apply monotasking to their lives in the digital age.

SPEAKING

A Read the tasks aloud. Note that the two tasks are almost identical, but in the second one, students spell the sentence after they have finished writing their name instead of while they are writing it. Give students enough time to complete each task. Make sure partners know that they should be timing each other.

B Have each pair take turns explaining their results to the class. Encourage them to also talk about how they felt while doing each of the two tasks. Was one more stressful than the other? Did they feel more focused in one than the other?

Content Note

In the interview titled "How to do one thing at a time: The secret to improving your focus" on today.com, Earl Miller talks about the constant distractions we deal with because of modern technology and the short attention spans that have resulted from this. He says that the human brain works best when it's focused on one thing, so switching back and forth between tasks is not to our advantage. Our brains operate at a higher capacity when we focus on one task at a time.

D Have students preview the task. Encourage them to guess the answers based on the content they heard in the first listening as well as the grammar in the language chart.

▶ **11.5** Play the audio/video again. Have students work individually to complete the activity. Check answers as a class.

E Have students work individually. Tell them to use the information in the language chart to help them decide which article is needed, if any.

▶ **11.7** Play the audio/video to check answers. Ask students to share their mistakes. Go over them together.

F Have students work individually before checking answers in pairs.

11C

Your brain on nature

LESSON OVERVIEW

Aims: Read and comprehend an article about the importance of spending time outdoors; understand main ideas and details

Target Vocabulary: addiction, cognitive, evolved, intuitively, therapy

Reading Summary: The forests of South Korea are being declared areas for healing mental health. The government is partly funding the development of "forest healing" facilities, and there is even a university degree in "forest healing" these days. Nature is being medicalized in this way because we are spending too little time in nature, so we need programs to learn the benefits of spending time outdoors. Being in nature has been shown to calm stress levels, reduce blood pressure, and even improve heart disease and diabetes. It also makes us happier by making us more energetic and even more creative. Spending less than an hour a day walking in nature has been proven to improve our brain function and moods.

PRE-READING

Read the questions aloud. Give students time to look over the photo and think about their answers. Note that students will likely project on the man in the photo the same types of feelings that they have while in nature. Check answers by eliciting a class discussion about how nature makes students feel. Make sure the discussion environment is open so that students who don't enjoy nature can also talk freely. Encourage students to share any personal stories about time they've spent in nature.

▶ **11.8** Play the audio/video as students read along. Go over any unfamiliar language. See **Language Note**.

11C Your brain on nature

PRE-READING Predicting Answers will vary.

Look at the photo. How do you think the man in the photo is feeling? How do you feel when you are surrounded by nature?

▶ **11.8**

1 After a morning hike in the Saneum Healing Forest east of Seoul, 46-year-old firefighter Kang Byoung-wook sips tea made from the bark of an elm tree, practices yoga, enjoys an
5 arm massage, and makes a collage from dried flowers. He is one of about 40 firefighters taking part in a three-day program sponsored by the local government. The aim of the program is to offer "forest healing"; the firefighters all have post-
10 traumatic stress disorder.

Saneum is one of three official healing forests in South Korea, which offer a range of programs from meditation to woodcraft to camping. Soon there will be 34 more. South Koreans—many of
15 whom suffer from work stress, digital **addiction**, and intense academic pressures—have embraced the medicalization of nature with great enthusiasm. In fact, Korea's Chungbuk University offers a "forest healing" degree program, and the government
20 is investing a hundred million dollars in a healing complex next to Sobaeksan National Park.

There is increasing evidence that being outside in a pleasant natural environment is good for us. But how many of us get to enjoy nature regularly? Fewer
25 and fewer, it seems. According to Lisa Nisbet, a psychology professor at Canada's Trent University, evidence for the benefits of nature is pouring in at a time when we are most disconnected from it. The pressures of modern life lead to long hours
30 spent working indoors. Digital addiction and strong academic pressure add to the problem. In America, visits to parks have been declining since the

dawn of email, and so have visits to the backyard. Research indicates that only about 10 percent of
35 American teens spend time outside every day. "We don't think of [being outdoors] as a way to increase happiness," says Nisbet. "We think other things will, like shopping or TV." But some countries, like South Korea, are starting to challenge this mindset.
40 So what are some of the benefits of nature that Nisbet refers to? Being surrounded by nature has one obvious effect: It calms us and reduces our stress levels. This has been shown to lower blood pressure, heart rates, and levels of the
45 stress hormone cortisol, as well as reduce feelings of fear or anger. But studies also indicate that spending time in nature can do more than provide an improved sense of well-being; it can lower rates of heart disease, asthma, and diabetes. This is
50 probably because we **evolved** in nature and are adapted to understanding its signs.

144

⭐ **CHALLENGE** Write the term *forest healing* on the board. Have students scan the passage to find its meaning. Elicit an explanation.

➡ **EXTENSION ACTIVITY** Have students work individually to keep a record of time spent in nature over the last week. What did they do? How did they feel? After they write their journals, ask them to evaluate if they think their time spent in nature was enough. Then have students come back and re-evaluate at the end of the lesson.

A hiker in Washington State's Olympic National Park

Spending time outdoors also makes us happier and can lead to a boost of energy—a sense of being more alive. Just 20 minutes a day in nature
55 is enough to make a significant difference. "Nature is fuel for the soul," says psychology professor Richard Ryan.

Another experiment conducted by psychologist Stephen Kaplan and his colleagues
60 found that people who took a 50-minute walk in a park had better attention and short-term memory than those who took a walk along a city street. "Imagine a **therapy** that had no known side effects, was readily available, and could
65 improve your **cognitive** functioning at zero cost," the researchers wrote in their paper. It exists, they continued, and it's called "interacting with nature."

Perhaps what's more surprising is that nature
70 may also make us more creative. David Strayer, a cognitive psychologist at the University of Utah, demonstrated as much with a group of participants, who performed 50 percent better on creative problem-solving tasks after
75 three days of wilderness backpacking. When we slow down, stop the busywork, and take in beautiful natural surroundings, he says, not only do we feel restored, but our mental performance improves too.

80 We all **intuitively** know that nature is good for us. Now we are beginning to understand the many ways it benefits us and just what effects it has on the mind and body. According to Strayer, we may never know exactly what nature does to the brain.
85 Something mysterious will always remain, and maybe that's as it should be. "At the end of the day," he says, "we come out in nature not because the science says it does something to us, but because of how it makes us feel."

Language Note

To *sponsor* (line 7) something means to give money to fund its development.

Woodcraft (line 13) refers to making things out of wood. The activity is also called *woodwork*. The profession of building pieces of furniture out of wood is called *carpentry*.

The verb *medicalize* refers to making something a medical issue that usually isn't considered to be one. The word is often used in a negative way. However, in the passage, the noun *medicalization* (line 17) in reference to nature simply describes how the healing benefits of nature are becoming more accepted in general.

A *complex* (line 21) is a series of buildings that are together in one area and usually built for a similar purpose.

The expression *the dawn of* (lines 32–33) refers to when something first began. The author refers to *the dawn of email* to talk about the time when email first came into our lives.

Short-term memory (lines 61–62) refers to the ability to recall events that happened recently.

A *cognitive psychologist* (line 71) focuses on how humans process thought, including memory, problem-solving, and attention span.

Content Note

The driving philosophy behind South Korea's forest healing programs is that the increase in chronic illnesses is partly a result of the disconnect from nature. By 2017, South Korea will be home to 36 therapy forests, with over 500 trained instructors in forest healing.

This interest in forest healing is spreading to other countries as well. Forest service representatives in South Korea and Japan have met about bringing the same forest healing idea to Japan, which is a heavily forested country with a similar natural topography to South Korea.

UNDERSTANDING MAIN IDEAS

Have students work individually. Explain that they will choose the new title based on the main idea of the entire passage. Note that the two other choices could be used as subheadings, but do not reflect enough of the main idea. Check answers as a class.

UNDERSTANDING DETAILS

Give students time to monotask during this activity. Tell them to slowly go back through the passage to focus on the statements in the activity and find whether they are in the passage or not.

Check answers as a class. Ask students to comment on whether teenagers in their home countries are spending less time outdoors as well.

BUILDING VOCABULARY

A Ask students to go back to the reading to see each word used in context. Have students work individually and then check answers as a class.

B Encourage students to practice "slow learning." Give them time to slowly work through each sentence to choose the correct word and understand the sentence's complete meaning. Check answers as a class, eliciting a paraphrase of the meaning of each sentence.

C **CRITICAL THINKING** Read the questions aloud as students read along. Point out that it is OK for students' opinions and answers to be very different from each other. Encourage pairs to have a lively discussion about how to get themselves and their peers back in nature.

Elicit a class discussion to hear students' ideas. Ask students especially about how the government could get involved in helping people spend more time in nature. Encourage the class to brainstorm some program ideas that they can use for the **Extension Activity**.

UNDERSTANDING MAIN IDEAS

Choose the best alternative title for the passage.

- **a** South Korea's Natural Wonders
- **(b)** The Power of Nature
- **c** Getting Closer to Nature

UNDERSTANDING DETAILS

Which of the following does the passage mention? Check (✓) your answers.

- ☐ We need to take better care of the natural environment, particularly our forests and national parks.
- ☑ Outdoor activities like hiking and camping are useful for treating stress and attention disorders.
- ☑ "Forest healing" is offered as a university course in South Korea.
- ☐ Pollution is one of the reasons fewer and fewer Americans are spending time outdoors.
- ☐ Teenagers are less likely to spend time outside than adults.
- ☑ Spending time outdoors has both a calming and an energizing effect on us.
- ☑ Being in nature enhances our short-term memory and problem-solving abilities.
- ☐ Government officials should do more to increase people's access to nature.

BUILDING VOCABULARY

A Match the words in blue from the passage to their definitions.

1. addiction — a condition that results when a person's need to regularly do something interferes with ordinary life responsibilities
2. evolved — developed gradually
3. therapy — the treatment of an illness or injury, whether physical or mental
4. cognitive — concerned with the act or process of thinking
5. intuitively — knowing or understanding something based on feelings rather than facts or proof

B Complete the sentences using the words in **A**.

1. Her company has _____evolved_____ from a hobby into a thriving business.
2. A key contributing factor to today's fast-paced lifestyle is people's _____addiction_____ to technology.
3. Language and memory are examples of basic _____cognitive_____ abilities.
4. Contact with nature is increasingly used as a form of _____therapy_____ by mental health professionals.
5. Some entrepreneurs prefer to make decisions _____intuitively_____ instead of relying on data or asking other people for advice.

C **CRITICAL THINKING** Answers will vary.

Analyzing What things could you do to spend more time outdoors in nature? What could the government do to help? Discuss with a partner.

146

⊙ EXTENSION ACTIVITY Have students work in groups. Ask them to plan a government-sponsored program to get students better in touch with nature. Have students prepare a sample one-day schedule of what participants will do at the event.

11D Cloudy with a chance of joy

TEDTALKS

GAVIN PRETOR-PINNEY is a science writer. His writing combines science with an appreciation of the natural wonders around us. He co-founded *The Idler* magazine, a publication that encourages people to take time out of their busy routines to enjoy their surroundings. He also founded the Cloud Appreciation Society, an organization devoted to the idle pursuit of cloud watching.

Gavin Pretor-Pinney's idea worth spreading is that we can all benefit from looking up and admiring the beauty of the clouds over our heads.

PREVIEWING

Read the sentences. Choose the option that has a similar meaning to each **bold** word. You will hear these words in the TED Talk.

1 Extreme weather events like hurricanes can cause fallen trees and road **obstructions**.

   (a) obstacles   **b** signs

2 Most explorers have a **fondness** for the natural world.

   a ambition   **(b)** affection

3 **Meditation** is a good way to relax and relieve stress.

   (a) quiet thought   **b** nervousness

4 You've got to **stand up for** what you believe in.

   (a) defend   **b** dismiss

5 Some common things people **moan** about are heavy traffic, bad weather, and slow Wi-Fi.

   a care   **(b)** complain

VIEWING

A ▶ **11.9** Watch Part 1 of the TED Talk. Would Gavin Pretor-Pinney agree with the following statements? Circle **Y** for yes or **N** for no.

1 A lot of people don't notice how beautiful clouds really are.   **(Y)**   **N**

2 Clouds are annoying because they block the sun.   **Y**   **(N)**

3 Clouds can stimulate our imagination.   **(Y)**   **N**

4 Cloud watching is more fun when you're young.   **Y**   **(N)**

5 How we think or feel can influence what shapes we see in the clouds.   **(Y)**   **N**

147

LESSON OVERVIEW

Aims: Watch and understand a talk about cloudspotting; observe and practice being enthusiastic

Target Vocabulary: fondness, meditation, moan, obstruction, stand up for

TED Talk Summary: Gavin Pretor-Pinney is a writer fascinated with clouds, and he explains more about these often overlooked occurrences in nature. He encourages us to use them as an opportunity to slow down. Not only are clouds overlooked, but they've been given so many negative associations in our language and culture that we see them as something undesirable. Pretor-Pinney uses visuals to go over the various kinds of clouds while also talking about how cloudspotting can force us to take a moment to enjoy an aimless pursuit.

PREVIEWING

Have students first read the paragraphs about the speaker. Ask students to comment on why he might be so interested in clouds, and how cloudspotting fits into the overall theme

---

11D

Cloudy with a chance of joy

of the unit. Note that the paragraphs do not contain the vocabulary words. For the task, tell students to pay attention to how each word is used in context in each sentence in order to understand its meaning. Have students work individually before checking answers in pairs. Remind students of the **Warm Up** preview clip. Tell them to use all the language and information they have learned so far to support their viewing of the TED Talk.

➡ **EXTENSION ACTIVITY** Have students work in pairs to go online to *The Idler*'s website. Tell them to look at the titles and pictures and draw conclusions about the magazine's readers as well as its editor-in-chief, Gavin Pretor-Pinney. Ask pairs to share their conclusions with the class.

VIEWING

A Have students preview the task. Explain that students will infer some points based on what the speaker says. Note that some of the statements are ones that he infers other people would agree with.

▶ **11.9** Play Part 1 of the TED Talk. Check answers as a class. Write on the board the expression by Aristophanes that Pretor-Pinney refers to: *the patron goddesses of idle fellows.* Elicit an explanation of the meaning of this expression. An idle fellow is a person who is not very active and enjoys living in the slow lane. The Greek playwright means that clouds offer an opportunity for those living the slow life to have a spiritual moment.

Elicit the meaning of any unfamiliar language. Suggestions for Part 1 include *bad rap, doom-and-gloom, omnipresent,* and *harboring.*

B Have students preview the task by looking over the pictures carefully as well as the label name for each type of cloud. Point out that both **B** and **C** will use Part 2 of the talk, so students may want to preview both tasks.

▶ **11.10** Play Part 2 of the TED Talk. Don't check answers until students complete the next activity.

C Have students complete the task without watching the video again. Check answers to **B** and **C** as a class or play the check-your-answers part of the video.

Write on the board the following quote from Part 2: *Not a very snappy name. Needs a rebrand.* Ask students to identify the cloud that the speaker was talking about (Kelvin-Helmholtz) and elicit the meaning of his joke. He is saying that name is not very interesting compared to the other cloud names and that scientists might want to consider a new name for this type of cloud.

Elicit or explain the meaning of any unfamiliar language. Suggestions for Part 2 include *troposphere, brushstroke, bombing along, UFO, flying saucer,* and *egalitarian.*

Content Note

The Kelvin-Helmholtz cloud is named after a mathematic principle that also explains how those cloud shapes form. This instability theory was introduced by Lord Kelvin and Hermann von Helmholtz, two physicists who lived in the 19th century.

D Have students preview the task. Tell them that they will have to use inference based on what Pretor-Pinney says to choose the statements he would agree with. Point out that students can probably guess some of the statements based on what they already know about Pretor-Pinney even before watching Part 3. Note that background knowledge can be of great use in this way when completing comprehension tasks.

▶ **11.11** Play Part 3 of the TED Talk. Check answers as a class. Elicit or explain the meaning of any unfamiliar language. Suggestions for Part 3 include *aimless, gazing, pointless,* and *legitimizes.*

B ▶ **11.10** Watch Part 2 of the TED Talk. Match the clouds (**1–4**) to the pictures.

1 cirrus

2 lenticularis

3 fallstreak holes

4 Kelvin-Helmholtz

a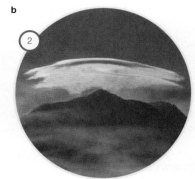

b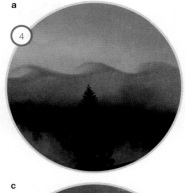

c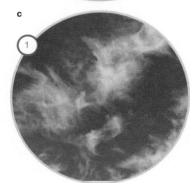

d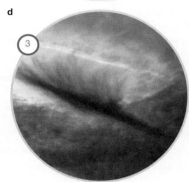

C Match the types of clouds to their descriptions.

1 cirrus — formed when the wind rises to pass over mountains

2 lenticularis — formed when water droplets in the cloud start to freeze into ice crystals

3 fallstreak holes — caused by different wind speeds above and below the cloud layer

4 Kelvin-Helmholtz — high up; made of ice crystals that are blown by strong winds

D ▶ **11.11** Watch Part 3 of the TED Talk. Check (✓) the statements that Gavin Pretor-Pinney would agree with.

☐ The cumulonimbus storm cloud is the best cloud for finding shapes in.

☐ Cloudspotting on a sunny day is a waste of time.

☑ Cloudspotting is important because there's no real point in doing it.

☑ Feeling that you're in the present moment is beneficial in many ways.

⊙ **EXTENSION ACTIVITY** Have pairs work together to go online and learn more about the Kelvin-Helmholtz cloud and look at more pictures of that type of cloud formation. Ask pairs to then brainstorm some new names for the cloud. Have each pair present their name to the class. Then have a class vote to choose the best name.

E CRITICAL THINKING Answers will vary.

Synthesizing Compare Gavin Pretor-Pinney's recommendations with the advice given by Julian Treasure in Unit 10. How are they similar? Discuss with a partner.

VOCABULARY IN CONTEXT

▶ **11.12** Watch the excerpts from the TED Talk. Choose the correct meaning of the words. 1.b; 2.a; 3.b

PRESENTATION SKILLS Being enthusiastic

It's important to be enthusiastic about your topic. Your audience will become more involved and will pay more attention to what you're saying. You can show your enthusiasm by:

- varying the speed and volume of your delivery;
- using facial expressions and body language that convey the interest you feel in the topic;
- using questions and gestures to invite the audience to share your enthusiasm;
- using visuals that show what there is to enjoy about your topic.

A ▶ **11.13** Watch part of Gavin Pretor-Pinney's TED Talk. Which of the techniques above does he use? All – He varies the speed and volume of his speech; he moves his arms as he talks; he involves the audience; and he shows photos of the clouds.

B Choose a topic you know a lot about or an activity you enjoy doing. It could be a place, a sport, or a hobby. Make brief notes on three things you want to communicate about your topic, and practice your presentation. Try to use at least one of the techniques in the Tip box.
Answers will vary.

C Work in small groups. Take turns giving your presentations. Note the ways your group members show their enthusiasm. Answers will vary.

Mick Ohrberg (Member 14,198)
Kansas City, Missouri, US

149

E **CRITICAL THINKING** Read the direction line and question aloud. Give students time to go back to **Unit 10** to review Julian Treasure's talk. The communications expert said that the fast pace of today's modern world is causing our listening skills to decline, which is negatively affecting the way we understand each other and the world we live in. Both speakers are offering ways to step away from the distractions of today's world and reconnect by becoming focused on one task, instead of many. After students discuss in pairs, have a class discussion about how the speakers' messages are

similar. Have students also share what they are taking away from both talks.

Language Note

Part 1
The expression *bad rap* refers to having an unsavory reputation, often one that is not deserved. The term *doom-and-gloom* describes a sad or negative feeling. Something that is *omnipresent* is everywhere—a common occurrence. To *harbor* a thought or feeling means to keep it in your mind secretly.

Part 2
The *troposphere* is the lowest level of Earth's atmosphere. A *brush-stroke*

shape refers to something that looks like a mark made by a paintbrush. Pretor-Pinney uses the term *bombing along* to explain that the clouds are moving very fast. Both a *UFO* (unidentified flying object) and a *flying saucer* are popular names to describe airships that people think are operated by aliens. Something that is *egalitarian* is based on the principle of equality.

Part 3
Something or someone described as *aimless* is without a clear direction. To *gaze* at something means to look at it intently, usually for a long time. Something that is *pointless* is considered to have no meaning. To *legitimize* something means to make it permissible.

VOCABULARY IN CONTEXT
▶ **11.12** Play the video. If necessary, play it again.

PRESENTATION SKILLS

A Read the Presentation Skills paragraph **Being enthusiastic** aloud. Go over each of the suggestions for showing enthusiasm. Remind students that being authentic is also an important skill, so their enthusiasm shouldn't be so over the top that it seems inauthentic.

Have students preview the task.

▶ **11.13** Play the video. Check answers as a class.

B Read the direction line aloud. Have students work individually to prepare notes and ideas for their presentation. Tell them to choose a topic that they genuinely feel enthusiastic about. Give students enough time to think about how they want to show enthusiasm as they introduce their topic to their groups.

C Divide the class into small groups. Tell each group member to speak for at least one minute on the topic. Encourage them to practice all the presentation skills from the textbook, especially being enthusiastic. Afterwards, elicit a class discussion to hear how students showed enthusiasm. Use this as an opportunity to review the presentation skills taught so far.

Changing the pace

11E Changing the pace

LESSON OVERVIEW

Aims: Plan an organization to support the Slow Movement; write an advertisement

COMMUNICATE

A Have students work in groups. Explain that they should gather all the ideas about slow living that they've learned throughout the unit and discuss how to apply the principles of the movement. If necessary, give students an example of Cittaslow, an organization that is explained in the **Content Note** of **Lesson A**. Point out that organizations only need to focus on one aspect of daily life. Encourage groups to choose a topic that all members are interested in. Tell them to brainstorm a list of ways in which the organization will help people slow down. Give students time to take the notes from their discussion and write down the key information in the chart.

B Have groups practice their presentations before giving them to the class. Tell them that each group member must have a speaking role in the presentation. Encourage students to use many of the relevant presentation skills that they have learned in the book to help improve their presentations. Explain that listeners should think of questions to ask groups as well. Read the box **Handling questions** aloud. Remind students of the language they learned in **Unit 10** for asking follow-up questions (*Can you elaborate on that, please? Can you give an example?*).

C Encourage students to think about which organization they think does the best job of spreading the message of the Slow Movement. Tell students to vote for the organization they would personally like to join. If necessary, make the vote anonymous by

COMMUNICATE Slow movement organizations *Answers will vary.*

A Work in small groups. You are going to create an organization that encourages people to slow down, appreciate simple things, and live more in the present. It could focus on nature, food, travel, or your own idea. Make notes in the chart below.

Name of organization	Area of focus	Activities or programs offered

B As a group, tell the class about your organization and how it helps people enjoy life more. Invite your classmates to ask follow-up questions.

> **Handling questions**
> *Thank you for asking. We plan to …*   *That's a great question. Our strategy is to …*

C Which organization would you like to join? Hold a class vote.

WRITING An advertisement *Answers will vary.*

Choose either your own organization or one of the other organizations you heard about above, and write an advertisement for it. Explain what the organization does and how it will benefit people.

> Fancy a surfing vacation? Tired of the usual "touristy" beaches? Look no further. At Surf Spot, we help surfers avoid all the usual tourist traps of a beach vacation, and instead, put more emphasis on the local communities and culture. We can help you …

Sedgefield, South Africa—a member of the Slow Town movement—attracts many surfers.

150

having students write their favorite organization on a piece of paper and then tallying the votes.

WRITING

Explain that students can write an advertisement for any organization that they heard about in the presentations. Read the example aloud. Point out that it's written to engage an audience and make them interested in going somewhere, not as a public service message about the benefits of slowing down. Give students enough time to write their advertisements.

⭐ **CHALLENGE** Have students read their advertisements aloud to the class as radio advertisements. Encourage them to use animated voices, vary their tones as they speak, and/or use background music, such as is typical in radio commercials.

12 Make Yourself Heard

" So how do organizations think? Well, for the most part, they don't ... because the people inside of them are too afraid of conflict. **"**

Margaret Heffernan
Management thinker, TED speaker

UNIT GOALS

In this unit, you will ...

- talk about people who had the courage to express their views.
- read about famous whistleblowers.
- watch a TED Talk about the importance of challenging accepted wisdom.

WARM UP

▶ **12.1** Watch part of Margaret Heffernan's TED Talk. Answer the questions with a partner.

1 Why do you think the executives were afraid to raise their issues or concerns? Answers will vary.

2 How do you usually react when you disagree with someone? Do you keep quiet or voice your opinion?
Answers will vary. **151**

12

Make Yourself Heard

Idea Worth Spreading

Employees who aren't afraid to disagree are actually supporting an organization by trying to improve it.

WARM UP

Have students look over the picture, caption, and quote on the page. Read the quote aloud. Ask students to infer what they think the speaker means by *organizations.* She is referring to governments and other institutions and agencies as well as businesses. Note that the quote will not be heard in the video clip.

Draw students' attention to the **Unit Goals**. Ask them to read the three points. Then elicit a paraphrase of each. *Courage to express* views means to share an opinion even when it's in opposition to what most others seem to think. A *whistleblower* is an employee at an organization who brings attention to possibly illegal or dangerous activities happening within the organization. The term *accepted wisdom* describes thinking that is generally accepted as right by most people.

▶ **12.1** Play the preview clip of the TED Talk.

For question 1, explain that an executive is someone in a senior position in a company. Have students share their ideas after discussing in pairs. Encourage them to recognize that even those in positions of power may be hesitant to express opposition to their company or colleagues, as it may lead to them being labeled difficult to work with—or get them fired.

For question 2, ask students to share personal stories about their own experiences with disagreement, and how they react to it. How do they feel about conflict? How is a person who disagrees with others viewed in their culture?

UNIT GOALS

In this unit, students will read, watch, and talk about bringing attention to a situation in which something unethical is happening. Students learn language for talking about conflict and whistleblowing. They will use third and mixed conditionals to talk about what could have happened in certain situations if things had been different. Students are asked to think about standing up for what they think is right, and are encouraged to find benefits and value in the act of disagreeing.

TED Speaker

Margaret Heffernan is an entrepreneur, a former CEO, and an author. She has given several TED Talks.

TED Talk Summary

Heffernan begins her talk with an anecdote about a doctor whose research in regard to preventing childhood cancer was ignored for 25 years. People who find something problematic within their field and speak out against conventional ways are often marginalized and labeled as troublemakers. Heffernan says that we need to be more open to people who bring up issues of wrongdoing in organizations to improve the way we do things.

12A

Expressing yourself

Pakistani student Malala Yousafzai speaks before the United Nations Youth Assembly.

12A Expressing yourself

LESSON OVERVIEW

Aims: Learn language for talking about disagreeing; listen to a true story about a whistleblower; practice talking about people who stand up for their beliefs

Target Vocabulary: assert, clarify, conflict, persuade, resolve

VOCABULARY

A Have students work individually to complete the sentences.

▶ **12.2** Play the audio/video and check answers as a class, going over meaning. Elicit additional example sentences for each vocabulary word.

B Have students work individually. Then have students check answers in pairs. For item 1, remind students that they heard an interview with a mediator in **Unit 10** (page 129).

C Read the question aloud. Have students work in pairs to share as much information as they know about Malala Yousafzai. Tell students to take notes to keep a record of what they know about her.

⟶ **EXTENSION ACTIVITY** Have students work in pairs to go online and find out more about Malala. Ask them to look at their notes in **C** and formulate questions about any missing information. Then have them go online to find the answers. If time permits, have pairs share the information that they learned with the class.

VOCABULARY Voicing an opinion

A ▶ **12.2** Complete the sentences using the correct form of the words from the box. Then listen and check your answers.

clarify	persuade	conflict	assert	resolve

1 Despite the evidence against him, he has continued to _____assert_____ his innocence.

2 The company's problems were finally _____resolved_____ when the unpopular CEO resigned.

3 The politician was asked to _____clarify_____ his position on the recent tax cuts.

4 In order to avoid _____conflict_____, he decided to keep his opinion to himself.

5 It can sometimes be hard to _____persuade_____ people to do the right thing.

B Complete the sentences. Circle the correct words.

1 Mediators help to (**assert** / **resolve**) family disputes.

2 Both countries were hoping for a peaceful (**conflict** / **resolution**) to the crisis.

3 During court cases, lawyers often appeal to the jury's emotions in order to make their arguments more (**persuasive** / **assertive**).

C Work with a partner. Look at the picture of Malala above. What do you know about her? Answers will vary.

152

Content Note

Malala Yousafzai is the youngest person to win a Nobel Peace Prize. Born in 1997 in Pakistan, the young activist became a victim of violence when she began blogging and speaking out against the Taliban's ban on girls attending school. In 2012, she was shot in the head by a Taliban assassin on her school bus while on her way home from taking an exam. She survived the incident, and has since continued her activism for education even more fervently, gaining an international audience of support. In 2014, she was awarded the Nobel Peace Prize for her efforts. While she is still often bullied in the press in Pakistan, she continues to stand up for what she believes is right. In 2015, at the age of 18, she opened a school in Lebanon for Syrian refugees.

LISTENING The *Challenger* disaster

> **Listening for stressed words**
> Not every word in a sentence is stressed in spoken English. We tend to stress "information" words, such as nouns, verbs, adjectives, and adverbs. Grammatical words—like prepositions, auxiliaries, and articles—tend not to be stressed.

A ▶ **12.3** Watch a description of the space shuttle *Challenger* disaster. How was NASA involved?

   a NASA made decisions based on incorrect data.

   ⓑ NASA ignored critical data.

B ▶ **12.3** Watch again. Check (✓) the effects that whistleblowing had on Roger Boisjoly.

   ☑ He became isolated and lonely.

   ☑ His health deteriorated.

   ☐ He was immediately fired from his job.

C **CRITICAL THINKING**　　Answers will vary.

   Analyzing What does the *Challenger* disaster suggest about the organizational culture in NASA at the time? Discuss with a partner.

The final launch of the space shuttle *Challenger*

SPEAKING Standing up for your beliefs

A ▶ **12.4** What did Susan B. Anthony do?　She fought for women's rights.

   A: Have you decided who to write about for your social studies assignment?

   B: Yeah. I'm writing about Susan B. Anthony.

   A: I don't think I've heard of her before.

   B: She was an American civil rights leader in the early twentieth century who asserted that women should have equal rights to men. She stood up for her beliefs and fought for women's right to vote.

   A: Wow, she must have been very courageous.

   B: She was. She also called for equal educational opportunities for boys and girls. In 1900, she finally persuaded the University of Rochester to admit women.

   A: Did she ever come into conflict with the authorities for her beliefs?

   B: Yes, she did. She was arrested for voting in 1872. But she didn't let that stop her. She devoted the rest of her life to fighting for women's rights.

B Practice the conversation with a partner.

C Work with a partner. Talk about other famous people who have stood up for their beliefs. Use the expressions in blue above to help you.　Answers will vary.

> Can you think of someone famous who stood up for their beliefs?
>
> Malala Yousafzai. She fights for …

153

disaster as well as how his warnings were ignored before. Boisjoly's initial warning about the problem was probably ignored partly because NASA felt pressure to move forward with an important media event. The *Challenger* had a civilian on board—a high school teacher—and the event was set to be televised live so school children across the country could witness the first American teacher in space. Sadly, they instead watched the disaster happen live on TV.

SPEAKING

A Read the question aloud. Ask students to read along as they watch.

   ▶ **12.4** Play the audio/video. Check answers as a class. Point out the expression *devoted the rest of her life to*. Explain that when you devote your life to something, it becomes a cause that you are committed and dedicated to until you die.

B Model the conversation aloud with a student. Then have students work in pairs to practice. Make sure they alternate between A and B roles.

C Read the task aloud. Have students work with partners from different countries, if possible. Tell students to think of someone they have heard of who was committed to an important moral issue, such as the individuals mentioned in the lesson so far, and to share whatever they know about that person. Encourage students to use the language in the lesson in their discussions. Model the example with a volunteer.

➡ EXTENSION ACTIVITY Have students work individually to make a poster about the famous person they spoke about in **C**. Give them time to search online to learn more about the person. Ask them to include a picture or other visual in their posters. Have students each present their poster to the class and talk about the famous person who stood up for what was right. Tell students to include details about how the person was treated after daring to disagree.

LISTENING

A Read **Listening for stressed words** aloud as students read along. A word that is stressed is pronounced with greater emphasis than the other words being said. Note that the information explains that prepositions, auxiliaries, and articles tend not to be stressed. In fact, they are often spoken so softly or quickly that they become reduced and are not heard clearly. Read the question aloud and tell students to listen for the answer.

▶ **12.3** Play the audio/video. Check answers as a class. Ask students if they've heard of the *Challenger* disaster.

B Have students preview the task.

▶ **12.3** Play the audio/video. Check answers as a class. Elicit any words that they heard the speaker stress while telling the story of Roger Boisjoly.

C **CRITICAL THINKING** Read the question aloud. If necessary, explain the meaning of *organizational culture*. Encourage students to focus on how Boisjoly was treated after the

LESSON OVERVIEW

Aims: Read an infographic about tragic accidents that could have been avoided; discuss having a moral dilemma

Infographic Summary: The infographic gives a summary of three tragic events that happened due to avoidable errors, explaining how each disaster resulted after warnings were ignored.

LANGUAGE FOCUS

A Read the questions aloud.

▶ **12.5** Play the audio/video as students read along. Then give them additional time to look over the infographic.

Have students work in pairs. Ask them to retell as much of the story of the disaster as they know: why it happened and if it could have been avoided. If students don't know a disaster to talk about, ask them to retell in their own words the story of one from the infographic. Elicit a class discussion about which disaster in the infographic was most easily avoidable, and why.

B Read the question aloud. Note that students can guess part of the answer based on the information they read in the infographic.

▶ **12.6** Play the audio/video. Check answers as a class.

C Have students read over the language chart. Tell them to pay attention to the formation and use of the verbs in blue. Note that all of these sentences are imaginary or unreal, focusing on something that did not actually happen.

▶ **12.7** Play the audio/video. Direct students to page 190 for more information.

12B Disasters

LANGUAGE FOCUS Disasters that could have been prevented

A ▶ **12.5** Read the information. Do you know about any other famous disasters? What happened? What caused them? *Answers will vary.*

PREVENTABLE DISASTERS

Throughout history, there have been many disasters that could have been avoided. Here are a few examples.

1912

TITANIC DISASTER

R.M.S. *Titanic* sank after hitting an iceberg. The crew had received multiple **iceberg warnings** and were advised to slow down, but didn't. Also, the ship had only enough lifeboats to save about half the people on board. Many lifeboats were lowered before they were full.

Casualties: over 1,500 people killed

1986

CHALLENGER DISASTER

The space shuttle *Challenger* exploded after an O-ring seal failed at lift-off. The O-ring was not designed to fly under unusually cold conditions, as in this launch. Engineers had pleaded with NASA to **postpone the launch**, but NASA rejected their advice.

Casualties: all seven crew members killed

2007

MINNEAPOLIS BRIDGE COLLAPSE

The I-35W Mississippi River Bridge collapsed suddenly in 2007. For nearly two decades before the collapse, U.S. government officials knew the bridge was **"structurally deficient."** But instead of replacing it, they relied on "patchwork repairs."

Casualties: 13 people killed, 145 others injured

B ▶ **12.6** Listen to the conversation. What caused the sinking of *Titanic*?
It sank after hitting an iceberg. Overconfidence of the captain and crew also played a part.

C ▶ **12.7** Watch and study the language in the chart.

Talking about the imaginary past

If the captain of *Titanic* had taken the ice warnings seriously, the ship probably would have missed the iceberg.

If the crew of *Titanic* had been trained properly in evacuation procedures, more people would have survived.

If the engineers employed by NASA hadn't provided critical information to investigators, we wouldn't have found out the truth about the *Challenger* disaster.

If government officials had carried out sufficient repairs on the Mississippi River Bridge, it might still be standing today.

If the Internet hadn't been invented, we wouldn't have access to so much information.

For more information on **third conditional** and **mixed conditionals**, see Grammar Summary 12 on page 190.

154

Grammar Note

The language chart introduces third and mixed conditionals. Note that students were introduced to the first and second conditionals in **Unit 9** (page 116).

The third conditional talks about an impossible result that is not going to happen but could have happened if something else had occurred. The sentences in the chart all use the past perfect tense (*had* + past participle) in the first clause and the modal *would have* + past participle in the second.

Note that the modal *could have* can also be used to talk about something that didn't happen in the second clause of a sentence in the third conditional.

A sentence with an unreal or impossible topic that has a different tense (past, present, future) in each clause is a mixed conditional.

D ▶ **12.6** Listen to the conversation in **B** again. Complete the sentences from the conversation.

1 "If the ship _____had gone_____ slower, it probably _____would have had_____ time to avoid the iceberg."

2 "If there _____had been_____ the right number of lifeboats, more people _____would have survived_____."

3 "If the captain _____had taken_____ all the necessary precautions, we probably _____wouldn't_____ still _____be_____ talking about *Titanic* today."

E Read the information. Then complete the sentences below using the correct form of the words in parentheses.

Fires were common in London in the 17th century. Most buildings were made of wood and were very close together, so they caught fire easily. King Charles II had even warned the mayor of London about the dangers of a major fire. After a particularly hot and dry summer in September 1666, a fire broke out in a tiny bakery on Pudding Lane. The fire quickly got out of control, as a strong wind that day caused it to spread rapidly. The fire—now known as the Great Fire of London—continued to burn for four days. By the time it was over, it had destroyed 80 percent of the city and over 13,000 buildings. Luckily, only a few people died. The fire did have one positive effect, however: It killed thousands of rats that had carried the plague, and helped stop the spread of the deadly disease.

An illustration of the Great Fire of London

1 If the buildings _____hadn't been_____ (**be**) made of wood, they wouldn't have burned so easily.

2 If the mayor of London _____had taken_____ (**take**) the king's warning seriously, the fire probably wouldn't have been so bad.

3 If there hadn't been a strong wind that day, the fire _____wouldn't have_____ (**have**) spread so rapidly.

4 If there hadn't been a fire, the rats carrying the plague _____would have_____ (**have**) continued to spread the disease.

SPEAKING A moral dilemma   Answers will vary.

Work with a partner. Read the information about a fictitious disaster. Then discuss your answers to the questions below.

> In order to cut costs, a toy factory used cheap materials in its production process. A few assembly line workers knew about the dangers but were too afraid to speak up. As a result, several children were harmed while playing with the toy products, and the company is being sued by the children's families.

1 How could the disaster have been prevented?

> If the toy factory hadn't used cheap materials, no children would have been harmed.

> If the assembly line workers had informed the media beforehand, the public would have known ...

2 What would you have done if you were one of the assembly line workers? Why?

155

EXTENSION ACTIVITY Have students look up other famous disasters that could have been avoided (see **Content Note** for examples). Ask students to choose one and write a paragraph, similar to the one on the Great Fire of London, explaining how the disaster could have been avoided.

Content Note

Some other famous disasters that likely could have been avoided if warnings had been heeded ahead of time:

The British Petroleum Deepwater Horizon Oil Spill (Gulf of Mexico)

The Pike River Coal Mine Explosion (New Zealand)

The Levee Collapse in New Orleans after Hurricane Katrina (United States)

The Yungay Avalanche (Peru)

SPEAKING

Read the task aloud. Then give students time to read the information about the imaginary disaster. Have them also read the discussion questions. Model the example aloud with a volunteer. Ask partners to take turns sharing their thoughts in a style similar to the example conversation. After pairs discuss, elicit a class discussion for students to share their opinions and ideas.

EXTENSION ACTIVITY Have students write a letter to the toy company. Tell them to pretend that they are an assembly line worker who is writing to report concern about the products being sold.

D Have students preview the task. Encourage them to guess the answers based on the content they heard in the first listening as well as the grammar in the language chart.

▶ **12.6** Play the audio/video again. Have students work individually to complete the activity. Check answers as a class.

E Have students work individually to read the paragraph and then complete the sentences. Tell them to use the information in the language chart to help them. Check answers as a class. Elicit a summary in students' own words about how the Great Fire of London could have been avoided.

Whistleblowers

12C Whistleblowers

LESSON OVERVIEW

Aims: Read and comprehend an article about famous whistleblowers; understand main ideas and details

Target Vocabulary: anonymous, classified, discredit, retaliate, unprecedented, wrongdoing

Reading Summary: Is there a difference between whistleblowers who work for companies and whistleblowers who work for the government? The author thinks perhaps so. Examples are first given of individuals who stood up for what was right when they saw corrupt and dangerous practices occurring at their places of work. However, when government employees blow the whistle, damage can be done to national security, which ends up putting a lot of people at risk. The author concludes that whistleblowing is a complex topic, and while some situations of whistleblowing are clearly justified, others can be argued to cause more harm than good.

PRE-READING

Read the questions aloud. Review the meaning of *whistleblower*. Elicit a class discussion to check answers. Ask students to first name some famous whistleblowers and explain as much as they can about what happened. Then encourage students to share their opinions about these people. Note that whistleblowers are often viewed as disloyal, even though what they are doing is morally correct.

▶ **12.8** Play the audio/video as students read along. Go over any unfamiliar language. See **Language Note**.

PRE-READING Predicting   Answers will vary.

Do you know of any famous whistleblowers? What is your opinion of them?

▶ **12.8**

1 In late 2014, an **anonymous** source contacted a German newspaper. The source offered access to millions of internal documents from the secretive Panama law firm Mossack Fonseca.
5 Over the following year, the whistleblower leaked an **unprecedented** number of documents. The amount was so huge—over 11 million documents—that the newspaper coordinated with the International Consortium of Investigative Journalists (ICIJ) to
10 distribute the documents to around 100 media organizations in 80 countries. It took journalists over a year to analyze all this data, now known as the Panama Papers.

The Panama Papers reveal how the rich and
15 famous—including important politicians, well-known athletes, business tycoons, and even criminals— avoided paying taxes by using complicated offshore arrangements to hide their wealth. This was one of the biggest leaks in journalistic history, but it almost certainly
20 won't be the last. Statistics from the U.S. Securities and Exchange Commission show that from 2012 to 2015, the number of whistleblower tips it received grew by more than 30 percent. As technological advances make it increasingly easy for people to share files, we
25 can expect this trend to continue. So what motivates whistleblowers? And is what they do positive?

While some whistleblowers may be driven by revenge or self-enrichment, others may be dedicated individuals who want to make positive
30 changes to their organizations or bring **wrongdoing** to light. In 1996, Jeffrey Wigand—an employee of Brown & Williamson, an American cigarette company—exposed the tobacco industry's lies about the dangers of smoking. He revealed that
35 tobacco companies were intentionally increasing the amount of nicotine in cigarettes, despite knowing that it was highly addictive and could cause cancer. Few would argue now that what Wigand did was a bad thing. But what about revealing
40 government secrets? Does the public have a right to know everything? Or should we trust that our governments know what they're doing?

Edward Snowden is probably the most famous whistleblower in recent years. While working for the
45 CIA and National Security Agency (NSA), he was shocked to discover how extensive the government's reach was in terms of domestic surveillance of civilians. He regarded these practices as an invasion of privacy and an abuse of power. In 2013, he leaked
50 thousands of **classified** documents from the NSA's

Language Note

People who call attention to a moral or legal problem are referred to as *whistleblowers* because they are like referees in a game blowing a whistle to stop play. The term was originally used by a civic activist to applaud people who took a stand against unethical behavior in organizations; however, the term has since come to have a negative connotation since many view whistleblowers as disloyal, even if they are exposing unethical, illegal, and often dangerous goings-on.

Edward Snowden speaks via video to an audience in Hamburg, Germany.

surveillance program to journalists, after which he was charged by the U.S. government with violating the Espionage Act. He then fled to Russia to avoid arrest. His actions have fueled much discussion
55 about the balance between information privacy and national security.

Whistleblowers often pay a high price for their actions, as organizations may **retaliate** or try to **discredit** them. Wigand received anonymous death
60 threats and required round-the-clock bodyguards. His wife divorced him, and their two daughters went to live with her. Eventually, he moved to a new city to make a fresh start. As for Snowden, he was forced to leave the country altogether. American intelligence officials
65 have stated that by releasing classified information, Snowden has damaged national security and put

people's lives in danger: especially military troops and secret agents. Many people therefore view him as a criminal or a traitor who betrayed his own country. But
70 there are others who see him as a hero for standing up for freedom of speech and information.

Clearly, the consequences of whistleblowing can be very difficult to live with. This helps explain why many whistleblowers—including the source of
75 the Panama Papers—prefer to remain anonymous. There are many motivations that lie at the heart of whistleblowing, and our reactions to whistleblowers vary. In situations related to public health and safety, exposing wrongdoing seems hard to criticize.
80 However, when it comes to revealing government secrets, blowing the whistle is a much more complex issue that raises many ethical and moral questions.

157

UNDERSTANDING MAIN IDEAS

Have students work individually. Explain that they should infer the author's purpose for writing the passage based on what they read. Students should recognize the author offers two different views on whistleblowers to show the complexity of the topic. Check answers as a class.

UNDERSTANDING DETAILS

Explain that students should check only the statements that the author would definitely agree with. Tell them to use what they read to infer the author's opinions on each topic. Check answers as a class.

BUILDING VOCABULARY

A Have students work individually to complete the activity. Tell them to observe how each word is used in context in the passage in order to guess the meaning.

B Have students work individually to complete the sentences. Check answers to **A** and **B** as a class.

C **CRITICAL THINKING** Read the question aloud as students read along. Have students first work individually to write a list of questions that would be interesting for them to hear Snowden answer. Encourage students to stay focused on the topic of whistleblowing. After pairs discuss, elicit a class discussion to hear their ideas for questions. Write all the questions on the board for students to use in the **Extension Activity**.

Content Note

Some questions Edward Snowden has been asked during interviews include:

In your mind, though, are you blameless?
What did you report (as a whistleblower)?
What was the response?
What would you do if you had an audience with the President right now?
Do you see yourself as a patriot?
Have you met Putin in Russia?
Were you trained as a spy?

UNDERSTANDING MAIN IDEAS

The main purpose of the passage is to _____.

    a explain why it is wrong for whistleblowers to do what they do

    ⓑ discuss the complexities of whistleblowing

    c present personal stories about the experiences of whistleblowers

UNDERSTANDING DETAILS

Check (✓) the statements that the author would agree with.

    ☐ Whistleblowers generally do more harm than good.

    ☐ Whistleblowing cases are likely to decrease in the future.

    ☑ Jeffrey Wigand is an example of a whistleblower who did the right thing.

    ☑ Edward Snowden broke the law, but he had good intentions behind his actions.

    ☑ Some cases of whistleblowing are easier to justify than others.

BUILDING VOCABULARY

A Match the words in blue from the passage to their definitions.

    1 anonymous — illegal or dishonest behavior

    2 unprecedented — to damage someone's reputation

    3 wrongdoing — not identified by name

    4 classified — having no previous example

    5 retaliate — to attack or injure someone as a response to a hurtful action

    6 discredit — officially secret and available only to authorized people

B Complete the sentences using the correct form of the words in **A**.

    1 There are a number of cases where organizations have _____retaliated_____ against whistleblowers.

    2 Releasing _____classified_____ documents is against the law.

    3 Many whistleblowers prefer to stay _____anonymous_____ out of fear for their safety.

    4 Companies sometimes try to _____discredit_____ whistleblowers by making them appear untrustworthy.

    5 A cover-up is an attempt to hide evidence of _____wrongdoing_____.

    6 One whistleblower, Bradley Birkenfeld, received a(n) _____unprecedented_____ reward of $104 million from the U.S. government.

C **CRITICAL THINKING**   Answers will vary.

    Reflecting If you were able to interview Edward Snowden, what questions would you ask him? Discuss with a partner.

158

⊙ EXTENSION ACTIVITY Have students work in pairs to go online and try to find answers to some of the questions on the board. Snowden has been interviewed by various media outlets, and videos of his interviews as well as transcripts can be found online. Tell pairs to choose three questions from the questions on the board. After students find some answers, have the class gather again to share the information that they learned. If time permits, have a debate about whether or not Snowden should be allowed to return to the United States.

12D Dare to disagree

TEDTALKS

MARGARET HEFFERNAN is an entrepreneur, a writer, and the former CEO of several companies. She studies how organizations think—in particular, how an all-too-common culture of conflict avoidance can lead organizations and managers astray.

Margaret Heffernan's idea worth spreading is that if we want the best results at work, we can't be afraid to challenge our colleagues and must dare to disagree with conventional wisdom.

PREVIEWING

Read the paragraph below. Match each **bold** word to its meaning. You will hear these words in the TED Talk.

Alice Stewart was a British physician and a pioneer in social medicine. After World War II, she specialized in the study of childhood leukemia. She found that the practice of X-raying pregnant women was causing leukemia in children. The medical community, afraid of the controversy this would **provoke**, strongly opposed her finding and tried to **disprove** it. Stewart became **embroiled** in a 25-year battle to get her research recognized. Finally, in the 1970s, experts were persuaded and the practice of X-raying pregnant women was stopped.

1 to show to be incorrect _____ disprove _____

2 deeply involved in a difficult situation _____ embroiled _____

3 to cause a reaction, especially a negative one _____ provoke _____

VIEWING

A ▶ 12.9 Watch Part 1 of the TED Talk. Choose the correct options.

1 What made Alice Stewart and George Kneale good collaborators?

   a Both of them loved working with numbers.

   b Both of them were very friendly people.

   ⓒ Both of them were good at dealing with conflict.

2 Which of the following best summarizes their model of thinking?

   a Hard facts and statistics are more reliable than personal opinions.

   ⓑ Finding evidence that disproves a theory is just as important as finding evidence that confirms it.

   c Finding a middle ground compromise is crucial to resolving personality differences between co-workers.

159

LESSON OVERVIEW

Aims: Watch and understand a talk about whistleblowing; observe and practice using pauses

Target Vocabulary: disprove, embroiled, provoke

TED Talk Summary: Margaret Heffernan begins with the story of Alice Stewart, a British doctor who discovered that X-rays were causing cancer in children. Although her findings were ignored for 25 years by the medical industry, she was positive her results were accurate because she had a helpful collaborator who tried very hard to prove her wrong. Heffernan explains why this kind of collaboration is ideal. When we are able to challenge each other and openly disagree, our work becomes stronger in the end. People who find something problematic within their work and speak out against it are often marginalized and labeled as troublemakers. Heffernan says that we need to be more encouraging of people who bring up issues of wrongdoing, as they are the ones helping those organizations to improve.

12D

Dare to disagree

PREVIEWING

Have students read the paragraphs about the speaker first. Ask students to comment on what the *culture of conflict avoidance* means. Then give them enough time to read the paragraph about Alice Stewart. Note that the version of the TED Talk that students hear has been edited so that the full story of Dr. Stewart will not be heard. The paragraph provides the missing background information that students need in order to understand the beginning of the TED Talk. For the vocabulary task, tell students to pay attention to how each word is used in context. Have them work individually before checking answers in pairs. Remind students of the **Warm Up** preview clip. Tell them to use the language and information they have learned about whistleblowing to support their viewing of the TED Talk.

VIEWING

A Have students preview the task. Note that the question format is similar to comprehension questions on exams such as TOEFL® and TOEIC®. The answer choices paraphrase what students will hear in the video, which requires an understanding of overall meaning.

▶ 12.9 Play Part 1 of the TED Talk. Check answers as a class. Write on the board the last sentence that students heard in Part 1: *They saw it as thinking.* Elicit an explanation of what Heffernan meant. Who are *they* and what is *it*? Dr. Alice Stewart and George Kneale worked so successfully together because they viewed conflict as the path to getting a better result. Elicit or explain the meaning of any unfamiliar language. Suggestions for Part 1 include *fight on her hands, statistician, crunching the data,* and *echo chamber.*

B Have students preview the task by looking over the statements first. Encourage students to guess the answers based on what they've learned so far in the lesson and unit.

▶ **12.10** Play Part 2 of the TED Talk. Check answers as a class. Elicit or explain the meaning of any unfamiliar language. Suggestions for Part 2 include *constructive conflict* and *embroiled*.

⭐ **CHALLENGE** Have students work in pairs and go back to the statements in **B**. Ask them to say which statement they agree or disagree with the most strongly and to give reasons why.

C Have students preview the task. Tell them to listen for the words and how Heffernan uses them in her talk.

▶ **12.11** Play Part 3 of the TED Talk. Check answers as a class. Note that the word *crank* is a form of slang used to describe someone who complains a lot. The word has a strongly negative tone. It is also used to describe a person who others find irritating. Elicit or explain the meaning of any other unfamiliar language. Suggestions for Part 3 include *margins of error* and *raise concerns*.

D **CRITICAL THINKING** Read the questions aloud. For question 1, write on the board: *thinking partners who aren't echo chambers*. Heffernan is saying that a successful collaboration is not about always agreeing with each other, as this is actually not the best way to show support. Instead, disagreement helps co-workers come up with better ideas and makes a company stronger and more successful in the end.

⟲ **EXTENSION ACTIVITY** Have students work in groups to extend their discussion of question 2 in **Critical Thinking**. Ask them to compare Heffernan's opinion of whistleblowers with that of the author of the **Lesson C** reading passage. Would Heffernan encourage government whistleblowers? Tell students to use what they've learned about Heffernan's views from her TED Talk as support for what they think her view would be.

B ▶ **12.10** Watch Part 2 of the TED Talk. Would Margaret Heffernan agree with the following statements? Circle **Y** for yes or **N** for no.

1 People who have similar points of view make the most effective collaborators. Y (N)

2 Constructive conflict requires a lot of patience and energy. (Y) N

3 The biggest problems we face have come from individuals, not organizations. Y (N)

4 A successful organization is one that knows how to avoid conflict. Y (N)

5 Many European and American executives are afraid to raise concerns at work. (Y) N

6 Many CEOs pay more attention to recruiting employees instead of examining the organization's culture and how it thinks. (Y) N

C ▶ **12.11** Watch Part 3 of the TED Talk. Match the terms used by Margaret Heffernan to their corresponding situations.

1 allies

2 whistleblower

3 crank

4 leader

Pablo informed the media about a faulty product being manufactured by his company.

Melissa is good at organizing and guiding teams as well as managing conflict.

A few of Pablo's colleagues share the same concerns as him and are on his side.

Gina is a very negative and bad-tempered person, and seems to like to cause conflict.

D **CRITICAL THINKING** Answers will vary.

Inferring **Discuss these questions with a partner. Then compare answers with your classmates.**

1 Margaret Heffernan says, "It's a fantastic model of collaboration—thinking partners who aren't echo chambers." What does she mean by this?

2 What is Heffernan's opinion of whistleblowers?

VOCABULARY IN CONTEXT

A ▶ **12.12** Watch the excerpts from the TED Talk. Choose the correct meaning of the words.
1.b; 2.a; 3.c; 4.a

B Complete the sentences with the words from the box.

crunch data	dare to	bound to	stand up to

1 Surveys show that employees these days are increasingly willing to report corruption and wrongdoing. Whistleblowing is therefore _____ bound to _____ increase.

2 Thanks to new computer software, we can _____ crunch data _____ faster than ever before.

3 Increased legal protection will give workers more confidence to _____ stand up to _____ their employers.

4 If you were a whistleblower, would you _____ dare to _____ reveal your identity?

160

VOCABULARY IN CONTEXT

A ▶ **12.12** Play the video. If necessary, play it again.

B Have students work individually to complete the sentences. Check answers as a class.

⭐ **CHALLENGE** Have students work in pairs to share their answers to the question in item 4 in **Vocabulary in Context B**. Would they reveal their identity or not? Ask students to also talk about the typical corporate culture or organizational culture in their home countries. How are whistleblowers treated?

TEDTALKS

Using pauses in your presentation is an effective way to emphasize your main points.

- Pause when you want to draw the audience's attention to your next point. Maintain eye contact with your audience to show that the pause is intentional.
- Pause at the end of a point to give the audience time to process what you have said.
- Pause after a joke to allow the audience time to laugh.
- Pause when you show a new slide to give the audience time to read it.

A ▶ **12.13** Watch part of Margaret Heffernan's TED Talk. Mark with a **/** where she pauses in each excerpt below.

1 "Because it was only by not being able to prove **/** that she was wrong, **/** that George could give Alice the confidence she needed **/** to know that she was right."

2 "It's a fantastic model **/** of collaboration **/** —thinking partners who aren't echo chambers. **/** I wonder how many of us have, or **/** dare to have, **/** such collaborators."

3 "So how do organizations **/** think? **/** Well, for the most part, **/** they don't. **/** And that isn't because they don't want to, **/** it's really because they can't. **/** And they can't because the people inside of them **/** are too afraid **/** of conflict."

4 "In surveys of European and American executives, fully 85 percent of them acknowledged that they had issues or concerns at work **/** that they were afraid **/** to raise."

B Work in pairs. Look at the paragraph about Alice Stewart on page 159. Imagine this is part of a presentation you are giving. Mark with a **/** where you think you should pause. Then compare and discuss your answers with your partner. Answers will vary.

C Work with a new partner. Think of a time when you disagreed with someone. It could be a friend, a family member, or a teacher. Make notes about the story. Then tell the story to your partner, using pauses where effective. Answers will vary.

" I think we need to be teaching these skills to kids and adults at every stage of their development. **"**

161

C Give students enough time to write their notes. Then have them work in pairs to share their stories. Ask for volunteers to share their story with the class. Then have the class comment on any techniques used in the delivery, and how the pauses affected their understanding of the story as listeners.

Language Note

Part 1
The expression *to have a fight on someone's hands* is used to describe a conflict that is especially challenging for a person. Often, it is used in cases when one person opposes a large or powerful group.

The job of a *statistician* is to analyze data. When someone spends a lot of time going over numerical data, it's referred to as *crunching the data*.

An actual *echo chamber* is an enclosed space that echoes, or reverberates, sound back. The term is commonly used metaphorically to describe a situation where ideas or opinions are validated by agreement or by being repeated back to the person who first said them.

Part 2
The idea behind the term *constructive conflict* is that disagreement can be beneficial as it can help us gain better end results. To be *embroiled* in a conflict or argument means to be heavily involved in it.

Part 3
The term *margin of error* is a term statisticians use that basically explains the percentage of chance for error within the data.

To *raise concerns* about something means to introduce or explain a topic that you are worried about.

PRESENTATION SKILLS

A Read the Presentation Skills paragraph **Using pauses** aloud. Go over each example of how a pause can be used as a tool for effective communication. Note that Heffernan also demonstrates the Presentation Skill **Using a case study** that students learned in **Unit 8**. Elicit how this skill was used in Heffernan's TED Talk. She tells the story of her client named Joe, which is an example of a case study. Note that the story of Dr. Alice Stewart is not a case study, but an example of using an anecdote.

Have students preview the task.

▶ **12.13** Play the video. Check answers as a class. Elicit the most likely reason Heffernan paused in each case.

B Read the task aloud. Have students work individually to decide where they would pause. Then have them work in pairs and take turns reading the paragraph to each other with their pauses. Tell them to compare the differences and talk about why they chose to insert pauses where they did. Did the pauses change the meaning of the paragraph?

What should we do?

COMMUNICATE

A Have students work in pairs, assigning them as Student A or Student B. Read aloud the scenario that students are going to role-play. Note that they have to decide whether to stop using the chemical that may cause harm to their customers but probably helps the product sell well. Student B is the employee who is bringing the problem to the attention of Student A, the manager. Have students turn to the information for their roles to read about the background situation that may influence their decisions. Ask them to think about what position they want to take. Tell them to plan to take the position of constructive conflict, which they heard about in Heffernan's TED Talk.

B Read the steps aloud that students will follow in the role-play. Note that students are being asked to apply the techniques of conscious listening that they learned in **Unit 10**. Elicit a review of the meaning of RASA as well as details on how to apply each technique (receive, appreciate, summarize, ask).

Give students time to prepare what they want to say. Encourage them to take notes about arguments they want to make, as well as counter arguments in anticipation of what the other speaker is going to say. Read the box **Suggesting solutions to a problem** aloud. Also remind students of the language they learned in **Unit 10** for asking follow-up questions (*Can you elaborate on that, please? Can you give an example?*).

Model the example aloud with a volunteer. Point out that students should try to guide their conversation to reach some kind of resolution. Make

sure students understand that they are expected to give a detailed solution in **C**, so they should discuss in specifics what they want to do, rather than just deciding whether to stop using the chemical.

C Have each pair share with the class what their resolution was and how they were able to negotiate during their discussion. Once the role-play is completed, have students share with their partners the concerns outlined for them in their information.

WRITING

Read the task aloud. Explain that students should continue the role play by writing an email to the CEO with their suggestions. Point out that the two roles should have different styles and approaches in writing the email. For example, the manager needs to show the CEO that the company's reputation is being protected, too.

12E What should we do?

COMMUNICATE A company meeting Answers will vary.

A Work in pairs. You and your partner work for a company that produces food products. An employee has discovered that a chemical is being added to the products to make them tastier. The chemical has been banned in several countries but not yours. There is mixed evidence about its health risks to consumers. **Student A:** You are the senior manager. Turn to page 167. **Student B:** You are the employee. Turn to page 168.

B Student A is meeting Student B to discuss what to do next. Follow the steps below. You may take notes if necessary.

> **1** Student A: Welcome Student B to the meeting.
>
> **2** Student B: Explain your concerns to Student A and what you think the company should do.
>
> **3** Student A: As you listen to Student B, apply the RASA techniques (page 136). Then suggest ways to solve the problem.
>
> **4** Student B: As you listen to Student A, apply the RASA techniques (page 136).
>
> **5** Try to reach an agreement on what to do to fix the problem.

> **Suggesting solutions to a problem**
> *Let's find out more about ...   Maybe we should ...*

> I think we should stop using the chemical immediately and recall all the products.

> Yes, I have temporarily halted production and ordered everyone to stop using the chemical. But before we recall the product, let's find out more about the health risks.

C Share the results of your discussion with your classmates. What are the different solutions suggested?

WRITING An email Answers will vary.

Write an email to the CEO of the company, explaining your role and the decisions reached. Give your reasons.

> Dear Mr. Jones,
>
> I met with _____ today to discuss the problem as you requested, and we were able to come to an agreement. We have decided that we need to ...

An internal company meeting

Presentation 4

MODEL PRESENTATION

A Complete the transcript of the presentation using the words in the box.

rushing	get away	suggested that	hadn't gone
a few	high-stress	relationships	leisurely

Hi, everybody. I'm Brenda. Tell me, how many of you sometimes feel like there aren't enough hours in the day? Right, almost everyone. I know exactly how you feel. I'm a newspaper reporter. It's a [1] <u>high-stress</u> job that keeps me very busy, so I often feel like I'm [2] <u>rushing</u> through life instead of actually living it.

[3] <u>A few</u> months ago, I decided I needed to [4] <u>get away</u> from work for a while and take a vacation. A friend [5] <u>suggested that</u> I go to El Nido in the Philippines. Some of you may not have heard of it before. El Nido is a coastal town that's known for its white-sand beaches and clear waters. My sister came with me, and we stayed in a beautiful resort. We took long, [6] <u>leisurely</u> walks together, and went snorkeling and scuba diving. Picture yourself on a beach, feeling the warm sun on your face. After spending a couple of days like that, I felt refreshed and so much happier.

If I [7] <u>hadn't gone</u> on this trip, I'm sure I'd be even more stressed out now and less productive at work. So my advice to all of you is to slow down, develop more meaningful [8] <u>relationships</u> with your loved ones, and spend more time interacting with nature. Thanks for listening.

B ▶ **P.4** Watch the presentation and check your answers.

C ▶ **P.4** Review the list of presentation skills from Units 1–12 below. Which does the speaker use? Check (✓) them as you watch again. Then compare with a partner.

The speaker …
- ✓ asks the audience questions
- ✓ asks the audience to imagine themselves in a particular situation
- ☐ uses examples the audience is familiar with
- ☐ uses props
- ☐ begins with a strong statement
- ☐ explains technical words that the audience may not understand
- ✓ raises their hand above their head
- ☐ includes a quote
- ✓ smiles and shows enthusiasm while presenting
- ✓ pauses after asking a question to give the audience time to reflect

163

B ▶ **P.4** Play the video to check answers.

C Have students preview the task.

▶ **P.4** Play the video again. Check answers as a class.

As a quick reminder, elicit the presentation skills from Units 1–9 and examples of each:

1. Involving the audience
2. Knowing your audience
3. Using props
4. Beginning with a strong statement
5. Explaining technical words
6. Being authentic
7. Using body movements and gestures
8. Using a case study
9. Referring to visuals

Then elicit the presentation skills in Units 10–12:

10. Using acronyms to summarize
11. Being enthusiastic
12. Using pauses

Elicit more details about the language and techniques that the speaker uses. Point out that even though the speaker uses an example the audience may not be familiar with (El Nido), she then gives a brief description of it (*El Nido is a …*). Ask students to comment on how the speaker communicates enthusiasm through tone and body language.

Review the presentation skills from Units 10–12 in more detail. Elicit the language options or techniques for each that students can use in **Your Turn**.

Presentation 4

LESSON OVERVIEW

Aim: Students give a presentation to a partner about a vacation spot, using each of the presentation skills they've learned in Units 9–12 as well as relevant ones from previous units.

MODEL PRESENTATION

A Have students work individually to complete the sentences. Elicit some basic points about the presentation:

1. What is the topic? (a relaxing vacation)
2. Where did the speaker go? (the Philippines)
3. What is the speaker's main message? (Taking time to slow down is essential for well-being.)
4. What is the speaker's purpose? (to encourage others to take a similar vacation to slow down)

YOUR TURN

A Have students preview the task. Note that students are asked to talk about a vacation spot, but it does not have to be based on personal experiences as in the example. Tell students that they can also talk about their dream vacation spot if they prefer that. Ask students to brainstorm some ideas first and then use the chart to outline the points they want to talk about in their presentation.

Remind students that the focus is slowing down, which they learned about in Unit 11. If necessary, let students look back at Unit 11 for a review of the topic. Give students five or ten minutes to write down and organize their ideas.

B Read the useful phrases aloud as students repeat. Give students more time to revise their notes and decide what language to use in their presentations. Encourage students to use pauses and to show enthusiasm. Challenge them to also use an acronym.

C Remind students that they have two important roles in the activity: speaker and listener. Explain that they need to give their partner their full attention in order to evaluate in **C** and give effective feedback in **D**. Encourage listeners to ask follow-up questions after the presentation is finished.

YOUR TURN Answers will vary.

A You are going to plan and give a short presentation about a vacation spot that encourages people to slow down and enjoy nature. Think of the location, what activities you can do there, and how visiting this place will benefit people. Make notes in the chart below.

Location
Activities
Benefits

B Look at the useful phrases in the box below. Think about which ones you will need in your presentation.

> **Useful phrases**
>
> **Asking the audience questions:** *Tell me, how many of you …?*
> *Would you like to …?*
>
> **Describing places:** *beautiful, picturesque, unspoiled, peaceful*
>
> **Explaining the benefits of something:** *This will help …*
> *… is a good idea for people who …*

C Work with a partner. Take turns giving your presentation using your notes. Use some of the presentation skills from Units 1–12 below. As you listen, check (✓) each skill your partner uses.

The speaker …
- [ ] asks the audience questions
- [ ] asks the audience to imagine themselves in a particular situation
- [ ] uses examples the audience is familiar with
- [ ] uses props
- [ ] begins with a strong statement
- [ ] explains technical words that the audience may not understand
- [ ] raises their hand above their head
- [ ] includes a quote
- [ ] smiles and shows enthusiasm while presenting
- [ ] pauses after asking a question to give the audience time to reflect

D Give your partner some feedback on their talk. Include at least two things you liked and one thing that could be improved.

D Remind students that when offering feedback, it's good to start with some praise. Elicit simple phrases for students to praise each other: *You did great; Fantastic job; That was riveting.*

Explain that after giving praise, students should then offer some positive feedback (*I could really feel your enthusiasm*), and then offer any points that need to be improved (*I wish you could have tried pausing more often for effect*).

⭐ **CHALLENGE** Have students take the feedback from their partners into account and then give their presentation again to the entire class.

Workbook Answer Key

UNIT 1

1A

VOCABULARY

A **1.** feels; **2.** experience; **3.** cope with; **4.** relieve; **5.** reduce; **6.** handle

B Answers will vary.

LISTENING

A a

B **1.** do some exercise; **2.** use gadgets; **3.** relax

COMMUNICATION

1. b; **2.** b; **3.** a; **4.** b

1B

LANGUAGE FOCUS

A **1.** having; **2.** becoming; **3.** to work; **4.** to work; **5.** to look

B **1.** b; **2.** a; **3.** a; **4.** b

C **1.** Y; **2.** N; **3.** Y; **4.** Y; **5.** N; **6.** N

LISTENING FOCUS

B **1.** Hajime doesn't plan to do a Master's. He wants to do a Ph.D.

2. My parents always encouraged me to become a doctor.

3. My sister can't imagine having a desk job.

4. I considered doing a degree in Spanish, but I chose English in the end.

C **1.** a; **2.** b; **3.** a; **4.** a

1C

READING

A a

B **1. Job:** being in the military; **Causes of stress:** tough nature of job, physically and mentally; **2. Job:** firefighting; **Causes of stress:** physical danger and demands of job, dealing with the public; **3. Job:** pilot; **4. Causes of stress:** being in the public eye, possibility of real danger; **5. Job:** event coordinator; **Causes of stress:** deadlines, organizational and people skills required, dealing with problems quickly; **6. Job:** public relations officer; **Causes of stress:** facing the public, sorting out problems that can't be predicted; **7. Job:** senior executives; **Causes of stress:** heavy responsibilities, anxiety about making the wrong decision; **8. Causes of stress:** deadlines, being in the public eye; **9. Job:** field reporters; **10. Job:** taxi driver; **Causes of stress:** dealing with people, rush hour traffic, long hours

LISTENING

A b

B **1.** c; **2.** b; **3.** b

C Answers will vary.

VOCABULARY BUILDING

A **1.** anxiety; **2.** responsibilities; **3.** recession; **4.** generation

B **1.** Social responsibility; **2.** take responsibility; **3.** sense of responsibility; **4.** delegate responsibility

1D

TED PLAYLIST

A b

B **1.** c; **2.** a; **3.** b

C Answers will vary.

1E

WRITING

B Answers will vary.

C Answers will vary.

UNIT 2

2A

VOCABULARY

1. inspiration; **2.** role models; **3.** character; **4.** ideals; **5.** hero; **6.** influence

LISTENING

A **1.** b; **2.** a; **3.** b; **4.** a

B **1.** Man; **2.** Man and Woman; **3.** Woman; **4.** Woman

COMMUNICATION

1. a; **2.** b; **3.** a; **4.** a

2B

LANGUAGE FOCUS

A **1.** which; **2.** that/which; **3.** who; **4.** which

B **1.** Comedies that make you laugh a lot can help lower your stress.; **2.** The girl who won the race trained very hard.; **3.** Nine in ten people who took part in the study said movies were important to them.; **4.** The documentary, which focused on the life of an amazing woman, had a powerful influence on the viewers.

C **1.** a; **2.** b; **3.** b; **4.** b

LISTENING FOCUS

B 1. inspired by; 2. first three; 3. found that; caused people's; blood pressure; 4. raised people's; 5. impressed by; 6. must be

C 1. b; 2. b; 3. a; 4. b

2C
READING

A c

B 1. because she knew that games encouraged people to be determined, optimistic, creative, and to seek help; 2. because it encouraged her to fight things in her life that caused pain and to look for pleasant things; 3. improve problem-solving skills, motor skills, and accuracy; develop strategic thinking, reading, and math skills; strengthen memory and concentration; encourage teamwork and cooperation; 4. games that encourage people to help and support others

LISTENING

A 1. c; 2. a

B a, b, and e

C **Positive effects of video games:** encourage people to be determined, optimistic, creative, and to seek help; can improve problem-solving skills, motor skills, and accuracy; develop strategic thinking, reading, and math skills; strengthen memory and concentration; encourage teamwork and cooperation; pro-social games encourage people to help and support others in real life. **Negative effects of video games:** correlation exists between playing violent video games and aggressive behavior; children who watch violent video games are likely to be more violent and less empathetic towards others in real life; children are taught negative values and bad behavioral models; some games enhance negative stereotypes, particularly of female characters; the addictive nature of video games can lead to children playing for too long and this can negatively impact on their academic achievement; children addicted to games have higher levels of anxiety and depression; children may find distinguishing fantasy and real life difficult; long-term concentration may be damaged. Answers will vary.

VOCABULARY BUILDING

A 1. transfer; 2. virtual; 3. exposure; 4. well-adjusted; 5. underlying

B 1. role models; 2. leadership role; 3. key role

2D
TED PLAYLIST

A c

B 1. b; 2. a; 3. c

C Answers will vary.

2E
WRITING

B Answers will vary.

C Answers will vary.

UNIT 3
3A
VOCABULARY

1. priorities; 2. struggle; 3. accomplish; 4. ambitious; 5. trend; 6. aspirations; 7. altruistic

LISTENING

A 1. a; 2. b

B 1. d; 2. c; 3. a; 4. b; 5. e

COMMUNICATION

A a. 2; b. 3; c. 5; d. 7; e. 6; f. 4; g. 1; h. 8

B Answers will vary.

3B
LANGUAGE FOCUS

A 1. has been increasing; 2. has been decreasing; 3. grew; 4. expanded

B 1. developing; 2. increasing; 3. risen; 4. changed; 5. moved; 6. raised

C 1. finished; 2. been working; 3. been writing; 4. written; 5. made

LISTENING FOCUS

B 1. has been introduced; 2. has been an increase; 3. has been found; 4. have been using; 5. Have you been following; 6. Has there been

C 1. b; 2. a; 3. b; 4. a

3C
READING

A c

B 1. b, c, d; 2. a, c, f

LISTENING

A 1. b; 2. b; 3. a

B c, d, e

C Answers will vary.

VOCABULARY BUILDING

A 1. correlation; 2. paradox; 3. decline; 4. threshold; 5. surge

B 1. coordination; 2. co-workers; 3. coexist; 4. co-founder

3D
TED PLAYLIST

A 1. b; 2. c; 3. a

B 1. Nic Marks; 2. because he wanted to measure how much each country contributes to (or takes away from) the planet and humanity; 3. It prioritizes the world's problems based on how cost-effective the solutions are.

C Answers will vary.

3E
WRITING

B Answers will vary.
C Answers will vary.

UNIT 4

4A
VOCABULARY

1. an element of truth; **2.** the absolute truth; **3.** a white lie;
4. stretched the truth; **5.** a total lie

LISTENING

A a
B **a.** 5; **b.** 6; **c.** 4; **d.** 3; **e.** 2; **f.** 1

COMMUNICATION

1. a; **2.** a; **3.** a; **4.** b

4B
LANGUAGE FOCUS

A **1.** can't; **2.** might; **3.** could; **4.** may not
B **1.** may/might; **2.** must; **3.** can't/couldn't; **4.** may/might;
5. can't/couldn't
C Answers will vary.

LISTENING FOCUS

B **1.** must have been; **2.** might become; **3.** could have come;
4. can't have
C **1.** a; **2.** b; **3.** b; **4.** a

4C
READING

A c
B **1.** b; **2.** a; **3.** c

LISTENING

A c
B b, d, e, f
C Answers will vary.

VOCABULARY BUILDING

A **1.** honesty; **2.** dishonesty; **3.** truthful; **4.** network; **5.** deception
B **1.** taken for a ride; **2.** tall tales; **3.** lying through her teeth; **4.** a
pack of lies; **5.** two-faced

4D
TED PLAYLIST

A **1.** c; **2.** a; **3.** b
B **1.** that we are predictably irrational and can be influenced in ways
we can't grasp; **2.** He says that it keeps us honest because cell
phones and online platforms leave a record of verifiable facts.;
3. She says we should celebrate when very young children start
lying as it is a normal part of their development.
C Answers will vary.

4E
WRITING

B Answers will vary.
C Answers will vary.

UNIT 5

5A
VOCABULARY

1. breaking; **2.** pushed; **3.** endured; **4.** reaching; **5.** set

LISTENING

A c
B **1.** c; **2.** a; **3.** b

COMMUNICATION

1. a; **2.** b; **3.** b; **4.** b

5B
LANGUAGE FOCUS

A **1.** had been training; **2.** had already won; **3.** hadn't shown **4.** had
been working; became
B **1.** had already been running; joined; **2.** was; had started; **3.** had
been speaking; had just begun; arrived; **4.** had submitted; was
C **1. A:** Had she seen a koala before her visit to Australia?;
B: She'd only seen them on TV.; **2. A:** How long had you been
waiting when he called to cancel?; **B:** I'd been waiting two whole
hours.; **3. A:** Had he won any races before he started training
professionally?; **B:** He'd won one race.

LISTENING FOCUS

B **1.** had been reading; **2.** had he reached; **3.** had already become;
4. Had she been training; **5.** had already been living
C **1.** a; **2.** a; **3.** b; **4.** b

5C
READING

A c

B **1. a.** He was fired from his job because his boss thought he wasn't creative enough.; **b.** His first company went bankrupt.; **c.** Universal Studios took both his cartoon character Oswald the Rabbit and his employees.
2. Company 1: Chicago; failure; **Company 2:** New York; failure; **Company 3:** Pennsylvania; success; **Company 4:** Derry Township; success
3. a. Both had experienced failure early on—Walt Disney in his first job, Milton Hershey at school.; **b.** Both had companies that had failed/had succeeded.; **c.** Both persevered and didn't give up.

LISTENING

A c
B **a.** 2; **b.** 4; **c.** 3; **d.** 1
C **a.** Reasons may vary.

VOCABULARY BUILDING

A **1.** amazement; **2.** stunts; **3.** endurance; **4.** reaction; **5.** transformed
B **1.** key ingredients; **2.** direct experience; **3.** achieve success; **4.** smooth path; **5.** Research suggests

5D

TED PLAYLIST

A c
B **1.** c; **2.** a; **3.** b
C Answers will vary.

5E

WRITING

B Answers will vary.
C Answers will vary.

UNIT 6

6A

VOCABULARY

A **1.** earned a living; **2.** contribute; **3.** donate; **4.** make a donation; **5.** contributed; earns interest
B Answers will vary.

LISTENING

A a
B **1.** a way of getting funding for a specific goal from a large number of people; **2.** The Statue of Liberty was crowdfunded.; **3.** People log on to a website, identify a project they are interested in, and contribute money online.; **4.** People know that the money will go directly to the project they have chosen, and they get regular updates on how the money is being spent.

COMMUNICATION

A **1.** a; **2.** a; **3.** a; **4.** b
B Answers will vary.

6B

LANGUAGE FOCUS

A **1.** comes to; **2.** look into; **3.** figure out; **4.** broke down; **5.** do without; **6.** find out; **7.** taking out; **8.** put aside
B **1.** c; **2.** d; **3.** a; **4.** b
C Answers will vary.

LISTENING FOCUS

B **1.** -; **2.** -; **3.** can; **4.** -; **5.** and
C **1.** a; **2.** b; **3.** a

6C

READING

A b
B **Issues with common trading practices:** (Answers will vary.) **1.** Producers don't get a fair share of the profits.; **2.** Producers may have to endure tough working conditions.; **3.** Some workers are children.; **4.** Production methods may harm the environment.; **Benefits of Fairtrade:** (Answers will vary.) **1.** Provides a fairer system of trade./Fairtrade is fairer to workers.; **2.** A small amount of money from purchases is invested back into the community./Fairtrade empowers workers.; **3.** Fairtrade empowers workers./encourages workers to invest in their own future.; **4.** Fairtrade protects the environment./is sustainable.

LISTENING

A a
B **1.** a; **2.** b
C Answers will vary.

VOCABULARY BUILDING

A **1.** poverty; **2.** Foundation; **3.** pledge; **4.** take off; **5.** celebrities
B **1.** d; **2.** b; **3.** c; **4.** a

6D

TED PLAYLIST

A **1.** b; **2.** c; **3.** a
B **1.** b; **2.** c; **3.** a

6E

WRITING

B Answers will vary.
C Answers will vary.

UNIT 7

7A
VOCABULARY

A **1.** invented; designed; **2.** discovered; **3.** innovations
B Answers will vary.

LISTENING

A **1.** a; **2.** a
B **1.** M; **2.** M; **3.** M; **4.** B

COMMUNICATION

A **a.** 3; **b.** 6; **c.** 2; **d.** 5; **e.** 1; **f.** 4
B Answers will vary.

7B
LANGUAGE FOCUS

A **1.** will; **2.** ought to; **3.** won't; **4.** will; **5.** could
B **1.** a; **2.** a; **3.** b
C Answers will vary.

LISTENING FOCUS

B **1.** Robots might take over from doctors eventually.; **2.** Surgeons won't be replaced by machines for a long time.; **3.** New technology has led to many medical innovations.; **4.** Scientists are developing robots that look like human beings.; **5.** Medical scientists should be able to learn a lot from the space program.
C **1.** That cookie was meant for your brother!; **2.** The company organized a blood donation drive.; **3.** My grandfather suffered from Alzheimer's disease.; **4.** I bought these really cool shoes for a bargain!; **5.** Mama Rosa's bakery is the best place to buy fresh bread.; **6.** Scientists have found a way to extend the lifespan of mice.; **7.** San Francisco's Golden Gate is a popular tourist attraction.; **8.** The manager called a meeting to discuss the team's next project.; **9.** Mixed marriages are becoming more common these days.; **10.** The huge bear charged towards him.

7C
READING

A c
B **Materials used:** plastic, carbon fiber, metal; **Recent innovation:** incorporation of computer chips into prosthetics; **What it does:** These chips can read the electrical signal that a muscle sends when it contracts, and this activates motors in the prosthetic limb.; **TMR: What it does:** redirects nerves from the amputated part to a healthy muscle elsewhere in the body; **Result:** Users can control their prosthetics just by thinking, like they would a real limb.

LISTENING

A c
B **1.** T; **2.** F; **3.** T; **4.** T

C Answers will vary. They both involve interface between the prosthetic limb and nerves in the body.

VOCABULARY BUILDING

A **1.** modified; **2.** three-dimensional; **3.** customize; **4.** traditional; **5.** Synthetic
B **1.** approach; **2.** cultures; **3.** values; **4.** role; **5.** methods

7D
TED PLAYLIST

A c
B **1.** c; **2.** a; **3.** b
C Answers will vary.

7E
WRITING

B Answers will vary.
C Answers will vary.

UNIT 8

8A
VOCABULARY

1. putting off; **2.** raise a family; **3.** pursue a career; **4.** get a degree; **5.** settling down

LISTENING

A a
B **1.** 33; **2.** society; **3.** seven, 50; **4.** over 30; **5.** 80, 50

COMMUNICATION

A **a.** 7; **b.** 6; **c.** 1; **d.** 3; **e.** 2; **f.** 4; **g.** 5
B Answers will vary.

8B
LANGUAGE FOCUS

A **1.** finished; **2.** have been studying; **3.** have lived; **4.** have been dating; **5.** graduated
B **1.** a; **2.** a; **3.** a; **4.** b
C Answers will vary.

LISTENING FOCUS

B **1.** She'll have finished; **2.** You won't have passed; **3.** He won't have finished; **4.** You'll have arrived; **5.** I'll have started
C **1.** b; **2.** b; **3.** a; **4.** a

8C

READING

A b

B **1.** prime; **2.** stress at work; **3.** a house; **4.** children;
5. self-confident; **6.** happy; **7.** are less satisfied than women.;
8. increasingly happy; **9.** sense of well-being; **10.** higher

LISTENING

A **1.** b; **2.** c; **3.** a

B **1.** M; **2.** M; **3.** M; **4.** W; **5.** W

C Answers will vary.

VOCABULARY BUILDING

A **1.** peaks; **2.** extending/extended; **3.** coast; **4.** trivialized; **5.** defining moment

B **1.** exploit; **2.** exceed; **3.** exceptions; **4.** extinct; **5.** exclude; **6.** exchanged

8D

TED PLAYLIST

A **1.** b; **2.** c; **3.** a

B **1.** c; **2.** b; **3.** b

8E

WRITING

B Answers will vary.

C Answers will vary.

UNIT 9

9A

VOCABULARY

1. assembled; **2.** function; **3.** remote-controlled; **4.** operate;
5. program

LISTENING

A c

B **1.** slow biological evolution; **2.** evolve; **3.** monitor and control;
4. benefit society

COMMUNICATION

1. a; **2.** b; **3.** a; **4.** b

9B

LANGUAGE FOCUS

A **1.** c; **2.** e; **3.** d; **4.** b; **5.** a

B **1.** see; **2.** were; **3.** wait; **4.** could; **5.** cancel; **6.** were; **7.** approve

C **1.** a; **2.** b; **3.** a; **4.** b

LISTENING FOCUS

B **1.** everybody; **2.** average; **3.** temperature; **4.** camera; **5.** several

C **1.** a; **2.** b; **3.** b; **4.** a; **5.** a

9C

READING

A c

B **1. a.** machines began to do jobs people had done in the past;
b. electricity allowed mass production of goods; **c.** introduction
of computers and IT; **d.** Rapid changes in technology, robotics,
and AI (artificial intelligence); **2.** Cobots are robots that collaborate
with people. They are cheaper, can be easily programmed and
moved. **3.** They will replace a lot of people in small to medium-
sized businesses.

LISTENING

A a

B c, d

C b, c, e

VOCABULARY BUILDING

A **1.** poses a hazard; **2.** surveillance; **3.** humanitarian; **4.** civilians;
5. drawbacks; **6.** carrying out

B **1.** orders; **2.** attack; **3.** mission; **4.** tasks; **5.** research

9D

TED PLAYLIST

A c

B **1.** Markus Fischer and Auke Ijspeert;
2. Answers will vary. They can help us to understand the human
body better; Assist in rescuing people/saving lives in disaster
situations; Help designers to create more efficient designs for
industry.; **3.** They are safer for people and can work more quickly.

C Answers will vary.

9E

WRITING

B Answers will vary.

C Answers will vary.

UNIT 10

10A

VOCABULARY

1. a; **2.** b; **3.** b; **4.** a; **5.** b

LISTENING

A b

B **1.** a; **2.** c; **3.** d; **4.** b

COMMUNICATION

A **1.** a; **2.** b; **3.** b; **4.** b
B Answers will vary.

10B
LANGUAGE FOCUS

A **1.** a; **2.** b; **3.** e; **4.** c; **5.** d
B **1.** He asked Chris if he had been able to focus on her lecture.; **2.** She promised to finish the report that day.; **3.** They said (that) his speech had been really long.; **4.** She told Kyle to present his paper to the class.
C (Answers may vary.) **1.** She told them to listen quietly to what she was going to say.; **2.** He promised (that) he wouldn't get distracted and (that) he would listen carefully.; **3.** They said they were sorry (that) they had been/were late, and that there had been an accident on the way and they had been delayed.; **4.** He told Andy not to be late for the presentation.; **5.** She asked Karen to hand in her homework the following day.

LISTENING FOCUS

B **1.** That was a <u>terrible</u> movie.; **2.** I <u>really</u> enjoyed that lecture.; **3.** Don't you think that was a <u>difficult</u> test?; **4.** I <u>highly</u> recommend you hire him. He's a very good worker.; **5.** She's a <u>rude</u> child!
C **1.** b; **2.** a; **3.** b; **4.** a

10C
READING

A b
B **1.** They treated it with respect and participated in the experiment.; **2.** Answers may vary. Isay probably means that in the media today, it's rare to hear real people telling authentic stories about their lives. As a result, the StoryCorps stories have a powerful effect on listeners.; **3.** Because they are hearing something authentic and pure.; **4.** Answers may vary. StoryCorps provides an opportunity for ordinary people to tell their personal stories and it provides the opportunity to hear something that is authentic and pure.

LISTENING

A a
B a; c; d; f
C Answers will vary.

VOCABULARY BUILDING

A **1.** overestimated; **2.** disruptive; **3.** rapport; **4.** enhances; **5.** pioneer
B **1.** discriminate; **2.** disapproved; **3.** disappointed; **4.** dislike; **5.** discourage

10D
TED PLAYLIST

A **1.** b; **2.** a; **3.** c
B **1.** c; **2.** a; **3.** b
C Answers will vary.

10E
WRITING

B Answers will vary.
C Answers will vary.

UNIT 11

11A
VOCABULARY

1. restore; **2.** meaningful; **3.** leisurely; **4.** juggle; **5.** appreciation; **6.** mindful

LISTENING

A b
B **1.** c; **2.** a; **3.** b

COMMUNICATION

1. a; **2.** a; **3.** b; **4.** a

11B
LANGUAGE FOCUS

A **1.** a little bit of; **2.** every time; **3.** a lot of; **4.** a large number
B **1.** an, the; **2.** a, the; **3.** the, x; **4.** the, a
C **1.** The pace of life today is much faster than it was 30 years ago.; **2.** An increasing number of people like to disconnect and go tech-free at times.; **3.** Spending a day or two in nature is a great way to unwind.; **4.** Without the internet, life and work would be very different.; **5.** Jun has a large number of urgent emails to respond to.

LISTENING FOCUS

B **1.** a; **2.** b; **3.** b; **4.** a; **5.** a
C **1.** a trip; **2.** the city; **3.** the beach; **4.** a while; **5.** a quiet hotel

11C
READING

A c
B **1.** T; **2.** T; **3.** T; **4.** NG; **5.** T; **6.** F

LISTENING

A b
B **1.** local traditions, retain their uniqueness, and preserve nature.; **2.** preserve its traditions, and natural environment.; **3.** an increase in tourism.; **4.** There are clear benefits to becoming a slow city.
C Answers will vary.

VOCABULARY BUILDING

A **1.** cognitive; **2.** evolved; **3.** addiction; **4.** therapy; **5.** intuitively
B **1.** shopping addiction; **2.** gaming addiction; **3.** gambling addiction

11D
TED PLAYLIST

A **1.** c; **2.** a; **3.** b

B **1.** The desire to be happy.; **2.** They both talk about taking time for stillness.; **3.** Pico Iyer

C Answers will vary.

11E
WRITING

B Answers will vary.

C Answers will vary.

UNIT 12

12A
VOCABULARY

A **1.** assert; **2.** resolve; **3.** clarify; **4.** conflict; **5.** persuaded

B **1.** Answers will vary.; **2.** Answers will vary.

LISTENING

A b

B **1.** a; **2.** a

COMMUNICATION

1. a; **2.** b; **3.** b; **4.** a

12B
LANGUAGE FOCUS

A **1.** hadn't been, would still be; **2.** hadn't fallen, wouldn't have; **3.** hadn't been, wouldn't have; **4.** hadn't sounded, wouldn't have; **5.** hadn't been, wouldn't have

B **1.** a; **2.** b; **3.** a

C **2.** If there hadn't been a big leak of classified documents, you wouldn't know the company's problems.; **3.** If I didn't believe in the power of real stories, I wouldn't have become a journalist.; **4.** If they hadn't received threats, they wouldn't have kept quiet about the wrongdoing.; **5.** If she hadn't signed up for the skiing trip, she wouldn't be joining us tomorrow.

LISTENING FOCUS

B **1.** a; **2.** a; **3.** a; **4.** b; **5.** b

C **1.** wouldn't have, they didn't; **2.** would have been, we'd taken; **3.** would have, you'd invited; **4.** hadn't been; would have; **5.** I'd known, would have

12C
READING

A b

B **1.** The illegal wildlife trade is worth up to $20 billion and is the 4th largest illegal trade in the world. The criminal gangs are more sophisticated than ever before, and people who know about what is going on are often reluctant to talk about it.; **2.** WildLeaks does not leak information it receives to the media. Instead, it verifies it and then decides what action to take.; **3.** Answers will vary. WildLeaks probably carries out independent investigations when they do not trust the local law enforcement officers.

LISTENING

A c

B **1.** T; **2.** F; **3.** T; **4.** T; **5.** F

C Answers will vary.

VOCABULARY BUILDING

A **1.** wrongdoing; **2.** classified; **3.** retaliate; **4.** discredit; **5.** unprecedented; **6.** anonymous

B **1.** level; **2.** access; **3.** number; **4.** growth; **5.** opportunity

12D
TED PLAYLIST

A a

B **1.** a; **2.** c; **3.** b

C Answers will vary.

12E
WRITING

B Answers will vary.

C Answers will vary.

Audio and Video Scripts

UNIT 1

1.1 TED TALK PREVIEW CLIP

For years I've been telling people, stress makes you sick. It increases the risk of everything from the common cold to cardiovascular disease. Basically, I've turned stress into the enemy. But I have changed my mind about stress, and today, I want to change yours.

Let me start with the study that made me rethink my whole approach to stress. This study tracked 30,000 adults in the United States for eight years, and they started by asking people, "How much stress have you experienced in the last year?" They also asked, "Do you believe that stress is harmful for your health?"

1.2 LISTENING PART 1

What causes stress?

Many of us experience stress when we feel that too much is demanded of us or if we feel that we are being judged. It's natural to feel stress when taking a test, going for a job interview, or going to a social event, for example. These stressful situations and the physical discomfort we feel are usually temporary and fairly manageable. However, at times, stress can build up and become overwhelming, leading to chronic stress. This is becoming more common as we try to cope with the increasing demands of modern technology, in addition to our other work, school, and family obligations.

Why is it important to deal with stress?

When we become stressed, the brain undergoes chemical and physical changes that affect how it functions. If left unmanaged over time, stress can lead to changes in brain structure that can cause fatigue and health problems. Stress also makes it harder for us to manage our emotions. So our ability to deal with stress effectively is essential for our well-being.

1.3 LISTENING PART 2

How can we reduce stress?

The activities that can help us relieve stress vary from person to person. For some people, physical or creative activities such as sports, art, or music can reduce stress and help them relax. Many people also find that meditation helps to calm the mind and relieve bodily tension. Getting enough sleep and rest is also vital. And perhaps even more importantly, greater social connection with our friends, family, and even pets can trigger the release of stress-reducing hormones in the brain and improve our mental well-being.

1.6 INFOGRAPHIC CONVERSATION

[Speaker A is male; Speaker B is female]

A: Hey, Sophie. I barely get to see you these days. I guess work keeps you really busy.

B: Don't even ask. I've been so over-worked lately.

A: I thought you always wanted to be a pilot. How are you coping?

B: I didn't expect to work such long hours. I just got back from a 14-hour flight to Brazil. I'm exhausted. And I have to turn around and fly to Tokyo tomorrow.

A: That sounds really tiring.

B: It is. It's really stressful too—being in charge of the safety of all the passengers. Anyway, how's your job going, William?

A: It's great! I love being a professor.

B: Do you ever feel stressed at work?

A: I do have crazy deadlines sometimes. I have to submit a paper for a journal next week, but before I do that my colleagues have to read my paper and give me their opinions.

B: I can't imagine writing papers and having people evaluate them. That's too much like school!

A: Good thing I didn't encourage you to become a professor then!

1.10 TED TALK PART 1

For years I've been telling people, stress makes you sick. It increases the risk of everything from the common cold to cardiovascular disease. Basically, I've turned stress into the enemy. But I have changed my mind about stress, and today, I want to change yours.

Let me start with the study that made me rethink my whole approach to stress. This study tracked 30,000 adults in the United States for eight years, and they started by asking people, "How much stress have you experienced in the last year?" They also asked, "Do you believe that stress is harmful for your health?" And then they used public death records to find out who died.

(Laughter)

OK. Some bad news first. People who experienced a lot of stress in the previous year had a 43 percent increased risk of dying. But that was only true for the people who also believed that stress is harmful for your health.

(Laughter)

People who experienced a lot of stress but did not view stress as harmful were no more likely to die. In fact, they had the lowest risk of dying of anyone in the study, including people who had relatively little stress.

[…] So this study got me wondering: Can changing how you think about stress make you healthier? And here the science says yes. When you change your mind about stress, you can change your body's response to stress.

1.11 TED TALK PART 2

Now to explain how this works, I want you all to pretend that you are participants in a study designed to stress you out. It's called the social stress test. You come into the laboratory, and you're told you have to give a five-minute impromptu speech on your personal weaknesses to a panel of expert evaluators sitting right in front of you, and to make sure you feel the pressure, there are bright lights and a camera in your face, kind of like this.

(Laughter)

And the evaluators have been trained to give you discouraging, non-verbal feedback, like this.

(Exhales)

(Laughter)

[…] If you were actually in this study, you'd probably be a little stressed out. Your heart might be pounding, you might be breathing faster, maybe breaking out into a sweat. And normally, we interpret these physical changes as anxiety or signs that we aren't coping very well with the pressure.

But what if you viewed them instead as signs that your body was energized, was preparing you to meet this challenge? Now that is exactly what participants were told in a study conducted at Harvard University.

[…] Now, in a typical stress response, your heart rate goes up, and your blood vessels constrict like this. And this is one of the reasons that chronic stress is sometimes associated with cardiovascular disease. It's not really healthy to be in this state all the time. But in the study, when participants viewed their stress response as helpful, their blood vessels stayed relaxed like this. Their heart was still pounding, but this is a much healthier cardiovascular profile. It actually looks a lot like what happens in moments of joy and courage. Over a lifetime of stressful experiences, this one biological change could be the difference between a stress-induced heart attack at age 50 and living well into your 90s. And this is really what the new science of stress reveals, that how you think about stress matters.

So my goal as a health psychologist has changed. I no longer want to get rid of your stress. I want to make you better at stress.

1.12 TED TALK PART 3

I want to finish by telling you about one more study. And listen up, because this study could also save a life. This study tracked about 1,000 adults in the United States, and they ranged in age from 34 to 93, and they started the study by asking, "How much stress have you experienced in the last year?" They also asked, "How much time have you spent helping out friends, neighbors, people in your community?" And then they used public records for the next five years to find out who died.

OK, so the bad news first: For every major stressful life experience, like financial difficulties or family crisis, that increased the risk of dying by 30 percent. But—and I hope you are expecting a "but" by now—but that wasn't true for everyone. People who spent time caring for others showed absolutely no stress-related increase in dying. Zero. Caring created resilience.

And so we see once again that the harmful effects of stress on your health are not inevitable. How you think and how you act can transform your experience of stress. When you choose to view your stress response as helpful, you create the biology of courage. And when you choose to connect with others under stress, you can create resilience. Now I wouldn't necessarily ask for more stressful experiences in my life, but this science has given me a whole new appreciation for stress.

[…] Thank you.

UNIT 2

2.1 TED TALK PREVIEW CLIP

The movies are very, very focused on defeating the villain and getting your reward, and there's not a lot of room for other relationships and other journeys. It's almost as though if you're a boy, you are a dopey animal, and if you are a girl, you should bring your warrior costume.

2.2 LISTENING

My favorite movie when I was a young girl was a movie called *Space Camp*. It was released in 1986. Every time I watched it, I got lost in my imagination—like I was Kathryn, the lead character who wanted to be the first female space shuttle commander. Or maybe I had a robot friend named Jinx who could send me into space. I could practically feel the vibrations every time I watched it. I already wanted to be an astronaut. But because of that movie, it inspired me even more to fly into space some day.

The character of Kathryn from *Space Camp* was one of my very first role models as a young girl. It's amazing to think that this fictional character inspired me on my journey—from growing up in a small town plagued by gangs and drugs to becoming an engineer for NASA. Hollywood movies can be a big influence on kids, and I'm living proof of that. It's a serious responsibility.

There are many other TV shows and movies that could easily be credited for inciting an interest in space and engineering, like *Apollo 13* or *Star Trek*. Or Disney Junior's spacefaring cartoon, *Miles from Tomorrowland*. These shows appeal to both boys and girls. They're about possibility, about exploration and imagination. But most importantly, they're about not giving up on your dreams.

2.5 INFOGRAPHIC CONVERSATION

[Speaker A is female; Speaker B is male]

A: Hi, Steve. How was your weekend?

B: Pretty good. I watched the movie *The Avengers* with my little brother.

A: Your little brother? But he's so young. Are you sure that was a good idea?

B: Sure, why not? He seemed to enjoy it.

A: But there's a lot of violence in that movie. I don't think it's very age-appropriate for him.

B: What do you mean?

A: I read an article recently about the impact that violent movies can have on young children. It said that kids who are exposed to violence in movies and on TV tend to show higher levels of aggressive behavior once they grow up.

B: I don't think that's true, Jennifer. My brother's smart enough to know it's just a movie. Besides, I watched stuff like this all the time when I was a kid and I've turned out OK.

A: I hope you're right. But I'd prefer it if my younger brother watches movies like *Finding Dory*, which is funny and inspiring.

2.9 TED TALK PART 1

You know, my favorite part of being a dad is the movies I get to watch. I love sharing my favorite movies with my kids, and when my daughter was four, we got to watch *The Wizard of Oz* together. It totally dominated her imagination for months. Her favorite character was Glinda, of course. It gave her a great excuse to wear a sparkly dress and carry a wand.

But you watch that movie enough times, and you start to realize how unusual it is. Now we live today, and are raising our children, in a kind of children's-fantasy-spectacular-industrial complex. But *The Wizard of Oz* stood alone. It did not start that trend. Forty years later was when the trend really caught on, with, interestingly, another movie that featured a metal guy and a furry guy rescuing a girl by dressing up as the enemy's guards. Do you know what I'm talking about? (Laughter) Yeah.

Now, there's a big difference between these two movies, a couple of really big differences between *The Wizard of Oz* and all the movies we watch today. One is there's very little violence in *The Wizard of Oz*. The monkeys are rather aggressive, as are the apple trees. But I think if *The Wizard of Oz* were made today, the wizard would say, "Dorothy, you are the savior of Oz that the prophecy foretold. Use your magic slippers to defeat the computer-generated armies of the Wicked Witch." But that's not how it happens.

Another thing that's really unique about *The Wizard of Oz* to me is that all of the most heroic and wise and even villainous characters are female.

2.10 TED TALK PART 2

Now I started to notice this when I actually showed *Star Wars* to my daughter, which was years later, and the situation was different. At that point I also had a son. He was only three at the time. He was not invited to the screening. He was too young for that. But he was the second child, and the level of supervision had plummeted. (Laughter) So he wandered in, and it imprinted on him like a mommy duck does to its duckling, and I don't think he understands what's going on, but he is sure soaking in it.

And I wonder what he's soaking in. Is he picking up on the themes of courage and perseverance and loyalty? Is he picking up on the fact that Luke joins an army to overthrow the government? Is he picking up on the fact that there are only boys in the universe except for Aunt Beru, and of course this princess, who's really cool, but who kind of waits around through most of the movie so that she can award the hero with a medal and a wink to thank him for saving the universe, which he does by the magic that he was born with?

Compare this to 1939 with *The Wizard of Oz*. How does Dorothy win her movie? By making friends with everybody and being a leader. That's kind of the world I'd rather raise my kids in—Oz, right?—and not the world of dudes fighting, which is where we kind of have to be. Why is there so much Force—capital F, Force—in the movies we have for our kids, and so little yellow brick road?

[…] The movies are very, very focused on defeating the villain and getting your reward, and there's not a lot of room for other relationships and other journeys. It's almost as though if you're a boy, you are a dopey animal, and if you are a girl, you should bring your warrior costume. There are plenty of exceptions, and I will defend the Disney princesses in front of any of you. But they do send a message to boys, that they are not, the boys are not really the target audience. They are doing a phenomenal job of teaching girls how to defend against the patriarchy, but they are not necessarily showing boys how they're supposed to defend against the patriarchy. There's no models for them. And we also have some terrific women who are writing new stories for our kids, and as three-dimensional and delightful as Hermione and Katniss are, these are still war movies.

2.11 TED TALK PART 3

Now, almost none of these movies pass the Bechdel Test. I don't know if you've heard of this. It has not yet caught on and caught fire, but maybe today we will start a movement. Alison Bechdel is a comic book artist, and back in the mid-'80s, she recorded this conversation she'd had with a friend about assessing the movies that they saw. And it's very simple. There's just three questions you should ask:

Is there more than one character in the movie that is female who has lines? So try to meet that bar.

And do these women talk to each other at any point in the movie?

And is their conversation about something other than the guy that they both like? (Laughter)

Right? Thank you. (Applause) Thank you very much.

Two women who exist and talk to each other about stuff. It does happen. I've seen it, and yet I very rarely see it in the movies that we know and love.

[…] I think our job in the Netflix queue is to look out for those movies that pass the Bechdel Test, if we can find them, and to seek out the heroines who are there, who show real courage, who bring people together, and to nudge our sons to identify with those heroines and to say, "I want to be on their team," because they're going to be on their team.

[…] I want more quests like that. I want fewer quests where my son is told, "Go out and fight it alone," and more quests where he sees that it's his job to join a team, maybe a team led by women, to help other people become better and be better people, like the Wizard of Oz. Thank you.

UNIT 3

3.1 TED TALK PREVIEW CLIP

I still remember the day in school when our teacher told us that the world population had become three billion people, and that was in 1960. I'm going to talk now about how world population has changed from that year and into the future, but I will not use digital technology, as I've done during my first five TED Talks. Instead, I have progressed, and I am, today, launching a brand new analog teaching technology that I picked up from IKEA: this box.

3.2 LISTENING PART 1

Linda, please tell us a bit about the work you do at Save the Children.

Save the Children is a leading independent organization for children around the world. A big part of what we do is support children who are affected by war and disasters. My work focuses specifically on the Asia region. I help design monitoring and evaluation systems that track how effective our programs are in healthcare, education, and so on. Then, based on that evidence, we work with governments to develop better policies and design projects aimed to improve children's lives.

3.3 LISTENING PART 2

What made you want to work in international development?

When I was 12, I went on a family holiday to Myanmar. I met a boy near the pagodas where he was selling postcards. I was writing in my notebook, and he came over to me and asked me if he could have my pen, instead of trying to sell me the postcards. So I asked him a little bit about his life, and he told me that he had an ambition to be a doctor and to learn to write in school, et cetera. So I was searching in my bag for everything that I could give to him because my school taught us that everyone had a right to education, and so I felt that any little piece of information or material that I could [give] to help someone fulfil their potential, I would do so. When I left, I went back to Singapore and I volunteered in hospitals and schools for children as part of my school activities—children with special needs in particular. This helped me realize what it is that I wanted to work in the future—in particular, in international development and the aid industry.

What tips do you have for people who want to get a job in international development?

Well, I studied Geography and Development Studies in university, and I did an Honors year in Indonesia after the tsunami—six years after the tsunami—and it helped me gain valuable skills and insights into issues on the ground. And I'd also say that interning is extremely important to get a better idea of what it is that you want, and to see whether all the hard work in trying to get into the industry is in fact what you want to spend your efforts on. So I interned in Save the Children during university, to try out different positions within the organization. And I really believe that the aid industry is a very difficult industry to get into, so if this is really your passion, never give up on your passion, and find a way to get in. And persist—that's the biggest advice I can give.

3.6 INFOGRAPHIC CONVERSATION

[Speaker A is male; Speaker B is female]

A: Hey, Grace. How's school going? Are you enjoying your classes?

B: Hi, Joseph. School's great. I'm really enjoying my geography class right now. We've just been learning about the MINT countries.

A: MINT? What's that?

B: MINT stands for Mexico, Indonesia, Nigeria, and Turkey.

These four countries are considered to be the next economic giants.

A: Turkey's located on the border of Europe and Asia, isn't it?

B: That's right. Its strategic location should encourage international trade. Also, all four MINT countries have a growing young population, which means that the labor force in these countries has been increasing.

A: But what about other problems like corruption and poverty? I heard that many people in Mexico and Nigeria live in poverty.

B: Unfortunately, poverty and inequality have worsened in many emerging countries. But I think this situation is starting to improve. The Indonesian government has been making significant efforts to reduce poverty levels in recent years.

A: I wonder if all the MINT economies will become real giants in the future. It'll be interesting to watch their progress over the next few decades.

3.10 TED TALK PART 1

I still remember the day in school when our teacher told us that the world population had become three billion people, and that was in 1960. I'm going to talk now about how world population has changed from that year and into the future, but I will not use digital technology, as I've done during my first five TED Talks. Instead, I have progressed, and I am, today, launching a brand new analog teaching technology that I picked up from IKEA: this box.

This box contains one billion people. And our teacher told us that the industrialized world, 1960, had one billion people. In the developing world, she said, they had two billion people. And they lived away then. There was a big gap between the one billion in the industrialized world and the two billion in the developing world. In the industrialized world, people were healthy, educated, rich, and they had small families. And their aspiration was to buy a car. And in 1960, all Swedes were saving to try to buy a Volvo like this. This was the economic level at which Sweden was. But in contrast to this, in the developing world, far away, the aspiration of the average family there was to have food for the day. They were saving to be able to buy a pair of shoes. There was an enormous gap in the world when I grew up. And this gap between the West and the rest has created a mindset of the world, which we still use linguistically when we talk about "the West" and "the Developing World." But the world has changed, and it's overdue to upgrade that mindset and that taxonomy of the world, and to understand it.

3.11 TED TALK PART 2

But the world has changed, and it's overdue to upgrade that mindset and that taxonomy of the world, and to understand it.

And that's what I'm going to show you, because since 1960 what has happened in the world up to 2010 is that a staggering four billion people have been added to the world population. Just look how many. The world population has doubled since I went to school. And of course, there's been economic growth in the West. A lot of companies have happened to grow the economy, so the Western population moved over to here. And now their aspiration is not only to have a car. Now they want to have a holiday on a very remote destination and they want to fly. So this is where they are today. And the most successful of the developing countries, they have moved on, you know, and they have become emerging economies, we call them. They are now buying cars. And what happened a month ago was that the Chinese company, Geely, they acquired the Volvo company, and then finally the Swedes understood that something big had happened in the world. (Laughter)

So there they are. And the tragedy is that the two billion over here that is struggling for food and shoes, they are still almost as poor as they were 50 years ago. The new thing is that we have the biggest pile of billions, the three billions here, which are also becoming emerging economies, because they are quite healthy, relatively well-educated, and they already also have two to three children per woman, as those [richer also] have. And their aspiration now is, of course, to buy a bicycle, and then later on they would like to have a motorbike also. But this is the world we have today, no longer any gap. But the distance from the poorest here, the very poorest, to the very richest over here is wider than ever. But there is a continuous world from walking, biking, driving, flying—there are people on all levels, and most people tend to be somewhere in the middle. This is the new world we have today in 2010.

3.12 TED TALK PART 3

Here I have on the screen my country bubbles. Every bubble is a country. The size is population. The colors show the continent. The yellow on there is the Americas; dark blue is Africa; brown is Europe; green is the Middle East; and this light blue is South Asia. That's India and this is China. Size is population. Here I have children per woman: two children, four children, six children, eight children—big families, small families. The year is 1960. And down here, child survival, the percentage of children surviving childhood up to starting school: 60 percent, 70 percent, 80 percent, 90, and almost 100 percent, as we have today in the wealthiest and healthiest countries. But look, this is the world my teacher talked about in 1960: one billion Western world here—high child-survival, small families—and all the rest, the rainbow of developing countries, with very large families and poor child survival.

What has happened? I start the world. Here we go. Can you see, as the years pass by, child survival is increasing? They get soap, hygiene, education, vaccination, penicillin, and then family planning. Family size is decreasing. [When] they get up to 90-percent child survival, then families decrease, and most of the Arab countries in the Middle East is falling down there [to small families]. Look, Bangladesh catching up with India. The whole emerging world joins the Western world with good child survival and small family size, but we still have the poorest billion. Can you see the poorest billion, those [two] boxes I had over here? They are still up here. And they still have a child survival of only 70 to 80 percent, meaning that if you have six children born, there will be at least four who survive to the next generation. And the population will double in one generation.

So the only way of really getting world population [growth] to stop is to continue to improve child survival to 90 percent. That's why investments by Gates Foundation, UNICEF and aid organizations, together with national government in the poorest countries, are so good; because they are actually helping us to reach a sustainable population size of the world. We can stop at nine billion if we do the right things. Child survival is the new green. It's only by child survival that we will stop population growth. And will it happen? Well, I'm not an optimist, neither am I a pessimist. I'm a very serious "possibilist." It's a new category where we take emotion apart, and we just work analytically with the world. It can be done. We can have a much more just world. With green technology and with investments to alleviate poverty, and global governance, the world can become like this.

And look at the position of the old West. Remember when this blue box was all alone, leading the world, living its own life. This will not happen [again]. The role of the old West in the new world is to become the foundation of the modern world—nothing more, nothing less. But it's a very important role. Do it well and get used to it.

Thank you very much.

UNIT 4

4.1 TED TALK PREVIEW CLIP

OK, now I don't want to alarm anybody in this room, but it's just come to my attention that the person to your right is a liar.

(Laughter)

Also, the person to your left is a liar. Also, the person sitting in your very seats is a liar. We're all liars. What I'm going to do today is I'm going to show you what the research says about why we're all liars, how you can become a liespotter, and why you might want to go the extra mile and go from liespotting to truth seeking, and ultimately to trust building.

4.2 LISTENING PART 1

Erin, could you tell us a bit about your job?

I'm a recruiter and project manager for an international IT organization, with experience in recruitment across the Asia-Pacific region. As part of my day-to-day work, I interview candidates for a variety of roles within my organization.

Have you ever met someone who lied in a job interview?

Absolutely. Every candidate wants to present themselves the best way they possibly can to increase their chances of getting a job. But it's *my* job to identify what the candidates may be hiding that could hurt the organization in the long run.

4.3 LISTENING PART 2

What do people usually lie about in a job interview?

One of the most common things candidates lie about is why they left their previous organization, or why they want to leave their current company. Sometimes, I need to figure out if they're looking to leave because of the company's culture, or if they were fired due to poor performance.

Most people will lie or stretch the truth a little bit if they think they can get away with it. For example, I've interviewed candidates who claimed to be skilled in certain IT systems. But when I questioned them more closely—which maybe they weren't expecting—they couldn't give detailed descriptions about how the systems actually work.

Generally, people won't lie about facts that can be easily verified. But once, I had a candidate who provided a false certificate on his credentials. And another time, a candidate lied on his résumé about the years of experience he had working in different companies. Needless to say, he didn't get the job.

4.6 INFOGRAPHIC CONVERSATION

[Speaker A is male; Speaker B is female]

A: Hey, Heidi. Have you checked Facebook lately?

B: Not since last week. Why?

A: Sally's just changed her profile picture to a photo of a tattoo on her shoulder! Do you think she really got one?

B: You're kidding! There's no way Sally got one. It must be a picture of someone else's tattoo.

A: That's what I thought at first. But the tattoo is of a dog's paw print, and I know she loves her dog a lot. It might be real.

B: I don't know, Matt. Sally doesn't seem like the type of person who would get a tattoo.

A: Then why post the photo on her Facebook page?

B: Who knows? She could have posted it just to see how people would react. Or maybe she was trying to make herself seem cooler somehow.

4.10 TED TALK PART 1

OK, now I don't want to alarm anybody in this room, but it's just come to my attention that the person to your right is a liar.

(Laughter)

Also, the person to your left is a liar. Also, the person sitting in your very seats is a liar. We're all liars. What I'm going to do today is I'm going to show you what the research says about why we're all liars, how you can become a liespotter, and why you might want to go the extra mile and go from liespotting to truth seeking, and ultimately to trust building.

[…] And we all kind of hate to admit it. We wish we were better husbands, better wives, smarter, more powerful, taller, richer—the list goes on. Lying is an attempt to bridge that gap, to connect our wishes and our fantasies about who we wish we were, how we wish we could be, with what we're really like. And boy are we willing to fill in those gaps in our lives with lies.

On a given day, studies show that you may be lied to anywhere from 10 to 200 times. Now granted, many of those are white lies. But in another study, it showed that strangers lied three times within the first 10 minutes of meeting each other.

(Laughter)

Now when we first hear this data, we recoil. We can't believe how prevalent lying is. We're essentially against lying. But if you look more closely, the plot actually thickens. We lie more to strangers than we lie to co-workers. Extroverts lie more than introverts. Men lie eight times more about themselves than they do other people. Women lie more to protect other people. If you're an average married couple, you're going to lie to your spouse in one out of every 10 interactions. Now, you may think that's bad. If you're unmarried, that number drops to three.

4.11 TED TALK PART 2

Trained liespotters get to the truth 90 percent of the time. The rest of us, we're only 54 percent accurate. Why is it so easy to learn? Well, there are good liars and there are bad liars. There are no real original liars. We all make the same mistakes. We all use the same techniques.

[…] Now this brings us to our next pattern, which is body language. With body language, here's what you've got to do. You've really got to just throw your assumptions out the door. Let the science temper your knowledge a little bit. Because we think liars fidget all the time. Well guess what, they're known to freeze their upper bodies when they're lying. We think liars won't look you in the eyes. Well guess what, they look you in the eyes a little too much just to compensate for that myth. We think warmth and smiles convey honesty, sincerity. But a trained liespotter can spot a fake smile a mile away. Can you all spot the fake smile here? You can consciously contract the muscles in your cheeks. But the real smile's in the eyes, the crow's feet of the eyes. They cannot be consciously contracted, especially if you overdid the Botox. Don't overdo the Botox; nobody will think you're honest.

Now we're going to look at the hot spots. Can you tell what's happening in a conversation? Can you start to find the hot spots to see the discrepancies between someone's words and someone's actions? Now, I know it seems really obvious, but when you're having a conversation with someone that you suspect of deception, attitude is by far the most overlooked but telling of indicators.

4.12 TED TALK PART 3

An honest person is going to be cooperative. They're going to show they're on your side. They're going to be enthusiastic. They're going to be willing and helpful to getting you to the truth. They're going to be willing to brainstorm, name suspects, provide details. They're going to say, "Hey, maybe it was those guys in payroll that forged those checks." They're going to be infuriated if they sense they're wrongly accused throughout the entire course of the interview, not just in flashes; they'll be infuriated throughout the entire course of the interview. And if you ask someone honest what should happen to whomever did forge those checks, an honest person is much more likely to recommend strict rather than lenient punishment.

Now let's say you're having that exact same conversation with someone deceptive. That person may be withdrawn, look down, lower their voice, pause, be kind of herky-jerky. Ask a deceptive person to tell their story, they're going to pepper it with way too much detail in all kinds of irrelevant places. And then they're going to tell their story in strict chronological order. And what a trained interrogator does is they come in and in very subtle ways over the course of several hours, they will ask that person to tell their story backwards, and then they'll watch them squirm, and track which questions produce the highest volume of deceptive tells.

Why do they do that? Well, we all do the same thing. We rehearse our words, but we rarely rehearse our gestures. We say "yes," we shake our heads "no." We tell very convincing stories, we slightly shrug our shoulders. We commit terrible crimes, and we smile at the delight in getting away with it.

[...] Science has surfaced many, many more indicators. We know, for example, we know liars will shift their blink rate, point their feet towards an exit.

[...] They'll alter their vocal tone, often making their vocal tone much lower.

Now here's the deal. These behaviors are just behaviors. They're not proof of deception. They're red flags.

[...] When you combine the science of recognizing deception with the art of looking, listening, you exempt yourself from collaborating in a lie. You start up that path of being just a little bit more explicit, because you signal to everyone around you, you say, "Hey, my world, our world, it's going to be an honest one. My world is going to be one where truth is strengthened and falsehood is recognized and marginalized." And when you do that, the ground around you starts to shift just a little bit.

And that's the truth. Thank you.

(Applause)

UNIT 5

5.1 TED TALK PREVIEW CLIP

As a young magician, I was obsessed with Houdini and his underwater challenges. So, I began, early on, competing against the other kids, seeing how long I could stay underwater while they went up and down to breathe, you know, five times, while I stayed under on one breath. By the time I was a teenager, I was able to hold my breath for three minutes and 30 seconds. I would later find out that was Houdini's personal record.

5.2 LISTENING PART 1

When did you run your first marathon?

I ran my first marathon when I was 14 years old. Back then, I didn't have any proper training or running experience. But I was inspired to do it after watching a marathon on TV. That first race was one of the most painful experiences of my life. I broke down in tears and felt like giving up halfway through. But my dad, who was running with me that day, kept telling me that I could do it and to believe in myself. He taught me the power of mental strength that day and helped me reach the finish line. After that, I started training seriously and running more marathons every year. In 2013, I became the youngest Latin-American woman in the world to run 100 marathons. Now, at the age of 32, I've completed 128 marathons, in addition to other adventure races and triathlons.

5.3 LISTENING PART 2

Why do you like running marathons?

Running is a sport against yourself. It tests both your mind and your body. The more I push myself, the more I learn about myself. So running helps me grow as a person and become the best person I can be.

What is the biggest challenge in a marathon?

Without doubt, the pain. No matter how hard you train, it's impossible to avoid feeling pain when running a marathon. You need a lot of mental toughness to push through it. Ultimately,

on race day it comes down to: How bad do you want it? Do you believe in yourself? If you can overcome the mental barrier, your body will follow.

5.6 INFOGRAPHIC AUDIO

1. She had turned 40 when she learned to speed read. She says she doesn't have any special power. Her success comes from hard work and practice.

2. He had been studying Eastern philosophy for several years when, in the winter of 1979, he decided to jump into some icy water. He wanted to test the connections between the body and the mind.

3. By the age of five, she had already started earning money for her family by performing at schools and businesses, showing her amazing ability with numbers.

4. When he set his world record for cutting the fastest tennis ball with a sword, he had been practicing the Samurai way of life for many years.

5. She had been showing off her strength for about 60 years before she finally set a world record in 2009—as the world's strongest granny!

6. You could say that he had been preparing for this challenge for most of his life. He had been running regularly since kindergarten, and completed his first marathon before he graduated from high school.

5.10 TED TALK PART 1

As a young magician, I was obsessed with Houdini and his underwater challenges. So, I began, early on, competing against the other kids, seeing how long I could stay underwater while they went up and down to breathe, you know, five times, while I stayed under on one breath. By the time I was a teenager, I was able to hold my breath for three minutes and 30 seconds. I would later find out that was Houdini's personal record.

[...] So, I started researching into pearl divers. You know, because they go down for four minutes on one breath. And when I was researching pearl divers, I found the world of free-diving. It was the most amazing thing that I ever discovered, pretty much. There is many different aspects to free-diving. There is depth records, where people go as deep as they can. And then there is static apnea. That's holding your breath as long as you can in one place without moving. That was the one that I studied.

The first thing that I learned is when you're holding your breath, you should never move at all; that wastes energy. And that depletes oxygen, and it builds up CO_2 in your blood. So, I learned never to move. And I learned how to slow my heart rate down. I had to remain perfectly still and just relax and think that I wasn't in my body, and just control that. And then I learned how to purge. Purging is basically hyperventilating. You blow in and out—

(Breathing loudly)

You do that, you get lightheaded, you get tingling. And you're really ridding your body of CO_2. So, when you hold your breath, it's infinitely easier. Then I learned that you have to take a huge breath, and just hold and relax and never let any air out, and just hold and relax through all the pain.

5.11 TED TALK PART 2

I started learning about the world record holder. His name is Tom Sietas. And this guy is perfectly built for holding his breath. He's six foot four. He's 160 pounds. And his total lung capacity is twice the size of an average person. I'm six foot one, and fat. We'll say big-boned.

(Laughter)

I had to drop 50 pounds in three months. So, everything that I put into my body, I considered as medicine. Every bit of food was exactly what it was for its nutritional value. I ate really small controlled portions throughout the day. And I started to really adapt my body.

[Individual results may vary.]

(Laughter)

The thinner I was, the longer I was able to hold my breath. And by eating so well and training so hard, my resting heart rate dropped to 38 beats per minute. Which is lower than most Olympic athletes. In four months of training, I was able to hold my breath for over seven minutes. I wanted to try holding my breath everywhere. I wanted to try it in the most extreme situations to see if I could slow my heart rate down under duress.

(Laughter)

I decided that I was going to break the world record live on primetime television.

[…] So, I started full focus. I completely trained to get my breath-hold time up for what I needed to do. But there was no way to prepare for the live television aspect of it, being on Oprah. But in practice, I would do it facedown, floating on the pool. But for TV they wanted me to be upright so they could see my face, basically. The other problem was the suit was so buoyant that they had to strap my feet in to keep me from floating up. So, I had to use my legs to hold my feet into the straps that were loose, which was a real problem for me. That made me extremely nervous, raising the heart rate.

5.12 TED TALK PART 3

When I made it to the halfway mark, at eight minutes, I was 100 percent certain that I was not going to be able to make this. There was no way for me to do it.

[…] I kept pushing to 10 minutes. At 10 minutes you start getting all these really strong tingling sensations in your fingers and toes. And I knew that that was blood shunting, when the blood rushes away from your extremities to provide oxygen to your vital organs. At 11 minutes I started feeling throbbing sensations in my legs, and my lips started to feel really strange.

[…] At 15 minutes I was suffering major O_2 deprivation to the heart. And I started having ischemia to the heart. My heartbeat would go from 120 to 50, to 150, to 40, to 20, to 150 again. It would skip a beat. It would start. It would stop. And I felt all this. And I was sure that I was going to have a heart attack.

So, at 16 minutes what I did is I slid my feet out because I knew that if I did go out, if I did have a heart attack, they'd have to jump into the binding and take my feet out before pulling me up. I was really nervous. I let my feet out, and I started floating to the top. And I didn't take my head out. But I was just floating there waiting for my heart to stop, just waiting.

They had doctors with the "Pst," you know, sitting there waiting. And then suddenly I hear screaming. And I think that there is some weird thing—that I had died or something had happened. And then I realized that I had made it to 16:32. So, with the energy of everybody that was there, I decided to keep pushing. And I went to 17 minutes and four seconds.

(Applause)

[…] As a magician, I try to show things to people that seem impossible. And I think magic, whether I'm holding my breath or shuffling a deck of cards, is pretty simple. It's practice, it's training, and it's—It's practice, it's training and experimenting, while pushing through the pain to be the best that I can be. And that's what magic is to me, so, thank you.

UNIT 6

6.1 TED TALK PREVIEW CLIP

Bill Gates: Oh yeah. If you take from the most wealthy and give to the least wealthy, it's good. It tries to balance out, and that's just.

Melinda Gates: But you change systems. In the U.S., we're trying to change the education system so it's just for everybody and it works for all students. That, to me, really changes the inequality balance.

6.2 LISTENING

I understand you co-founded the company Piper. Can you tell us a bit about Piper and how you founded it?

Piper is a product that lets kids play Minecraft and interact with the virtual game while building electronics in the real world. It comes in a toolbox with wires and switches, and basically, kids have to assemble it themselves and hook it up to their computer to play. The reason my co-founder and I actually started Piper was to create more fun tools for kids to get them interested in technology. So we launched a Kickstarter crowdfunding campaign back in March 2015, and the company's been growing ever since.

How does crowdfunding work?

In crowdfunding, a project is basically funded by the public using an online platform. Since Piper was a completely new product, we wanted to make sure that there was a demand for it first. So we shared information about Piper on the Kickstarter website, and then people from all over the world who wanted to support it could donate money—usually a small amount each. Our goal was to raise $50,000, but we actually had so many donors that we ended up raising $280,000, which we used to begin production.

What do people who contribute get in return?

Crowdfunding backers usually get rewards in exchange for being the first people to believe in a product. Our backers received personalized toolboxes with their names printed on the back, Piper T-shirts, and Piper keychains. You can kind of think of it as a customer loyalty program. Thanks to our incredible backers, thousands of kids are playing with Piper now all over the world.

6.5 INFOGRAPHIC AUDIO

1. It's going to be big, with about 200 guests. We're having the ceremony on the beach, then we'll have a big party in a hotel, just next to the beach. We're putting aside about two hundred dollars a month right now. We haven't set a date yet.

2. I don't feel I can take a vacation right now, because I don't have any savings. I just started working, and I need to save money in case I lose my job or my car breaks down or something like that. I want to be ready for these things.

3. We're bringing up two kids, and we just have a small flat that we're renting. We want a house of our own, and we want our kids to have their own rooms, so that's what we're saving for.

4. I've been working a lot of extra shifts lately and saving as much money as I can. My plan is to take six weeks off next year and go backpacking around Europe.

5. I'm saving to buy a mini-van. I can't afford a brand new one, so I'm planning to buy it secondhand. Since I have a big family, I'll need a 7-seater.

6. I haven't figured out what I want to study, but I definitely want to go to university. So when I graduate from high school, I'm going to work for a year and save as much money as I can, and think about which university to go to.

6.8 TED TALK PART 1

Chris Anderson: Bringing up three children when you're the world's richest family seems like a social experiment without much prior art. How have you managed it? What's been your approach?

Bill Gates: Well, I'd say overall the kids get a great education, but you've got to make sure they have a sense of their own ability and what they're going to go and do, and our philosophy has been to be very clear with them—most of the money's going to the foundation—and help them find something they're excited about. We want to strike a balance where they have the freedom to do anything but not a lot of money showered on them so they could go out and do nothing. And so far, they're fairly diligent, excited to pick their own direction.

CA: You've obviously guarded their privacy carefully for obvious reasons. I'm curious why you've given me permission to show this picture now here at TED.

Melinda Gates: Well, it's interesting. As they get older, they so know that our family belief is about responsibility, that we are in an unbelievable situation just to live in the United States and have a great education, and we have a responsibility to give back to the world. And so as they get older and we are teaching them—they have been to so many countries around the world—they're saying, you know, we do want people to know that we believe in what you're doing, Mom and Dad, and it is okay to show us more. So we have their permission to show this picture, and I think Paul Farmer is probably going to put it eventually in some of his work. But they really care deeply about the mission of the foundation, too.

CA: You've easily got enough money despite your vast contributions to the foundation to make them all billionaires. Is that your plan for them?

BG: Nope. No. They won't have anything like that. They need to have a sense that their own work is meaningful and important. We read an article long, actually, before we got married, where Warren Buffett talked about that, and we're quite convinced that it wasn't a favor either to society or to the kids.

6.9 TED TALK PART 2

CA: And I think you've pledged that by the time you're done, more than, or 95 percent of your wealth, will be given to the foundation.

BG: Yes.

CA: And since this relationship, it's amazing—(Applause) And recently, you and Warren have been going around trying to persuade other billionaires and successful people to pledge to give, what, more than half of their assets for philanthropy. How is that going?

BG: Well, we've got about 120 people who have now taken this giving pledge. The thing that's great is that we get together yearly and talk about, OK, do you hire staff, what do you give to them? We're not trying to homogenize it. I mean, the beauty of philanthropy is this mind-blowing diversity. People give to some things. We look and go, "Wow." But that's great. That's the role of philanthropy is to pick different approaches, including even in one space, like education. We need more experimentation. But it's been wonderful, meeting those people, sharing their journey to philanthropy, how they involve their kids, where they're doing it differently, and it's been way more successful than we expected. Now it looks like it'll just keep growing in size in the years ahead.

MG: And having people see that other people are making change with philanthropy, I mean, these are people who have created their own businesses, put their own ingenuity behind incredible ideas. If they put their ideas and their brain behind philanthropy, they can change the world. And they start to see others doing it, and saying, "Wow, I want to do that with my own money." To me, that's the piece that's incredible.

6.10 TED TALK PART 3

CA: It seems to me, it's actually really hard for some people to figure out even how to remotely spend that much money on something else. There are probably some billionaires in the room and certainly some successful people. I'm curious, can you make the pitch? What's the pitch?

BG: Well, it's the most fulfilling thing we've ever done, and you can't take it with you, and if it's not good for your kids, then let's get together and brainstorm about what can be done. The world is a far better place because of the philanthropists of the past, and the U.S. tradition here, which is the strongest, is the envy of the world. And part of the reason I'm so optimistic is because I do think philanthropy is going to grow and take some of these things government's just not good at working on and discovering and shine some light in the right direction.

CA: The world's got this terrible inequality, growing inequality problem that seems structural. It does seem to me that if more of your peers took the approach that you two have made, it would make a dent both in that problem and certainly in the perception of that problem. Is that a fair comment?

BG: Oh yeah. If you take from the most wealthy and give to the least wealthy, it's good. It tries to balance out, and that's just.

MG: But you change systems. In the U.S., we're trying to change the education system so it's just for everybody and it works for all students. That, to me, really changes the inequality balance.

BG: That's the most important. (Applause)

UNIT 7

7.1 TED TALK PREVIEW CLIP

Disability in our age should not prevent anyone from living meaningful lives. My hope and desire is that the tools and processes we develop in our research group can be used to bring highly functional prostheses to those who need them.

7.2 LISTENING PART 1

Can you tell us about some of the work you've done in drug discovery and development?

That's a big question. I think I'm going to focus on my research in diabetes, and on two drugs in particular that I helped to develop—Symlin and Byetta. I'm particularly proud of the fact that they're both "first in class" drugs. That means they're original, and there have never been any drugs like them before.

7.3 LISTENING PART 2

How did you develop these two drugs?

Both drugs are based on natural products. Symlin is based on a human hormone called amylin, and it is for people with Type 1 diabetes. When Type 1 diabetics take symlin with insulin, their bodies control blood sugar much better than with insulin alone.

Byetta, on the other hand, is for the far more common type of diabetes, Type 2. It's based on a hormone found in the body of a large lizard called the gila monster. Byetta helps control blood sugar in Type 2 diabetics, and can delay the need for insulin for many years.

What are the steps involved in bringing a "first in class" drug to the market?

To start, we make sure there's no drug like it out on the market already. Then we see if the drug is safe in animals. After that, we check the drug's safety in humans. We see how well the drug works when real patients take it. Then, if it works the way we expect, we send all the data to the U.S. Food and Drug Administration, otherwise known as the FDA. Finally, after getting FDA approval, we start an advertising campaign for the new drug.

7.6 INFOGRAPHIC AUDIO

Nanoparticles are very small particles that exist in the natural world and are also man-made. They're so small that you can't even see them with a microscope. Nanoparticles have important uses in medicine, such as in cancer treatment. They can be designed to go to specific types of cells in the body and kill cancer cells. Researchers are also hopeful that nanoparticles will one day be used to treat diabetes by delivering insulin to targeted cells. In addition, nanoparticles should be able to deliver vaccines in the future. Nanoparticle-based vaccination is expected to be much cheaper than vaccinations used today. It could therefore make a big difference to public health, particularly in the developing world.

7.9 TED TALK PART 1

I was born and raised in Sierra Leone, a small and very beautiful country in West Africa, a country rich both in physical resources and creative talent.

However, Sierra Leone is infamous for a decade-long rebel war in the '90s when entire villages were burnt down. An estimated 8,000 men, women, and children had their arms and legs amputated during this time. As my family and I ran for safety when I was about 12 from one of those attacks, I resolved that I would do everything I could to ensure that my own children would not go through the same experiences we had. They would, in fact, be part of a Sierra Leone where war and amputation were no longer a strategy for gaining power.

As I watched people who I knew, loved ones, recover from this devastation, one thing that deeply troubled me was that many of the amputees in the country would not use their prostheses. The reason, I would come to find out, was that their prosthetic sockets were painful because they did not fit well.

7.10 TED TALK PART 2

The prosthetic socket is the part in which the amputee inserts their residual limb, and which connects to the prosthetic ankle. Even in the developed world, it takes a period of three weeks to often years for a patient to get a comfortable socket, if ever. Prosthetists still use conventional processes like molding and casting to create single-material prosthetic sockets. Such sockets often leave intolerable amounts of pressure on the limbs of the patient, leaving them with pressure sores and blisters. It does not matter how powerful your prosthetic ankle is. If your prosthetic socket is uncomfortable, you will not use your leg, and that is just simply unacceptable in our age.

So one day, when I met Professor Hugh Herr about two and a half years ago, and he asked me if I knew how to solve this problem, I said, "No, not yet, but I would love to figure it out." And so, for my Ph.D. at the MIT Media Lab, I designed custom prosthetic sockets quickly and cheaply that are more comfortable than conventional prostheses. I used magnetic resonance imaging to capture the actual shape of the patient's anatomy, then use finite element modeling to better predict the internal stresses and strains on the normal forces, and then create a prosthetic socket for manufacture. We use a 3-D printer to create a multi-material prosthetic socket which relieves pressure where needed on the anatomy of the patient. In short, we're using data to make novel sockets quickly and cheaply.

7.11 TED TALK PART 3

Disability in our age should not prevent anyone from living meaningful lives. My hope and desire is that the tools and processes we develop in our research group can be used to bring highly functional prostheses to those who need them. For me, a place to begin healing the souls of those affected by war and disease is by creating comfortable and affordable interfaces for their bodies. Whether it's in Sierra Leone or in

Boston, I hope this not only restores but indeed transforms their sense of human potential.

Thank you very much.

(Applause)

UNIT 8

8.1 TED TALK PREVIEW CLIP

So, I specialize in 20-somethings because I believe that every single one of those 50 million 20-somethings deserves to know what psychologists, sociologists, neurologists, and fertility specialists already know: that claiming your 20s is one of the simplest, yet most transformative, things you can do for work, for love, for your happiness, maybe even for the world.

8.2 LISTENING PART 1

In your book, *Age of Opportunity*, you write about how adolescence now lasts longer than ever before. Could you tell us more about this?

Adolescence starts when kids go through puberty, and ends when they've settled into traditional adult roles. These would include finishing formal education, entering the labor force, getting married, and becoming economically independent from their parents. By the time I was 25, I had finished graduate school, moved away from home, started my first job as a professor, was no longer receiving help from my parents, and was engaged to be married. But people nowadays are reaching these milestones at a much later age. Today, compared with my generation, twice as many 25-year-olds are still in school, only half as many are married, and 50 percent more are receiving financial assistance from their parents. It's a different world.

8.3 LISTENING PART 2

Do you think it's a worrying sign that many young people today are putting off adulthood?

Lots of people worry about this trend. They see it as a sign that today's young people are immature, lazy, or spoiled. But I don't see it that way. I think delaying these transitions is a rational response to a changing world. The world we live in today is so competitive. You need more education to get a decent job. So you're going to stay in school longer, which keeps you financially dependent on your parents, which in turn delays starting a family of your own. I don't see any evidence that young people today are any less mature than my generation was, for example.

8.6 INFOGRAPHIC CONVERSATION

[Speaker A is female; Speaker B is male]

A: Graduation's just a few weeks off! What are your plans after college, Ian?

B: Well, I hope to get a good job in banking. I need to pay off my student loans.

A: When do you think you'll have paid off your loans?

B: Hopefully by the time I'm 30.

A: Oh, that's not too bad.

B: What about you, Julia? What are your plans after college?

A: I want to do some traveling and see the world, particularly China. Hopefully, I'll have saved enough money by the time I start my trip. I'm thinking about doing some volunteer work in China, too.

B: That's a great idea! You speak Mandarin fluently, don't you?

A: Yeah, I do. By the time I graduate, I'll have been learning Mandarin for six years.

8.10 TED TALK PART 1

So, I specialize in 20-somethings because I believe that every single one of those 50 million 20-somethings deserves to know what psychologists, sociologists, neurologists, and fertility specialists already know: that claiming your 20s is one of the simplest, yet most transformative, things you can do for work, for love, for your happiness, maybe even for the world.

[…] I want to change what 20-somethings are doing and thinking.

Here's a story about how that can go. It's a story about a woman named Emma. At 25, Emma came to my office because she was, in her words, having an identity crisis. She said she thought she might like to work in art or entertainment, but she hadn't decided yet, so she'd spent the last few years waiting tables instead. Because it was cheaper, she lived with a boyfriend who displayed his temper more than his ambition. And as hard as her 20s were, her early life had been even harder. She often cried in our sessions, but then would collect herself by saying, "You can't pick your family, but you can pick your friends."

Well, one day, Emma comes in and she hangs her head in her lap, and she sobbed for most of the hour. She'd just bought a new address book, and she'd spent the morning filling in her many contacts, but then she'd been left staring at that empty blank that comes after the words "In case of emergency, please call …" She was nearly hysterical when she looked at me and said, "Who's going to be there for me if I get in a car wreck? Who's going to take care of me if I have cancer?"

8.11 TED TALK PART 2

So over the next weeks and months, I told Emma three things that every 20-something, male or female, deserves to hear.

First, I told Emma to forget about having an identity crisis and get some identity capital. By "get identity capital," I mean do something that adds value to who you are. Do something that's an investment in who you might want to be next. I didn't know the future of Emma's career, and no one knows the future of work, but I do know this: Identity capital begets identity capital. So now is the time for that cross-country job, that internship, that startup you want to try. I'm not discounting 20-something exploration here, but I am discounting exploration that's not supposed to count, which, by the way, is not exploration. That's procrastination. I told Emma to explore work and make it count.

Second, I told Emma that the urban tribe is overrated. Best friends are great for giving rides to the airport, but 20-somethings who huddle together with like-minded peers limit who they know, what they know, how they think, how they speak, and where they work. That new piece of capital, that new person to date, almost always comes from outside the inner circle. New things come from what are called our weak ties, our friends of friends of friends. So yes, half of

20-somethings are un- or under-employed. But half aren't, and weak ties are how you get yourself into that group. Half of new jobs are never posted, so reaching out to your neighbor's boss is how you get that unposted job. It's not cheating. It's the science of how information spreads.

Last but not least, Emma believed that you can't pick your family, but you can pick your friends. Now this was true for her growing up, but as a 20-something, soon Emma would pick her family when she partnered with someone and created a family of her own. I told Emma the time to start picking your family is now.

Now you may be thinking that 30 is actually a better time to settle down than 20, or even 25, and I agree with you. But grabbing whoever you're living with or sleeping with when everyone on Facebook starts walking down the aisle is not progress. The best time to work on your marriage is before you have one, and that means being as intentional with love as you are with work. Picking your family is about consciously choosing who and what you want rather than just making it work or killing time with whoever happens to be choosing you.

8.12 TED TALK PART 3

So what happened to Emma? Well, we went through that address book, and she found an old roommate's cousin who worked at an art museum in another state. That weak tie helped her get a job there. That job offer gave her the reason to leave that live-in boyfriend. Now, five years later, she's a special events planner for museums. She's married to a man she mindfully chose. She loves her new career, she loves her new family, and she sent me a card that said, "Now the emergency contact blanks don't seem big enough."

Now Emma's story made that sound easy, but that's what I love about working with 20-somethings. They are so easy to help. Twenty-somethings are like airplanes just leaving LAX, bound for somewhere west. Right after takeoff, a slight change in course is the difference between landing in Alaska or Fiji. Likewise, at 21 or 25 or even 29, one good conversation, one good break, one good TED Talk, can have an enormous effect across years and even generations to come.

So here's an idea worth spreading to every 20-something you know. It's as simple as what I learned to say to Alex. It's what I now have the privilege of saying to 20-somethings like Emma every single day: Thirty is not the new 20, so claim your adulthood, get some identity capital, use your weak ties, pick your family. Don't be defined by what you didn't know or didn't do. You're deciding your life right now.

Thank you.

(Applause)

UNIT 9

9.1 TED TALK PREVIEW CLIP

The robot I'm holding in my hand is this one, and it's been created by two students, Alex and Daniel. So this weighs a little more than a tenth of a pound. It consumes about 15 watts of power. And as you can see, it's about eight inches in diameter.

9.2 LISTENING

I'm Robert Wood, and I create robots. I like to observe insects like bees. They are small but efficient. Most people think of robots as big, powerful machines. But I thought it would be useful if I could build a small robot that can go to places humans can't go, like deep oceans or space. My team is making robots that are smaller, cheaper, and faster than traditional robots. We are making robots the size of insects, and robots made from completely soft materials. We get ideas from nature. Right now, we are working on creating a group of robot bees. We believe that 20 years in the future, robots like these can help us do dangerous tasks, such as search-and-rescue operations. We face many challenges while building the robots. We can't find robot parts in the shops, so we have to build everything ourselves. Many of our designs don't work. We build and test the robots over and over again. But every time we fail, we're able to learn something new and improve our designs. Bees can't do much on their own, but when they work in groups, they can do so much more. My team wants to build robots that behave in the same way. And that will eventually make a big difference to all our lives.

9.5 INFOGRAPHIC CONVERSATION

[Speaker A is female; Speaker B is male]

A: Hey, Jason. What do you think of driverless cars?

B: I think they're a great idea, Elizabeth.

A: Really? Why?

B: I hate driving. It stresses me out. If I had a driverless car, I'd feel a lot more relaxed because I wouldn't have to worry about parking.

A: I guess that's true.

B: Also, if everyone had a driverless car, there'd be less traffic.

A: What do you mean?

B: Well, those cars have detection systems, so they can coordinate with each other and avoid creating traffic jams. We might not even need traffic lights in the future.

A: But have you considered the potential risks? If the software fails, it'll probably cause a car crash.

B: You know what, Elizabeth? I actually think there's a higher chance of human drivers becoming distracted and causing accidents. Let's face it—that happens all the time.

A: Hmm. I don't know. I think I'd prefer to be in control of the car.

9.9 TED TALK PART 1

The robot I'm holding in my hand is this one, and it's been created by two students, Alex and Daniel. So this weighs a little more than a tenth of a pound. It consumes about 15 watts of power. And as you can see, it's about eight inches in diameter.

[…] So why build robots like this? Well, robots like this have many applications. You can send them inside buildings like this, as first responders to look for intruders, maybe look for biochemical leaks, gaseous leaks. You can also use them for applications like construction. So here are robots carrying beams, columns and assembling cube-like structures. I'll tell you a little bit more about this. The robots can be used for transporting cargo. So one of the problems with these small robots is their payload-carrying capacity. So you might want to have multiple robots carry payloads. This is a picture of a recent experiment we did—actually not so recent anymore—in Sendai, shortly after the earthquake. So robots like this could be sent into collapsed buildings, to assess the damage after natural disasters, or sent into reactor buildings, to map radiation levels.

[…] Here, you have overhead motion-capture cameras on the top that tell the robot where it is 100 times a second. It also tells the robot where these obstacles are. And the obstacles can be moving. And here, you'll see Daniel throw this hoop into the air, while the robot is calculating the position of the hoop, and trying to figure out how to best go through the hoop. So as an academic, we're always trained to be able to jump through hoops to raise funding for our labs, and we get our robots to do that.

(Applause)

So another thing the robot can do is it remembers pieces of trajectory that it learns or is pre-programmed. So here, you see the robot combining a motion that builds up momentum, and then changes its orientation and then recovers. So it has to do this because this gap in the window is only slightly larger than the width of the robot. So just like a diver stands on a springboard and then jumps off it to gain momentum, and then does this pirouette, this two and a half somersault through and then gracefully recovers, this robot is basically doing that. So it knows how to combine little bits and pieces of trajectories to do these fairly difficult tasks.

9.10 TED TALK PART 2

So I want to change gears. So one of the disadvantages of these small robots is its size. And I told you earlier that we may want to employ lots and lots of robots to overcome the limitations of size. So one difficulty is: How do you coordinate lots of these robots? And so here, we looked to nature. So I want to show you a clip of Aphaenogaster desert ants, in Professor Stephen Pratt's lab, carrying an object. So this is actually a piece of fig. Actually, you take any object coated with fig juice, and the ants will carry them back to the nest. So these ants don't have any central coordinator. They sense their neighbors. There's no explicit communication. But because they sense their neighbors and because they sense the object, they have implicit coordination across the group.

So this is the kind of coordination we want our robots to have. So when we have a robot which is surrounded by neighbors—and let's look at robot I and robot J—what we want the robots to do, is to monitor the separation between them, as they fly in formation.

[…] So what I want to show you next is a video of 20 of these little robots, flying in formation. They're monitoring their neighbors' positions. They're maintaining formation. The formations can change. They can be planar formations, they can be three-dimensional formations. As you can see here, they collapse from a three-dimensional formation into planar formation. And to fly through obstacles, they can adapt the formations on the fly. So again, these robots come really close together. As you can see in this figure-eight flight, they come within inches of each other. And despite the aerodynamic interactions with these propeller blades, they're able to maintain stable flight.

(Applause)

So once you know how to fly in formation, you can actually pick up objects cooperatively. So this just shows that we can double, triple, quadruple the robots' strength, by just getting them to team with neighbors.

9.11 TED TALK PART 3

So all these experiments you've seen thus far, all these demonstrations, have been done with the help of motion-capture systems. So what happens when you leave your lab, and you go outside into the real world? And what if there's no GPS? So this robot is actually equipped with a camera, and a laser rangefinder, laser scanner. And it uses these sensors to build a map of the environment. What that map consists of are features—like doorways, windows, people, furniture—and it then figures out where its position is, with respect to the features. So there is no global coordinate system. The coordinate system is defined based on the robot, where it is and what it's looking at. And it navigates with respect to those features.

So I want to show you a clip of algorithms developed by Frank Shen and Professor Nathan Michael, that shows this robot entering a building for the very first time, and creating this map on the fly. So the robot then figures out what the features are, it builds the map, it figures out where it is with respect to the features, and then estimates its position 100 times a second, allowing us to use the control algorithms that I described to you earlier. So this robot is actually being commanded remotely by Frank, but the robot can also figure out where to go on its own. So suppose I were to send this into a building, and I had no idea what this building looked like. I can ask this robot to go in, create a map, and then come back and tell me what the building looks like. So here, the robot is not only solving the problem of how to go from point A to point B in this map, but it's figuring out what the best point B is at every time. So essentially it knows where to go to look for places that have the least information, and that's how it populates this map.

So I want to leave you with one last application. And there are many applications of this technology. I'm a professor, and we're passionate about education. Robots like this can really change the way we do K-12 education. But we're in Southern California, close to Los Angeles, so I have to conclude with something focused on entertainment. I want to conclude with a music video. I want to introduce the creators, Alex and Daniel, who created this video.

(Applause)

So before I play this video, I want to tell you that they created it in the last three days, after getting a call from Chris. And the robots that play in the video are completely autonomous. You will see nine robots play six different instruments. And of course, it's made exclusively for TED 2012. Let's watch.

(Sound of air escaping from valve)

(Music)

(Whirring sound)

(Music)

(Applause) (Cheers)

UNIT 10

10.1 TED TALK PREVIEW CLIP

We are losing our listening. We spend roughly 60 percent of our communication time listening, but we're not very good at it. We retain just 25 percent of what we hear.

10.3 LISTENING PART 1

What kinds of issues do you deal with as a mediator?

Well, I deal mainly with disputes between neighbors. It's pretty common for neighbors to complain about things like loud music or shouting, or children behaving badly. So what I do is, I'll arrange a meeting between all the parties to the dispute, and help them resolve the situation.

Can you give us an example of a situation you helped resolve?

There was one case involving a family with two children. Their neighbors had complained about really loud noise and bad behavior from the children, and even wanted the local police to take action. During the mediation meeting, I listened carefully to everyone's side of the story. The family revealed that one of the children had autism, a condition that makes her behavior very hard to control. The neighbors didn't know this. So after that, I helped everyone reach an agreement about how to communicate better in future and avoid further disputes.

10.4 LISTENING PART 2

It sounds like listening is extremely important in mediation. What advice do you have to help people improve their listening skills?

First, don't interrupt when somebody else is talking. As a mediator, it's important to draw out the other person's story and pick up on the details. Second, remove all distractions. Don't check your phone or look out of the window—focus on what's being said. And finally, observe the emotions behind the words. In mediation meetings, people are often angry and emotional. Part of my job is helping people to express their feelings in an appropriate and productive way.

10.7 INFOGRAPHIC CONVERSATION

[Speaker A is female; Speaker B is male]

A: Hey, Tom. How did your presentation go this morning?

B: Not that great, unfortunately. It looked like half the people weren't really interested.

A: Really? Why would you say that?

B: Well, no one asked any follow-up questions. And a lot of people looked bored and kept checking their cell phones.

A: Did you use any visuals in your presentation?

B: Not many. Why?

A: I recently read an article which said that most people process words using their short-term memory. But images go directly into long-term memory. So when you're giving a presentation, adding visuals can help grab the audience's attention and make a more lasting impact.

B: OK, thanks for the suggestion, Jane. I'll try to use more visual aids and slides tomorrow. Hopefully I'll get a better response from the audience.

A: Don't worry. I'm sure you'll do fine.

10.10 TED TALK PART 1

We are losing our listening. We spend roughly 60 percent of our communication time listening, but we're not very good at it. We retain just 25 percent of what we hear. Now not you, not this talk, but that is generally true. Let's define listening as making meaning from sound. It's a mental process, and it's a process of extraction.

We use some pretty cool techniques to do this. One of them is pattern recognition. (Crowd Noise) So in a cocktail party like this, if I say, "David, Sara, pay attention," some of you just sat up. We recognize patterns to distinguish noise from signal, and especially our name. Differencing is another technique we use. If I left this pink noise on for more than a couple of minutes, you would literally cease to hear it. We listen to differences, we discount sounds that remain the same.

And then there is a whole range of filters. These filters take us from all sound down to what we pay attention to. Most people are entirely unconscious of these filters. But they actually create our reality in a way, because they tell us what we're paying attention to right now. Give you one example of that: Intention is very important in sound, in listening. When I married my wife, I promised her that I would listen to her every day as if for the first time. Now that's something I fall short of on a daily basis. (Laughter) But it's a great intention to have in a relationship.

10.11 TED TALK PART 2

But that's not all. Sound places us in space and in time. If you close your eyes right now in this room, you're aware of the size of the room from the reverberation and the bouncing of the sound off the surfaces. And you're aware of how many people are around you because of the micro-noises you're receiving. And sound places us in time as well, because sound always has time embedded in it. In fact, I would suggest that our listening is the main way that we experience the flow of time from past to future. So, "Sonority is time and meaning"—a great quote.

I said at the beginning, we're losing our listening. Why did I say that? Well, there are a lot of reasons for this. First of all, we invented ways of recording—first writing, then audio recording and now video recording as well. The premium on accurate and careful listening has simply disappeared. Secondly, the world is now so noisy, (Noise) with this cacophony going on visually and auditorily, it's just hard to listen; it's tiring to listen. Many people take refuge in headphones, but they turn big, public spaces like this, shared soundscapes, into millions of tiny, little personal sound bubbles. In this scenario, nobody's listening to anybody.

We're becoming impatient. We don't want oratory anymore, we want sound bites. And the art of conversation is being replaced—

dangerously, I think—by personal broadcasting. I don't know how much listening there is in this conversation, which is sadly very common, especially in the U.K. We're becoming desensitized. Our media have to scream at us with these kinds of headlines in order to get our attention. And that means it's harder for us to pay attention to the quiet, the subtle, the understated.

This is a serious problem that we're losing our listening. This is not trivial. Because listening is our access to understanding. Conscious listening always creates understanding. And only without conscious listening can these things happen—a world where we don't listen to each other at all, is a very scary place indeed. So I'd like to share with you, […] tools you can take away with you, to improve your own conscious listening. Would you like that?

(Audience: Yes.) Good.

10.12 TED TALK PART 3

The first one is silence. Just three minutes a day of silence is a wonderful exercise to reset your ears and to recalibrate so that you can hear the quiet again. If you can't get absolute silence, go for quiet, that's absolutely fine.

Second, I call this the mixer. (Noise) So even if you're in a noisy environment like this—and we all spend a lot of time in places like this—listen in the coffee bar to how many channels of sound can I hear? How many individual channels in that mix am I listening to? You can do it in a beautiful place as well, like in a lake. How many birds am I hearing? Where are they? Where are those ripples? It's a great exercise for improving the quality of your listening.

Third, this exercise I call savoring, and this is a beautiful exercise. It's about enjoying mundane sounds. This, for example, is my tumble dryer. (Dryer) It's a waltz. One, two, three. One, two, three. One, two, three. I love it. Or just try this one on for size. (Coffee grinder) Wow! So mundane sounds can be really interesting if you pay attention. I call that the hidden choir. It's around us all the time.

[…] And finally, an acronym. You can use this in listening, in communication. If you're in any one of those roles—and I think that probably is everybody who's listening to this talk—the acronym is RASA, which is the Sanskrit word for juice or essence. And RASA stands for Receive, which means pay attention to the person; Appreciate, making little noises like "hmm," "oh," "OK"; Summarize, the word "so" is very important in communication; and Ask, ask questions afterwards.

[…] So I invite you to connect with me, connect with each other, take this mission out and let's get listening taught in schools, and transform the world in one generation to a conscious listening world—a world of connection, a world of understanding, and a world of peace.

Thank you for listening to me today.

(Applause)

UNIT 11

11.1 TED TALK PREVIEW CLIP

Clouds. Have you ever noticed how much people moan about them? They get a bad rap. If you think about it, the English

language has written into it negative associations towards the clouds.

11.2 LISTENING

Can you tell us a bit about the Slow Movement and what its aim is?

Slow means being present, living each moment fully, and putting quality before quantity in everything we do. A lot of people nowadays are rushing through life instead of actually living it. This can hurt our health, our work, and our relationships, as I found out from personal experience. So the Slow Movement is about doing things at the *right* speed for ourselves. This doesn't mean that we should do everything slowly—that would be unreasonable. But faster isn't always better.

When did you realize you needed to slow down your pace of life?

I realized this when I started speed-reading bedtime stories to my son. I'd be reading *Snow White* and skipping paragraphs, even whole pages. My son would complain, and we argued about it constantly. Then one day I considered buying a collection of *One-Minute Bedtime Stories*—think *Snow White* in 60 seconds. That's when I realized my fast-paced lifestyle was hurting my relationship with my son, and I needed to slow things down.

How can we slow down in our everyday lives?

Start with small changes and then build from there. I began by dropping a few things from my schedule that weren't essential, switching off my phone for periods of time, taking more breaks at work to rest or meditate. Like I said before, it's about finding your own ways to do things at the right speed for you instead of doing them as fast as possible.

11.5 INFOGRAPHIC CONVERSATION

[Speaker A is male; Speaker B is female]

A: Hey, Sarah. I'm so sorry I'm late. I got here as fast as I could.

B: That's OK, Nicholas. What happened? Did you get lost?

A: Yeah. I had to stop the car a couple of times to check the directions.

B: Was the address I gave you wrong?

A: No, the address was correct. It was my fault. I had to take a work call while I was driving. I guess I got distracted and took a wrong turn somewhere.

B: You mean you were driving and using your cell phone at the same time?

A: Yeah, but don't worry. I used a hands-free kit.

B: You shouldn't do that. A lot of accidents happen because people try to multitask while driving. Even listening to your cell phone while driving can cause you to lose focus. That's why you got lost.

A: You're right, it's a bad habit. I really should try not to do that.

11.9 TED TALK PART 1

Clouds. Have you ever noticed how much people moan about them? They get a bad rap. If you think about it, the English language has written into it negative associations towards the clouds. Someone who's down or depressed, they're under a cloud. And when there's bad news in store, there's a cloud on the horizon. I saw an article the other day. It was about problems with computer processing over the Internet. "A cloud over the cloud," was the headline. It seems like they're everyone's default doom-and-gloom metaphor. But I think they're beautiful, don't you? It's just that their beauty is missed because they're so omnipresent, so, I don't know, commonplace, that people don't notice them. They don't notice the beauty, but they don't even notice the clouds unless they get in the way of the sun. And so people think of clouds as things that get in the way. They think of them as the annoying, frustrating obstructions, and then they rush off and do some blue-sky thinking. (Laughter) But most people, when you stop to ask them, will admit to harboring a strange sort of fondness for clouds. It's like a nostalgic fondness, and they make them think of their youth. Who here can't remember thinking, well, looking and finding shapes in the clouds when they were kids? You know, when you were masters of daydreaming? Aristophanes, the ancient Greek playwright, he described the clouds as the patron goddesses of idle fellows two and a half thousand years ago, and you can see what he means. It's just that these days, us adults seem reluctant to allow ourselves the indulgence of just allowing our imaginations to drift along in the breeze, and I think that's a pity. I think we should perhaps do a bit more of it. I think we should be a bit more willing, perhaps, to look at the beautiful sight of the sunlight bursting out from behind the clouds and go, "Wait a minute, that's two cats dancing the salsa!" (Laughter) (Applause) Or seeing the big, white, puffy one up there over the shopping center looks like the Abominable Snowman going to rob a bank. (Laughter)

[…] Perhaps you're having a moment of existential angst. You know, you're thinking about your own mortality. And there, on the horizon, it's the Grim Reaper. (Laughter)

[…] But one thing I do know is this: The bad press that clouds get is totally unfair. I think we should stand up for them, which is why, a few years ago, I started the Cloud Appreciation Society. Tens of thousands of members now in almost 100 countries around the world. And all these photographs that I'm showing, they were sent in by members. And the society exists to remind people of this: Clouds are not something to moan about. Far from it. They are, in fact, the most diverse, evocative, poetic aspect of nature. I think, if you live with your head in the clouds every now and then, it helps you keep your feet on the ground. And I want to show you why, with the help of some of my favorite types of clouds.

11.10 TED TALK PART 2

Let's start with this one. It's the cirrus cloud, named after the Latin for a lock of hair. It's composed entirely of ice crystals cascading from the upper reaches of the troposphere, and as these ice crystals fall, they pass through different layers with different winds and they speed up and slow down, giving the cloud these brush-stroked appearances, these brush-stroke forms known as fall streaks. And these winds up there can be very, very fierce. They can be 200 miles an hour, 300 miles an hour. These clouds are bombing along, but from all the way

down here, they appear to be moving gracefully, slowly, like most clouds. And so to tune into the clouds is to slow down, to calm down. It's like a bit of everyday meditation.

Those are common clouds. What about rarer ones, like the lenticularis, the UFO-shaped lenticularis cloud? These clouds form in the region of mountains. When the wind passes, rises to pass over the mountain, it can take on a wave-like path in the lee of the peak, with these clouds hovering at the crest of these invisible standing waves of air, these flying saucer-like forms, and some of the early black-and-white UFO photos are in fact lenticularis clouds. It's true.

A little rarer are the fallstreak holes. All right? This is when a layer is made up of very, very cold water droplets, and in one region they start to freeze, and this freezing sets off a chain reaction which spreads outwards with the ice crystals cascading and falling down below, giving the appearance of jellyfish tendrils down below.

Rarer still, the Kelvin-Helmholtz cloud. Not a very snappy name. Needs a rebrand. This looks like a series of breaking waves, and it's caused by shearing winds—the wind above the cloud layer and below the cloud layer differ significantly, and in the middle, in between, you get this undulating of the air, and if the difference in those speeds is just right, the tops of the undulations curl over in these beautiful breaking wave-like vortices.

All right. Those are rarer clouds than the cirrus, but they're not that rare. If you look up, and you pay attention to the sky, you'll see them sooner or later, maybe not quite as dramatic as these, but you'll see them. And you'll see them around where you live. Clouds are the most egalitarian of nature's displays, because we all have a good, fantastic view of the sky. And these clouds, these rarer clouds, remind us that the exotic can be found in the everyday. Nothing is more nourishing, more stimulating to an active, inquiring mind than being surprised, being amazed. It's why we're all here at TED, right? But you don't need to rush off away from the familiar, across the world to be surprised. You just need to step outside, pay attention to what's so commonplace, so everyday, so mundane that everybody else misses it.

One cloud that people rarely miss is this one: the cumulonimbus storm cloud. It's what produces thunder and lightning and hail. These clouds spread out at the top in this enormous anvil fashion stretching 10 miles up into the atmosphere. They are an expression of the majestic architecture of our atmosphere. But from down below, they are the embodiment of the powerful, elemental force and power that drives our atmosphere. To be there is to be connected in the driving rain and the hail, to feel connected to our atmosphere. It's to be reminded that we are creatures that inhabit this ocean of air. We don't live beneath the sky. We live within it. And that connection, that visceral connection to our atmosphere feels to me like an antidote. It's an antidote to the growing tendency we have to feel that we can really ever experience life by watching it on a computer screen, you know, when we're in a wi-fi zone.

11.11 TED TALK PART 3

But the one cloud that best expresses why cloudspotting is more valuable today than ever is this one, the cumulus cloud.

Right? It forms on a sunny day. If you close your eyes and think of a cloud, it's probably one of these that comes to mind. All those cloud shapes at the beginning, those were cumulus clouds. The sharp, crisp outlines of this formation make it the best one for finding shapes in. And it reminds us of the aimless nature of cloudspotting, what an aimless activity it is. You're not going to change the world by lying on your back and gazing up at the sky, are you? It's pointless. It's a pointless activity, which is precisely why it's so important. The digital world conspires to make us feel eternally busy, perpetually busy. You know, when you're not dealing with the traditional pressures of earning a living and putting food on the table, raising a family, writing thank you letters, you have to now contend with answering a mountain of unanswered emails, updating a Facebook page, feeding your Twitter feed. And cloudspotting legitimizes doing nothing. (Laughter) And sometimes we need—(Applause) Sometimes we need excuses to do nothing. We need to be reminded by these patron goddesses of idle fellows that slowing down and being in the present, not thinking about what you've got to do and what you should have done, but just being here, letting your imagination lift from the everyday concerns down here and just being in the present, it's good for you, and it's good for the way you feel. It's good for your ideas. It's good for your creativity. It's good for your soul. So keep looking up, marvel at the ephemeral beauty, and always remember to live life with your head in the clouds. Thank you very much. (Applause)

UNIT 12

12.1 TED TALK PREVIEW CLIP

In surveys of European and American executives, fully 85 percent of them acknowledged that they had issues or concerns at work that they were afraid to raise.

12.3 LISTENING

On the cold morning of January 28, 1986, the space shuttle *Challenger* exploded 73 seconds after lift-off, killing all seven astronauts on board. Millions of people watched the live television broadcast in horror as *Challenger* exploded over the Atlantic Ocean. It remains one of the worst accidents of the American space program.

A few weeks after the accident, two engineers who had worked on the space shuttle talked to National Public Radio on condition that they would not be named. They revealed that prior to lift-off, they had warned NASA about the cold-weather risk. They were concerned that the cold temperature would stiffen the rubber O-ring seals, making them useless, which could cause the shuttle to blow up. The engineers had therefore recommended delaying the launch. However, NASA—under intense pressure to meet its promise of affordable space travel and eager to prove the program a success—rejected this advice and proceeded with the launch, with fatal consequences.

One of the engineers, Roger Boisjoly, later provided documents to investigators that proved the disaster could have been prevented. He became widely known as a whistleblower and was shunned by colleagues and friends. He was also cut off from space work. As his situation grew more difficult, he became sick and depressed—a condition doctors diagnosed as post-traumatic stress disorder. Boisjoly hung on for six months before deciding to take long-term disability leave. He did not return to his job.

12.6 INFOGRAPHIC CONVERSATION

[Speaker A is male; Speaker B is female]

A: You know, even though *Titanic* sank over 100 years ago, there's still a lot we can learn from it.

B: Really? Like what? The ship sank after hitting an iceberg, right?

A: Yes, that's true. But apparently, the crew received numerous warnings about heavy ice in the area and were advised to slow down. Unfortunately, they didn't take the warnings seriously.

B: Why not?

A: Some people believe that the captain ignored the warnings because he wanted to beat a speed record and impress people. If the ship had gone slower, it probably would have had time to avoid the iceberg.

B: Are you serious? How could the captain have been so reckless?

A: Mm. That's not all, though. *Titanic* only carried enough lifeboats for about half the people on board. If there had been the right number of lifeboats, more people would have survived. Over 1,500 people died that night.

B: Why didn't they have more lifeboats on board? That's shocking to me.

A: Well, a lot of people believed *Titanic* was unsinkable, and I think they just became overconfident. If the captain had taken all the necessary precautions, we probably wouldn't still be talking about *Titanic* today.

12.9 TED TALK PART 1

So for 25 years, Alice Stewart had a very big fight on her hands. So, how did she know that she was right? Well, she had a fantastic model for thinking. She worked with a statistician named George Kneale, and George was pretty much everything that Alice wasn't. So, Alice was very outgoing and sociable, and George was a recluse. Alice was very warm, very empathetic with her patients. George frankly preferred numbers to people. But he said this fantastic thing about their working relationship. He said, "My job is to prove Dr. Stewart wrong." He actively sought disconfirmation. Different ways of looking at her models, at her statistics, different ways of crunching the data in order to disprove her. He saw his job as creating conflict around her theories. Because it was only by not being able to prove that she was wrong, that George could give Alice the confidence she needed to know that she was right.

It's a fantastic model of collaboration—thinking partners who aren't echo chambers. I wonder how many of us have, or dare to have, such collaborators. Alice and George were very good at conflict. They saw it as thinking.

12.10 TED TALK PART 2

So what does that kind of constructive conflict require? Well, first of all, it requires that we find people who are very different from ourselves. That means we have to resist the neurobiological drive, which means that we really prefer people mostly like ourselves, and it means we have to seek out people with different backgrounds, different disciplines, different ways of thinking and different experience, and find ways to engage with them. That requires a lot of patience and a lot of energy.

[…] So it's one thing to do that in a one-to-one relationship. But it strikes me that the biggest problems we face, many of the biggest disasters that we've experienced, mostly haven't come from individuals, they've come from organizations, some of them bigger than countries, many of them capable of affecting hundreds, thousands, even millions of lives. So how do organizations think? Well, for the most part, they don't. And that isn't because they don't want to, it's really because they can't. And they can't because the people inside of them are too afraid of conflict.

In surveys of European and American executives, fully 85 percent of them acknowledged that they had issues or concerns at work that they were afraid to raise. Afraid of the conflict that that would provoke, afraid to get embroiled in arguments that they did not know how to manage, and felt that they were bound to lose. Eighty-five percent is a really big number. It means that organizations mostly can't do what George and Alice so triumphantly did. They can't think together. And it means that people like many of us, who have run organizations, and gone out of our way to try to find the very best people we can, mostly fail to get the best out of them.

12.11 TED TALK PART 3

So how do we develop the skills that we need? Because it does take skill and practice, too. If we aren't going to be afraid of conflict, we have to see it as thinking, and then we have to get really good at it. So, recently, I worked with an executive named Joe, and Joe worked for a medical device company. And Joe was very worried about the device that he was working on. He thought that it was too complicated and he thought that its complexity created margins of error that could really hurt people. He was afraid of doing damage to the patients he was trying to help. But when he looked around his organization, nobody else seemed to be at all worried. So, he didn't really want to say anything. After all, maybe they knew something he didn't. Maybe he'd look stupid. But he kept worrying about it, and he worried about it so much that he got to the point where he thought the only thing he could do was leave a job he loved.

In the end, Joe and I found a way for him to raise his concerns. And what happened then is what almost always happens in this situation. It turned out everybody had exactly the same questions and doubts. So now Joe had allies. They could think together. And yes, there was a lot of conflict and debate and argument, but that allowed everyone around the table to be creative, to solve the problem, and to change the device.

Joe was what a lot of people might think of as a whistleblower, except that like almost all whistleblowers, he wasn't a crank at all, he was passionately devoted to the organization and the higher purposes that that organization served. But he had been so afraid of conflict, until finally he became more afraid of the silence. And when he dared to speak, he discovered much more inside himself and much more give in the system than he had ever imagined. And his colleagues don't think of him as a crank. They think of him as a leader.

So, how do we have these conversations more easily and more often? Well, the University of Delft requires that its Ph.D. students have to submit five statements that they're prepared to defend. It doesn't really matter what the statements are about, what matters is that the candidates are willing and able to stand up to authority. I think it's a fantastic system, but I think leaving it to Ph.D. candidates is far too few people, and way too late in life. I think we need to be teaching these skills to kids and adults at every stage of their development, if we want to have thinking organizations and a thinking society.

Unit 1 Quiz: Embrace Stress!

A CONVERSATION

Complete the conversation below using the words in the box.

cope	responsibilities	handle	relief	anxiety	feel

A: Your job seems very stressful. You have so many important ¹_____ . How do you
²_____ the stress?

B: I've learned to ³_____ with it in a number of ways. Sometimes, I take short breaks at
work to meditate. And I like to go fishing on the weekends. Being out on the water in the peace and
quiet is a great stress ⁴_____ .

A: Do you experience less ⁵_____ now than you used to?

B: Yes. I used to ⁶_____ it all the time and had trouble sleeping. But now things are
better.

B GRAMMAR

Complete the sentences with your own words. Start with a gerund or infinitive.

Example: I like <u>working at the clothing store</u>.

1 I enjoy _____ .

2 I want _____ .

3 I am considering _____ .

4 I prefer _____ .

5 I hope _____ .

C TED TALK

Complete the paragraph using the words in the box.

chronic	experiences	relatively	transform

Everyone ¹_____ some kind of stress. According to Kelly McGonigal, some of
us respond to stress better than others. People who view stress as harmful and try to avoid
stressful situations may start to experience ²_____ stress, which can lead
to cardiovascular disease. However, those who view stress as natural and normal may feel
³_____ less stress and have a lower risk of dying from stress-related causes.
McGonigal believes that our attitudes towards stress can ⁴_____ the way it
affects our bodies.

Unit 2 Quiz: Media Influences

A CONVERSATION

Complete the conversation. Circle the correct words.

A: Are you going to JD's concert?

B: No, my parents won't let me go.

A: Why not?

B: They don't think he's a good [1](**theme** / **influence**).

A: You can still enjoy someone's music even if they're not a good [2](**villain** / **role model**).

B: I agree, but I don't like his music anyway. I don't find any [3](**inspiration** / **characters**) in it. He doesn't sing about things that are important to me.

A: You and your high [4](**ideals** / **idols**)! I just like JD's music because it makes me want to dance.

B GRAMMAR

Match each sentence to its missing clause.

____ **1** Batman, … , is mostly good, but he also has a dark side.

____ **2** Watching movies … can make people more violent and aggressive.

____ **3** The lyrics to this song, … , always make me cry.

____ **4** Angelina Jolie, … , is a good role model for other actors.

____ **5** The evening news, … , may make people fearful of leaving their homes.

a which are very sad

b that have a lot of fight scenes

c who is the hero of a comic book series

d which broadcasts stories of crime daily

e who has helped many children around the world

C TED TALK

Complete the paragraph using the words in the box.

assesses	heroic	quest	seek out	theme	villainous

Colin Stokes watches children's movies and [1]_____ them to see what they teach children. Most popular children's movies have the classic [2]_____ of good versus evil. The main character is often a man on a [3]_____ to save a beautiful woman from a "bad guy"—a [4]_____ character, such as an evil scientist or a monster. Stokes wants parents to [5]_____ movies with stronger female characters for their children. A [6]_____ female character shows boys and girls that women are also strong, not just beautiful.

Unit 3 Quiz: Development

A CONVERSATION

Complete the conversation. Circle the correct words.

A: According to an article I read, today's young people are more [1](**altruistic** / **enduring**) than previous generations.

B: Interesting. What's causing this [2](**priority** / **trend**)?

A: The article says there's [3](**an aspiration** / **a correlation**) between young people's altruism and their use of the Internet—they are more aware of problems around the world, so they want to make a difference.

B: Wow! I hope this is the start of [4](**an enduring** / **a declining**) movement. It would be great if everyone cared more about others.

A: Yeah, it would change the world if more people's [5](**aspirations** / **surges**) were to help the poor instead of just becoming rich. Some people's [6](**priorities** / **thresholds**) need to change.

B GRAMMAR

Complete the sentences with either the present perfect or present perfect progressive form of the verb in parentheses. Both are possible.

1 The global standard of living _____ (improve).

2 The unemployment rate _____ (fall) in our country.

3 Around the world, the number of villages without clean water _____ (shrink).

4 The government _____ (make) significant efforts to reduce income inequality.

5 The mayor is worried because the level of crime in the city _____ (increase).

6 Thanks to the work of conservationists, people's awareness of environmental issues _____ (grow) steadily.

C TED TALK

Match the terms from Hans Rosling's TED Talk with their definitions.

____ **1** developing world

____ **2** emerging economies

____ **3** industrialized world

a countries with healthy economies and hi-tech industries

b countries with few economic resources or hi-tech industries

c countries that used to lack technological and economic resources but are becoming more successful

Unit 4 Quiz: Secrets and Lies

A CONVERSATION

Complete the conversation below using the words in the box.

dishonest	element	lie	truth	white

A: My friend asked me how she looked, but I couldn't tell her the [1]_____.

B: Why not?

A: Well, the dress she was wearing didn't suit her. So I just said it was colorful.

B: That wasn't a total [2]_____, was it?

A: No, there was a(n) [3]_____ of truth in it. The dress was very bright. But I feel like I was being [4]_____.

B: Oh, don't worry. A little [5]_____ lie never hurt anybody.

B GRAMMAR

Read each situation. Then circle the correct words.

1 Katie said she was sick at home, but I saw her at the party.
   She (**might be** / **must have been**) lying.

2 Jim doesn't have a lot of money, but I saw him driving an expensive sports car the other day.
   It (**couldn't** / **must**) have been his car.

3 Jan has a habit of lying.
   When you talk to her, she (**could have been** / **may or may not be**) telling the truth.

4 There's a photo of a little girl lifting a piano on the cover of a magazine.
   That photo (**can't** / **might**) be real.

C TED TALK

Complete the paragraph using the words in the box.

body language	extroverts	fake	introverts	prevalent	sincere

Pamela Meyer talks about how [1]_____ lying is. Everyone does it, but some lies are more hurtful than others. She says that [2]_____, or people who are socially confident, lie more often than [3]_____. And you can tell if someone is lying by looking at their [4]_____. People who are dishonest have different gestures and behaviors from people who are [5]_____. For example, you can tell a(n) [6]_____ smile from a real one by looking at the person's eyes.

Unit 5 Quiz: To the Edge

A CONVERSATION

Complete the conversation below using the words in the box.

challenges	endure	goal	push	record

A: Why do you compete in marathons?

B: I like facing [1]_____ and overcoming them. For example, a lot of runners
[2]_____ pain from sore feet and muscles. It can be difficult to keep going during the
race. You need a lot of mental toughness to [3]_____ through the pain.

A: Did I hear that today you're hoping to break your personal [4]_____?

B: Yes, that's right. My [5]_____ is to improve my time to four hours.

B GRAMMAR

Correct the mistake in each sentence.

1 He had been compete internationally for many years before he was selected to go to the Olympics.

2 She had being a gymnast before she started her figure skating career.

3 By the age of 3, Annie had already learn how to play the piano.

4 Scott having been thinking about retiring when he was asked to extend his contract.

5 By the time Lee's classmates finished the first question, Lee had already turning in the test.

6 Josephine had been worked as a waitress for many years before she decided to open her own restaurant.

C TED TALK

Read the excerpt from David Blaine's TED Talk. Write the number of the underlined word next to its meaning.

As a young magician, I was [1]<u>obsessed</u> with [Harry] Houdini and his underwater challenges. So, I began, early on, competing against the other kids, seeing how long I could stay [2]<u>underwater</u> while they went up and down to breathe, you know, five times, while I stayed under on one breath …

As a [3]<u>magician</u>, I try to show things to people that seem [4]<u>impossible</u>. And I think magic, whether I'm holding my breath or shuffling a deck of cards, is pretty simple.

_____ **a** something that cannot happen

_____ **b** extremely interested in something

_____ **c** a person who performs special tricks that don't seem real

_____ **d** below the surface of a swimming pool or other body of water

Unit 6 Quiz: Money Matters

A CONVERSATION

Complete the conversation. Circle the correct words.

A: Tell me more about the charity you volunteer with.

B: It's actually a school. We teach job skills to people who are unemployed and unable to [1](**donate** / **earn**) a living. The goal is to help students gain an [2](**income** / **investment**) by using their new skills.

A: Do all the instructors work for free?

B: Yes, we [3](**donate** / **make**) our time and expertise. We believe we are making [4](**interest** / **an investment**) in the future of these people as well as in our community.

A: Wow, it sounds like you guys are really [5](**earning** / **making**) a difference.

B GRAMMAR

Rewrite the sentences by replacing the words in bold with a phrasal verb from the box. Some of the phrasal verbs are separable.

saving up	cut back on	gave away	go without	pay back

1 We **donated** all of our old DVDs.

_____

2 I need to **stop spending so much money on** eating out.

_____

3 Thanks for buying my coffee. I'll **return the money that I owe you** tomorrow.

_____

4 I am **putting money in a savings account every month** so that I can buy a new home.

_____

5 Karen knows designer jeans are expensive, but she says she can't **live unless she has** them.

_____

C TED TALK

Read the quotes from Bill and Melinda Gates's TED Talk and complete the sentences.

1 *Giving away our wealth has been the most satisfying thing we've done.*
Donating money makes the Gates feel (**good** / **sad that they can't do more**).

2 *These are people who have created their own businesses ... If they put their ideas and their brain behind philanthropy, they can change the world.*
The Gates hope that businesspeople will (**start new companies** / **support charitable causes**).

3 *Our philosophy has been to be very clear with them* [their children] *... help them find something they're excited about.*
The Gates (**don't have** / **have**) a specific set of ideas about parenting.

4 *... we have a responsibility to give back to the world.*
The Gates feel (**they don't have** / **it is their duty**) to help others.

5 *In the U.S., we're trying to change the education system so it's just for everybody and it works for all students.*
The Gates want the education system to be (**fairer** / **more challenging**).

Unit 7 Quiz: Medical Frontiers

A CONVERSATION

Complete the conversation. Circle the correct words.

A: I just read an article about a new [1](**designed** / **design**) for prosthetic limbs. Instead of a one-size-fits-all approach, the limbs can be [2](**customized** / **customizes**) for each individual person.

B: Interesting. I was just reading about laparoscopic surgery. Did you know that it was first [3](**invented** / **invention**) in the early 1900s?

A: What's laparoscopic surgery?

B: It's when doctors make very small cuts in the body to do an operation. It's one of the most important medical [4](**innovates** / **innovations**) of the 20th century.

A: Wow. What will people think of next? It seems like there's a new [5](**discover** / **discovery**) every day.

B GRAMMAR

Put the words in the correct order to make sentences.

1 _____ by the year 2050.
(population / about nine / The world / reach / should / billion)

2 In the future, _____
(live / should / to / be / able / people / even longer.)

3 _____ in the future.
(likely / Scientists / find / for cancer / are / to / a cure)

4 _____ but I doubt it.
(be / Certain medical / in the future, / treatments / could / cheaper)

5 _____ in the future?
(you / Do / fewer / there / be / diseases / think / will)

6 _____
(ever go / common cold / doubt that / away. / the / will / I)

C TED TALK

Read the information from David Sengeh's TED Talk. Then circle **T** for true or **F** for false.

1 Many people in Sierra Leone suffered from amputations during the civil war.   **T**   **F**
  Their arms or legs had been seriously injured.

2 David Sengeh felt the conventional way of making prosthetic arms or legs wasn't   **T**   **F**
  working. He wanted to make prosthetic arms and legs the same way as before.

3 David Sengeh's innovative prosthetic limbs have helped people live more active   **T**   **F**
  lives. He designed artificial organs, such as hearts and lungs.

4 David Sengeh's goal is to help people with disabilities feel more comfortable.   **T**   **F**
  He helps people who are missing arms and legs to feel better.

Unit 8 Quiz: Life Decisions

A CONVERSATION

Complete the conversation below using the words in the box.

| get | pursue | put | raise | settle |

A: So, what are your plans after graduation?

B: You know, the usual things. After I ¹_____ my college degree, I'll probably
²_____ a career, maybe ³_____ down and ⁴_____
a family. What about you?

A: I'd like to ⁵_____ off all those responsibilities for now. I think I'd like to travel around
the world for a year.

B GRAMMAR

Complete the sentences with your own words.

Example: By this time next year, <u>I will have studied English for four years</u>.
                        OR <u>I will have been studying English for four years</u>.

1 When I finish this English class, I _____.

2 By next summer, I _____.

3 Next year, I _____.

4 By the year 2030, I _____.

5 By the time I turn 60, I _____.

C TED TALK

Complete the paragraph using the words in the box.

| consciously | identity crisis | investment | peers | procrastinated |

Some 20-year-olds face a(n) ¹_____ when they realize they don't know what to do with
their lives. Perhaps they've noticed how their ²_____ have moved ahead by getting
married or starting a dream job, whereas they're still doing the same things they did as teenagers.
They've ³_____ on making any serious decisions because they just wanted to have fun.
Psychologist Meg Jay tells young adults that it's OK to explore and have fun, but they also need to make
a(n) ⁴_____ in their future. Do they enjoy traveling? If so, they could look for internships
overseas and perhaps consider a career in international business. By acting more ⁵_____
during their 20s, they'll pave the way for a much more successful future.

Unit 9 Quiz: Technology and Innovation

A CONVERSATION

Complete the conversation. Circle the correct words.

A: How do you [1](**operate** / **function**) this toy?

B: It's [2](**remote-controlled** / **driverless**), so you don't have to stand so close to it. And you can
[3](**install** / **program**) it to do different things.

A: Like what?

B: It has several [4](**functions** / **drawbacks**). It can move forwards and backwards, it can spin, and it can lift
small objects.

A: Cool! Did it come like this, or did you have to [5](**operate** / **assemble**) it yourself?

B: I put it together myself. But it wasn't too difficult.

B GRAMMAR

Circle the correct sentence.

1 a If you push this button, the drone will fly up.
   b If you will push this button, the drone flies up.

2 a If driverless cars become common, there will be less traffic on freeways.
   b If driverless cars became common, there will be less traffic on freeways.

3 a More people buy house-cleaning robots if they were cheaper.
   b More people would buy house-cleaning robots if they were cheaper.

4 a What will you do with a drone if you had one?
   b What would you do with a drone if you had one?

5 a If more people used driverless cars, cities need to be redesigned.
   b If more people use driverless cars, cities will need to be redesigned.

C TED TALK

Complete the answers to the questions using the words in the box.

assess	autonomous	cooperatively	first responders	obstacles

1 Q: How do Vijay Kumar's robots carry heavy objects?
   A: By working _____ .

2 Q: Can the robots sense things that are in their way?
   A: Yes, they can sense _____ .

3 Q: Who can these robots help?
   A: _____

4 Q: How can they help?
   A: They can _____ the damage after natural disasters.

5 Q: Does someone control the robots' every move?
   A: No, they're _____ .

Unit 10 Quiz: Connections

A CONVERSATION

Complete the conversation. Circle the correct words.

A: You should have been at the meeting today. Everyone was listening ¹(**anxiously** / **sympathetically**) to hear about the changes.

B: What changes?

A: Mr. Phillips was ²(**polite** / **reluctant**) to talk about it at first, but he finally told us that a bigger company has bought over our company. We'll have to be ³(**distracted** / **patient**) and see what happens, but we might lose our jobs.

B: That's terrible news. Are you sure you heard him correctly?

A: Yes, I was listening ⁴(**very carefully** / **with half an ear**). Mr. Phillips seemed to be ⁵(**disruptive** / **sympathetic**). He kept apologizing and said the company would help us find new jobs if necessary.

B GRAMMAR

Read the conversation. Then circle the correct words to complete the statements.

Joan: My sister invited us to her house tomorrow night. Mike, did you hear me?

Mike: Huh? What did you say?

Joan: Turn down the TV, please. It's too loud.

Mike: Maybe you should speak louder.

1 Joan (**said** / **told**) Mike that her sister had invited them over.

2 She asked him if he (**had heard** / **hears**) her.

3 Mike asked what she (**had said** / **did say**).

4 Joan told Mike (**to turn** / **turn**) down the TV.

5 Mike (**promised to** / **suggested that**) Joan speak louder.

C TED TALK

Select the correct meaning of the underlined words from Julian Treasure's TED Talk.

1 *This is a serious problem that we're losing our listening. This is not <u>trivial</u>.*

   a very important   **b** of little value

2 *<u>Conscious</u> listening always creates understanding.*

   a thoughtful   **b** creative

3 *It's harder for us to pay attention to the quiet, the <u>subtle</u>, ...*

   a extreme   **b** not easily noticeable

4 *This exercise I call <u>savoring</u>, and this is a beautiful exercise. It's about enjoying …*

   a keeping something for a long time   **b** finding pleasure in something

5 *It's about enjoying <u>mundane</u> sounds. This, for example, is my tumble dryer.*

   a everyday; normal   **b** electric; technological

Unit 11 Quiz: Life in the Slow Lane

A CONVERSATION

Complete the conversation below using the words in the box.

appreciate	juggling	leisurely	meaningful	restore

A: When is the last time you took a(n) ¹_____ walk in the park?

B: I can't remember. I run in the park for exercise sometimes. Why do you ask?

A: I feel like I'm constantly busy. I'm always ²_____ work and family responsibilities. I don't have time to stop and ³_____ simple things like a nice park.

B: It sounds like you need to take a break and ⁴_____ some balance in your life.

A: I do. I'd love to slow things down and have more ⁵_____ relationships with my family members.

B GRAMMAR

Circle the correct article or quantifier. If no article is necessary, circle **x**.

1 (**A** / **The**) sun is setting behind the clouds.

2 Spending time in (**the** / **x**) nature is important.

3 Just (**a little** / **every**) relaxation can help a person's stress level go down.

4 I'd like to go to (**a** / **the**) retreat, but I'm not sure which retreat to go to.

5 A large (**amount** / **number**) of my friends have started cloudspotting.

C TED TALK

Complete the paragraph below using the words in the box.

moan	fondness	obstructions	stands up for	meditation

Gavin Pretor-Pinney has a great ¹_____ for clouds. He loves looking at them. He says clouds are "like a bit of everyday ²_____." Unfortunately, many people tend to complain or ³_____ about clouds. They think of clouds as ⁴_____ that block the sun. But Pretor-Pinney ⁵_____ clouds. He encourages people to look up at the clouds and imagine what shapes the clouds are taking. Cloudspotting, he believes, can help us to live in the present and be more mindful of our surroundings.

Unit 12 Quiz: Make Yourself Heard

A CONVERSATION

Complete the conversation below using the words in the box.

assert	clarify	conflict	persuaded	persuasive	resolving

A: Thank you for speaking to us about human rights, Ms. Reynolds. Your speech was very [1]_____.

B: I'm glad you thought so. Have I [2]_____ you to do anything in particular?

A: Well, there has been some [3]_____ recently over a poor neighborhood in my community. The city wants to tear down the houses there to make space for a new shopping center, but that means the people who live there would be forced to move.

B: What is your plan?

A: I'd ask the city to [4]_____ its position on affordable housing for the poor. Then, I'd [5]_____ that everyone has a right to adequate housing and shelter.

B: Sounds good. I wish you luck in [6]_____ this problem!

B GRAMMAR

Match the two parts of the sentences.

____ **1** If we had known about the problem,

____ **2** If you hadn't caught the fire so early,

____ **3** If the *Titanic* had been going more slowly,

____ **4** If you had complained about your living conditions,

____ **5** If the employee hadn't told the truth about her boss,

____ **6** If Malala had listened to people who told her to be quiet,

a it might have missed the iceberg.

b we could have done something about it.

c the whole house would have burned down.

d she wouldn't be the inspiration that she is today.

e her boss would still be stealing money from the company today.

f the company would have provided you with a better apartment.

C TED TALK

Complete the paragraph below using the words in the box.

disprove	embroiled	provoke

Margaret Heffernan claims that people in the workplace are afraid to disagree with one another because they don't want to [1]_____ any anger. Some employees find themselves [2]_____ in difficult situations, but they stay quiet out of fear of conflict. Heffernan encourages colleagues to challenge one another. She gives an example of a doctor, Alice Stewart, whose colleague was determined to [3]_____ her research. When her colleague couldn't show that she was wrong, this gave Alice the confidence she needed to know that she was right.

Unit Quizzes Answer Key

UNIT 1

CONVERSATION

1. responsibilities; **2.** handle; **3.** cope; **4.** relief; **5.** anxiety;
6. feel

GRAMMAR

(Answers will vary.) **1.** I enjoy *(gerund)* …;
2. I want *(infinitive)* …; **3.** I am considering *(gerund)* …;
4. I prefer *(infinitive)* …; **5.** I hope *(infinitive)* …

TED TALK

1. experiences; **2.** chronic; **3.** relatively; **4.** transform

UNIT 2

CONVERSATION

1. influence; **2.** role model; **3.** inspiration; **4.** ideals

GRAMMAR

1. c; **2.** b; **3.** a; **4.** e; **5.** d

TED TALK

1. assesses; **2.** theme; **3.** quest; **4.** villainous; **5.** seek out;
6. heroic

UNIT 3

CONVERSATION

1. altruistic; **2.** trend; **3.** a correlation; **4.** an enduring;
5. aspirations; **6.** priorities

GRAMMAR

1. has improved / has been improving; **2.** has fallen / has been
falling; **3.** has shrunk / has been shrinking; **4.** has made / has
been making; **5.** has increased / has been increasing; **6.** has
grown / has been growing

TED TALK

1. b; **2.** c; **3.** a

UNIT 4

CONVERSATION

1. truth; **2.** lie; **3.** element; **4.** dishonest; **5.** white

GRAMMAR

1. must have been; **2.** couldn't; **3.** may or may not be; **4.** can't

TED TALK

1. prevalent; **2.** extroverts; **3.** introverts; **4.** body language;
5. sincere; **6.** fake

UNIT 5

CONVERSATION

1. challenges; **2.** endure; **3.** push; **4.** record; **5.** goal

GRAMMAR

1. He had been competing …; **2.** She had been …;
3. … Annie had already learned …; **4.** Scott had been
thinking …; **5.** … , Lee had already turned …;
6. Josephine had been working …

TED TALK

1. b; **2.** d; **3.** c; **4.** a

UNIT 6

CONVERSATION

1. earn; **2.** income; **3.** donate; **4.** an investment; **5.** making

GRAMMAR

1. We gave away all of our old DVDs. / We gave all of our
old DVDs away.; **2.** I need to cut back on eating out.; **3.** I'll
pay you back tomorrow.; **4.** I am saving up money so that
I can buy a new home.; **5.** Karen knows designer jeans are
expensive, but she says she can't go without them.

TED TALK

1. good; **2.** support charitable causes; **3.** have; **4.** it is their
duty; **5.** fairer

UNIT 7

CONVERSATION

1. design; **2.** customized; **3.** invented; **4.** innovations; **5.** discovery

GRAMMAR

1. The world population should reach about nine billion; **2.** people should be able to live even longer.; **3.** Scientists are likely to find a cure for cancer; **4.** Certain medical treatments could be cheaper in the future,; **5.** Do you think there will be fewer diseases; **6.** I doubt that the common cold will ever go away.

TED TALK

1. T; **2.** F; **3.** F; **4.** T

UNIT 8

CONVERSATION

1. get; **2.** pursue; **3.** settle; **4.** raise; **5.** put

GRAMMAR

(Answers will vary, but all will start with *will have* + past participle OR *will have been* + present participle.)

TED TALK

1. identity crisis; **2.** peers; **3.** procrastinated; **4.** investment; **5.** consciously

UNIT 9

CONVERSATION

1. operate; **2.** remote-controlled; **3.** program; **4.** functions; **5.** assemble

GRAMMAR

1. a; **2.** a; **3.** b; **4.** b; **5.** b

TED TALK

1. cooperatively; **2.** obstacles; **3.** First responders; **4.** assess; **5.** autonomous

UNIT 10

CONVERSATION

1. anxiously; **2.** reluctant; **3.** patient; **4.** very carefully; **5.** sympathetic

GRAMMAR

1. told; **2.** had heard; **3.** had said; **4.** to turn; **5.** suggested that

TED TALK

1. b; **2.** a; **3.** b; **4.** b; **5.** a

UNIT 11

CONVERSATION

1. leisurely; **2.** juggling; **3.** appreciate; **4.** restore; **5.** meaningful

GRAMMAR

1. The; **2.** x; **3.** a little; **4.** a; **5.** number

TED TALK

1. fondness; **2.** meditation; **3.** moan; **4.** obstructions; **5.** stands up for

UNIT 12

CONVERSATION

1. persuasive; **2.** persuaded; **3.** conflict; **4.** clarify; **5.** assert; **6.** resolving

GRAMMAR

1. b; **2.** c; **3.** a; **4.** f; **5.** e; **6.** d

TED TALK

1. provoke; **2.** embroiled; **3.** disprove